MW00655674

LNG

A NONTECHNICAL GUIDE

LNG

A NONTECHNICAL GUIDE

Michael D. Tusiani
Gordon Shearer

PennWell®

Disclaimer

The recommendations, advice, descriptions, and methods in this book are presented solely for educational purposes. The authors and the publisher assume no liability whatsoever for any loss or damage that results from the use of any of the material in this book. Use of the material in this book is solely at the risk of the user.

Copyright© 2007 by
PennWell Corporation
1421 South Sheridan Road
Tulsa, Oklahoma 74112-6600 USA

800.752.9764
+1.918.831.9421
sales@pennwell.com
www.pennwellbooks.com
www.pennwell.com

Marketing Manager: Julie Simmons
National Account Executive: Barbara McGee
Director: Mary McGee
Managing Editor: Marla Patterson
Production/Operations Manager: Traci Huntsman
Production Editor: Tony Quinn
Cover Designer: Charles Thomas
Book Designer: Sheila Brock
Book Layout: Brigitte Coffman

Cover photo courtesy of Statoil

Library of Congress Cataloging-in-Publication Data

Tusiani, Michael D.
LNG : a nontechnical guide / Michael D. Tusiani and Gordon Shearer.
p. cm.
ISBN 978-0-87814-885-1 (hardcover)
1. Liquefied natural gas industry. I. Shearer, Gordon. II. Title.
HD9581.2.L572T87 2007
338.2'7285--dc22

2007013934

All rights reserved. No part of this book may be reproduced, stored in a retrieval system, or transcribed in any form or by any means, electronic or mechanical, including photocopying and recording, without the prior written permission of the publisher.

Printed in the United States of America

1 2 3 4 5 11 10 09 08 07

CONTENTS

List of Illustrations . . . xiv
Acknowledgments . . . xix
Introduction . . . xxi

1 The Liquefied Natural Gas Industry . . . 1
Introduction . . . 1
The Global Natural Gas Industry . . . 5
The age of the gas turbine . . . 5
Competing against other fuels . . . 7
Natural Gas Resource Development . . . 10
Natural gas supply . . . 10
Natural gas resources . . . 10
Pipelines . . . 11
LNG Industry Development . . . 13
Historical background . . . 13
The essential ingredients of an LNG project . . . 15
Alternative methods of monetizing natural gas resources . . . 20
Notes . . . 24

2 The Evolution of the Global Gas and LNG Markets . . . 25
Introduction . . . 25
The U.S. Natural Gas and LNG Markets . . . 27
Deregulation of the natural gas industry . . . 29
Natural gas prices . . . 30
Outlook for supply and demand . . . 32
LNG Import Terminals . . . 33
LNG importation: The experience of the 1970s . . . 33
Existing LNG import terminals in the United States . . . 33
New LNG terminals in the United States . . . 36
LNG developments in Canada . . . 37
LNG developments in Mexico . . . 38
Other terminals in North America . . . 39
Natural Gas and LNG Markets in the Caribbean . . . 42
Puerto Rico . . . 42
Dominican Republic . . . 42
Natural Gas and LNG Markets in Western Europe . . . 43
The United Kingdom . . . 45
Iberia . . . 46

France . . . 48
Italy . . . 48
Other European countries . . . 49
Natural Gas and LNG Markets in Asia . . . 49
Japan . . . 50
South Korea . . . 55
Taiwan . . . 57
New Asian Natural Gas and LNG Markets . . . 57
India . . . 58
China . . . 60
Niche Markets for LNG . . . 62
Chile . . . 62
New Zealand . . . 62
Pakistan . . . 62
Singapore . . . 63
Thailand . . . 63
Notes . . . 64

3 The LNG Chain: The Project Nature of the LNG Business . . . 67
Introduction . . . 67
The Physical Chain . . . 69
Upstream exploration and production . . . 69
Liquefaction . . . 71
Shipping . . . 72
Regasification terminals . . . 74
Markets . . . 74
The Ownership Chain . . . 75
Main ownership structures . . . 76
Shipping . . . 78
The Commercial and Financial Chain . . . 78
Cost and cost reduction along the LNG chain . . . 79
Exploration and production . . . 79
Liquefaction . . . 80
Shipping . . . 81
Regasification terminals . . . 83
Value generation along the LNG value chain . . . 83

4 Upstream Natural Gas . . . 87
Introduction . . . 87
Physical and Chemical Properties of Natural Gas . . . 88

Natural Gas Reserves 89
Geology of natural gas 92
Natural gas exploration 95
Natural gas production 100
Natural gas field processing 105
Natural gas pipelines 105
Notes 108

5 The Liquefaction Plant 109
Introduction 109
Siting Considerations 110
Liquefaction Process: Technology Overview 111
Feedgas purification and pretreatment 111
Liquefaction processes 112
Driver technology 121
Utilities 121
LNG Storage Tanks 121
Single-containment tanks 122
Double-containment tanks 123
Full-containment tanks 123
Membrane tank 124
LNG Loading Jetty 124
Project Development and Execution 125
Recent Trends 128
Larger trains 128
Reversal of cost reduction trends 130
Standardization and use of off-site fabricated modules 132
Offshore liquefaction facilities 133
Notes 135

6 LNG Tankers 137
Introduction 137
The Prototype LNG Ships 138
The First Purpose-Built Commercial Ships 139
LNG Ship Containment and Handling Systems 139
Self-supporting, independent tanks 141
Membrane tanks 141
Cargo-handling systems 143
LNG shipbuilding 143
Evolution of LNG Shipbuilding 144
Patents and licenses 149

Typical LNG Shipbuilding Project 150
Before contract signing 151
Project scheduling 151
Standards of construction 153
Typical Parameters of LNG Ships 153
The LNG Fleet 155
Drivers of growth 155
LNG tanker ownership 157
Ship Operations 158
Cooldown 158
Boil-off 159
Cargo loading/discharge 159
LNG Ship Safety and Accident Records 160
Maintenance and Life Extension (Ship Longevity) 160
LNG Maritime Industry Trends 161
Technology Developments 162
Engines and propulsion 162
Larger LNG ship sizes 162
Notes 163

7 LNG Import Terminals 165
Introduction 165
Storage and Sendout Capacity 165
Design and Construction 167
Cost 169
Main Components of LNG Import Terminals 170
Marine facilities 171
Storage tanks 172
Vaporizers 176
Boil-off gas facilities 179
Gas quality and treatment 180
Metering and pressure regulation station 182
Safety and Security 182
Peakshaving LNG Plants 184
Future Trends 184
Shipboard regasification 185
FSRUs 187
The HiLoad offshore LNG-unloading solution 188
Adaptation of existing infrastructure 189
GBS systems 190

The Bishop Process . . . 191
Offshore facilities—not the way forward after all? . . . 192
Notes . . . 193

8 The Evolution of the LNG Industry . . . 195
Introduction . . . 195
Who Imports LNG? . . . 198
Europe . . . 198
Asia . . . 198
The Americas . . . 199
The Evolution of the LNG Business Model . . . 200
The traditional LNG business . . . 200
Barriers to flexibility in traditional contracts . . . 201
Historical attempts to change the model . . . 203
Transformation of the Industry . . . 205
Gas and power market liberalization in the United States and Europe . . . 205
Decreases in capital costs . . . 206
Lower-cost financing . . . 207
Expansion of the LNG "club" . . . 207
Changing upstream strategies . . . 207
Critical and diversified mass . . . 208
New Business Strategies . . . 209
Uncommitted liquefaction . . . 209
Integration along the LNG chain . . . 209
Shipping . . . 212
Effect of the transformation of the industry . . . 213
The Short-Term and Spot LNG Market . . . 214
The rise of short-term trades . . . 214
Potential sources of surplus capacity . . . 215
Spot trades in the United States and Europe—driven by price . . . 217
Asian spot markets—still driven largely by relationships . . . 218
Challenges of spot transactions . . . 218
Future Possibilities . . . 219
Notes . . . 219

9 Orchestration and Financing of an LNG Project 223
Introduction 223
Monopoly Utilities and the Project-Chain Business Model 224
The Emergence of LNG Merchants 225
Supply Project Structure and Formation 228
Requirements for an LNG project 228
Project formation 229
LNG SPAs 231
LNG pricing 231
LNG off-take 233
Shipping 233
Funding 233
Evolving Project Venture Structures 234
Types of project ventures 235
The Atlantic Basin market and project development 238
The Asia-Pacific market and project development 240
LNG Industry Trends: The Emergence of Commercial LNG 242
Project Finance 244
History and motivation 244
Advantages of project finance 245
Risk mitigation 246
Structure and participants 248
Performance 249
Notes 250

10 Global Liquefaction Projects 253
Introduction 253
The Atlantic/Mediterranean Region 253
Algeria 254
Egypt 256
Equatorial Guinea 258
Libya 259
Nigeria 261
Norway 265
Russia (including the Pacific Basin project) 266
Trinidad and Tobago 268
The Middle East 271
Oman 271
Qatar 273
United Arab Emirates (UAE) 276
Yemen 278

The Asia-Pacific Region . . . 279
Australia . . . 279
Brunei . . . 283
Indonesia . . . 284
Malaysia . . . 288
The United States . . . 291
Notes . . . 293

11 The Economics of an LNG Project . . . 295
Introduction . . . 295
Project Capital Costs . . . 296
Upstream capital costs . . . 296
Pipeline Capital Costs . . . 297
Liquefaction capital costs . . . 298
Operating Costs . . . 300
Liquids Production . . . 300
Fiscal Terms . . . 302
Business Structure . . . 306
Shipping Costs . . . 306
Import Terminals . . . 308
Notes . . . 308

12 Upstream Gas Supply Agreements . . . 309
Introduction . . . 309
LNG Business Structures . . . 310
Separate upstream and downstream ventures . . . 311
Fully integrated LNG ventures . . . 311
Natural gas tolling ventures . . . 312
Typical Terms in a GSA . . . 313
Quantity . . . 313
Quality . . . 314
Delivery point . . . 315
Measurement and delivery conditions . . . 315
Natural gas sales price . . . 315
Allocation of the value of by-products . . . 317
Liabilities . . . 317
Force majeure . . . 318
Conclusion . . . 318

13 Sale and Purchase Contracts 319
Introduction 319
Historical Context 320
Long-Term Contracts 323
Quantities 323
Pricing 326
Alternative pricing mechanisms 329
Generic price provisions 330
Contract duration 331
Other Terms and Conditions 331
Gas quality 332
Transportation 333
Scheduling 334
Invoicing and payment 335
Measurement 335
Title transfer 338
Force majeure 338
Choice of law 337
Dispute resolution 338
Allocation of liabilities, liquidated damages, and termination 339
Spot contracts 340

14 LNG Tanker Contracts 341
Introduction 341
Charterparty Overview 341
Evolution of LNG Charterparties 343
LNG charterparties in the traditional shipping model 343
LNG transportation contracts in the new era 346
Controlling LNG Tankers: Adaptation to an Emerging Model 347
Owning LNG tankers 348
Chartering LNG tankers 350
Notes 354

15 Shipping Conventions and Regulations 355
Introduction 355
The Rise of Modern Shipping Regulations 356
Establishment and structure of the IMO 356
Major IMO conventions and codes applicable to LNG tankers 358
New LNG tanker construction rules and regulations 364

16 Import-Related Project Siting and Regulatory Issues 367
Introduction 367
LNG Import Terminal Design Basis 369
Codes and regulations 369
Location, location, location 369
Regulatory Issues 373
Terminal-licensing procedures 373
Terminal access 374
Offshore terminals 376
Notes 377

17 LNG Import Terminal Use Agreements 379
Introduction 379
Regulated Access 380
Proprietary access 384

18 Conclusion: The Future of LNG 389
Introduction 389
Global Demand and Supply 389
Technical Outlook 390
Commercial Trends 391
Regulatory Trends 394
Conclusions 396

Appendix A: Units of Measurement 397

Glossary 399

Bibliography 405

Index 407

About the authors 435

LIST OF ILLUSTRATIONS

Figures

2–1. Hurricanes Katrina and Rita: Next-day Henry Hub spot prices, May 2005–March 2006
2–2. Existing and proposed North American LNG import terminals
2–3. Prospective North American LNG import terminals
2–4. Japan's primary energy sources, 2005
2–5. Japan's power generation fuels, 2005
3–1. The LNG value chain
3–2. Illustrative break-even costs for a greenfield LNG project 10,000 miles from the U.S. East Coast
3–3. Forward integration
3–4. Backward integration
4–1. Gas trap created by folding
4–2. Fault-bounded gas trap
4–3. Gas traps created by salt dome intrusion
4–4. Onshore seismic survey
4–5. Onshore drilling rig
4–6. Offshore drilling rig
4–7. Well casing, showing diminishing diameter of casing with depth (exaggerated)
4–8. Christmas tree
4–9. Offshore gas production platform
4–10. Onshore gas pipeline construction
4–11. Offshore gas pipeline construction
5–1. Natural gas liquefaction flow diagram
5–2. Phillips Optimized Cascade process—ALNG Train 4
5–3. Propane-precooled mixed-refrigerant (C3-MR) process
5–4. APCI AP-X process
5–5. Axens Liquefin dual mixed-refrigerant (DMR) process
5–6. Statoil-Linde mixed-fluid cascade (MFC) process
5–7. Full-containment LNG storage tank
5–8. LNG export facility development phases
5–9. LNG train size growth
5–10. LNG plant unit costs
5–11. GBS/FPSO
6–1. Overview of LNG ship containment systems
6–2. Countries' entry into the LNG shipbuilding sector
6–3. Representative LNG membrane vessel newbuilding project schedule

6–4. LNG ship deliveries by year
7–1. An onshore baseload LNG receiving facility
7–2. LNG import terminal gas flow
7–3. ORV
7–4. SCV
7–5. STV
7–6. Excelerate's Energy Bridge, an LNG regasification vessel
7–7. Moss-type FSRU
7–8. HiLoad offshore LNG import terminal
7–9. Main Pass Energy Hub
7–10. GBS LNG facility
7–11. Gas processing by use of the Bishop Process Exchanger
8–1. Global LNG supply forecast to 2015
8–2. Global LNG demand forecast to 2015
8–3. LNG-exporting and -importing countries in 2005
8–4. Global LNG trade matrix, 2005
8–5. Emergence of spot and short-term LNG trades
9–1. Atlantic Basin LNG demand growth prospects
9–2. Asia-Pacific region LNG demand growth prospects
13–1. LNG pricing in Japan, 2005: JCC vs. weighted average LNG price
13–2. Moderation of price increases and decreases S-curve
14–1. Ocean transportation phase and typical charterparty contracts

Tables

2–1. Worldwide natural gas consumption, 1980–2004
2–2. U.S. natural gas consumption by end use
2–3. Japanese LNG import terminals
2–4. Korean LNG import terminals
4–1. Estimated proven reserves of the top 30 gas reserve holders, as of January 1, 2006
5–1. Liquefaction processes at LNG export plants worldwide, as of 2006
6–1. Main LNG ship containment tank designs
6–2. Europe: Active LNG shipyards
6–3. Japan: Active LNG shipyards
6–4. South Korea: Active LNG shipyards
6–5. China: Active LNG shipyard
6–6. Main LNG ship specifications, categorized by size
6–7. LNG ships: Size range, age profile, and trade allocation
7–1. Acceptable calorific values at onshore U.S. regasification facilities
7–2. Examples of average heating values by country

10–1. Algeria: Existing LNG export projects
10–2. Algeria: Planned LNG projects
10–3. Algeria: Contracted LNG volumes
10–4. Egypt: Existing LNG export projects
10–5. Egypt: Existing LNG project shareholdings
10–6. Egypt: Contracted Idku volumes
10–7. Egypt: SEGAS (Damietta) allocations, 2005–2010
10–8. Equatorial Guinea: LNG plant under construction
10–9. Libya: Existing LNG export project
10–10. Nigeria: Existing LNG export projects
10–11. Nigeria: LNG projects under construction or planned
10–12. Nigeria: LNG project shareholdings (under construction and planned)
10–13. Nigeria: Contracted Nigeria LNG volumes
10–14. Norway: LNG export project
10–15. Norway: Contracted LNG volumes
10–16. Russia: Planned LNG projects
10–17. Russia: Contracted Sakhalin II volumes
10–18. Trinidad: LNG projects existing or under construction
10–19. Trinidad: LNG project shareholdings (existing and under construction)
10–20. Trinidad: Contracted LNG volumes
10–21. Omani LNG export projects
10–22. Omani LNG sales contracts
10–23. Qatari LNG export facilities
10–24. Existing Qatari LNG project shareholdings
10–25. Qatari LNG projects under construction
10–26. Ownership of Qatari LNG projects under construction
10–27. Qatari contracted LNG volumes
10–28. ADGAS LNG project ownership
10–29. ADGAS LNG sales contracts
10–30. Yemen: LNG project under development
10–31. Yemen: Contracted LNG volumes
10–32. Australia: Darwin LNG sales agreements
10–33. Australia: Business structure of the Darwin LNG project
10–34. Australia: NWS LNG project export facilities
10–35. Australia: Signed NWS LNG sales contracts
10–36. Brunei LNG project structure
10–37. Brunei LNG sales contracts
10–38. Indonesia: Arun LNG export project
10–39. Indonesia: Bontang LNG export project

10–40. Indonesia: Arun LNG sales contracts
10–41. Indonesia: Bontang LNG sales contracts
10–42. Indonesia: Tangguh LNG project structure
10–43. Indonesia: Tangguh LNG project sales
10–44. Malaysia: LNG export facilities
10–45. Malaysia: Signed LNG sales contracts
10–46. Malaysia: LNG project business structures
10–47. Alaska: LNG export project summary
10–48. Alaska: Signed LNG sales contracts
13–1. Pricing formula for LNG in Europe
14–1. Key commercial terms in an LNG time charterparty

ACKNOWLEDGMENTS

The writing of this book began as a hobby about 10 years ago. At that time, I sensed that the LNG industry would grow at a much greater pace than in the past and that, as a result, new industry participants would seek a single source of comprehensive information about it. What I had not anticipated were the rapid changes soon to occur in most aspects of the industry itself. I began to realize that, on completion, every chapter had to be updated and, at times, entirely rewritten. At that point, given the staggering task at hand, I sought the assistance of my colleagues—some of the most knowledgeable individuals in the LNG field. This book is theirs more than mine. My ever-patient publisher kindly bore with the reiterated delays, to my utmost astonishment. To accelerate the research and writing process, I asked my colleague and friend Gordon Shearer to coauthor this book. When Gordon, one of the world's leading LNG experts, graciously accepted the task, I knew that what had once seemed a monumental and endless endeavor would soon be brought to fruition. Without Gordon's most welcome collaboration, this book would have long remained in the realm of good intentions.

I thank the following talented and dedicated colleagues, past and present, who worked on this book from the very beginning and to whom a boundless debt of gratitude is due—specifically, Fred Adamchak, Gabriel Avgerinos, Romain Grandbesançon, Anne Marie Johnson, Demetri Karousos, Francois Khawam, Mickey Kwong, Majed Liman, Blair MacIntyre, John Malone, Reinhardt Matisons, Nelly Mikhaiel, Roy Nersesian, David Nissen, Lawrence Noto, Theo Oerlemans, and Frank Spadine. So many others from Poten & Partners' LNG commercial and consulting groups and Hess LNG contributed tangentially but no less effectively.

Four names, however, stand out as worthy of my deepest thankfulness: Amy Biehl, Jeanine Prezioso, Colleen Taylor Sen, and in particular, Nelly Mikhaiel. With great devotion they reviewed, researched, wrote, rewrote, organized, annotated, and verified the entire material. To them I express my profound appreciation.

Were I to express all my praises to the many friends and colleagues who have enriched my life with their knowledge, insight, and advice throughout my career, numerous pages would be required. I must, however, single out the late Henning Ebsen-Petersen and Michael R. Naess, for introducing me to the world of LNG. Rene Boudet, the man with the vision about the future of liquefied natural gases and the courage to gamble on it, heightened my curiosity and inspired my perseverance in the field. My dear friend, Lucio A. Noto, with selfless generosity provided me with the wisdom of his counsel throughout the years and placed his friendship at my disposal.

Finally, I thank my wife, Beatrice, and my children, Paula and Michael, and their families for all their tireless support of my work habits over the years. My brother, Joseph, remains my mentor and guardian angel. Pamela, though you are no longer with us, you are more than ever present. This book is for you.

Michael D. Tusiani

October 6, 2006

New York City

Michael has already recognized our colleagues at Poten & Partners and others who provided so much help and support in the writing of this book. I can only reiterate and emphasize that without their help this would never have happened, and I join him in offering my thanks and praise for all their efforts.

I would also like to briefly acknowledge the many friends and colleagues with whom I have had the pleasure to work over the years in this industry and who have helped me in one of the most satisfying careers that I can imagine anyone would want. I spent almost 25 years at Cabot Corporation, one of the early pioneers in the global LNG business (literally, as the holder of the first known patents in the industry). In particular, I acknowledge my first supervisor, and later friend and colleague, John Cabot, who lived through the ups and downs of the U.S. LNG industry for longer than I have; Sam Bodman, who gave me the chance to run Cabot's LNG business and revive it when the consensus was that LNG would never work again in America; my many colleagues at Cabot LNG/Distrigas who came to share the vision; and the many friends I made on both sides of the negotiating tables over these past years, including our lawyers from BakerBotts, my friends at Sonatrach and the National Gas Company of Trinidad and Tobago, and many, many others in this industry whom I have had the fortune to know and, more important, who have helped me to learn so much.

I offer my thanks to my colleagues at Poten & Partners and Hess LNG, for shouldering more than their share of the load when I was taking time to work on this book; to Aleksandra, who has been a source of love, patience, and understanding; and finally and especially, to Michael, my colleague, friend, and mentor, who showed me that there was life after Boston and who has been for so long such a pillar of strength in our industry.

Gordon Shearer

October 6, 2006

New York City

INTRODUCTION

Natural gas is today considered by many as the fuel of the future. Years ago, when oil companies drilled for oil and found gas, their effort was deemed a failure. The gas, if associated, often had to be either reinjected or flared or, if dry, left for another day. When flaring was branded as wasteful by producing countries, companies had to find an alternative use for gas. Consequently, liquefied natural gas (LNG) projects were evaluated and, if viable, pursued. As oil prices rose and production costs fell, LNG became more economically feasible. Consuming nations with long-term vision were willing to pay a premium to secure clean energy from diverse and reliable producers. Projects were undertaken on a case-by-case basis, with close cooperation between buyers and sellers on every aspect of the LNG chain—production, liquefaction, transportation, and regasification.

Today companies continue to explore for oil and gas and are delighted to find one or the other or both! Nevertheless, as oil demand grows and the future supply of oil becomes ever more constrained, natural gas is the most viable energy alternative. Many experts believe that our industry will soon be referred to as gas and oil, rather than oil and gas—today's common description.

With the demand for gas ever growing while production is falling in the main consuming regions, LNG, as a result of technological advances and commercial maturity, has become a more attractive and economical option. LNG is an increasingly important part of the world's energy mix. As this book was being written, LNG was the fastest-growing segment of the world's hydrocarbon industry, and there is little reason to believe that this trend will change anytime soon.

Project development, however, is becoming much more complex. Partnering issues have emerged, since more companies are involved in gas development activities, and producing countries, having gained knowledge and experience, are seeking a more active role in the development and monetization of their natural resources. LNG trading patterns are expanding, and maximization of value is being sought by all parties. Many more speculative participants have emerged, willing to gamble large sums of capital on the industry's future needs. Capital costs fell, then began to rise; yet, because of technological advances, the delivered cost of gas has decreased. An exciting platform for future growth has been created.

A multitude of studies have been undertaken on natural gas and LNG, but in more than a decade, no single book has been written that covers all the salient aspects of the LNG industry in a comprehensive manner. The intent of this volume is to give the reader as complete an understanding of the whole LNG picture as possible. As previously stated, change seems to have become a constant in the LNG business; consequently, rather than continuing to update or rewrite, we have decided to choose this date as a cut-off point. Natural gas—and especially LNG—is the fuel of the future, and the future has arrived.

THE LIQUEFIED NATURAL GAS INDUSTRY 1

INTRODUCTION

At the dawn of the 21st century, the world has renewed its interest and concern over energy. Energy supply, security, and prices are dominant themes in the news media and the subject of political debates around the globe. Oil prices remain stubbornly above $50 per barrel (bbl), natural gas prices have reached record highs in most markets, and even coal prices have climbed along with the price of many other basic commodities. Energy demand grows inexorably with the growth of the world economy, and China and India have emerged as major, rapidly growing consumers. Concerns over global warming have not abated, but the promise of alternative renewable energy is proving slow to realize. Nuclear power appears to be on the verge of a revival, but the problems of waste disposal and proliferation remain unsolved. Speculation as to whether the world has seen peak oil production abounds, and many of the same commentators assume that natural gas may not be far behind in reaching its production peak.

In this context, the global energy industry faces new challenges. Remaining reserves of oil are concentrated in increasingly fewer countries, not all friendly to the principal consuming nations. State oil companies have grown in importance as high prices and ready access to technology have increasingly enabled them to operate independently of the major and large independent oil companies on whom they traditionally depended. These same private oil companies are now struggling to grow profitably, even with access to large cash flows, as their access to oil reserves becomes more constrained and as the competition from other producers, including from the state oil companies of the emerging new oil markets, proves fierce. While the natural gas industry has suffered from some of the same pressures, it has evolved somewhat differently than oil. With a more benign emissions profile than other hydrocarbons, broader resource distribution throughout the world, and a more complex market structure, natural gas has become the increasing focus of the oil and gas industry. Long gone are the days when the geologist returned home to report the good news and the bad news about his recent exploration endeavors—the bad news being that he didn't find oil, but the good news being that he didn't find natural gas.

In the 1970s, the era of the last worldwide concern over limitations to commodity production, natural gas was seen as being a fuel of limited scope, too precious to consume in many applications. In fact, some producers took to describing natural gas as the noble fuel, worthy of being sold at a premium. Government policies among the developed nations encouraged this perception. But what a difference a decade makes. By the early 1980s, natural gas prices were falling in the primary markets, and a glut of the fuel, earlier disguised by political considerations, quickly emerged. Low prices, coupled with its clean-burning characteristics, quickly made natural gas a favored fuel. At the beginning of the 21st century, natural gas is one of the fastest-growing sources of primary energy. This growth is expected to continue for at least the next several decades. Although oil remains the largest component of primary energy, accounting for about 37% of total world energy demand in 2004, its share has slipped from over 40% in the early 1980s, while the share of natural gas has increased from 19% to nearly 24% in the same time frame.[1]

Natural gas use is nearly on par with coal and is projected to become the secondmost widely used fuel after 2020.[2] Despite the strong growth in consumption, especially over the past decade, the worldwide reserves of natural gas have grown faster than consumption and, at current rates of production, are sufficient to last almost 70 years. By contrast, the world's oil reserves now represent just over 40 years of consumption at current production rates.

In 2005, world natural gas marketed production grew 2.1% to 2,819.4 Bcm (99.5 Tcf).[3] Lower prices, coupled with the advent of competition in traditional gas and power markets, promoted higher gas use. Advances in combined-cycle gas turbine (CCGT) technology in particular have enhanced the economics of generating electricity from gas, as lower capital costs and markedly higher operating efficiencies of the CCGTs have given natural gas a competitive edge over coal, along with superior emissions characteristics.

To meet this growing demand, there has been a steady rise in the share of natural gas that is traded internationally. Compared to other fossil fuels, natural gas is expensive and more technically challenging to transport over long distances, by pipeline or by ship as LNG. As a result, the global natural gas industry has evolved as a series of regional and even local markets. Yet despite this, natural gas exports rose 9% in 2004, to 680 Bcm (24 Tcf), representing 25% of total world consumption. Pipeline deliveries accounted for 74% of these exports; the balance was delivered as LNG.[4] LNG's shares of overall world natural gas consumption, now around 6.6%, and of the world natural gas trade have risen steadily since the first deliveries in the mid-1960s. As regional demand begins to exceed regional supply, the resulting demand pressure appears certain to lead to a significant expansion of the LNG industry in the coming decades. Even by low estimates, global LNG trade is forecast to double between 2000 and 2020.[5] Tens of billions of dollars will need to be invested in order to make this supply available. In contrast to the oil industry, however, LNG represents a more technically, financially, and commercially challenging energy delivery system, well suited to the strengths and competencies of the major oil and gas-producing companies. There is no world price for natural gas or LNG, and many end-use markets remain essentially closed to competition, under the control of regulated utilities. Simply having access to large untapped reserves of natural gas does not ensure that these reserves will be monetized easily or quickly.

These dynamics have resulted in a growing interest in this industry by national governments on both the producing and consuming sides, as well as by the energy industry and investment communities, who perceive the challenges as allowing more opportunity for investments, access to reserves, and production growth. By way of anecdotal evidence of this trend, in 2005 ExxonMobil added 1.7 billion barrels of oil equivalent (BOE) to its reserves. About 95% of this total was attributable to gas reserves associated with the company's LNG projects in Qatar.

In simple terms, the LNG industry involves identifying large reserves of natural gas with little or no prospect of securing local markets, producing then liquefying the natural gas at very low temperatures (–163°C), shipping the LNG in specially designed tankers to markets, and storing and regasifying (or vaporizing) it before injecting it into a pipeline grid, at which point it becomes indistinguishable from pipeline gas for the end user. In its liquid form, natural gas shrinks to less than 1/600th of its gaseous state, making its transportation and storage more efficient. However, little is simple about LNG. Bridging the gap between supply and demand is one

The LNG industry is based largely on a series of virtually self-contained projects made up of interlinking chains of large-scale facilities, requiring huge capital investments, bound together by complex, long-term contracts, and subject to intense oversight by host governments and international organizations at every stage of the process.

of the energy industry's most challenging and intricate problems. The LNG industry is based largely on a series of virtually self-contained projects made up of interlinking chains of large-scale facilities, requiring huge capital investments, bound together by complex, long-term contracts and subject to intense oversight by host governments and international organizations at every stage of the process. Ironically, this effort is applied to the simplest hydrocarbon, methane, and involves no chemical or other changes to the commodity, except to its temperature, from the time it is produced until it reaches the final consumer.

Even though LNG has represented a major source of natural gas and a significant share of primary energy for decades in Japan and other areas of the world, it was for many years considered a high-cost niche segment within the energy industry. Given the numerous hurdles and uncertainties that faced each project and the need to coordinate the multiple disparate elements involved, many projects failed to achieve realization or collapsed before they had run their course, often at a cost in the tens or even hundreds of millions of dollars. Skeptics warned of impending disasters that would threaten the safety, economics, or operations, and in some parts of the world, the public and the media attacked the industry on safety grounds. Each project took years to develop and had to chart new territory, so that it took decades for the industry to reach a critical mass of well-functioning projects and prove that the technical and commercial model could be successful. Conventional wisdom held that even the "successful" LNG projects had marginal economic returns, and many energy companies avoided the LNG sector or exited it as quickly as they could. For the first few decades, the industry had relatively few participants and was loosely known as "the club." Yet club members were already cognizant of what the rest of the world is only now realizing—that well-executed LNG projects can generate highly profitable and stable financial returns over many decades.

Notwithstanding the hurdles, the industry has proven its reliability and stability under a variety of market and economic conditions, accompanied by a safety record second to none for an operation of its scale and scope. Currently, demand growth and high energy prices, coupled with advances in technology, are driving more planned and proposed LNG projects than at any point in history. There is no question now about the important, growing role that LNG plays in meeting global natural gas demand.

THE GLOBAL NATURAL GAS INDUSTRY

Although the ancient Greeks, Romans, and Chinese made limited use of natural gas, it was only in the 20th century that it became a significant source of energy, thanks to technological advances in long-distance, high-pressure pipeline transportation that permitted it to be widely distributed and allowed it to substitute for town gas produced from coal, which had been introduced to many cities in the late 19th century. World demand has grown steadily throughout the 20th century and has more than doubled since 1970.

The U.S. Department of Energy's (DOE) Energy Information Administration (EIA) has projected that world gas consumption will grow nearly 70% between 2002 and 2025.[6] Natural gas is used extensively for heating and cooking in residential and commercial settings and as a process fuel and feedstock for industrial consumers. However, while the number of customers for these applications continues to grow, overall consumption growth is muted as equipment efficiencies improve. The future of gas demand reflects the future of electricity demand. The electric power sector is expected to account for more than half of the growth in gas demand, because of the environmental benefits and efficiency of natural gas, compared with other energy sources. Technological advances in CCGT power plants have shifted the economics of power generation away from coal in favor of natural gas, even with gas's higher prices. Historically, gas-fired power generation was primarily used for peak generation in simple-cycle gas turbines or when prices justified, as a direct substitute for residual fuel oil in steam boilers, since the variable costs of generating baseload electricity using other fuels, such as coal and nuclear, were lower.

The age of the gas turbine

Until the 1970s, coal and oil were the principal fuels used to generate electricity. However, the use of oil for electricity generation has been shrinking in the wake of the oil shocks of the mid-1970s. This, in turn, contributed to the rapid expansion of nuclear generation from the 1970s through the 1980s. By the mid-1980s, public opposition and escalating construction costs brought nuclear development to an abrupt halt in many countries. At the same time, environmental concerns associated with greenhouse gas emissions began to slow the development of coal-fired generation. Many countries also began a process of liberalizing their wholesale electric markets, and this brought an increased focus on the overall costs and efficiencies of the power generation technologies, with costs no longer guaranteed recovery as they had been under the classic utility regulatory environment. Lower-capital-cost technologies with shorter construction times began to win favor. The stage was now set for the emergence of natural gas.

The first gas-fired generating units, built in the United States during the 1960s, were small turbines and relatively inexpensive to build, but they were often inefficient and depended on high-cost natural gas supplied through gas distribution utilities. Gas supply was often curtailed during periods of peak gas demand. As a result, these peaking units were employed to provide a rapid source of power only during periods of peak demand, which largely occurred during the summer months. With the exception of Japan, natural gas was rarely used for power generation outside the United States, since it had to be imported and these imports were expensive and often raised issues of supply security. Moreover, many countries adopted policies prohibiting the use of natural gas in power generation—including the United States, through the Fuel Use Act of 1978. Japan was an unusual case, where natural gas was used widely by the large power utilities in direct substitution for oil in classic, steam turbine power plants. This served two purposes: Japan could diversify its energy supply, shifting from overdependence on Middle East oil to sources closer to home; and the baseload nature of the Japanese power utility demand helped to underwrite the success of the early LNG exports project by assuring a stable, secure, and financially appealing market.

With the introduction of CCGTs in the 1980s, the removal of prohibitions on the use of gas for power generation, and the introduction of competition in wholesale electric markets, the boom in gas turbine generation was under way. (In a combined-cycle plant, a gas turbine is combined with a steam turbine, which uses the waste heat from the gas turbine to increase efficiency.) Modern CCGT plants have thermal efficiencies approaching 60%, compared to efficiencies of closer to 40% in modern coal-fired power plants. During most of the 1980s, annual sales of gas turbines hovered around 300–400 units, with an average size of only 30 megawatts (MW), reflecting their use in peaking applications. By 1990, annual sales exceeded 600 units, soaring to 900 units by mid-decade and 1,500 units in 2000. Turbine size increased dramatically as well, reaching up to 500 MW.

Deregulation has also put in play other factors supporting the popularity of CCGTs. The introduction of wholesale competition in the power sector is increasing the demand for these units. Gas turbines can be deployed rapidly, which reduces market risk, since developers can match their investment decisions more closely with fluctuating market requirements. Capital costs are much lower, making financing easier and reducing the risk that the developer may be left with stranded assets.

During the 1980s and '90s, natural gas was cheap and there was a common consensus that it would remain cheap and plentiful for the foreseeable future. Finding a site for a gas-fired power plant is easier than for a coal plant, which is widely viewed as dirtier, or for a nuclear facility, which the public considers too dangerous. Gas-fired plants were often the only generation choice which could meet regional air quality restrictions. These developments contributed to a major increase in the use of gas for power generation between 1973 and 2000. From 1980 to 2000, oil's share of the U.S. energy mix dropped from 46% to 39%, while natural gas rose from 19% to 23%.[7] Between 1990 and 2004, natural gas-fired power plants accounted for some 95% of all new power plants installed in the country—a total of over 100,000 MW of power capacity. Yet natural gas-fired power is not the answer to everything. The bankruptcy of companies such as Calpine and Mirant demonstrated that single-minded bets on natural gas carried their own risks—in this case, the risks associated with rapidly increasing fuel prices which could not be recovered in the wholesale power markets.

Competing against other fuels

While natural gas may continue to gain market share at the expense of other hydrocarbon resources, coal is fighting back, nuclear is showing new signs of life, and new renewable fuels are helping to change the energy mix. Still, expectations for the potential of renewable fuels and associated technologies are often overstated, and reducing coal's environmental impact is a nontrivial undertaking.

Oil, long the king of energy consumption, comprises the biggest share of global energy supply and will continue to do so for the foreseeable future. Oil is relatively cheap to ship globally, and international markets are well established. Transportation fuel demand, especially in India, China, and other emerging countries, will continue to expand. Natural gas does not yet economically compete with oil for transportation. Until technological breakthroughs occur and/or legislation passes favoring natural gas or other alternative transportation fuels, oil will continue to dominate these markets in most areas of the globe, and transportation use will continue to dominate oil demand, accounting for some 70% of the petroleum market.

In the past, the lack of infrastructure to transport and distribute natural gas was a barrier to increasing gas consumption. However, the 1970s oil shocks provided an impetus for the improvement of infrastructure, leading to the construction of major pipelines from the North Sea, Russia, and North Africa to Europe and to significant expansion of existing networks in North America.

In regions where natural gas pipeline infrastructure is not in place, oil continues to be used for residential and commercial heating purposes. Natural gas is slowly making inroads in developing countries, especially Latin America (Mexico), South America (Venezuela, Brazil, and Argentina), Eastern Europe and the former Soviet Union, and Asia (China, India, and Thailand). The EIA forecasts that gas use will grow 63% in Eastern Europe and the former Soviet Union over the 2002–20 period and will nearly triple in emerging Asia, including India and China. Gas demand will grow at a slower rate (1.3% annually) in the mature market economies, whose share of the global natural gas demand is expected to decline from 50% in 2002 to 43% by 2025.[8]

In places without indigenous supply, infrastructure, or existing consumers, electric power projects or industrial projects are often built first as anchor customers to secure sufficient baseload gas demand and justify a supply project. Later, distribution networks are added to reach smaller consumers. This is the pattern followed by Japan in the 1970s and '80s.

Another reason for the recent growth in popularity of natural gas is that it is the cleanest-burning fossil fuel. Its low carbon content per unit of energy, compared to oil and coal, contributes to its attractiveness. Following the Kyoto Treaty, many developed countries have adopted targets to reduce CO_2 emissions and intend to enforce these targets through a combination of emission-trading regimes and fines for noncompliance, further improving the comparative economics of natural gas.

Although coal, nuclear, and hydro have historically been the dominant fuels for power generation owing to their low costs, the improved economics of natural gas-fired power generation, coupled with its environmental benefits, will allow gas to capture new markets where gas infrastructure can be built and gas can be delivered on a cost-effective basis. New gas-fired power plants have the lowest capital costs per megawatt of any power plant and are easier to site than most other types of plants.

The coal industry is moving to address the concerns associated with emissions. New technologies are more fuel efficient and produce fewer and cleaner emissions. Power companies are looking at the development of carbon sequestration as a way to address CO_2 emissions. While these are expensive solutions, government policy (especially in the United States) will favor them to further energy supply diversity and security. The advantage of natural gas over nuclear energy has much to do with public perception. There are widespread safety concerns about nuclear power because of the perceived risks, such as radiation leaks, long-term spent fuel disposal, and nuclear proliferation; by contrast, public opinion of natural gas-fired generation is typically positive or neutral. The negative sentiment associated with nuclear power makes constructing new plants difficult. Nuclear facilities have enormous capital costs, and even though new technologies and standardization of designs could lower the costs of constructing new plants, natural gas does not stand to lose market share to nuclear. The greatest potential for nuclear additions would be through government policies aimed at removing risks associated with siting the plants and a desire to ensure energy supply diversity. Public perception may also be shifting as people's concerns over the negative impacts of global warming overcome the more speculative and sensationalist aspects of nuclear power with its lower emissions footprint.

With the exception of hydroelectricity, renewable sources have historically not been economically competitive with fossil fuels. Hydroelectric power generation is restricted to certain areas and is subject to variations in weather. Major hydroelectric power projects carry their own environmental risks and can force the migration of local populations, as was seen in the Three Rivers project in China. New construction is more likely in locations remote from local populations, but the cost of long-distance power transmission is another factor.

Solar power and wind power have clear environmental benefits over natural gas for power generation. The economics of wind energy have changed as costs decline, and wind increasingly appears competitive with other fuels, often aided by favorable government tax treatment. Large-scale wind farms, virtually nonexistent before the 1990s, are becoming increasingly common in North America and Europe. As wind becomes cheaper to build, its incremental costs could be competitive with those of natural gas for power generation. Wind stands to be the fastest growing of all energy sources in the coming decades. However, the construction of massive wind farms, both onshore and offshore, is facing opposition in some communities. While wind will undoubtedly capture some of the natural gas-fired power generation market, natural gas is considered more reliable and economical and will remain the dominant fuel for new power generation over the next few decades. Solar power is also advancing but at a slower pace than wind, because the technological challenges appear to be more difficult to surmount. However, solar is developing natural niche markets in remote and isolated locations where other sources of electricity prove too expensive to deliver. While alternative energy has a rapidly expanding future, it still will not account for more than 9% of the global primary energy supply by 2020.

NATURAL GAS RESOURCE DEVELOPMENT

Natural gas supply

Historically, natural gas reserves that were remote from markets were viewed as a nuisance that potentially impeded the development of oil reserves. These remote gas reserves are often termed "stranded." As the options for monetizing natural gas have expanded, however, some previously stranded reserves discovered decades earlier are finally being developed. For many of the major energy companies, increasingly denied access to oil reserves or being forced to settle for onerous financial conditions to develop them, gas is becoming the "new oil." In addition to technology improvements in exploration and production, the energy industry has doubled worldwide natural gas reserves between 1980 and 2000, and reserves continue to climb. At present consumption levels, there is enough gas to last through the next seven decades.

Natural gas resources

Proponents of the gas era point to the large size of the world's natural gas resource. At the end of 2005, world gas reserves totaled 6,112 Tcf (173 trillion cubic meters [Tcm]), equivalent to 1,107 billion bbl of oil, just slightly less than proven petroleum reserves of 1,293 billion bbl.[9] Proven natural gas reserves will last for 70 years at current production levels, and prospects to increase total reserves are excellent as the energy industry increasingly focuses on natural gas. By contrast, the global oil resource base would be depleted in 40 years at today's production rates, and the prospects for significantly expanding the resource base seem less certain.

While gas resources are ample on a global basis, they are not evenly distributed. They are often far from major demand centers and have not been developed. About 75% of the world's reserves are located in the former Soviet Union and the Middle East. However, consumption is dominated by North America and Europe (including Russia), accounting for at least 56% of global gas consumption. The comparative ratio of reserves to production (R/P ratio), which indicates the number of years that it would take to deplete proven reserves at current production levels, also highlights this regional disparity. For example, proven reserves in the Middle East would last for 257 years, and there is clearly room to prove up additional gas resources with relatively little effort. By contrast, the R/P ratio in North America is less than 10 years, and regional hydrocarbon basins have been explored extensively and are considered mature. However, R/P ratios alone do not tell the full story of the ultimate resource base, since the U.S. R/P ratio has varied between 9 and 13 years for several decades, illustrating the ability of the industry to find new reserves, often in response to economic signals.

The imbalance between the location of gas resources and gas markets necessitates a major expansion in the international gas trade, by long-distance pipelines and in the form of LNG. However, building the infrastructure to move natural gas long distances requires multibillion-dollar investments. This raises the question of whether incremental gas supply can be delivered long distances to markets at competitive prices or whether high prices will moderate gas demand growth below current expectations. The power sector in particular, faced with gas supply and price concerns, may reevaluate the potentials of clean coal and nuclear technologies.

Pipelines

One of the first modern commercial applications for natural gas was in streetlamps in the eastern United States and northwestern Europe in the 19th century. When nations became electrified, gas lamps became obsolete, and natural gas did not play a major role in the energy picture until pipelines were constructed to transport the fuel from producing areas to consumers. Although natural gas had been transported in wooden pipelines in other areas of the globe much earlier, the first metal natural gas pipeline was built in 1872. Stretching five and a half miles, it brought gas from a producing well to the town of Titusville, Pennsylvania. These first metal pipelines were extremely inefficient. It was not until after World War II, when pipeline technology dramatically improved, that natural gas became a major part of the energy mix. In Europe, the foundation of the gas transmission system was laid between 1970 and 1975, fueled by the giant gas discovery in Groningen, The Netherlands.[10]

The pipeline industry groups natural gas pipeline systems according to three definitions: gathering systems, transmission lines, and distribution pipelines. For the most part, in this book, the term "pipelines" refers to transmission pipelines, which transport natural gas from supply areas to markets. These long-haul pipelines are usually between 16 and 48 inches in diameter and can extend for thousands of miles, operating at high pressures maintained by compressor stations along the route. In mature markets, such as the United States and Europe, a complex web of transmission pipelines connects to other transmission pipelines, storage facilities, large end users, and distribution systems.

Gathering systems generally comprise smaller-diameter pipelines that take gas from the wellhead to central processing facilities, where impurities are extracted. However, offshore gathering systems may be physically indistinguishable from transmission lines. Gathering-line pressures can vary significantly, usually as a function of the wellhead pressure of the producing well. Distribution pipelines also tend to be smaller in diameter and disseminate natural gas to consumers in market areas. Distribution lines normally operate at medium to low pressures. While very large consumers, such as a steel mill or an electric generator, may be directly connected to a transmission pipeline, the vast majority of medium to small consumers obtain their gas through a distribution system, which is often run by a local distribution company (LDC).

From an environmental and safety perspective, pipelines pass with flying colors. Aside from the initial impacts associated with construction, the pipelines themselves have very little environmental impact. Thanks to safety and security systems that detect corrosion or leaks, most problems can be identified and corrected before they become significant. Although accidents happen from time to time, the system is considered one of the safest modes of transportation.

Pipelines remain the major mode of transporting the world's natural gas to consumers, accounting for over 90% of natural gas deliveries. The United States alone has over 180,000 miles of interstate pipelines.[11] As natural gas demand grows, the number of major international pipeline projects continues to increase. The industry has faced and met increasingly complex challenges of distance and terrain and long, deep underwater crossings. Some existing and proposed pipeline projects are nearly four thousand miles long and cost billions of dollars to build. Generally speaking, an offshore pipeline is more expensive than a similar onshore one.

Despite technical advances, it is not always possible or desirable to link supply to market by a pipeline, because of terrain, right-of-way issues, politics, and/or distance. Sometimes geographical features, such as underwater faults or coral reefs, may prevent construction, or a planned pipeline may interfere with an environmentally protected area or other public infrastructure already in place. Landowners may not allow (or be required to allow) the pipeline to be built on their territory. A route may traverse politically unstable regions or countries that are on unfriendly terms with the supplying or consuming country. These factors may prevent a pipeline from being built or may render it uneconomical.

LNG INDUSTRY DEVELOPMENT

Historical background

Petroleum products were first transported by tankers in the 1860s, but a century passed before natural gas was transported by ship.[12] One reason for this delay was the rapid evolution of the global oil industry, spurring the long-haul transportation of petroleum. Another reason was the significant technical challenges of transporting natural gas on oceangoing tankers. It is relatively easy to store, load, and transport oil or other petroleum products, but natural gas has to be turned into a liquid at very low temperatures, then stored and transported in this form.

Two 17th-century physicists, Robert Boyle and Edme Mariotte, are credited with discovering that air is compressible; this led to insights into how gas might be pressurized and condensed. Numerous subsequent experiments were conducted to establish the optimum method of reducing the volume of natural gas, and it was determined that increasing the density of gas could be achieved by extreme pressure, extreme cooling, or a combination of the two. Compressed natural gas was generally considered too difficult and dangerous to be transported around the world because of the lack of suitable materials to contain the high pressures and the risk of explosion in the case of a sudden release of gas. However, with extreme cooling to below its boiling point (in this case, –163°C), natural gas could be reduced in volume by a factor of over 600 times, then stored and shipped at normal atmospheric pressure. In its liquid form, natural gas exhibits an unusual property known as auto-refrigeration, whereby continuous evaporation draws heat away from the liquid and does not require anything more than insulation to maintain the gas in liquid form as long as the evaporated gas, known as boil-off, is removed from the storage tank.

The process of cooling natural gas to extremely low temperatures began as a means of extracting helium from natural gas for use in U.S. military balloons in the early 1900s. Shortly thereafter, through advances in metallurgical techniques, metals, notably aluminum and steel alloys, were produced in Europe and the United States that would not become brittle at extremely low temperatures, as most metals do. Storage facilities could thus be built for the supercooled liquid.

Godfrey Cabot devised the first conceptual scheme for LNG in 1914, when he patented a barge-based system to demonstrate that waterborne transportation of gas was technically feasible. However, he never pursued the idea. In 1939, the first commercial LNG peakshaving plant was built in West Virginia. Two years later, the East Ohio Gas Company built a second facility in Cleveland. This peakshaving plant operated without incident until 1944, when the facility was expanded to include a larger tank. However, World War II created a shortage of the best available stainless steel alloys (stainless steel could withstand the very cold temperatures without fracturing as mild steel does when exposed to LNG), and a storage tank was built using steel with inadequate nickel content. In 1944, the tank ruptured and natural gas leaked into the sewer system and into peoples' homes, where it ignited, killing 128 people—the largest disaster in LNG history. Subsequent investigations resulted in new standards for the materials used with LNG, preventing this from happening in the future. However, this incident put LNG development on hold, and commercialization of the technology was not attempted again until a decade later.

In the 1950s and '60s, William Wood Prince, president of the Union Stock Yards of Chicago, was faced with escalating electricity rates and began to study the liquefaction of natural gas in Louisiana and the possibility of barging it up the Mississippi River to Chicago. The British Gas Council was also looking to transport natural gas to supplement gas supplies in areas thinly stretched by manufacturing and household use. The Union Stock Yards subsequently joined forces with Continental Oil Company and the British Gas Council to turn an old World War II dry bulk carrier into an LNG ship, the Methane Pioneer. This vessel was used to transport LNG from Lake Charles, Louisiana, on the Gulf of Mexico, to Canvey Island, in the United Kingdom, in 1959, in what was the first maritime shipment of LNG. After a major natural gas discovery in Algeria, the United Kingdom and France signed contracts with Algeria in 1961 and 1962, respectively, and the first commercial-scale LNG "chain" with a liquefaction plant at Arzew, Algeria, and receiving terminals in France and the UK, became operational in 1964.

In many countries, an LNG project is the largest investment ever undertaken, and a country's future creditworthiness may hang in the balance. Unfulfilled commitments for any reason can lead to millions of dollars of losses.

During the 1960s and '70s, liquefaction plants were built in Alaska, Libya, Brunei, Abu Dhabi, and Indonesia, as well as Algeria. Import terminals were developed in Japan, France, the United States, and Italy, later joined by terminals in Belgium, Spain, Taiwan, and Korea. However, owing to an oversupply of gas in the Atlantic markets in the 1980s, only two new export projects (in Australia and Malaysia) were added in that decade, while expansions continued in Indonesia. Most of the capacity added in the 1980s was designed to serve Asian LNG markets, which were growing rapidly and did not have the same access to domestic gas or pipeline imports as Europe or North America. In the early 1990s, demand was catching up with supply in the Western hemisphere. Consequently, a rebirth of LNG projects was targeted toward those markets, and the first output from Qatar, Nigeria, Oman, and Trinidad occurred between 1996 and 2000.

The essential ingredients of an LNG project

Unlike many other energy delivery systems, LNG has tended to be organized on a project basis, involving the development of not only upstream infrastructure and gas production, gathering, and liquefaction facilities but also shipping and import terminals. This reflects the very high capital investment needed for each unit of energy delivered, as well as the historical separation between the LNG suppliers (large international oil companies, both private and state owned) and the LNG buyers (principally gas and electric utilities, both private and state owned). As the industry matures—and as the traditional sellers move downstream while the buyers move upstream—these challenges may lessen but will be replaced by others, though perhaps not as severe.

Between the start of the commercial LNG business in 1964 and the year 2000, the industry grew at a very deliberate pace, adding fewer than 20 projects in a dozen countries. During this time, it remained a closed industry dominated by a handful of players and strong bilateral contracts. For many years, every new project announcement was met with skepticism and predicted failure, even when the existing projects could demonstrate years of successful trade.

There is good reason for doubt, as each new project faces substantial risks and challenges. The principal reason for the apparently slow pace of development of the business is the scale of requirements (and, consequently, the requisite investments), which have few parallels in any industry. Except for a few long-distance pipelines and nuclear power, no other type of energy project consistently rivals LNG in costs. In many countries, an LNG project is the largest investment ever undertaken, and a country's future creditworthiness may hang in the balance. Unfulfilled commitments for any reason can lead to millions of dollars of losses. To mitigate participants' financial risks, each project weaves together a complex web of contracts and agreements. The challenge of managing a project where buyer and seller have disparate interests and are both subject to scrutiny from and/or involvement of their host governments cannot be overestimated.

Other considerable barriers to successful project execution are the many commercial, technical, and legal challenges. Addressing these challenges requires the coordination of dozens of experts, including lawyers, engineers, contractors, shipowners, bankers, government representatives, and consultants.

The complex issues involved in developing an LNG project will be discussed in detail in chapter 9. The following is a summary of some of the main issues, emphasizing the major conditions necessary for development to proceed. The first consideration is to ensure that the physical locations, resources, and commercial conditions are favorable.

Sufficient gas reserves. By the time an LNG project is under consideration, the existence of ample low-cost gas reserves has usually been confirmed. A project must have dedicated proven reserves that allow the project to operate at its design level for 20–30 years, with an additional reserve margin to protect against unexpected production declines. This helps ensure the financial viability and the financeability of the project. The cost of producing the reserves must be fairly low to make the LNG project economical. If the gas is too expensive to produce, it will be left in the ground. The presence of liquid hydrocarbons, along with the gas, can also improve project prospects, as this can create an additional, high-value revenue stream for the project.

Long-term commitments from buyers. While a liquefaction facility may have varying degrees of its capacity reserved for short-term or spot trades, the capital costs required in order to build a facility usually dictate that a downstream buyer or buyers, who will contract for the majority of the plant's output, must be secured. This ensures a stable off-take for the supplier. In most contracts in the LNG industry, the buyer takes most of the volume risk with limited flexibility, while the seller takes most of the price risk, with limited opportunity to revisit those terms. This traditional structure is now being modified, as the industry matures and the options and opportunities for buyers and sellers expand.

Unlike the oil business, where the production profile tends to build gradually over time and the commodity may be shipped relatively inexpensively to any number of markets on tankers that can be contracted on relatively short notice, liquefaction plants generally produce large quantities of LNG shortly after they come on line, and access to LNG tankers and market outlets is more limited and can be significantly more expensive. Under ideal conditions, production and consumption should be maximized as early as possible and maintained at this level for the duration of the project. For this reason, it is preferable to market LNG to buyers with access to well-established gas markets. In countries with small or nonexistent natural gas markets, an LNG sales contract might be anchored by an electric generating plant or an industrial buyer that can consume large volumes of the gas, with smaller customers added later, as a distribution network is built out from the terminal.

Access to capital. Any LNG project requires access to sizeable shareholders with the ability to fund major capital investments, either on an equity basis or through borrowings. Project (or limited recourse) financing can play a major role in securing the funding for LNG projects, even those involving the largest oil and gas companies. Successful project financing requires a well-constructed project concept with robust and stable commercial arrangements, which can ensure the repayment of billions of dollars of financing over many years in a potentially volatile energy price environment.

Strong relationships. Although the hardest to define in concrete terms, the relationships, reputations, and experience of the various stakeholders are among the most important aspects of an LNG project. Strong relationships between project sponsors, customers, governments, lenders, and contractors are a key to long-term project success. The reason that trust and relationships are so important is simple: in an enterprise spanning many decades, subject to many evolutionary changes unimagined at the outset, the underlying commercial and legal agreements may be inadequate to ensure the project's success, and the relationship between the parties provides the only guarantee that the business can address the inevitable problems that will arise. These relationships are especially important at the outset, when the project is least defined and the parties are preparing to spend significant sums of money without any assurance that the project they are envisioning will in the end achieve commercial reality. It can take years to build these types of trusting relationships and reputations, and for prospective new entrants, breaking into the LNG industry can be more challenging as a result.

Technical details. All physical links in the LNG chain require technical analysis, including feasibility studies, engineering designs, project execution, and operational plans. These will determine the technologies that are used; the size, compatibility, and integration of each component of the facilities; and any additional infrastructure that is required.

Unique logistical challenges have been faced (and overcome) on each project. Planning for these sometimes-tangential details may be projects in their own right. For example, when the Nigeria liquefaction plant was being constructed, it was necessary to house over 10,000 people at a remote site where there were no existing accommodations. Such related undertakings can cost the project millions of dollars.

Commercial issues. At the outset of a proposed project, the most important work involves agreeing on the commercial terms. This involves the project structure and ownership of various components of the project, including shareholders' agreements and project development agreements; negotiating and structuring a set of end-to-end contracts covering the production of natural gas at the wellhead, all the way to sales to the end users; defining the host government's role and share in the revenues; negotiating the contracts for the plant design and construction; and financing the project.

Safety and siting. Safety is of paramount importance in the LNG industry. The assets are so expensive that any repairs required by a major accident could amount to tens of millions of dollars plus the loss of significant revenues. A major accident could mar the industry's reputation and set back any proposed projects. Finally, insurance costs are a major expense for project investors, and an accident could drive them so high that profitability might be significantly reduced. Lenders will require an independent technical analysis of the facilities' design, as well as confirmation of their compliance with regulatory requirements and good industry practice. For all of these reasons, companies go to great lengths to design safety into the facilities from the outset and to provide continual training and resources for employees working on and around LNG facilities and ships, to ensure LNG's safe transportation and storage.

These considerations are most acute for regasification terminals, since the most desirable locations from an infrastructure standpoint are often near densely populated areas. There is widespread misunderstanding with regard to the safety of these terminals. In an era when the threats of global terrorist activities have dramatically increased, siting new terminals or moving tankers near populated areas has become even harder, particularly in the United States.

In the case of a greenfield project, both supplier and buyer must control sufficient land to accommodate their respective facilities and must ensure legal compliance with safety and environmental conditions. To accommodate tanker access, these sites must have access to waterways that are either already of sufficient depth or capable of being dredged to accommodate the LNG tankers. Expansions of existing facilities generally do not create the same level of concerns.

External advisers. Legal issues are present from the outset of a proposed project. Lawyers are instrumental in the drafting of contract and project terms. The contracts and agreements associated with an LNG project are complex, especially when it comes to allocating and mitigating the parties' risks and addressing contingencies for unforeseen circumstances. Lawyers also must advise on—and in certain cases help decide—the applicable law that will govern each element of a project. Legal issues are a major component of every project.

Each project will also involve the input of a variety of other technical advisers who will provide expert support to the project sponsors. These include consultants who will help prepare the necessary environmental impact statements, evaluate the gas reserves and markets, and make provisions related to shipping alternatives, insurance, safety, and security, among other tasks. The project sponsors, buyers, and financiers will all seek independent evaluations of the various aspects of the project as part of their own due-diligence exercise, leading up to the final investment decision (FID).

Government regulations. In most aspects of an LNG project, government regulations can play a significant role—though much more so downstream of the liquefaction facility. Most liquefaction plants are constructed in relatively remote locations and often in countries that do not have well-developed environmental, safety, or other regulatory guidelines. In these cases, the project sponsors will utilize regulations from other countries or guidelines issued by the World Bank or best practices promulgated by industry associations. Adopting these guidelines is often a prerequisite to securing international financial support for the project.

Downstream beyond the liquefaction plant, the degree of government scrutiny and involvement will rise. The LNG tankers are subject to a variety of regulations and conventions issued by the International Maritime Organization (IMO), the tanker's flag state, and the maritime regulatory bodies of the countries in which the tanker is expected to load and unload its cargo. The regasification terminals also are subject to stringent regulatory guidelines in their host countries, governing safety, security, and environmental aspects of the terminal and the vessels calling on it. In addition, the importing country may exercise economic regulation over the import terminals, requiring open access and the filing of tariffs governing the terminals' use. In particular, this will be the case when the LNG terminal is owned by a public utility.

Alternative methods of monetizing natural gas resources

LNG is not always the best choice for gas monetization. Given a large, remote gas field, a producer's best option may be to leave the gas in the ground. Often, gas reserves are too expensive and/or too far from a viable market to warrant the huge costs of development. However, declining costs, rising prices, improving technology, and expanding markets are leading developers to reexamine some of their remote reserves. Options for monetizing gas that are available to gas resource holders and developers include the following:

Local market. Depending on the location of the gas field and its proximity to developed areas, gas can be monetized by selling it into a local market. National governments generally prefer such a scheme, since it allows the development and internal use of a state resource. A steady supply of local gas can encourage industries that use natural gas as a feedstock (e.g., methanol and fertilizer production) or whose operations require large quantities of cheap power (e.g., aluminum smelters). It also promotes investment in infrastructure and creates jobs in the host country.

Many large gas finds are in areas that are too remote or inhospitable to make use of the gas as a local energy source. In these cases, some method must be found to monetize the gas as an export commodity. Sometimes, at the insistence of the host government, the development of gas export projects will go hand in hand with supply to local markets. Conversely, host nations can contract gas developers to build infrastructure to supply internal markets with gas, and the developers are then given the right to build gas export facilities in parallel.

LNG or pipeline? In the development of gas reserves, the choice between LNG or pipeline development can be relatively simple, as the LNG project in Trinidad illustrates. In Trinidad, there were significant reserves of stranded gas, and there were no nearby markets of any size—and none that could be reached economically by pipeline. On the market side, Japan is an example of a country with little or no indigenous gas reserves, concentrated population centers on the coast, and no nearby pipeline-accessible sources of gas (at least not when the early Japanese import projects were being developed). It goes without saying that ready access to the ocean is an essential ingredient of any successful LNG project! Beyond this, the trade-offs and decisions become more complex.

Economic trade-offs. In its early evolution, LNG was seen as a high-cost option and the last choice for countries with potential access to pipeline gas. Now that LNG technology has matured and costs have come down, LNG can generally compete with pipeline deliveries—at least over longer distances (generally greater than 2,000 kilometers) and even over shorter distances where there are major impediments to pipeline construction. Today in Japan, LNG remains the preferred import approach because of the disconnected nature of the Japanese markets, which would make it difficult to bring a large pipeline to the country and arrange for onward transmission and distribution. Japan's markets are viewed as prohibitively expensive and too legally complex to integrate into a single grid, foreclosing the pipeline option.

Security advantages. LNG has security advantages that can override economics. On the one hand, LNG is generally transported across international waters, so that only the seller and buyer governments are involved. On the other hand, unlike ships, pipelines are not vulnerable to the vagaries of weather and are simpler to maintain. Pipelines can provide a secure and stable method of delivering set volumes of gas on a year-round basis.

Pipelines often have to cross several international boundaries, which means that several governments may be involved, increasing the relative complexity of development. This may also raise the potential of supply interruptions through diversion of gas volumes, attack on the infrastructure, or having the intermediary country close the valve for political reasons. Gas buyers and sellers in a pipeline trade are essentially hostage to events in the countries crossed by their pipeline. A good example is the potential gas trade between India and Iran. The most obvious and economical method for bringing Iranian gas to Indian markets would be via an onshore pipeline across southern Pakistan, a scenario fraught with obvious political difficulties. LNG projects are not entirely immune to these kinds of difficulties. For example, historical distrust between Bolivia and Chile led to the demise of a scheme to export Bolivian LNG from a facility located on the Chilean coast.

One of the major reasons that countries have decided to import LNG has been to diversify their energy supply portfolios. They may be to diversify away from another energy commodity, as in

One of the major reasons that countries have decided to import LNG has been to diversify their energy supply portfolios. They may be to diversify away from another energy commodity, as in the case of Japan, which initially imported LNG to lessen its reliance on oil, or to reduce reliance on any single gas supplier, as in the case of European nations.

the case of Japan, which initially imported LNG to lessen its reliance on oil, or to reduce reliance on any single gas supplier, as in the case of European nations.

Exporters may favor the LNG option because, unlike a pipeline project, they can diversify their revenue sources by selling to multiple buyers and markets. Exporters reliant on a pipeline are at the mercy of a single market that has to be fully developed at some cost prior to construction. If demand slackens in that market, the asset remains stranded, whereas LNG may be able to find other markets when demand patterns change. More flexible schemes like LNG can get smaller commitments from a number of different buyers to reach the necessary threshold for project investment.

Security of supply and security of markets are central themes in the 21st-century energy marketplace.

Options for monetizing gas that are available to gas resource holders and developers other than LNG or long distance gas transmission lines include the following:

Gas to liquids (GTL). This term often is used to refer to the reprocessing of methane into longer-chain hydrocarbons that are liquid at atmospheric temperatures and pressures. The GTL process entails the generation of syngas, a mixture of CO and H_2 derived by combining methane with H_2O and/or O_2 at high temperatures. This syngas is then subject to the Fischer-Tropsch (FT) reaction or another similar process, in which the syngas is reacted in the presence of a catalyst to produce longer-chain hydrocarbons that are liquid at normal pressures and temperatures. These hydrocarbons can then be processed using standard refining techniques. The primary product to date has been a form of very clean diesel fuel, which can be handled and used in the same way as diesel refined from crude oil.

GTL competes primarily against more traditional oil products, rather than LNG. An advantage of GTL is that it is stable, liquid under normal conditions (and therefore easily transportable), and very clean. Like oil and unlike LNG, GTL is a fungible commodity. These characteristics make GTL especially valuable in developed markets that are highly sensitive to environmental concerns. Because GTL competes against refined petroleum products for markets, it is highly sensitive to oil price, though usually capable of attracting a premium price for its environmental value, and may offer a "portfolio" benefit to a gas resource holder who is otherwise largely captive to natural gas markets and pricing. With advances in technology and scale, capital costs for GTL projects have dropped significantly, from more than $100,000/bbl of installed capacity to $25,000–$30,000/bbl in mid-2005 (compared with around $15,000/bbl for conventional petroleum refining).

Rising oil prices starting in 2002 have made GTL increasingly more attractive to gas producers as a monetization method. As a result, gas-rich countries, such as Qatar, Iran, Russia, Nigeria, Australia, and Algeria, are examining or initiating demonstration-scale GTL projects. Furthermore, the development of a GTL project needs less gas reserves than an LNG project of comparable investment size and therefore can be appealing to countries with limited gas reserves.

Compressed natural gas (CNG). For shorter-distance trades or for relatively small reserves (<2 Tcf [56.7 Bcm]), another monetization option is CNG. In a CNG scenario, natural gas is compressed to between 2,000 and 4,000 pounds per square inch (psi) and is transported to market aboard specially outfitted ships. These ships are essentially floating pipelines. A number of different containment systems for the compressed gas have been proposed, each consisting of a series of high-pressure pipes into which gas is pumped at high pressure.

An advantage of CNG is that it does not require expensive infrastructure in the host countries. Political risk in the (often developing) nations that hold much of the world's gas reserves can raise the cost of capital for projects. The facilities for a CNG project in a host nation downstream of the pipeline consist solely of compression and (if necessary) gas-processing facilities, so that substantially less capital is at risk than for an LNG or GTL project. The most expensive assets—the ships—are mobile. A drawback is that the lack of infrastructure in the gas-producing country means less tax revenue and fewer jobs.

The major disadvantage of CNG vis-à-vis LNG is cost. CNG ships cost roughly the same as LNG ships but can deliver only about a quarter of the volume per ship. As more CNG ships are built, the cost is expected to go down, but the shipping cost will still be at a premium relative to LNG. The nature of the CNG trade, which requires a constant rotation of vessel deliveries to maintain a steady gas flow, is also somewhat of a drawback (although this could be mitigated by gas storage on the receiving end). The weight and complexity of CNG vessels could make maintenance difficult.

Variations on the CNG theme have been proposed, mainly in the form of hybrids between CNG and LNG technologies. They take advantage of the fact that both pressurization and cooling reduce the volume of natural gas and make it easier to transport. However, no successful schemes have been developed to date. Independent players, rather than the oil and gas majors, are pursuing most of the projects currently under consideration. The technology is unproven in long-term service, which also raises issues of financeability and market acceptance. Other factors that remain to be fully addressed are the acceptability of the high-pressure tankers into the importing countries and the siting of the facilities to unload them and connect them to the gas grid.

NOTES

[1] BP. 2005. Statistical Review of World Energy 2005. London: BP.

[2] EIA. 2005. International Energy Outlook 2005. http://www.eia.doe.gov/oiaf/archive/aeo05/pdf/0383(2005).pdf.

[3] 2004. Worldwide look at reserves and production. *Oil and Gas Journal*. 102 (47): 22–23.

[4] Cedigaz. 2005. The 2004 Natural Gas Year in Review.

[5] EIA. International Energy Outlook 2005.

[6] Ibid., p. 3.

[7] EIA. International Energy Annual 2001.

[8] EIA. International Energy Outlook 2005, p. 37.

[9] BP. Statistical Review of World Energy 2005.

[10] Mabro, Robert, and Ian Wybrew-Bond. 1999. Gas to Europe: The Strategies of Four Major Suppliers. Cambridge: Oxford University Press.

[11] Interstate Natural Gas Association of America Web site. http://www.ingaa.org.

[12] Tusiani, Michael D. 1996. The Petroleum Shipping Industry. 2 Vols. Tulsa: PennWell.

THE EVOLUTION OF THE GLOBAL GAS AND LNG MARKETS 2

INTRODUCTION

In most markets, the gas business developed within a regulatory environment that reflected the principle that transmission and distribution of natural gas (the pipes end of the business) were activities that created a natural monopoly and as such were to be franchised and regulated by governmental authorities. Transmission lines and gas distribution systems were built under cost-of-service tariff structures, which guaranteed that the owners would recover their costs, their capital, and a fair or just and reasonable return on their investments. Each component of the supply chain—production, gathering, transmission, and distribution—was often functionally and legally separated from the others. In countries with indigenous production, regulators often set the price of gas at the wellhead. In the case of imported gas, regulators often had the right to approve the supply contracts before they could come into effect.

Natural gas producers and suppliers sold gas to transmission companies under long-term purchase contracts with high take-or-pay obligations, to help the producer justify the exploration risks and high production investments. In turn, the transmission companies (unless they were integrated with the distribution companies, as was usually often the case in Europe) resold the gas, under similar arrangements, to the distributors. The guiding concept was the regulatory bargain, or compact. The monopoly operator was permitted to recover its costs and earn a reasonable, assured return on its investments (provided these were deemed prudent); in turn, the operator was obligated to provide a public service, namely, the assured supply of natural gas to the consumers (i.e., the obligation to serve). The actual cost of the natural gas purchases (whether from producers or transmission companies) itself was generally treated as a "pass-through" and was fully recovered from the next buyer along the chain, all the way to the burner tip.

It is now widely believed that although the traditional, cost-plus structure provided security of supply, it resulted in higher prices, especially in those markets in which the business was mature. Inflated energy costs became unacceptable, especially when the emerging global economy introduced new competitive pressures. Starting with the production functions, opening up gas and power markets to competition is now seen as a way of lowering energy costs to industry, as well as to residential and commercial consumers. Regulators have adopted policies of separating facility ownership and operation, providing open access to the pipeline infrastructure, and bringing competition to supply and marketing. This in turn is expected to contribute to a more competitive marketplace for gas and has led to the emergence of gas trading hubs—prerequisites for the development of a commodity market with transparent pricing. These hubs usually develop where several pipelines meet, often near large storage facilities such as Henry Hub, Louisiana, in the United States, and the Zeebrugge LNG terminal, in Belgium. In the case of the United Kingdom, the hub is a notional one, the National Balancing Point (NBP).

Questions have been raised about the value of these market liberalization policies. Will real price reductions be realized from a competitive environment? And how will funding be obtainable for projects in such an environment ensuring that supplies are available for customers? The answer is somewhat mixed: While large consumers are generally perceived to have benefited from competition, the record for smaller and especially residential consumers is less clear. In the two most competitive markets, the results are notably different. In the United Kingdom, competition appears to be working in all segments of the market. However, in the United States, residential consumers have seen little market competition. Nonetheless, the move toward liberalized utility markets appears irreversible in the West.

Market liberalization is now advanced in the United States, Canada, and the United Kingdom. In Western Europe, it is being promoted by the European Union (EU) and at the national level, although the pace of implementation varies widely. Progress toward market liberalization is moving at a more restrained pace in Asia.

Whatever the pace of gas and power sector liberalization in global gas markets may be, the general consensus in the gas (and LNG) industry is that demand will continue to grow for the foreseeable future. However, forecasts of demand growth and, consequently, LNG prices have been tempered in the face of persistently high oil prices. According to historic data from the EIA, oil prices have remained above $55/bbl since January 2006.[1] This has led to lower gas demand forecasts as a result of gas demand destruction or migration (especially in the power generation and industrial sectors in the developed economies) and/or conservation measures. However, even with lower demand expectations, the need for LNG seems destined to rise inexorably as major consuming countries, such as the United States, the United Kingdom, and Canada suffer apparently irreversible declines in their domestic production.

As the world advances into the gas era, some people have questioned whether the industry is capable of supplying large volumes on a reliable basis and at acceptable prices over long periods of time. There is no doubt that worldwide reserves are adequate, as discussed in chapter 1, even though the industry focused its drilling activity on the search for oil. There are sufficient gas resources to last for 70 years at current production levels, compared with 42 years for oil. While gas resources are ample, they are not evenly distributed around the world—and certainly not where the demand is greatest. For example, although North America holds less than 5% of global reserves, it accounts for 28% of world consumption. By contrast, Middle East nations hold 36% of global gas reserves but consume only 10% (table 2–1).

THE U.S. NATURAL GAS AND LNG MARKETS

The U.S. gas market, which accounts for one-quarter of the global consumption of natural gas and 85% of the North American total, is the world's largest and probably most competitive wholesale gas market. Natural gas represents about one-quarter of the country's primary energy. The electric power and industrial sectors are the largest consumers of gas for generation of electric power, for plant process fuel, and as an industrial feedstock. Natural gas also has the largest share of residential heating and cooking. Natural gas enjoyed the fastest growth in the power generation sector since the mid-1990s, reflecting the impact that competition has had on fuel preferences of power generators (table 2–2).

Table 2–1. Worldwide natural gas consumption, 1980–2004 (*Source:* EIA, International Energy Outlook 2006)

Year	Consumption (Bcf)															
	Canada	France	Germany[1]*	Indonesia	Iran	Italy	Japan	Nether-lands	Former U.S.S.R.	Russia	Saudi Arabia	Ukraine	United Kingdom	United States	Uzbek-stan	Other	World
1980	1,883	981	2,621	195	232	972	903	1,493	13,328	—	334	—	1,702	19,877	—	8,369	52,890
1981	1,842	1,003	2,513	232	155	942	925	1,421	14,440	—	564	—	1,740	19,404	—	8,333	53,513
1982	1,859	979	2,334	218	200	944	956	1,511	15,522	—	430	—	1,743	18,001	—	8,931	53,628
1983	1,863	999	2,397	302	310	967	1,020	1,451	16,822	—	418	—	1,815	16,835	—	9,427	54,626
1984	2,017	1,079	2,584	365	476	1,135	1,372	1,540	18,512	—	620	—	1,851	17,951	—	10,189	59,692
1985	2,165	1,110	2,546	513	600	1,151	1,468	1,624	20,302	—	716	—	1,991	17,281	—	10,777	62,244
1986	2,130	1,129	2,595	441	536	1,217	1,494	1,620	21,522	—	890	—	2,020	16,221	—	11,303	63,118
1987	2,112	1,038	2,733	542	565	1,346	1,543	1,672	22,462	—	946	—	2,079	17,211	—	12,062	66,312
1988	2,331	963	2,716	492	706	1,460	1,618	1,513	24,092	—	1,028	—	1,972	18,030	—	12,628	69,548
1989	2,427	984	2,835	546	784	1,581	1,731	1,550	24,529	—	1,052	—	1,951	19,119	—	13,549	72,638
1990	2,378	997	2,669	547	837	1,674	1,851	1,535	24,961	—	1,077	—	2,059	19,174	—	13,611	73,370
1991	2,400	1,131	2,776	557	811	1,775	1,976	1,715	25,014	—	1,130	—	2,218	19,562	—	13,841	74,907
1992	2,596	1,146	2,739	673	883	1,760	2,023	1,669	—	16,482	1,201	3,503	2,170	20,228	1,095	16,868	75,036
1993	2,691 [R]	1,158	2,830	850	938	1,801	2,034	1,714	—	16,185	1,268	3,871	2,412	20,790	1,541	17,005	77,086 [R]
1994	2,738 [R]	1,157	2,965	965	1,123	1,748	2,180	1,654	—	15,214	1,331	3,327	2,542	21,247	1,229	17,400	76,820 [R]
1995	2,872 [R]	1,183	3,172	1,061	1,243	1,921	2,207	1,701	—	14,507	1,343	2,970	2,690	22,207	1,349	18,297	78,723 [R]
1996	2,917	1,314	3,163	1,108	1,416	1,984	2,390	1,874	—	14,504	1,460	2,935	3,182	22,609	1,434	19,939 [R]	82,231 [R]
1997	2,887	1,300	3,012	1,125	1,663	2,048	2,439	1,763	—	13,434	1,601	2,832	3,013	22,737	1,455	20,825 [R]	82,136 [R]
1998	2,798 [R]	1,313	3,130	983	1,828	2,205	2,535	1,752	—	14,045	1,653	2,606	3,072	22,246	1,409	21,357 [R]	82,930 [R]
1999	3,108 [R]	1,383	3,151	1,124	2,112	2,396	2,736 [R]	1,705	—	14,013	1,632	2,755	3,259	22,405	1,423	21,995 [R]	85,196 [R]
2000	2,991 [R]	1,403	3,098	1,081	2,221	2,498	2,833 [R]	1,725	—	14,130	1,759	2,779	3,373	23,333	1,511	23,538 [R]	88,275 [R]
2001	3,121 [R]	1,471 [R]	3,239	1,182	2,478	2,505	2,831 [R]	1,769	—	14,412	1,896	2,617	3,338	22,239	1,596	24,804 [R]	89,499 [R]
2002	3,173 [R]	1,528 [R]	3,204	1,218 [R]	2,798	2,488 [R]	2,928 [R]	1,767 [R]	—	14,567	2,002	2,779	3,379 [R]	23,007	1,642	26,170 [R]	92,653 [R]
2003	3,373 [R]	1,511 [R]	3,566 [R]	1,222 [R]	2,910 [R]	2,732 [R]	3,045 [R]	1,775 [R]	—	15,291	2,121	3,023	3,358 [R]	22,277 [R]	1,670	28,086 [R]	95,960 [R]
2004[P]	3,385	1,604	3,576	1,309	3,021	2,847	2,950	1,812	—	16,022	2,319	3,051	3,477	22,430	1,773	30,088	99,665

Note: Totals may not equal sum of components due to independent rounding.

R = Revised. P = Preliminary. — = Not applicable.

[1] *Through 1990, this is East and West Germany. Beginning in 1991, this is unified Germany.

Table 2–2. U.S. natural gas consumption by end use (*Source:* EIA)

	Consumption (MMcf/d)					
	2000	2001	2002	2003	2004	2005
Total demand	23,333,121	22,238,624	23,007,017	22,276,502	22,430,225	21,871,008
Lease and plant fuel	1,150,948	1,118,552	1,113,082	1,122,283	1,097,902	1,067,820
Lease fuel	746,889	747,411	730,579	758,380	731,561	–
Plant fuel	404,059	371,141	382,503	363,903	366,341	–
Pipeline and distribution use	642,210	624,964	666,920	591,492	571,853	557,596
Volumes delivered to consumers	21,539,964	20,495,108	21,227,015	20,562,727	20,760,470	20,245,592
Residential	4,996,179	4,771,340	4,888,818	5,079,351	4,884,521	4,838,371
Commercial	3,182,469	3,022,712	3,144,170	3,179,493	3,141,653	3,058,963
Industrial	8,142,240	7,344,219	7,507,180	7,150,396	7,250,634	6,529,263
Vehicle fuel	12,752	14,536	14,950	18,271	20,514	22,259
Electric power	5,206,324	5,342,301	5,671,897	5,135,215	5,463,148	5,796,736

(*Source*: EIA)

Deregulation of the natural gas industry

The process of deregulation began with the Natural Gas Policy Act (NGPA) of 1978, which provided for the phased removal of controls from gas prices at the wellhead, price controls that had been in place since the 1950s. Wellhead deregulation was completed with the Wellhead Decontrol Act of 1989. In addition, the Federal Energy Regulatory Commission (FERC) developed new regulations for interstate pipelines, which changed their role in the delivery of natural gas. In 1985, faced with rising prices and falling demand, FERC Order 380 allowed customers (local distribution companies) to reject their take-or-pay obligations with the transmission companies, while leaving the transmission companies obligated to their suppliers for the corresponding contractual supply obligations that they had made. Order 380 also gave tacit recognition to the creation of transportation-only services on the transmission lines. In 1992, FERC Order 636 formally separated the merchant (gas supply) and transportation functions of interstate pipeline companies and essentially took the transmission companies out of the gas supply and marketing business.

Simultaneously, many states began moving to force electric power companies (which are largely regulated at the state level, in contrast to gas transmission companies, which are largely regulated at the federal level) to divest themselves of their power plants and create a competitive market in power generation. A new group of merchant energy firms emerged to take advantage of investment and trading opportunities crossing both business sectors. These firms were initially the darlings of Wall Street; however, following the collapse of Enron, they experienced a loss of investor confidence, and the value of their shares sharply declined. Abuses of trading positions and market power (most notoriously during the California energy crisis of 2000–2001) led FERC to become much more vigilant about monitoring gas and power transactions, and in June 2004, FERC established the Market Oversight and Investigations office. Its purpose is "to protect customers through understanding markets and their regulation, identifying and fixing market problems, and assuring compliance with Commission rules and regulations."[2]

Natural gas prices

Following the deregulation of wellhead gas prices and the unbundling of gas transportation and supply functions, an important trading hub developed at Henry Hub, in Louisiana, around which is set the most closely watched benchmark U.S. price. Hubs at other locations are more thinly traded. The New York Mercantile Exchange (NYMEX) prices for futures contracts are based on Henry Hub prices. North American wholesale gas prices are largely set by market conditions, and supply contracts are not contractually linked to competitive oil product prices or other indices, as is still the case in many other nations. Not only natural gas but also transportation and storage rights are now actively traded. During the latter part of the 1980s and most of the '90s, natural gas prices were low relative to other fossil fuels. During the 1990s, the Henry Hub benchmark price was typically about $2.00–$2.50 per million British thermal units (MMBtu). This led to a strong increase in natural gas demand, particularly in the industrial and power sectors. U.S. gas consumption increased from 19.2 Tcf (544.1 Bcm) in 1990 to 23.4 Tcf (663.2 Bcm) in 2000. The consensus view of the industry in 2001 was that gas demand would reach 30 Tcf (850.2 Bcm) by 2010.

The year 2000 signaled the end of low, stable gas prices in the United States. The rapid expansion in gas-fired power generation had a surprising impact. Unprecedented gas demand by the power sector to meet summer air-conditioning load resulted in underground storage below historical levels going into the winter. Early cold sent gas prices soaring, and Henry Hub prices reached a then-extraordinary peak of around $10/MMBtu in January

2001. High gas prices caused considerable demand loss—gas use declined by 1.1 Tcf (31.2 Bcm) in 2001—and stimulated a major drilling effort, which contributed to a restoration of a market balance.

By early 2002, gas prices had plummeted back to the $2.00–$2.50/MMBtu level, and industry pundits started to question their prognostications of gas shortages and higher gas prices. In 2002, the Henry Hub price averaged $3.05/MMBtu, compared to $3.75/MMBtu in 2001 and $4.34/MMBtu in 2000. However, relief to gas consumers proved to be temporary. A cold 2002–3 winter sent gas inventories to record low levels at winter's end, sending prices to over $7.50/MMBtu at Henry Hub, approximately $3.00/MMBtu more than the level recorded at the start of the heating season. Although prices decreased in the spring of 2003, gas demand by the power sector to meet summer air-conditioning load kept prices well above the $4.50/MMBtu mark through the summer.

As time passed, it appeared increasingly obvious that higher prices were here to stay. Henry Hub failed to dip below $5.30/MMBtu during 2004 and crept inexorably past the $6.00/MMBtu mark as the heating season of 2004–5 approached. In the summer and fall of 2005, the loss of production in the Gulf of Mexico caused by Hurricane Katrina drove gas prices to all-time highs that exceeded $14.00/MMBtu. By February 2006, they had fallen to $7.00/MMBtu, aided by warmer-than-normal winter weather in most of the country (fig. 2–1).

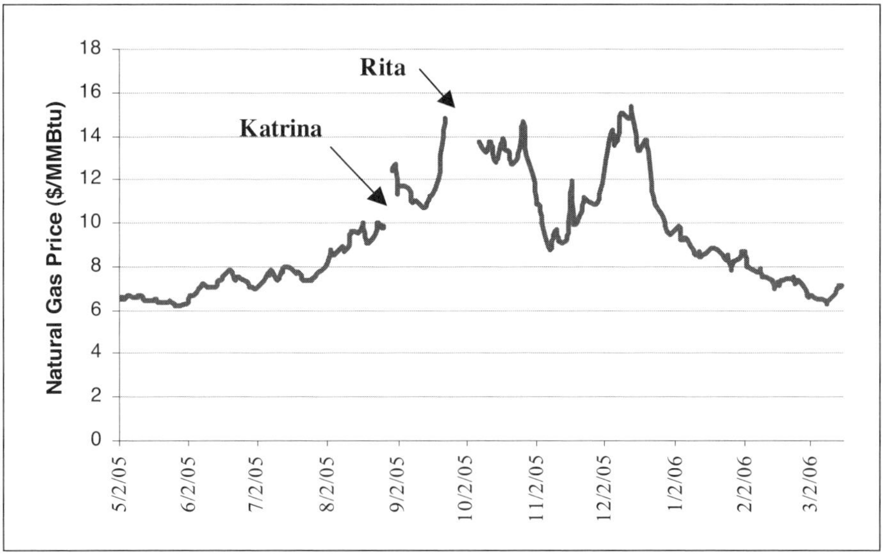

Fig. 2–1. Hurricanes Katrina and Rita: Next-day Henry Hub spot prices, May 2005–March 2006 (*Source:* EIA)

Outlook for supply and demand

While DOE and other organizations had anticipated a 30 Tcf (850.2 Bcm) U.S. gas market by 2010, the advent of an era of higher gas prices led them to moderate these expectations. By 2003, it was clear that domestic gas production was falling far short of the levels required in order to meet the demand of a market of this size. Prices needed to engender such a large supply response would not sustain a demand of this magnitude. Nevertheless, DOE is still projecting gas demand will reach 30 Tcf, albeit later than in its earlier outlook. In its 2005 forecast, DOE projected a 32–40 Tcf (906.9–1,133.6 Bcm) gas market in 2025, depending on economic scenarios. In its reference case, DOE projects natural gas use for power generation will increase from 5 Tcf (141.7 Bcm) in 2003 to over 9 Tcf (255.1 Bcm) in 2025, while industrial consumption is forecast to rise from 8 Tcf (226.7 Bcm) to over 10 Tcf (283.4 Bcm) during the same period.[3] Residential and commercial use is expected to remain essentially flat during this time period.

In the 1980s and '90s, the robust growth in gas consumption increasingly outpaced domestic supply. Drilling in the Lower 48 states was unable to significantly boost gas production capability, and the growing supply gap was largely filled by imports from Canada. However, the prolific Western Canadian Sedimentary Basin is also maturing and faces the same trends as the Lower 48 basins. More and more wells have to be drilled just to offset declines in producing fields. Thus, at the beginning of the 21st century, North American self-sufficiency finally came to an end, and the industry turned to more distant gas resources. This opened up opportunities for LNG imports and the development of frontier natural gas resources, such as Alaska's North Slope and Canada's Arctic resources. The cost of a 4 billion cubic foot per day (Bcf/d) (41.4 billion cubic meters per year [Bcm/y]) pipeline to deliver North Slope gas to the Lower 48 states is estimated at up to $27 billion and is unlikely to begin operations before 2015.[4] The Canadian Arctic gas resources involve less investment to bring to market but hold a smaller contribution potential. There is increasing acceptance of the view that LNG, benefiting from impressive cost reductions in production and delivery infrastructure, is cost-competitive with these frontier gas supplies. Qatar, for example, has established mega-sized liquefaction chains, employing the principles of economies of scale to deliver large quantities of gas to the distant United States at costs competitive with the best indigenous North American gas supplies. Moreover, sustained high Henry Hub prices have made even more distant LNG imports from Australia a feasibly profitable prospect. Of course, this assumes that Henry Hub prices will remain high for a prolonged period of time, which is an extremely risky presumption, as those who survived the price collapse of the late 1980s can attest.

LNG IMPORT TERMINALS

LNG importation: The experience of the 1970s

Skeptics about the long-term prospects for LNG imports into the United States are quick to point to the failed LNG trades from Algeria in the 1970s. At that time, four LNG import terminals and a number of tankers were built to deliver LNG from Algeria. These investments were made under a regulatory policy that "rolled in" high-priced new gas alongside low-priced gas already under contract to interstate pipelines—a policy that subsidized new gas, primarily LNG and imports from Canada, at the expense of domestic production. When this approach ended with the passage of the NGPA in 1978, new domestic gas prices rose and then fell, as domestic gas production increased and demand fell. The collapse of U.S. wellhead prices associated with the gas bubble of the 1980s resulted in Algerian LNG being priced out of the market, the collapse of the supply contracts (with extensive accompanying litigation), and the mothballing of terminals (except for the Everett terminal in Boston) and ships for significant periods of time. The regulators had approved the contract conditions supporting the earlier LNG trade and then, with Order 380, removed these underpinnings. It was ultimately the market, not regulations, that provided the foundation for the revived LNG trade into the United States in the late 1990s.

The four onshore import and regasification plants built to serve the earlier trade provided the foundation for the revival of LNG in the United States. When the United States experienced tightening gas supplies in the late 1990s, these terminals represented quickly available infrastructure to facilitate LNG imports. The cost of reactivating a mothballed terminal was far less than building a new terminal and could be done far more quickly. By mid-2003, all four terminals were receiving LNG cargoes, and plans were in place to add capacity to all of these facilities at a relatively low cost.

Existing LNG import terminals in the United States

Everett, Massachusetts. The sole LNG import terminal in the Northeast is located at Everett, Massachusetts, in Boston Harbor. This terminal is a critical component of regional gas supplies, since it provides approximately 20% of New England's annual needs—and an even larger share during the winter.[5] The Everett terminal was opened by Distrigas Corporation, a subsidiary of Cabot Corporation, in 1971 and started receiving LNG from Sonatrach, Algeria's national oil company (NOC). It imported Algerian LNG until 1985, when FERC Order 380 allowed customers to abandon their take-or-pay obligations and switch to cheaper pipeline gas. Unable to recover the costs of LNG imports which were too expensive to clear the market, the terminal was placed into bankruptcy reorganization. Following a settlement between Distrigas and Sonatrach in 1987, providing for new supply arrangements, the facility has remained in continuous operations.

Sonatrach supplied the bulk of the LNG to the facility until Trinidad's Atlantic LNG (ALNG) was commissioned in 1999. In September 2000, Cabot sold the terminal and related assets to Belgium's Tractebel, Inc., for $690 million. Tractebel was subsequently acquired by Suez, which owns and operates the terminal under its Suez Energy North America subsidiary. The Everett terminal houses two LNG storage tanks with a combined capacity of 3.6 Bcf (154,900 cubic meters). Everett's installed nameplate sendout capacity is over 1 Bcf/d (10.3 Bcm/y), with a sustainable daily throughput capacity of approximately 0.715 Bcf/d (7.4 Bcm/y). Everett also supplies large volumes of LNG by truck to an extensive network of satellite LNG peakshaving plants owned by local distribution companies throughout the Northeast.

Lake Charles, Louisiana. This plant was opened in 1980 by Trunkline LNG Corporation, a subsidiary of Panhandle Eastern Pipeline Corporation, but operated for only three years. During this period, it received LNG cargoes from Algeria, until low gas prices made this trade uneconomical. The terminal was reopened for business in 1987. Duke Energy subsequently acquired, then sold Panhandle (including the terminal) to CMS Energy in the spring of 1999. As interest in reviving LNG imports grew, CMS Energy held an open season in early 2001. BG LNG Services, Inc., won the rights to all available capacity at the terminal for 22 years from January 2002.

CMS Energy then sold Panhandle to Southern Union in 2003. The terminal's new owner promptly set about expanding the average sendout, from 0.63 Bcf/d (6.5 Bcm/y) to 1.2 Bcf/d (12.4 Bcm/y), and the storage capacity, from 6.3 Bcf (315,000 cubic meters) to 9 Bcf (425,000 cubic meters). In 2004, Trunkline LNG launched a phase II expansion to add another 0.3 Bcf/d (3.1 Bcm/y) of sendout and a new unloading dock. The phase II expansion was completed in the second quarter of 2006. BG is the sole capacity holder for both of these expansions. A third expansion is under consideration. In April 2006, BG signed an agreement with Southern Union to extend its terminal services contract for an additional five years, until 2028.

Elba Island, Georgia. This terminal was opened by Southern LNG, a subsidiary of Sonat, Inc., in 1978 and received Algerian LNG for two years before a pricing dispute ended this trade. After operating briefly in peaking service, the facility remained dormant until it was reopened for LNG imports in late 2001. When El Paso merged with Sonat in 1999, it assumed control over Sonat's pipeline system, as well as the Elba Island terminal. An affiliate,

El Paso Merchant Energy (EPME), won 100% of the capacity rights at the terminal in an open season. Enron subsequently challenged the award and negotiated supply rights for 43% of the capacity. These rights were later acquired by Marathon after Enron's bankruptcy.

Like many U.S. energy-trading companies, El Paso experienced financial difficulties in the wake of the Enron debacle, and in December 2003, the firm sold its entire capacity at Elba Island to BG, together with its related LNG supply agreements from Trinidad. In June 2003, Southern LNG started an expansion of the terminal, adding a 3.3 Bcf (160,000 cubic meters) storage tank, 0.36 Bcf/d (3.7 Bcm/y) of baseload sendout capacity, and two LNG tanker berths. This expansion, which was placed into service in early 2006, increased total storage capacity to 7.3 Bcf (347,500 cubic meters) and sendout capacity to 0.81 Bcf/d (8.3 Bcm/y). Shell acquired all of the rights to this expansion capacity.

In December 2005, Southern LNG announced plans to significantly expand Elba Island once again. This expansion would add 8.4 Bcf (420,000 cubic meters) of storage capacity at the facility and 0.9 Bcf/d (9.3 Bcm/y) of sendout capacity, thereby doubling the storage and sendout capabilities of the facility. BG and Shell will have exclusive rights to this expansion when it is completed in 2012. A Sonat affiliate is in the process of building a new pipeline, the Cypress Pipeline, from Elba Island to Jacksonville, Florida, to bring regasified LNG to the rapidly growing Florida market.

Cove Point, Maryland. The LNG terminal on the Chesapeake Bay, near Baltimore, was originally built by Columbia Gas and Consolidated Natural Gas, to serve the mid-Atlantic market. It began operations in 1979 but was mothballed in 1980. Consolidated sold its interest to Columbia in 1988, which partially reactivated the plant in 1995 to provide gas peaking service, liquefying pipeline gas in the summer and making this gas available for sendout during the winter peak demand periods.

In July 2000, Williams Corporation purchased the terminal and an associated 87-mile pipeline linking it to the interstate pipeline grid in Virginia. In 2002, Williams sold the terminal to Dominion Resources for $217 million. It reopened as an LNG terminal in 2003. BP, El Paso, and Shell won equal capacity rights at the terminal under an open season bidding process. El Paso subsequently sold its rights to Norway's Statoil.

In 2005, Cove Point applied for FERC authorization to add 0.8 Bcf/d (8.3 Bcm/y) of sendout capacity and 7.7 Bcf (385,000 cubic meters) of storage to its terminal in Maryland. The expansion will increase throughput capacity to 1.8 Bcf/d (18.6 Bcm/y) and will raise storage capacity to 14.6 Bcf (730,000 cubic meters). All of Cove Point's expansion capacity was contracted to

Statoil in 2005 under negotiated arrangements, open access no longer being required at U.S. LNG terminals.

Energy Bridge, Gulf of Mexico. The world's first offshore regasification terminal, the Gulf Gateway Deepwater Port terminal is located 116 miles off the coast of Louisiana and received its first cargo in March 2005. It is owned by Excelerate Energy, which acquired the rights to the technology from El Paso in 2003. In this innovative approach, an LNG tanker is fitted with vaporization equipment and connects with a Submerged Turret Loading buoy, based on technology that has been used in the North Sea. The facility can deliver 0.5 Bcf/d (5.2 Bcm/y) of gas through lines from the ship to undersea pipelines, which then deliver it onshore. However, Gulf Gateway received only two cargoes during its inaugural year.

New LNG terminals in the United States

As the industry gained confidence that the revived LNG trade into the United States was not simply a replay of the 1970s and it became clear that domestic production and Canadian imports would level off or even fall, many companies developed plans for LNG terminals. As of late 2006, four new terminals were under construction in the United States.

Cameron, Louisiana. Sempra is building the 1.5 Bcf/d (15.5 Bcm/y) Cameron LNG terminal on the Calcasieu River, some 15 miles south of Lake Charles, Louisiana. It is due to start operations in 2008. Sempra has announced that it has signed access agreements with Italy's Eni and Merrill Lynch. Sempra has also concluded heads of agreement for terminal access with Suez and Sonatrach. Sempra has applied to FERC to expand the sendout capacity from 1.5 Bcf/d to 2.65 Bcf/d (27.4 Bcm/y) and add one storage tank, bringing total storage capacity to 13 Bcf (650,000 cubic meters) by 2010.

Sabine Pass, Louisiana. Cheniere Energy, an independent developer of LNG terminals, is building an LNG terminal near Sabine Pass in Cameron Parish, Louisiana. Phase I will have 2.6 Bcf/d (26.9 Bcm/y) of sendout capacity and be capable of receiving vessels of up to 250,000 cubic meters. Capacity has been reserved by Chevron, Total, and a Cheniere affiliate. Cheniere has obtained authorization to expand the capacity to 4 Bcf/d (41.4 Bcm/y) and add additional storage. Start-up of phase I is targeted for early 2008, and phase II will start up in 2009.

Freeport, Texas. Freeport LNG Development, a partnership of Michael Smith, ConocoPhillips, and Cheniere, is building a terminal on Quintana Island, Texas. Phase I includes two LNG storage tanks with a capacity of 6.9 Bcf (345,000 cubic meters) and sendout capacity of 1.75 Bcf/d (18.1 Bcm/y).

Construction of the terminal began in January 2005 and should be completed by January 2008.

The terminal's Phase I capacity has been sold to ConocoPhillips, which will take two-thirds, and Dow, which will control the remaining one-third. Expansion applications were submitted to FERC in 2005 for a Phase II expansion. This includes a second LNG-unloading dock and 0.5 Bcf/d (5.2 Bcm/y) of additional sendout capacity. Phase II capacity has been sold to Mitsubishi and ConocoPhillips. Assuming approval of these applications in mid-2006, Phase II capacity is expected to be available in 2009. Future expansions of the terminal (up to 4 Bcf/d [41.4 Bcm/y]) are planned and will be constructed as additional capacity is sold.

Golden Pass LNG, Texas. This 2 Bcf/d (20.7 Bcm/y) terminal is largely owned by Qatar Petroleum (70%), while ExxonMobil and ConocoPhillips own the rest. It is the prime destination for volumes from the integrated RasGas III project in Qatar, which is sponsored by Qatar Petroleum and ExxonMobil. However, the terminal will also receive a portion of output from Qatar Petroleum and ConocoPhillips' Qatargas III project. Golden Pass LNG began construction in the summer of 2006, and it should be finished in 2009.

LNG developments in Canada

Canada has an estimated 57 Tcf (1,615.4 Bcm) of proven natural gas reserves and is the world's third-largest natural gas producer. It exports gas to the United States via pipeline. However, the production of conventional natural gas, mainly in Alberta, is projected to flatten or even decline. As a result, Canada is turning its attention to LNG, mainly in the Maritime provinces. Eight terminals have been proposed, of which one is in an advanced stage as of the end of 2005.

Canaport LNG, Saint John, New Brunswick. Irving Oil, a large independent refinery owner, and Repsol are constructing a 1 Bcf/d (10.3 Bcm/y) terminal near Irving Oil's existing refinery and deepwater marine terminal. It is scheduled to be in service in 2008. The regasified LNG will be sold in eastern Canada, to Irving's own refinery, and to New England via the Maritimes & Northeast Pipeline.

Bear Head Project, Canso Strait, Nova Scotia. Anadarko Petroleum began site preparation work on a 1 Bcf/d (10.3 Bcm/y) project in 2005. The gas was to be delivered to markets in the United States and Canada. However, in early 2006 Anadarko halted work on this project and in July 2006 announced that the project had been sold to a group of investors named US Venture Energy. Anadarko confirmed in a September 2006 filing to the Securities and

Exchange Commission that the sale had failed to materialize. In February 2007, Anadarko announced it had written off its investment in Bear Head. The further development of the terminal remains in doubt.

LNG developments in Mexico

Although Mexico has substantial natural gas resources, particularly in the Burgos Basin, the NOC, Petróleos Mexicanos (PEMEX), has focused its limited investment capital on oil, causing the development of the nation's gas resources to lag demand. The Mexican constitution prohibits the foreign ownership of oil and gas resources, which has further complicated the development of these reserves. Mexico has made some progress toward opening up its upstream sector through a new contractual arrangement known as the Multiple Service Contract (MSC). The idea is to increase production significantly by attracting foreign capital without foreign ownership of natural gas reserves. Nevertheless, the very concept of foreign involvement in the Mexican upstream remains problematic for many voters and politicians, not to mention the powerful PEMEX unions. As a result, little has been accomplished, and the ultimate development of these reserves is uncertain at best.

Demand for natural gas has been growing, especially in the power and industrial sectors. Residential and commercial consumption have also seen substantial growth due to the 1995 privatization of the transmission and distribution sector, which brought natural gas distribution systems into large cities. Mexico's gas demand is projected to grow 5.2% annually, from 5.7 Bcf/d (59 Bcm/y) in 2004 to 9.5 Bcf/d (98.3 Bcm/y) by 2014.[6] Mexico has depended on imports from the United States for some time, and indigenous gas production is expected to reach only 7.4 Bcf/d (76.5 Bcm/y) by 2015. With the United States now being less well positioned to export gas, Mexico is turning to LNG imports of its own, as well as providing a conduit for LNG deliveries to California. The Mexican Energy Secretariat forecasts that LNG imports will reach 1.8 Bcf/d (18.6 Bcm/y) by 2014.[7] This means that LNG will meet 19% of the total Mexican demand for gas. At least three terminals will be needed to provide this supply.

Proposals exist for at least 15 receiving terminals. As of late 2006, one was in operation and one was under construction.

Altamira. Shell, Total, and Mitsui have built the Altamira LNG terminal in the eastern state of Tamaulipas. This facility will have an initial sendout capacity of 0.65 Bcf/d (6.7 Bcm/y). The Mexican national power generation monopoly company Comisión Federal de Electricidad (CFE) has contracted for 0.5 Bcf/d (5.2 Bcm/y) of regasified LNG for 15 years. Other customers are likely to be found among the many industrial plants in the Altamira area. The terminal received its maiden cargo in August 2006, slightly ahead of the start of its commercial gas sales agreement with CFE.

Energia Costa Azul. Sempra LNG's Energia Costa Azul terminal in Baja California is expected to start up in 2008, with a phase I sendout capacity of 1.0 Bcf/d (10.3 Bcm/y). Sempra and Shell will share equally the terminal's phase I capacity, and there are plans to expand the capacity to up to 2.5 Bcf/d (25.9 Bcm/y) by 2010. It is expected that at least 40% of Energia Costa Azul's initial capacity will be directed to Baja California itself, while the remainder will be shipped over the border, for use in the United States.

Other terminals in North America

As of mid-2006, many more terminals were in various stages of the permitting process (figs. 2–2 and 2–3). Proposed terminals are those for which some aspect of the permitting process has been initiated. Potential terminals are those that companies have announced their intention to build.

Many of these terminals, however, will not be built because of local opposition, environmental and other siting factors, and economic infeasibility. Still, there is a growing recognition in Washington, D.C., Mexico City, and Ottawa that LNG will provide an important supplement to North American gas supplies in the future.

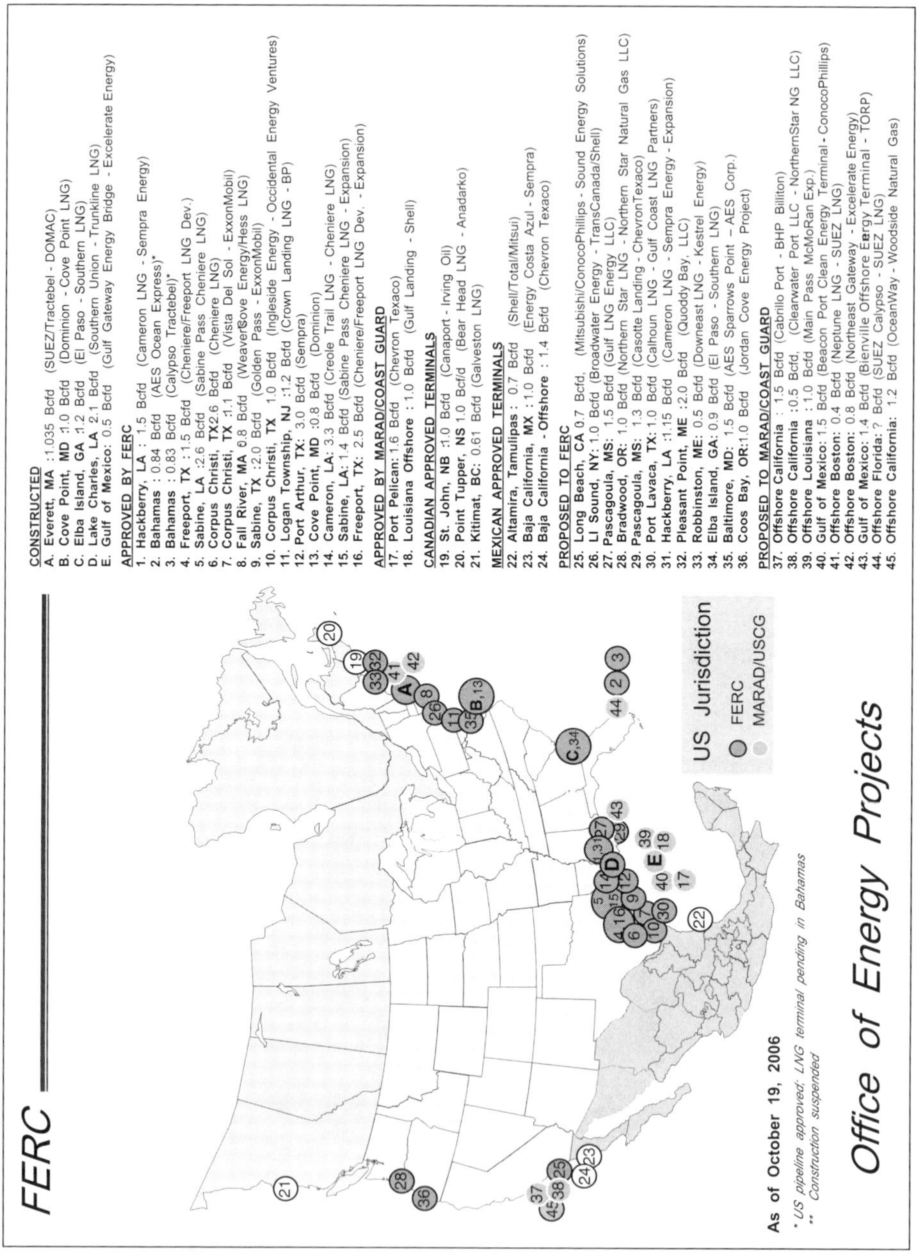

Fig. 2–2. Existing and proposed North American LNG import terminals (*Source:* FERC)

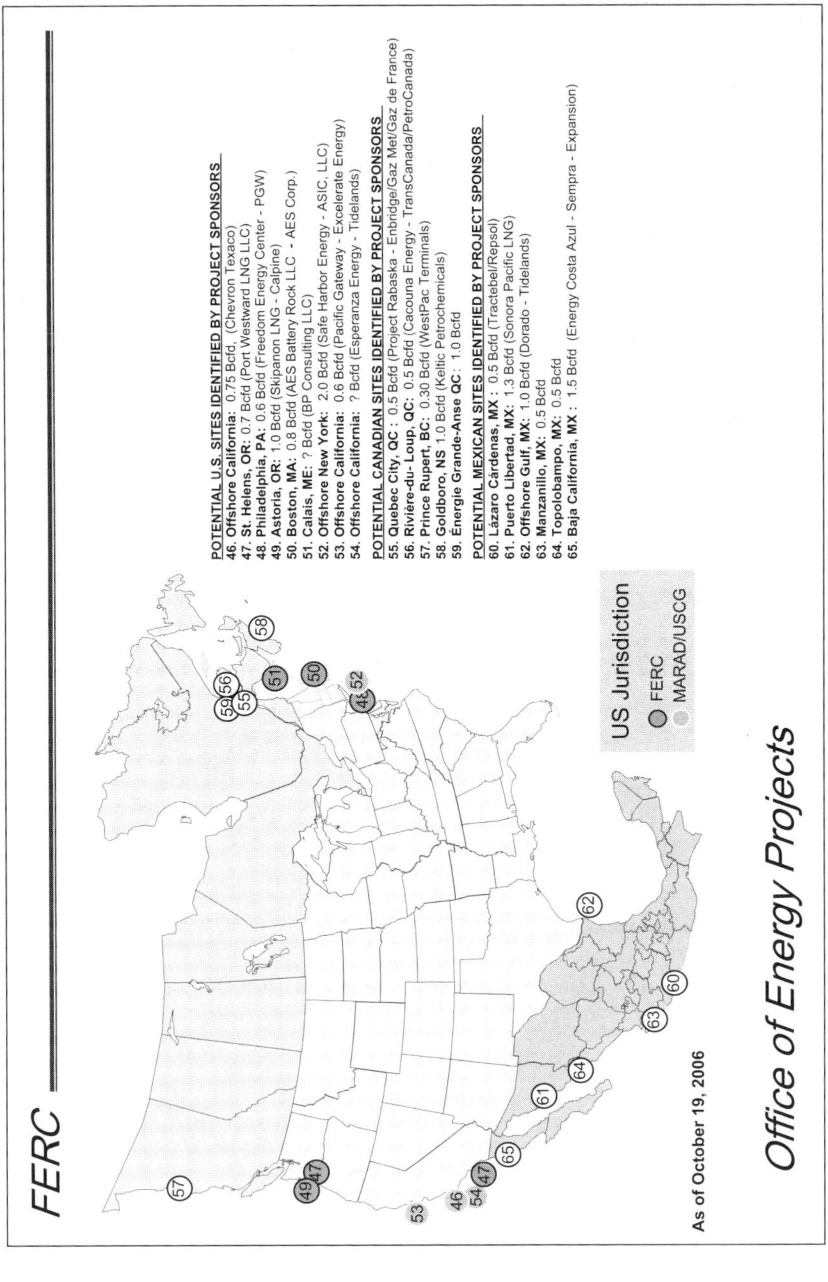

Fig. 2–3. Prospective North American LNG import terminals (*Source:* FERC)

NATURAL GAS AND LNG MARKETS IN THE CARIBBEAN

Puerto Rico

Enron and its partner Kenetech completed the EcoElectrica power plant and adjacent LNG import terminal in Guayanilla, on Puerto Rico's south coast, in 1999. The 500 MW combined-cycle plant initially ran on propane delivered into Enron's existing liquefied petroleum gas (LPG) terminal. On completion of the adjacent LNG import terminal in July 2000, the facility switched over to LNG supplied under a long-term contract by Cabot LNG (now Suez). In mid-2003, Spain's Gas Natural, which holds contracts for Trinidad LNG, purchased Enron's stake in EcoElectrica and became the project operator. The facility is now owned by International Power/Mitsui (50%), Gas Natural (47.5%), and GE Capital (2.5%). An expansion of the terminal and development of downstream pipelines to other customers on the island are now under consideration.

Dominican Republic

AES followed a similar business model in developing the Caribbean's second LNG import terminal, in the Dominican Republic. The U.S.-based power generator built an LNG import terminal and associated 310 MW gas-fired power plant, which began operations in 2002. The Puerto Rico and Dominican Republic terminals are both supplied by Trinidad's ALNG project, which started up in 1999. BP's contract to supply LNG to the Dominican Republic contained a commercial innovation. While Trinidad will likely be the source of most LNG delivered under this contract, it was not designated as the dedicated source, allowing the British firm to hail this as a sale of "branded LNG." However, the terminal has been extremely underutilized, largely because Dominican electric distributors failed to pay for the electricity produced by the power plant.[8] This in turn has forced AES to cancel contracted LNG deliveries from BP. As of mid-2006, no LNG had been delivered for about three years.

NATURAL GAS AND LNG MARKETS IN WESTERN EUROPE

Although Western European nations individually represent modest gas markets, when aggregated this market is very large, equivalent to about 60% of the U.S. market. In 2005, gas consumption in the 25 EU countries rose 2.9% from the previous year, to 540 Bcm (18.9 Tcf).[9] Six countries accounted for about 75% of this total: the United Kingdom with 94.8 Bcm (3.36 Tcf), followed by Germany with 93.3 Bcm (3.3 Tcf), Italy with 85.4 Bcm (3.0 Tcf), France with 49.4 Bcm (1.7 Tcf), the Netherlands with 43.5 Bcm (1.5 Tcf), and Spain with 33.6 Bcm (1.2 Tcf).[10] Spain is one of the fastest-growing European gas markets and is highly desirable for Atlantic Basin and Middle East LNG sellers, given its limited access to pipeline gas.

Western Europe relies heavily on pipeline gas from the Netherlands, the North Sea, Russia, and Algeria, which together provided more than 40% of its supplies in 2004, with a further 42% being produced within the EU's own borders.[11] LNG, with a 12% share of the market, is becoming an increasingly important source, on both cost and strategic grounds.[12] Algeria and Libya were Europe's original LNG suppliers, followed by Egypt, Nigeria, Oman, Qatar, and Trinidad.

Beginning in the 19th century, Europe developed localized gas businesses based on manufactured gas or nearby gas resources. The discovery of the huge Groningen gas field in the Netherlands in 1959 provided the foundation for international gas trade in continental Europe. The Dutch sought a wider European market to secure revenues, and annual exports grew from only 10 Bcm (0.4 Tcf) in the early 1970s to 45 Bcm (1.6 Tcf) by middecade. Groningen gas was the basis for the early development of continental Europe's gas pipeline grid and gas market.

The oil price increase of 1973 provided a large boost to the European gas business. Indigenous and regional gas was viewed as a more secure energy source than Middle Eastern oil. Furthermore, contractual time lags in gas contracts provided gas with a competitive advantage over oil, even where gas prices were tied to oil prices. By the late 1970s, the development of markets and infrastructure and higher prices encouraged new supplies from the Soviet Union, Algeria, and Norway. Gas-buying consortia comprising national monopolies typically contracted for gas supplies at oil-linked prices. Security and supply diversity were also key considerations. These powerful consortia provided critical credit support and volume assurances underpinning the construction of international pipelines to deliver gas into Europe from the Soviet Union, Algeria, and Norway.

International politics also played a role. The 1980s were a time of difficult U.S.-Soviet relations, reflected in U.S. attempts to obstruct Soviet plans to build a new pipeline from the vast Urengoy gas field to Europe. The United States feared that increasing dependence on Soviet gas supplies would enable the Soviet Union to influence European policies. In fact, the reverse happened, as natural gas sales became a key source of hard currency for the Soviet Union. However, in early 2006, concerns about the reliability of Russian supplies again became a matter of concern, when the Russians temporarily cut off supplies to Ukraine over a pricing dispute. The cutoff then fed through to other European buyers who depended on transit routes through the Ukraine to deliver their Russian supplies. With rising oil prices and an increasingly assertive Gazprom acting as an arm of the Russian state, security of supply and geopolitical considerations once again have moved to the fore in the European gas industry.

In the late 1990s, the EU enacted legislation to end gas and power monopolies and to bring competition to end-use gas and power markets. This liberalization was already well advanced in the United Kingdom, which had developed in isolation from the continental pipeline grid and further evolved following the privatization and subsequent splitting up of British Gas. Liberalization of gas and power businesses is now being implemented in continental European markets, but at a much slower pace, as the entrenched monopolies (state and private) have battled to retain their market control for as long as possible.

Buoyed by its success in introducing a common currency, the euro, the EU is intent on establishing a unified energy market as well. However, in the meantime, market structures vary greatly by state, depending on the maturity and physical characteristics of each market, the level of competition and the number of established players and new entrants, and the way in which nations implement EU directives.

National gas and power monopolies are being privatized and split up. At the same time, national regulatory authorities are implementing third-party access to supply and transmission infrastructure. Incumbent monopolists are now competing in other national markets and are facing competition from new entrants on their home turf. At the same time, electric and gas utilities are competing on each other's traditional turf. As a result, the European gas market is on the brink of some of the biggest changes in its history, and the prospects for the expansion of LNG imports appear bright.

The United Kingdom

The United Kingdom became the world's first commercial LNG importer when a cargo of Algerian LNG was delivered into Canvey Island in 1964. By the 1970s, the discovery of large gas resources in the Southern Basin of the North Sea ended this trade, and the United Kingdom's only terminal was mothballed and dismantled. U.K. policy strongly encouraged the development of North Sea oil and gas, to stimulate the nation's economy and to reap tax revenues. Over time, the United Kingdom's supply sources expanded to include pipeline gas from Norway. Thus, the United Kingdom became self-sufficient in gas, prices fell, and government policy encouraged its use in power generation. Indeed, the original "dash for gas" by power generators was first witnessed in the United Kingdom. The United Kingdom was one of the first nations to fully open up its gas and power businesses to competition and arguably has seen the most successful implementation of competition in end-use markets. Natural gas could fuel around 50% of the country's electricity generation by 2010, up from only 5% in 1990.[13]

U.K. isolation from the continental grid ended in 1998, when the Interconnector pipeline, linking the United Kingdom's Bacton terminus to Zeebrugge, Belgium, was completed. The Interconnector was initially conceived to provide a continental outlet for surplus U.K. North Sea gas and was designed to transport 20 Bcm/y (1.9 Bcf/d) in forward flow from the United Kingdom to Belgium and only 8.5 Bcm/y (0.82 Bcf/d) in reverse. Compression was added to increase the reverse flow on the Interconnector to 16.5 Bcm/y (1.59 Bcf/d). By 2006, a further expansion will raise the U.K. import capacity to 23.5 Bcm/y (2.3 Bcf/d).

After decades of self-sufficiency, U.K. energy authorities began to realize that falling North Sea production and steadily increasing gas demand would transform the country into a net importer by 2005. In 2003, the Joint Energy Security of Supply Working Group forecast that Britain might have to import 50% of its gas requirements by 2010 and warned that this dependency could rise above 80% by 2020.[14]

Construction began on a second pipeline—connecting Balgzand, in the Netherlands, to Bacton, in the United Kingdom—in late 2004. The 16 Bcm/y (1.5 Bcf/d) pipeline, known as the Balgzand Bacton Line (BBL), entered service in late 2006. While these lines can be used to supply Dutch and Norwegian gas to the United Kingdom, they could provide a link for Russian gas as well. Prospects for Russian gas supply to the United Kingdom would rise considerably if the proposed North Transgas line through the Baltic Sea were built. Russia's Gazprom is promoting the pipeline, together with Germany's BASF and E.ON. The 27.5 Bcm/y (2.7 Bcf/d) line would extend

1,200 kilometers from Vyborg, on the Gulf of Finland, to Germany's Baltic coast. Once in the continental grid, the gas could be directed into the Interconnector or into an expanded BBL. The North European Gas Pipeline (NEGP) project envisions a second pipeline, doubling the transmission capacity to 55 Bcm/y (5.3 Bcf/d).

Norwegian gas producers are also targeting the United Kingdom for additional sales. The partners in the Ormen Lange field plan to deliver 20 Bcm/y (1.93 Bcf/d) of gas to British consumers via a 1,166-kilometer, $3.2 billion subsea pipeline to the Easington/Dimlington terminals in eastern England. The giant Ormen Lange field has gas reserves of some 400 Bcm (14 Tcf); development costs are estimated at $10.8 billion.[15]

LNG is seen as an additional way of bridging the United Kingdom's gap between supply and demand. In 2005, National Grid Transco, the pipeline grid's owner and operator, finished converting its peakshaving plant on the Isle of Grain, in Kent, into an LNG terminal, called Grain LNG. Initial capacity at the 4.4 Bcm/y (0.43 Bcf/d) terminal was awarded to BP and Sonatrach, and first deliveries began in 2005. Grain LNG immediately began expanding the terminal by another 9.1 Bcm/y (0.88 Bcf/d), which should be completed by mid-2008. At the end of 2005, a third expansion was under evaluation, to add another 6.9 Bcm/y (0.67 Bcf/d) of capacity by 2010–11.

Meanwhile, two separate groups are building LNG terminals in Milford Haven, Wales. They are Dragon LNG, which is a consortium comprising Petroplus, BG, and Petronas, with a capacity of 10 Bcm/y (0.97 Bcf/d); and South Hook LNG, which is a joint venture between ExxonMobil and Qatar Petroleum, with a capacity of 21.8 Bcm/y (2.1 Bcf/d). Both terminals should be completed by the end of 2007. By the end of 2005, there were at least five other proposals for U.K. LNG import terminals under consideration. After an absence of 25 years, the United Kingdom is now poised to become a major importer of LNG.

Iberia

Spain is Europe's fastest-growing market for natural gas, virtually all of it imported. Consumption increased nearly threefold in the 1990s, following a similar rise in the '80s. It was driven by the industrial and power generation markets and was facilitated by a major expansion of the national pipeline system and import infrastructure.

In 2005, LNG accounted for almost two-thirds of Spain's overall supply of 33.6 Bcm. Algeria was the main supplier with 44%, followed by the Middle East and Nigeria. Spain also receives natural gas via pipeline from Algeria.

The Maghreb-Europe (GME) pipeline has a capacity of nearly 13 Bcm/y (1.2 Bcf/d), most of it targeted for Spain, with small volumes delivered to Portugal.

Originally, Gas Natural dominated the Spanish gas market, not only as a supplier but also via its 91% ownership of the nation's gas infrastructure owner and operator, Enagás. However, Gas Natural was forced in 2002 to reduce its ownership in Enagás in keeping with European liberalization laws, and it now owns only 5% of the company. Taking into account Gas Natural's loosening grip over gas sales and the growing influence of comparative newcomers such as power companies Endesa, Iberdrola, and Union Fenosa (not to mention international firms, e.g., BP, Eni, Shell, and Total), the Spanish gas market has seen dramatic changes since 2000. Evidence of new entrants' success is mirrored in the nation's official market statistics: in 2005, Gas Natural accounted for only 68.1% of gas sales to the liberalized gas market and 82.2% of sales to the regulated market compared to almost 100% of each sector just five years earlier.

Enagás provides nondiscriminatory third-party access on its infrastructure, including the nation's pipeline grid and Enagás' three LNG import terminals. However, third parties are also allowed to build LNG terminals in Spain. The Bahía de Bizkaia Gas consortium commissioned a 6 Bcm/y terminal near Bilbao, in northern Spain, in 2003, while the Regasificación de Sagunto (SAGGAS) joint venture commissioned a 6.6 Bcm/y (0.64 Bcf/d) facility near Valencia, in the south, in March 2006. A third greenfield terminal, known as Regasificadora del Noroeste (REGANOSA), is slated for startup in 2007. This 5.8 Bcm/y (0.56 Bcf/d) facility is located at Murgados, in northwestern Spain. None of these new terminals is owned by Enagás; rather they group together various new entrants to the Spanish gas market who plan to use LNG to meet their ambitious market growth goals. Spain's older LNG facilities at Barcelona, Huelva, and Cartegena (all owned by Enagás) are continually being expanded. By 2011, these facilities could have a combined sendout capacity of 61.6 Bcm/y (almost 6 Bcf/d).

Spain will need this additional LNG import capacity to meet projected gas demand growth. Demand is projected to grow aggressively to 40 Bcm (1.4 Tcf) by 2010 and 58 Bcm (2.05 Tcf) by 2020 from a 33.6 Bcm (1.2 Tcf) base in 2005. The country has lined up roughly 31 Bcm (1.1 Tcf) of LNG supplies annually to see it through 2010. Pipeline imports will satisfy the remaining demand. For example, seven companies have formed a consortium known as Medgaz, to build and operate a pipeline from Beni Saf, on the Algerian coast, up to landfall at Almeria, Spain, with an annual capacity of 8 Bcm/y (0.8 Bcf/d). The pipeline is also designed to connect to the south of France.

Medgaz's shareholders are Algeria's Sonatrach with a 36% share; Spanish oil company Compania Española de Petroleos, or Cepsa, and Iberdrola each holding a 20% share; and Gaz de France and Endesa each holding a 12% share. Each shareholder is also a shipper on the line. The pipeline began construction in December 2006 and is slated for completion in 2009.

Elsewhere on the Iberian Peninsula, Portugal's first receiving terminal began operation at Sines in 2003. The Sines facility can also be used to supply Spain.

France

Overall French gas demand is expected to grow at a strong 4.4% rate through 2010, reaching 57 Bcm (2.01 Tcf) from 44.7 Bcm (1.6 Tcf) in 2004. This rate will slow a little in the following decade, to around 3%, with total gas demand reaching 77 Bcm (2.7 Tcf) in 2020.

France's growing natural gas demand will be met with both LNG and pipeline imports. LNG is expected to slightly increase its share of the gas market, meeting 34% of overall demand in 2020, up from 31% in 2002. LNG imports are forecast to increase to 26.2 Bcm/y (2.53 Bcf/d) in 2020, a 12.2 Bcm/y (1.2 Bcf/d) increase from today's levels. These increased imports will be accommodated at (1) Gaz de France and Total's new LNG receiving terminal, Fos II, at Fos-sur-Mer, near Marseille; and (2) one other greenfield receiving facility, yet to be built. The Fos II terminal will likely receive Gaz de France's purchase of Egyptian LNG Train 1 volumes (5 Bcm/y).

Pipeline supplies will come from the North Sea, Russia, and potentially Algeria via a proposed Algeria-Spain pipeline (Medgaz). Some natural gas from this pipeline is projected to transit through Spain into the French market. Gaz de France and Sonatrach control around 4 Bcm/y (0.4 Bcf/d) of the pipeline's capacity.

Italy

Italy is the largest gas market in the Mediterranean and is mainly supplied by pipelines from Algeria, Russia, and the Netherlands, plus indigenous production. The Italian gas market is projected to grow at a 2.5% rate through 2020, from 74 Bcm (2.6 Tcf) in 2004 to 90 Bcm (3.2 Tcf) in 2010 and 110 Bcm (3.9 Tcf) in 2020.

Italy will remain largely a pipeline market, as new pipeline imports from Libya, Algeria, and Russia will limit terminal development. The inauguration of the Green Stream pipeline in late 2004—a joint venture between Agip-Eni

(75%) and Libya's NOC (25%)—introduced Libyan gas into the Italian natural gas grid. Green Stream is expected to deliver an average 8 Bcm/y (0.8 Bcf/d) of gas with a maximum capacity of 11 Bcm/y (1.1 Bcf/d). Further capacity upgrades are projected for the TransMed pipeline, connecting Algeria to Italy via Tunisia. Sources say capacity could reach up to 30 Bcm/y (2.9 Bcf/d) by 2010, up from 25 Bcm/y (2.4 Bcf/d) in 2004. An additional Algerian-Italian link through the Algeria-Sardinia Galsi pipeline could also provide a further 8 Bcm/y (0.8 Bcf/d) to Italy (this pipeline will likely also supply France).

LNG imports are forecast to increase to about 16.5 Bcm/y (1.6 Bcf/d) by 2020, compared to 3.5 Bcm/y (0.34 Bcf/d) from the only current terminal, at Panigaglia. Up to three new LNG import terminals could be built to meet increased gas demand, though many more are in the development stage. These projects include an 8 Bcm/y (0.8 Bcf/d) gravity-based offshore structure off Rovigo, which is under construction by Qatar Petroleum, ExxonMobil, and Edison; the Offshore Floating LNG Terminal Toscana (OLT), near Livorno; an 8 Bcm/y (0.8 Bcf/d) onshore terminal at Brindisi, in the southeast of Italy, sponsored by BG; another 8 Bcm/y (0.8 Bcf/d) onshore project in Sicily, backed by Shell and ERG; and two terminals proposed by Gas Natural.

Other European countries

Although currently supplied with LNG from Algeria, Belgium is also a major pipeline hub. The LNG terminal in Zeebrugge provides access to the gas to markets in Belgium, France, Germany, and the Netherlands. Fluxys is expanding the LNG terminal, and capacity has been awarded to Qatar Petroleum and ExxonMobil, Distrigas, and Suez Global LNG. After expansion, terminal capacity will be 14.1 Bcm/y (1.4 Bcf/d).

Greece and Turkey are expected to remain predominantly pipeline-supplied markets, with no major expansion or new terminals. Greece has one small import terminal, while Turkey has two, although the second has seen limited utilization. The Netherlands, Germany, Cyprus, Croatia and Poland all have plans, at various levels of advancement, to develop LNG import terminals.

NATURAL GAS AND LNG MARKETS IN ASIA

In Asia, most nations are taking a cautious approach to gas market liberalization. The region's main LNG importers (Japan, South Korea, and Taiwan) have no access to pipeline gas imports, and measures to introduce competition into their gas markets tend to take a backseat to security concerns and to face obstacles not encountered in more mature markets (e.g., the absence of an integrated pipeline grid in Japan). In Japan, the late 1990s saw the introduction of laws that opened about 30% of gas and electricity markets to competition. However, incursions by gas utilities into the franchise areas of one another, as well as gas utilities into the power sector and vice versa, have been relatively minor. Moreover, competition is limited because there is little room for competition on price: the various companies typically import LNG under similar price terms, and Japan has made no moves to open LNG terminals to third-party access. In South Korea and Taiwan, after initial enthusiasm for privatization and restructuring of the gas and electricity businesses, the governments are adopting go-slow, less aggressive restructuring programs. As yet, there are no gas-trading hubs in the Far East, and price linkage to oil remains intact.

Uncertainties remain about how gas demand in individual Asian nations will evolve. However, it is increasingly likely that robust growth, driven by the need for clean energy, will be realized across the region. India has already joined the list of LNG-importing nations, with two terminals operating (at Dahej and Hazira) and at least two more planned, not counting the planned completion of a mothballed terminal at Dabhol that was formerly owned by Enron.

China's first terminal, at Guangdong, began operations in 2006, and many more are planned in that country. Nevertheless, it may be difficult for the numerous Pacific Rim supply projects to sign up buyers as quickly as they would like. In China and India, the sharp rise in oil prices seen during 2005 and 2006 coupled with slower upstream LNG development than expected has made it increasingly difficult for these countries to secure additional LNG supplies at the very low prices achieved earlier, in what was clearly a buyer's market.

Japan

In 2005, Japan imported 58 million metric tons (MMt) (81.2 Bcm) of LNG, making it by far the world's largest LNG importer. Japan imported LNG under long-term contracts from eight countries: Abu Dhabi, Australia, Brunei, Indonesia, Malaysia, Oman, Qatar, and the United States. Indonesia was the largest exporter, but Indonesian exports to Japan have been steadily declining in the face of falling LNG production. Japan has 27 LNG terminals, almost all of which are owned and operated by Japanese regional gas and power utility companies and are dedicated to their exclusive use (table 2–3).

Table 2–3. Japanese LNG import terminals

Project	Region	Location	Sponsor	Sendout (Bcf/d)	Status	Start
Chita LNG Joint Terminal	Asia	Chita City	Chubu Electric, Toho Gas	0.77	Operating	1977
Chita LNG Terminal	AsiaIse Bay	Chubu	Electric	1.6	Operating	1983
Chita Midorihama	Asia	Chita Prefecture	Toho Gas	0.7	Operating	2001
Fukuoka	Asia	Kyushu Island	Saibu Gas	0.08	Operating	1993
Futtsu	Asia	Tokyo Bay	TEPCO	2.13	Operating	1985
Hatsukaichi	Asia	Hiroshima	Hiroshima Gas	0.05	Operating	1996
Higashi-Ohgishima	Asia	Tokyo Bay	TEPCO	1.96	Operating	1984
Himeji	Asia	Osaka	Osaka Gas	1.11	Operating	1977
Himeji Joint Terminal	Asia	Osaka	Osaka Gas, Kansai Electric	0.53	Operating	1985
Jyoetsu Kyodo	Asia	Joetsu	Chubu Electric, Tohoku Electric	TBD	Planned	2012
Kagoshima	Asia	Kyushu Island	Kagoshima Gas	0.01	Operating	1996
Kawagoe	Asia	Ise Bay	Chubu Electric (100%)	0.72	Operating	1997
Mizushima	Asia	Mizushima	Mizushima LNG	0.08	Operating	2006
Nagasaki	Asia	Nagasaki	Saibu Gas	0.01	Operating	2003
Negishi	Asia	Tokyo Bay	Tokyo Gas, TEPCO	1.78	Operating	1969
Nihonkai Niigata	Asia	Niigata	Tohoku EP	2.28	Operating	1983
Ohgishima	Asia	Tokyo Bay	Tokyo Gas (100%)	0.68	Operating	1998
Ohita	Asia	Kyushu Island	Kyushu Electric, Kyushu Oil, Chita Gas	0.68	Operating	1990
Sakai LNG	Asia	Sakai	Cosmo Oil, Iwatani, Kansai Electric, Ube Industries	0.95	Operating	2006
Sakaide LNG	Asia	Sakaide	Cosmo Oil, Shikoku Electric, Shikoku Electric	TBD	Under construction	2010
Senboku I	Asia	Osaka	Osaka Gas	0.33	Operating	1972
Senboku II	Asia	Osaka	Osaka Gas	1.75	Operating	1977
Shin Minato	Asia	Sendai	Sendai City Gas	1.07	Operating	1997
Sodegaura	Asia	Tokyo Bay	Tokyo Gas, TEPCO	3.7	Operating	1973
Sodeshi	Asia	Shimizu Bay	Shizuoka Gas	0.85	Operating	1996
Tobata	Asia	Kyushu Island	Kyushu Electric, Nippon Steel	0.85	Operating	1977
Wakayama	Asia	Wakayama	Kansai Electric	TBD	Planned	2013
Yanai	Asia	Hiroshima	Chugoku Electric	0.32	Operating	1990
Yokkaichi LNG Center	Asia	Ise Bay	Chubu Electric	0.94	Operating	1987
Yokkaichi Works	Asia	Ise Bay	Toho Gas	0.09	Operating	1991

The oil crisis of 1973 caused a revolution in Japanese energy planning. Japan found itself overexposed to oil, in terms of both price and supply. Policy makers decided that this was unacceptable and implemented plans to increase gas supplies in the form of LNG and to expand nuclear generation. LNG was seen as fuel whose supply sources would be more diversified, especially outside the Persian Gulf, and whose suppliers would be more closely bound to their Japanese buyers than was the case with oil suppliers. In 1970, Japan was dependent on oil for over 70% of its primary energy supply, and oil represented 60% of the fuel used in power generation. By 2004, oil's share of primary energy had been reduced to 52%, and its share of power generation had dropped to only 8%. The big winners in this transition were nuclear and LNG. Nuclear and gas account for approximately 13% each of primary energy and for 35% and 27%, respectively, of power generation (figs. 2–4 and 2–5).[16]

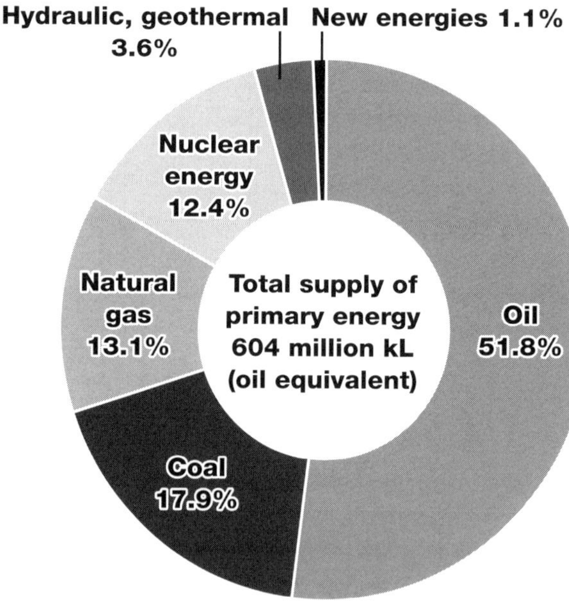

Fig. 2–4. Japan's primary energy sources, 2005 (*Source:* Government of Japan, Agency for Natural Resources and Energy)

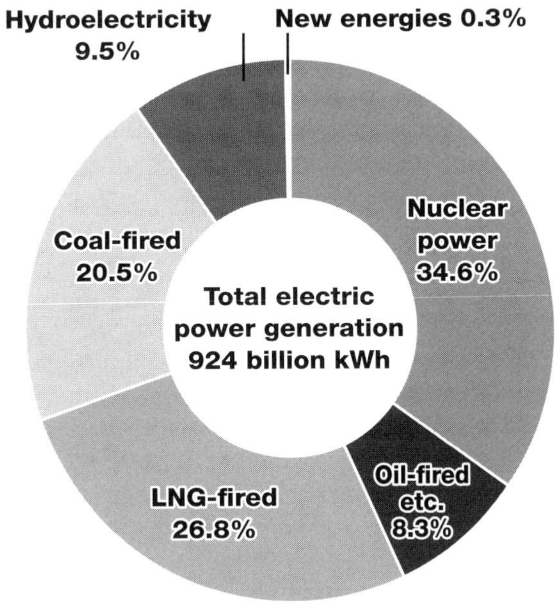

Fig. 2–5. Japan's power generation fuels, 2005

Japan emerged as the foundation buyer for the development of the Far East LNG industry. Although Japan's first LNG cargo was imported from Kenai, Alaska, in 1969, under a contract for 0.96 MMt/y (1.3 Bcm/y), rapid buildup did not begin until 1972, when a new liquefaction plant at Lumut, Brunei, started exporting to Japan. By 1977, this plant was supplying over 7 MMt/y (9.8 Bcm/y) to Japanese buyers. In the same year, Abu Dhabi and Indonesia joined the ranks of Japanese LNG suppliers. In 1983, Malaysia entered the trade, followed by Australia in 1989. In 1997, Japan received its first LNG cargo from Qatar, followed by Oman in 2000.

In the LNG trades to Japan, export project sponsors often enlisted Japanese trading companies as shareholders in the project company to facilitate sales. For example, Mitsubishi partnered in projects in Brunei and Malaysia, and Mitsui did the same in Abu Dhabi. Both firms participated in Australia's North West Shelf (NWS) venture and in Russia's Sakhalin II project. Nissho Iwai assisted in Indonesia, and Mitsubishi, Mitsui, and Itochu joined the Oman project. In Qatar, Mitsui and Marubeni hold shares in Qatargas, and Itochu and Nissho Iwai are participants in Ras Laffan LNG (RasGas). At the same time, extremely creditworthy Japanese buying consortia frequently lined up to purchase production from new production trains (at least in the earlier ventures), and Japanese shipyards built the vessels to deliver the cargoes to Japan. Meanwhile, Japanese banks financed the entire supply chain.

This comfortable structure has nevertheless eroded, for a number of reasons. Slower economic growth moderated growth in energy demand. At the same time, the potential for gas to displace other fuels diminished. In general, the requirement for large new LNG purchases appears to be limited, especially when compared to the scale of the export projects presently in development. Indeed, Japanese buyers are resorting to longer buildup periods in their purchase contracts, to ease new contracts into their supply portfolios. Japanese buyers can no longer simply band together and buy out new liquefaction trains, particularly as the size of these trains increase beyond 5 MMt/y (7 Bcm/y).

The most significant unknown in the outlook for LNG demand in Japan is the prospect for nuclear generation. About 87% of the new nuclear power generation capacity is being planned by electric utilities that are also LNG importers. These companies rely heavily on nuclear power generation to satisfy baseload demand, with gas-fired power plants addressing mid- and peak-load requirements only. Small shifts in nuclear power prospects can have magnified impacts on the demand for LNG. For example, gas-fired power generation was needed urgently in 2002 and 2003, when power generators such as Tokyo Electric (TEPCO) and Kansai Electric temporarily shut down their nuclear power plants to address severe operational safety concerns. Both companies were forced to scour the market for additional LNG to burn in their thermal power plants, which tightened the Pacific LNG supply situation dramatically; indeed, TEPCO's additional purchases alone totaled 3.6 MMt (5 Bcm), which at that time was equivalent to Italy's annual LNG demand.

With ongoing safety problems in many nuclear plants, Japanese utility companies are concerned that nuclear power may play a smaller role in the country's energy mix than was originally envisaged. To avoid being caught short in the future, firms that own both nuclear and gas-fired power capacity are expected to contract for more LNG than they actually require, in case plans for new nuclear power plants fail to materialize. Existing LNG importers are developing two-thirds of the 18 gigawatts (GW) of new nuclear power generation capacity planned for Japan by 2015. Only three of a planned 14 reactors are currently under construction, and plans for nuclear power plants are subject to increasingly stringent scrutiny from the Japanese nuclear regulators. As a result, Japanese electric utility companies may be forced to construct new gas-fired power plants to fulfill the power generation demand that was supposed to be supplied by nuclear capacity. If none of the proposed nuclear plants materializes, Japanese utility companies may be forced to contract for an additional 14 MMt/y (19.6 Bcm/y) of LNG by fiscal year 2015.

Over the years, there have been discussions of building a pipeline from Sakhalin Island to Japan. This project is known as the Sakhalin I project. As of the end of 2005, however, these plans were dormant. Phase I of the Sakhalin I venture will be dedicated to the Russian domestic market. Export of the remaining gas reserves via pipeline will commence when a contract is secured with a regional customer, likely China.

The ongoing (albeit conservative) effort to step up the pace of gas and power liberalization in Japan is another significant factor affecting Japanese LNG importers' plans. Gas and power utilities, which banded together in the past, can see a future in which they may be competing with each other. Thus, they are looking for competitive advantage in their gas purchase contracts as well, not just in the form of price but also in terms of volume flexibility and seasonality (which is especially important for the gas distribution companies). Japanese LNG buyers are also seeking outlets in foreign countries with more market flexibility, to better manage LNG demand uncertainty at home. They have shown interest in the acquisition of LNG import capacity in liberalized gas markets in the United Kingdom and the United States, but emerging niche markets such as Pakistan and Singapore may also offer attractive opportunities.

South Korea

The earliest challenge to Japanese dominance in the Far East LNG business came from South Korea. When state-owned Korea Gas Corporation (Kogas) made its first purchase of LNG, it meant that LNG export ventures were no longer totally dependent on Japan for sales. Kogas signed its first contract with Indonesia for LNG from the Arun complex in 1983, with deliveries starting in 1986. The Korean firm subsequently signed two more contracts for Indonesian LNG before entering into a short-term contract with Malaysia that was subsequently converted to a long-term arrangement. In the late 1990s, Kogas entered into several contracts for Middle East LNG supplies. LNG supplies from Qatar's RasGas project began in 1999, followed by supplies from Oman in 2000.

South Korea is the world's second-largest LNG importer, and Kogas is the largest buyer. Kogas owns and operates three LNG import terminals, at Incheon, Pyongtaek, and Tongyeong (table 2–4). Gas demand has risen at an annual pace of nearly 10% so far this decade, reaching 23 MMt (32.2 Bcm) in 2005, with supplies coming from eight countries. Qatar supplied 6.2 MMt (8.7 Bcm), followed by Indonesia with 5.6 MMt (7.5 Bcm), Malaysia with 4.7 MMt (6.6 Bcm), and Oman with 4.4 MMt (6.2 Bcm). According to a forecast prepared by the Korea Energy Economics Institute in January 2006, annual demand will rise from 25.4 MMt (35.6 Bcm) in 2006 to 30 MMt (42 Bcm) by 2010.[17]

Korean gas demand has large seasonal swings, which presents a significant logistical challenge and necessitates major investments in LNG storage at the terminals. As a result, Kogas has been a very active buyer of spot cargoes during the winter months. The firm has also entered into several medium-term contracts with deliveries heavily weighted to the winter months.

Table 2–4. Korean LNG import terminals (*Source:* Poten & Partners)

Project	Location	Sponsor	Sendout (Bcf/d)	Status	Start
GS Caltex	TBD	GS Caltex	1.3	Planned	2010
Incheon	Incheon	Kogas	3.85	Operating	1996
Incheon Expansion	Incheon	Kogas	0.63	Under construction	2006, 2009
POSCO	Kwangyang	POSCO	0.23	Operating	2005
Pyeongtaek	Pyeongtaek	Kogas	2.3	Operating	1986
Pyongtaek II	Pyeongtaek	Kogas	0.84	Planned	TBD
Tongyeong	Tongyeong	Kogas	1.6	Operating	2002
Unspecified	TBD	Kogas	1.3	Planned	TBD

(*Source:* Poten & Partners)

After putting forth a relatively aggressive gas market liberalization goal, Seoul has scaled back its program. However, private firms are now able to import LNG for their own use. Pohang Iron and Steel built the nation's first privately owned LNG import terminal and has signed a deal, along with SK Power, to import LNG from Indonesia. Imports began in mid-2005. Historically, Kogas has imported the LNG used in both the gas and power sectors. As of late 2005, however, the various regional generators spun off from Korea Electric Power (Kepco) were lobbying the Ministry of Commerce, Industry, and Energy (MOCIE) for authorization to secure their own supplies.

The Korean shipbuilding industry has played a major role in lowering costs in the LNG supply chain. After cutting their teeth on building LNG carriers for the Korean trade, the nation's shipbuilders—Daewoo Shipbuilding and Marine Engineering, Samsung Heavy Industries, and Hyundai Heavy Industries— successfully challenged the dominance of

Japanese shipyards starting in 1999, capturing the bulk of new orders and contributing to a major reduction in LNG tanker costs.

Taiwan

In Taiwan, Chinese Petroleum Corporation (CPC) remains the country's sole LNG importer. The firm owns and operates Taiwan's only LNG terminal, Yung An, located in the island's southwest. The Taiwan Power Company (Taipower), also state-owned but intended for privatization, consumes more than half of the country's LNG imports for power generation. Taiwan's relatively temperate winter limits gas use for space heating. However, its warm summer weather promotes the use of power generation for air-conditioning. As a result, power generation accounts for 70% of natural gas use in Taiwan, while city gas accounts for only 30%.

Power generation will be the main driver of LNG demand growth in the future. The most important developments in power generation are the construction of a fourth nuclear plant and a 4-GW gas-fired power generation complex, known as Ta Tan. Both are being developed in the north near Taipei and are scheduled to begin operating by the end of this decade.

Following a prolonged, tender process, CPC was mandated to construct a new import terminal in Taichung, north of the existing Yung An LNG terminal, to supply natural gas to the new Ta Tan power generation complex. The new facility will begin supplying natural gas to Ta Tan in 2008. CPC has arranged to fill the Taichung import terminal with up to 3 MMt/y (4.2 Bcm/y) of LNG from Qatar's RasGas II export project.

Taiwanese LNG imports are forecast to reach 9.5 MMt (13.3 Bcm) in 2010 and 12.4 MMt/y (17.4 Bcm) by 2015. By comparison, the import level was 7.1 MMt (9.9 Bcm) in 2005.

NEW ASIAN NATURAL GAS AND LNG MARKETS

China and India (with populations more than one billion each and rapidly growing economies) are potentially large gas and LNG markets. Both have some domestic production and actual or potential access to pipeline imports—China is already delivering natural gas from the remote Xinjiang Uygur Autonomous Region to the economic hub of Shanghai and other regions of the Yangtze River Delta via the 4,000-kilometer East-West Pipeline, and is considering pipeline imports from Sakhalin, while

India is discussing pipeline imports from Iran—but both governments also see a role for LNG in their supply portfolios. Another motivation for increasing gas use is improving air quality, since coal is their main source of energy. India was the first to bring an LNG terminal online, with Petronet's Dahej terminal taking its first cargo in 2003, and China following in 2006 with the start-up of the Guangdong terminal. A problem in both countries is the high price of imported gas relative to current wholesale and retail energy prices.

India

Inadequate regulatory and legal environments and energy prices kept artificially low by government controls undermine the feasibility of LNG import projects. End-user gas prices are low mainly because of state subsidies to major consumers, such as fertilizer and power plants. Conversely, removing subsidies and forcing prices up would dampen demand and could lead to public protests. Despite this, as of the end of 2005, two terminals were operating (the Petronet Dahej terminal, in Kochi, and Shell and Total's terminal, in Hazira), a third was being prepared for opening (Dabhol), and construction was about to start on a fourth (at Kochi).

Enron's failed Dabhol LNG import/power generation project serves as a high-profile example of the problems facing investment projects in India. The LNG terminal was never completed and was mothballed in 2001 because of a failure to resolve pricing disputes with the Maharashtra State Electricity Board, the main purchaser of power from the associated 2,200 MW power plant. In 2006, a new company, Ratnagiri Gas and Power, took over the LNG terminal and power plant as part of a comprehensive restructuring of the original project.[18] The partners reopened phase I of the power plant (740 MW) in mid-2006, using naphtha as a fuel, and there are plans to operate the power plant using LNG as soon as Ratnagiri can procure sufficiently cheap supplies of LNG and complete the construction of the LNG terminal and phase II of the power plant.

Petronet LNG, a partnership of four state-owned oil and gas companies, brought the nation's first LNG import terminal on stream in late 2003. The terminal at Dahej, in Gujarat, on the west coast, is supplied by Qatar's RasGas LNG venture. Development of this supply chain was quite a challenge despite the high-profile Indian firms involved and the support of the government. It has been extremely difficult for Petronet to enter into downstream sales agreements for the regasified LNG, and there has been ongoing pressure from India for the Qatari venture to lower the price, even though it stands well below current world LNG prices. Petronet was unable to obtain long-term financing for the Dahej terminal and funded the terminal with short-term debt. At the same time, RasGas was unable to attract international funding for the train being built to supply Dahej, owing to Indian risk, and had to bundle together this train with another being built for the Italian market, to improve the credit profile.

It has been difficult for both Ratnagiri and Petronet to secure LNG at a price acceptable to end users, who have long enjoyed highly subsidized prices. For example, Petronet agreed in mid-2005 to purchase LNG under a long-term contract from Iran at a price linked to $31/bbl crude. However, subsequent rises in the crude oil price caused the National Iranian Gas Export Company (NIGEC) to inform Petronet that the price was no longer valid. Since the Dabhol fiasco in 2001, it is clear that the main impediment to the advancement of the Indian LNG import business is a lack of reliable, creditworthy gas and power end users in India. Until the health of the country's gas and power sectors improves, the pressure will be on Indian LNG importers to seek extremely cheap LNG supplies to keep costs to an absolute minimum. However, with the steep increases in oil prices and corresponding increases in naphtha prices, Indian LNG importers have been able to pay world prices for LNG and resell the LNG to fertilizer manufacturers, whose alternatives are even more expensive. Whether this represents a change in philosophy or a temporary shift in the market may define India's medium-term role as an LNG buyer.

India's second terminal, at Hazira, also in Gujarat, went on line at the beginning of 2005. It is owned by Shell and Total. Shell built this plant with equity funding but with no long-term LNG supply contracts behind it. Shell planned to supply LNG from its diverse sources as downstream markets developed. This was a unique development for an industry that prizes long-term sale and purchase agreements (SPAs) with high take-or-pay obligations to fund supply chains. However, by the end of 2005, the Hazira terminal had received only two cargoes. Again, the unwillingness of end users to pay international prices was an obstacle. Thus, Shell made an agreement with what was then the Gas Authority of India Limited (now known as GAIL), allowing it to use the facility to import cargoes of LNG on a toll basis. The regasified LNG will enter GAIL's system through a 13-kilometer pipeline that connects to a new 475-kilometer pipeline being built from Dahej to Uran, in Maharashtra, near Mumbai. This will also allow Shell to market its gas to other customers.

A further challenge to Indian LNG developments is the potential for domestic gas production to expand, especially if the Indian government relaxes the price controls it now places on this segment of its natural gas industry. Likewise, although it may be a long way off, India could be supplied with pipeline gas from Iran or other Persian Gulf countries. However, this latter option would depend on significant shifts in the political relationships between several countries in that region of the world and seems remote today.

China

China has had some success in generating gas demand and building supply infrastructure through regulation and policy making, rather than through reliance on the market mechanism. For example, the 4,000-kilometer East-West Pipeline was completed in late 2004—a year ahead of schedule and without the participation of foreign partners. The $5.2 billion project is second in investment scale only to the Three Gorges Dam project.

The Chinese government concluded that certain coastal provinces will require LNG and has been an active promoter of these projects. The first terminal was built at Shenzhen by Guandong Dapeng LNG Company and began operations in June 2006. It is supplied from Australia's NWS venture. Partners are the state-owned China National Offshore Oil Company (CNOOC; 33%), BP (30%), and eight Chinese and Hong Kong companies (37%). Guangdong LNG signed contracts with 11 end users for the sale of up to 3.7 MMt/y (5.2 Bcm/y), of which 2.2 MMt/y (2.9 Bcm/y) will be used in power plants, 1.0 MMt/y (1.4 Bcm/y) will be used by residential users, and 0.6 MMt/y (0.9 Bcm/y) will be for buyers in Hong Kong..

China's second LNG terminal is located at Fujian and is scheduled to open in 2008. It will be owned and operated by CNOOC and Fujian Investment and Development Corporation. In 2002, a contract was signed with Indonesia's Tangguh LNG project for the purchase of 2.6 MMt/y (3.6 Bcm/y) for 25 years.

China broke new ground in the Asia-Pacific LNG business. Rather than entering into bilateral negotiations with LNG export ventures, the Guangdong venture issued a competitive tender for LNG supplies. Following this example, India's National Thermal Power Company, Taiwan's Taipower, and Korea's Pohang Iron and Steel also tendered for LNG supplies. In this competitive process, the Guangdong venture obtained extremely attractive prices from Australia. The Chinese then contracted LNG for Fujian under similar terms from the Tangguh LNG project in Indonesia, which had been competing with Qatar and Australia for the Guangdong project.

Guangdong pricing did not, however, emerge as the new benchmark for Far East LNG. The sharp rise in world oil prices, to $50/bbl and even higher, in 2005 led LNG producers to renegotiate the terms of their contract with the Chinese, which had a ceiling price linked to $25/bbl oil. The Indonesian government renegotiated the price of the LNG for Fujian, especially once it became clear that the terminal developers were having difficulty lining up downstream customers and were seeking to reduce their commitments to buy LNG during the early years of the contract. The sustained high-oil-price environment and the consequent higher LNG prices demanded by exporters have effectively prevented China from concluding additional SPAs for LNG, even while proposals existed for over a dozen Chinese LNG import terminals as of late 2005. Increased competition from a reemergent Japanese market and North America further reduced the attractiveness of China to LNG suppliers.

Consequently, China's LNG prospects appear less certain than earlier forecasts have assumed. Much remains to be seen as how quickly gas demand will materialize downstream from the country's terminals. LNG must be price competitive with indigenous and established energy forms—such as LPG, kerosene, and coal—to remain part of China's energy mix. Given the low costs of indigenous coal production, regasified LNG must be priced quite cheaply to displace coal in the power sector and remain affordable for the residential and commercial sectors. During the Chinese LNG industry's infancy, some form of government intervention may be essential for the downstream gas market to develop while ensuring the competitiveness of LNG imports for Chinese end users and guaranteeing a reasonable net back for the LNG export projects supplying China.

Following the Korean example, China decided to enter the shipbuilding business, and Chinese shipyards will first build LNG carriers to serve the China trade. Hudong Zhonghua is building the nation's first five LNG ships; the Dalian New Shipyard and the Jiangnan Shipbuilding Group are also licensed to build LNG carriers. It is unclear when they will compete in international tenders for LNG carriers. When they do, however, just as the Koreans did, they will likely have to offer attractive prices to break into this business.

NICHE MARKETS FOR LNG

When considered alone, the annual forecast LNG requirements of the emerging markets listed subsequently are modest. However, when considered as a whole, new regional demand centers, such as Chile, New Zealand, Pakistan, Singapore, and Thailand, may require 10–15 MMt/y (14–21 Bcm/y) of LNG by 2015—an amount similar to Taiwan's forecast demand in 2015.

Chile

Chile announced plans in 2004 to build an LNG import terminal to reduce dependency on pipeline gas purchases from neighboring Argentina. In June 2006, Chilean president Michelle Bachelet laid the cornerstone for the $400 million terminal at Quintero, in central Chile. The terminal is scheduled to start operations in late 2008, with full-scale activities beginning in 2009. It is being developed by a partnership of Empresa Nacional des Petroleo SA (ENAP), the BG Group, Endesa Chile, and Metrogas. It will have an initial capacity of close to 1 MMt/y (1.4 Bcm/y), with the potential to expand to around 3 MMt/y (4.2 Bcm/y). Two other projects are also under consideration in the country, further to the north.

New Zealand

New Zealand's largest gas field, Maui, could be depleted by 2007. Even with the Pohokura and Kupe fields coming on line over the next four years, New Zealand is expected to have an energy supply gap. Energy utility companies Contact and Genesis are evaluating a range of offshore and onshore LNG terminal solutions, but imports are not likely to begin before 2011 and might amount to no more than a modest 1 MMt/y (1.4 Bcm/y) by 2015.

Pakistan

Pakistani gas transmission and distribution company Sui Southern Gas Company (SSGC) is considering whether to build an LNG terminal to augment its domestic gas supplies. Pakistan's relatively modest gas reserve base, coupled with the political complexities of regional pipeline imports from neighboring Iran, has encouraged SSGC to consider LNG as a potential method of increasing its gas supply base. The most likely location for the import facility is the Port Qasim Terminal or the Karachi Port Trust area of Karachi. Initial throughput capacity will be a modest 2.5 MMt/y (3.5 Bcm/y).

Pakistan entertains hopes of commissioning an LNG import terminal by 2010, but the project is still in the very early stages of development.

Singapore

Singapore's Energy Market Authority awarded a feasibility study to Tokyo Gas Engineering Company in February 2005 that will determine whether the tiny island nation of 4.5 million people should import LNG. The country currently relies on imports of natural gas by pipeline from Indonesia and Malaysia but is looking to diversify its supply sources owing to security concerns. The feasibility study will examine LNG imports from 2010 and beyond. The quantity of imports and the location of a potential receiving terminal will be determined after evaluating the results of the feasibility study.

Thailand

Thailand is revisiting earlier plans (later shelved in the face of rising domestic supply) to introduce LNG into its energy mix. This rethinking comes amid a sharp rise in forecasted natural gas demand, with a projected average annual growth of 5%–6% through 2015. Thailand is currently supplied with gas by three major pipelines—two from domestic fields in Thailand and one from Myanmar. A fourth transmission line, from the Gulf of Thailand, is currently being developed, thus increasing future domestic supplies. Finally, a potential additional pipeline, the Trans Thailand Malaysia, is planned to open a new source of gas imported from neighboring Malaysia. The pipeline is designed to transport and process natural gas reserves in the Thailand/Malaysia Joint Development Area. Gas from Myanmar supplies close to 25% of Thailand's needs. Given the ongoing political uncertainty in Myanmar, Bangkok is re-evaluating the potential need for LNG in the country's energy mix. Energy authorities now forecast that LNG could meet 10% of Thailand's gas demand after 2010.

NOTES

[1] EIA. All countries spot crude oil price FOB weighted by estimated export volume (dollars per barrel). http://tonto.eia.doe.gov/dnav/pet/hist/wtotworldw.htm (accessed August 18, 2006).

[2] FERC. Market oversight and investigations. http://www.ferc.gov/cust-protect/moi.asp (accessed August 19, 2006).

[3] EIA. 2005. *Annual Energy Outlook* 2005. http://www.eia.doe.gov/oiaf/archive/aeo05/pdf/0383(2005).pdf.

[4] The Alaska Gas Project requires the largest capital investment in the world. A project to Alberta requires $15 billion for Point Thomson, the gas treatment plant, and pipelines and when other upstream capital expenditures are included requires $19 billion. Total capital expenditures to Chicago are $27 billion. See Petro van Meurs. 2006. Fiscal strategy of the stranded gas contract. Presentation to the Alaskan State Legislature, May 10, http://www.gov.state.ak.us/gasline/pdf/Meurs_GasPresentation_May10.pdf.

[5] Suez LNG North America. Our companies: Distrigas of Massachusetts facts and figures. http://www.suezenergyna.com/ourcompanies/lngna-domac.shtml (accessed August 19, 2006).

[6] Dirección general de planeación energética, Secretaría de Energía. 2006. Prospectiva del mercado de gas natural 2005–2014. Primera edición, p.16, http://www.energia.gob.mx/work/resources/LocalContent/2183/64/ProspecticaGasNatural.pdf.

[7] Ibid., pp. 102–104.

[8] This malaise has not been confined to the AES LNG terminal and associated power plant: Santo Dominico has been feuding for some time with the foreign electricity companies that own much of the country's power generation capacity. The companies have occasionally cut off electricity to the nation's distribution grid, contending that because the state-owned distribution companies have not paid their bills and that they cannot import the natural gas and oil needed to fuel their operations. That decision has placed the companies at the center of a political and economic maelstrom over blackouts lasting as long as 20 hours a day. See Simon Romero. 2004. Lights out in the Dominican Republic. *The New York Times*, August 14; and Andy Webb-Vidal. 2006. Why power to the people remains but a dream. *The Financial Times*, March 10.

[9] Jiménez, Ana. 2006. Statistical aspects of the natural gas economy in 2005. Eurostat, June. http://epp.eurostat.ec.europa.eu/cache/ITY_OFFPUB/KS-NQ-06-012/EN/KS-NQ-06-012-EN.PDF.

[10] Cedigaz. 2006. Consumption balance. *Statistics Cedigaz* 2005, July.

[11] According to the EU's own data, 2005 natural gas production in EU-25 amounted to 198.6 MMtoe, meaning that 42% of EU demand was produced in the EU itself. See Ana Jiménez. 2006. Statistical aspects of the natural gas economy in 2005. Eurostat, June. http://epp.eurostat.ec.europa.eu/cache/ITY_OFFPUB/KS-NQ-06-012/EN/KS-NQ-06-012-EN.PDF.

[12] Europe imports around 40 Bcm/y of LNG, a volume equivalent to 12% of total imports. See LNG set for extended European role despite limitations. *Energy Business Review*, January 31, 2006.

[13] Smith, Adrian. 2004. Past & future dash for gas in the UK. Presentation at the Future of Gas for Power Generation Workshop, Paris, June 14.

[14] UK Department of Trade and Industry 2003. *Joint Energy Security of Supply Working Group*. February, p. 18.

[15] The participating interests in Langeled (Ormen Lange pipeline) Joint Venture are Norsk Hydro (17.610%; operator for development phase), Gassco (0%; operator for the production phase), Petoro (32.954%), Shell (16.503%), Statoil (14.985%), Dong (10.222%), ExxonMobil (6.947%), and ConocoPhillips (0.779%). The costs quoted include Ormen Lange field development costs—complete with subsea installations, pipelines, and the land-based processing plant—but do not include the cost of the associated Langeled pipeline.

[16] Agency for Natural Resources and Energy. The Official Website of the Government of Japan. http://www.enecho.meti.go.jp/english/policy/nuclear/position.html.

[17] Korean Institute of Energy Economics. 2006. *Mid-term Energy Outlook*, 2005–2010. January.

[18] Ratnagiri Gas and Power is owned by National Thermal Power Corporation (28.33%), GAIL (28.33%), Industrial Development Bank of India-led institutions (28.33%), and the Maharashtra State Electricity Board (15%).

THE LNG CHAIN: THE PROJECT NATURE OF THE LNG BUSINESS 3

INTRODUCTION

The LNG business evolved as a collection of independent, disconnected projects. It originated in an environment with few potential customers or suppliers, where gas was seen as a nuisance, not a valuable commodity. When trying to bring remote gas reserves to market, it was logical to develop each business opportunity as a stand-alone project, essentially emulating a long-distance pipeline. Each project was designed to bring dedicated reserves to dedicated markets through a chain of separate but linked stages: upstream gas production and gathering, liquefaction, shipping, and regasification. Each step was connected to the others by long-term contractual relationships (fig. 3–1). Each project was developed with different technical and commercial considerations, government policies, and financing and fiscal terms, so that project developers often had to find unique solutions to the specific problems and opportunities created by each set of circumstances.

Because of the enormous capital investment at each stage, project developers try to reduce technical and commercial risks as much as is practicable. Technical risks can be lowered by adoption of proven designs, construction by experienced contractors, and operations that follow best practices and internationally accepted safety guidelines. All the energy companies involved, whether private or state-owned, international or domestic, as well as the international construction and engineering companies that can undertake these demanding projects, have built up over time their preferred way of tackling the manifold commercial, technical, safety, and organizational issues inherent in these projects.

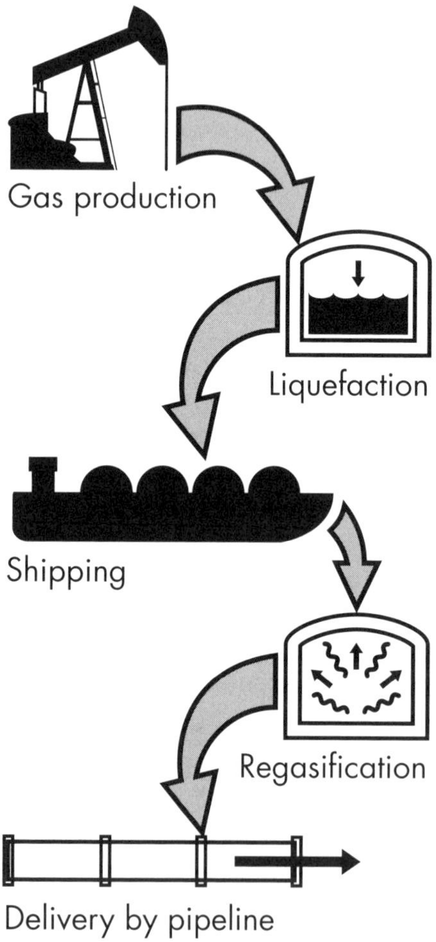

Fig. 3–1. The LNG value chain

In the end, the value of the gas and the overall economic viability of the project are realized only after regasification and sale in the final market. The final buyer of the LNG has traditionally been a major gas or power utility with a local or national franchise that is in a position to place the gas in its market with a high degree of certainty and has the ability to pass through the supply costs to its customers. The LNG supply contract with the utility provides the credit support for the project's long-term cash flow.

In this environment, the commercial structure creates an effective framework for long-term revenue and risk allocation between the various elements of the LNG chain. Establishing durable, long-term contracts between the different entities at each stage of a project reduces commercial risks. Once a project is reduced to its simplest elements, the LNG buyer takes the volume risk through take-or-pay provisions, obligating the buyer to pay for the gas even if he or she does not take it, and the upstream parties take the price risk. Contracts typically have terms of 20 years or longer and have limited volume flexibility.

The oil industry does not display similarly integrated project models, since the oil market is much more developed and globally accessible. Oil transportation costs are relatively low compared with the price of the product, whereas LNG shipping costs represent a significant component of overall project costs and delivered prices. A developer of an oil field can reasonably look at a multitude of potential outlets or customers around the globe; there is, therefore, no need to enter into contracts with customers before starting the construction of oil production facilities, as is the case with LNG.

THE PHYSICAL CHAIN

Upstream exploration and production

In the early days, natural gas was often discovered as a less desirable by-product of oil, but today exploration is increasingly aimed at the discovery of exportable gas reserves. Outside the United States and Europe, it was often difficult to develop gas reserves, because local markets were small and needed major efforts to grow to sufficient size to support large gas projects. Overseas markets were often inaccessible before the advent of LNG. Gas supplies often came from town gas (manufactured from coal or another feedstock) and served mainly domestic and commercial customers in highly localized markets. There was little or no demand for natural gas as a fuel for power generation; it was easier to burn coal or oil directly in power plants. The markets were therefore small. It was also complicated to convert town gas networks to natural gas since most appliances had to be retrofitted to handle the "richer" natural gas. In those circumstances, it was understandable that oil companies did not make any great efforts to explore for gas, let alone exploit it if they found any.

Gas is found onshore or offshore, as non-associated gas or as associated gas (where it forms part of an oil reservoir and is produced in conjunction with the oil). The non-associated gas can be dry—that is, nearly pure methane—or wet, containing higher-chain hydrocarbons, such as propane, butane, and condensates. In many oil-producing countries, such as Nigeria, associated gas is flared since it is too expensive to reinject into the reservoirs or to gather for sale to domestic or export markets. Other countries, such as Algeria, Qatar, and Trinidad, have large reserves of nonassociated gas. In all cases, the gas needs to be produced and treated before it can be processed in the liquefaction plant. Treating removes condensate and other heavier hydrocarbons, water, CO_2, and other contaminants.

The cost of the gas can vary substantially by location—depending on whether the gas is offshore (in which case, water depth and distance to shore are critical factors) or onshore, deep or shallow, wet or dry, associated or nonassociated. Gas well productivity and distance to the proposed liquefaction plant are also relevant. Compared with the other stages of the LNG chain, where most of the cost is incurred up front, gas production usually requires ongoing investment over the life of the project to offset the natural decline of the initial reservoirs.

When the gas is wet (i.e., contains condensates and LPG), the effective cost of the gas can be substantially reduced. These condensates may need to be stripped out of the gas before it enters the liquefaction plant, and sales of condensates can yield a substantial additional revenue stream. In some fields, such as those in Qatar and Oman, the condensate revenue can cover most of the upstream investment.

Exploration and production is usually covered by agreements between the host government and the energy companies. These agreements set out the terms under which producers can explore for, develop, and produce oil and gas. These terms often include provisions such as minimum exploration programs, cost recovery, tax treatment, and royalty payments. In the case of concession or license agreements, the oil and gas become the property of the producers, while in the case of production-sharing contracts, the government (often in the form of the state oil company) retains ownership and participation right in the reserves once discovered.

Traditionally, oil and gas companies have funded exploration and production expenditure with corporate funds because of the high risk involved. The large international majors tend to prefer this approach, but there is an increasing number of cases where large production installations, such as offshore production platforms, have been project financed by third-party funds.

Liquefaction

The heart of an LNG project and the largest single investment in the chain is the liquefaction plant. Gas composition, quantity, and location have important bearing on its design, but at heart, liquefaction plants are nothing more than giant refrigerators. Although each of the world's large baseload liquefaction plants is unique in design, they all perform a basic common task: first treating the gas to remove impurities and then liquefying it by cooling it to around −163°C, at which temperature the gas becomes a liquid at atmospheric pressure.

Plants are usually set up as a number of parallel processing units, called trains, each of which treats the gas and then liquefies it. The maximum capacity of each train is determined by the size of the equipment, such as heat exchangers and gas or steam turbines, which drive the compressors essential for the liquefaction process. Historically, parallel trains were developed to enable the plant to continue operating when one of the trains was shut down for maintenance or repair. Taking advantage of economies of scale and larger equipment sizes, unit train capacities have increased to almost 8 MMt/y (more than 11 Bcm/y) in new projects in Qatar, compared to 1 MMt/y (1.4 Bcm/y) capacity in the early plants (Libya, Algeria, Alaska, and Brunei).

After the gas leaves the upstream production facilities, it is metered and transported by pipeline to the liquefaction plant. Before leaving the production facilities or entering the liquefaction plant, the gas may be treated to remove impurities or heavier hydrocarbons that can turn into liquid in the line. Before the gas can be liquefied, it must be treated to remove carbon dioxide, sulfur, mercury, and water, which can freeze or cause corrosion inside the heat exchangers. Many heavier hydrocarbons are stripped out at this point, leaving mainly methane and some light hydrocarbons. Essentially, the gas at this stage needs to be of a quality that is saleable in the final market. Any heavier components removed in the plant (e.g., condensate and LPG) are shipped and sold separately, creating additional revenue for the project.

The liquefaction process equipment consists of compressors driven by steam or gas turbines and heat exchangers, where heat from the incoming gas is transferred to refrigerant gases (e.g., propane, ethylene, or mixtures thereof), which in turn transfer heat to an outside coolant (air or water or a combination). There are a number of proprietary processes, but the overall process concepts and costs are basically similar. In earlier plants, the compressors were largely driven by steam turbines, but today, gas turbines are the standard compressor drivers.

The storage and loading facilities are an important part of a liquefaction plant. After the gas is cooled to a liquid state, it must be stored in double-walled and insulated tanks. The tanks are designed to keep the LNG cold until it can be loaded on board LNG tankers. LNG tanks are usually built with an inner tank of cryogenic nickel/steel, surrounded by several feet of insulation and an outer tank constructed from prestressed concrete or mild steel. In the case of mild steel tanks, the tank is further surrounded by a berm, to contain the LNG in the unlikely event of a failure of the inner tank and provide a measure of protection to the remainder of the plant. No such berm is required for the reinforced concrete tank, which can contain the LNG if the inner tank fails. Early tanks had relatively small capacities, on the order of 50,000 cubic meters of liquid, but these have grown in scale to 200,000 cubic meters. The choice of tank design, size, and number is a function of the plant site size, LNG production rates, and the size and frequency of the LNG tankers calling at the plant.

The plant also needs a jetty and loading facilities that allow safe access for the LNG tankers. Often, breakwaters or harbors need to be constructed to protect the marine berths and the LNG tankers. LNG jetties have rigid loading arms, capable of handling the cryogenic temperatures, that are connected to the ship's manifold with special quick-disconnect couplings that can be released in the event of an emergency.

As LNG plants are often located in remote areas, significant infrastructure may be required (roads, airport, staff accommodation with schools, hospitals, laboratories, maintenance facilities, etc.), during both the construction and the operations phases of the project. A golf course is normally not far away! Up until now, all the existing liquefaction plants have been built onshore at coastal locations, although designs have been prepared for offshore floating plants integrated with offshore production facilities.

Safety is paramount during design, construction, and operation. Liquefaction plants have proven to be very safe and reliable, and most have generally produced well in excess of their initial design capacity and well beyond their initial design life. The Camel plant in Algeria, completed in 1964, was still in operation in 2006.

Shipping

After liquefaction and storage, the LNG is loaded onto specially designed ships built around insulated cargo tanks. LNG is sold either FOB (free on board), in which case the buyer is responsible for arranging the shipping and title to the cargo transfers on loading, or on a delivered ex-ship or CIF (cost, insurance, and freight) basis, in which case the seller arranges the shipping and title is transferred at the destination or after loading. LNG ships historically were custom built for and dedicated to specific projects, sailing in regular service between the LNG supplier and one or more customers. The size of LNG ships has steadily increased since the mid-1990s. Currently, ships with cargo capacities of 154,500 m^3 are being delivered, and 266,000 m^3 vessels are on order. LNG ships are specially designed with double hulls and other safety features. Unlike oil tankers, the double hulls on an LNG tanker provide both structural rigidity (which is not provided by the cargo tanks) and allow the ship to carry large quantities of ballast water since the cargo is so light. There are two basic types of cargo systems employed in the LNG fleet. Spherical tanks are essentially self-supporting, while membrane tanks rely on the ship and their insulation for support. These cargo systems are described in more detail in chapter 6.

Traditionally, LNG ships used steam turbines for propulsion, but as the relative price of oil and gas has changed and engine technology has improved, newer ships are more likely to employ slow-speed diesel engines, driving the propeller(s) either directly or indirectly through electrical generators. These diesel engines can be dual fueled or may only run on marine diesel fuel. While they are more expensive than steam turbines up front, they are generally less expensive to operate and maintain.

Regardless of the cargo system, some boil-off occurs during the voyage. On today's ships, up to 0.15% of the cargo boils off every day. LNG tankers do not usually have onboard reliquefaction facilities. Instead, the gas that boils off during a voyage is generally used as fuel for propelling the vessel. However, ships with onboard reliquefaction facilities, usually diesel engine ships that cannot burn gas, are currently being constructed in Korea. Besides having the capability of delivering all of the loaded cargo, these ships will be the biggest (209,000–266,000 m^3) LNG ships ever built and will serve the Qatari projects. After unloading their cargo, LNG ships usually retain a small amount of LNG, the heel, onboard during the ballast voyage. This LNG is kept on the ship to keep tanks cool for reloading. The heel is also sprayed within the tanks, to cool them further prior to loading. The colder the tanks are, the less boil-off occurs during loading and transport, which in turn affects loading time and the amount of LNG delivered. Warmer tanks may require cooldown, which is time-consuming.

Ship design, construction, and operation are all subject to very high standards. As a result, the track record of LNG ships is very good. No LNG cargo has ever been lost or spilled. Very few LNG ships have been scrapped, and there is general acceptance that with appropriate maintenance, these vessels can have a working life of 40 years or more.

Regasification terminals

LNG cargoes are discharged at regasification terminals (also called receiving or import terminals) that are located in the overseas customer's country. Usually, terminals are owned by the customer and operated on a proprietary basis; alternatively, the customer may arrange to lease capacity on a third-party access basis.

A terminal consists of one or more berths, each with a set of unloading arms, LNG storage tanks, and vaporization equipment to move the regasified LNG into the pipeline system. They may also include facilities for loading LNG onto tanker trucks for road delivery. Traditionally, terminals were funded by utilities, just as other gas distribution assets, and were included in the utilities' rate bases where they could earn a regulated rate of return. With the advent of open access, project financing is increasingly used to fund the construction of these terminals.

Markets

LNG sales from a project have classically been on a long-term basis (20 years or more) to a large utility, either a gas company or a large power company. These companies are often state owned or have a monopoly franchise area. They provided the long-term financial underpinnings that enabled shareholders and lenders to commit very large amounts of capital with confidence.

Pricing of LNG has until recently depended on the specific conditions of the customers' markets. In markets that have utility buyers and essentially no pipeline gas supplies, such as Japan and Korea, prices have been mainly set by reference to crude oil as a proxy price for LNG. In turn, these supply arrangements and prices were subject to approval by the governmental authorities that permitted the utilities to recover their fuel costs (but no associated profit) from their captive customers. Recent experience in the Far East in 2002–4 with India and China had suggested that this pattern could be varied through competitive tendering for LNG supplies, which appear to have broken the close links between oil and gas prices. Whether these terms were aberrations or set a new pattern is not yet known, but in 2006, there was no question that the market had slipped back toward a seller's market, in which security of supply again became as important as price. In Europe,

LNG competes with pipeline gas; therefore, LNG pricing tends to follow pipeline pricing, both being generally linked to oil or oil products when they are supplied under long-term contracts. In the United States, LNG pricing is driven by the U.S. gas market and is generally priced against the Henry Hub index, often with adjustments for basis (or location) differentials. However, the rapid evolution of an LNG spot market and the increased availability of shipping uncommitted to long-term contracts have resulted in an increasing globalization of spot LNG prices, driven on the margin by U.S. market prices. Whether LNG ultimately becomes a fungible commodity like oil and whether long-term contract pricing becomes driven by local gas market prices remain matters for debate. With little or no gas-on-gas competition in the Asian LNG markets—and, arguably, limited competition in some European markets—most of the world's long-term supply of LNG remains insulated from competitive market forces.

THE OWNERSHIP CHAIN

Every project tends to have its own organizational structure, which is determined by such local circumstances as legal and fiscal regimes, ownership of the gas resource and national ambitions, and the way the value chain is split up among the different project stages. In view of the technical complexity of the business and its need for large investments up front, the gas producers, often including or sometimes solely the national oil company, tend to be involved in the production and liquefaction stages and frequently take control of the LNG shipping, selling on an ex-ship or CIF basis. This structure evolved from the producers' desire to ensure control over the project's successful implementation and to protect their upstream interests. There is, however, a trend toward upstream participation by the customers, as a way of increasing their security of supply and gaining the right to invest in the more profitable components of the LNG chain, which were perceived as being financed on their credit and their markets. Increasingly, LNG buyers are acquiring control over LNG shipping and moving to purchases on an FOB basis. At the same time, LNG producers are moving downstream to secure market outlets through ownership or access rights in LNG terminals in the more competitive markets, to give themselves more control over the ultimate sale of the gas.

The entity owning the liquefaction plant may be controlled by just the gas producers and may buy the gas and sell the LNG (and other products) on an FOB or a delivered basis, taking some portion of the price risk. Alternatively, the liquefaction plant can be established as a tolling facility, in which case the gas producers pay a fee to convert their gas into LNG, keeping control of the product until sale to the ultimate customers.

While early projects were financed largely by equity contributed by the shareholders, it has become normal practice for liquefaction plants to be project financed by international banks and export credit agencies, sometimes with very high leverage (debt exceeding 80% of the total investment). Because of the long-term contract structure and the participation by experienced and highly regarded international companies, the credit rating of an LNG project can be higher than that of the host country, since the project's credit rating is often governed by the quality of the LNG buyers' contracts and credit ratings.

Main ownership structures

There are three primary models of project structure:

A. The same participants throughout the chain, with the point of sale either FOB (Sonatrach, RasGas) or delivered (Australia's NWS) and with the liquefaction profits integrated with the upstream profits.

B. The liquefaction plant as separate profit entity (company), owned mainly by the resource owners, buying gas and selling LNG, with margins reflecting both volume and prices of the LNG sales. This company can sell LNG on either an FOB basis (Oman LNG, ALNG Train 1) or a delivered basis (Malaysia LNG, Nigeria LNG, Brunei LNG).

C. The liquefaction plant as a cost center owned either by the national oil company (Indonesia) or by producers and customers (ALNG Train 2/3, ALNG Train 4, and Egyptian LNG). The liquefaction plant company can buy gas and sell LNG or operate on a toll basis, earning a utility margin in either case.

Model A has the advantage of a seamless structure and avoids the need to negotiate a transfer price and conditions for the gas supplied to the plant. However, the undivided joint venture concept used in the Australian NWS project can lead to management by committee and can also complicate project funding, as each participant needs to raise its own financing. Since the NWS model was driven by Australian legal and fiscal considerations, it may not be an issue in other settings.

Model B uses generally established company and management structures and is based on normally well-established fiscal and legal principles. While this structure requires the negotiation of the price of gas supplied to the liquefaction plant, it is flexible in accommodating shareholding interests that vary from the resource ownership interests. The company can also be used as a financing vehicle. The revenue of the company is created by its sale of LNG (and often condensate and LPG) to overseas buyers. Its main cost is the purchase of gas from the producers. The gas price is often set as a function (often expressed as a percentage) of the LNG price.

Model C is normally based on a fixed or semifixed toll-based fee structure that covers the plant's operating costs and can permit an assured profit margin, independent of fluctuations in the volume or price of the LNG sold. It has the same advantages as model B in that it uses well-established company and fiscal laws and permits flexibility in ownership. Properly structured, it can be easier and cheaper to project finance given the assured and relatively stable revenue stream. Often the tolling fees are subject to "hell or high water" provisions, payable by the producers independent of any upstream supply or downstream sales problems.

Except in model A, ownership interests can differ between the stages of a project. Major differences in shareholding between production, liquefaction, and shipping can create interface problems, such as transfer pricing, risk sharing, and project management issues, which have to be resolved through the project's commercial contract structure. Because of the different kind and level of risks in each stage, reaching agreement on the allocation of volume, price, and technical and political risks can be time consuming. The shareholding in the liquefaction plant and shipping is often based on the sharing of the resource base; in practice, this may be modified by ambitions of the host government or by LNG buyers seeking a stake in these components. Multiple participants and varying interests throughout the chain can create conflicts of interest and delays in agreement on terms, but addition of participants can enhance the project's financial attractiveness and may be a condition the project has to accept to achieve government support and market access.

Commercial and funding pressures can necessitate more complicated structures. For example, in the Australian NWS project, assets are commonly used but are owned by two different joint ventures with different shareholdings—one supplying pipeline gas to Western Australia, the other supplying LNG. In Egypt, Oman, and Trinidad, different trains in the plant are owned in different shareholdings, and in Trinidad, different trains have different commercial structures.

Shipping

The ships can be owned by sellers, either directly or through a special-purpose company, or they can be owned by buyers or third parties who charter ships out to the buyers or sellers. Ships are increasingly chartered from independent owners following competitive tenders and are project-financed by international banks. In many ways, LNG shipping has come to look more like a utility function, with the shipowners assured of a modest but stable long-term return—truly a gas pipeline equivalent!

Examples of delivered (ex-ship or CIF) sales are Australia's NWS, where the ships are owned mainly by its participants and are chartered by the joint venture; Brunei LNG, whose ships are chartered on a long-term basis from shipowner Brunei Tankers; and Nigeria LNG, most of whose ships are chartered from an associated company, Bonny Gas Transport.

Examples of FOB sales are Oman LNG and Qatar's RasGas LNG to Korea, where the ships are owned by Korean interests and chartered to Kogas; and Trinidad's ALNG, whose tankers are owned by a variety of owners and chartered back or owned outright by the buyers. Operation and management of the tankers are often delegated to experienced shipping companies.

THE COMMERCIAL AND FINANCIAL CHAIN

The buyers of LNG generate revenues from their gas or electric customers, such as industrial and commercial gas users, power generators, and residential consumers. From this, they pay for regasification terminal costs and margins, shipping (in the case of an FOB purchase), and the purchase of LNG. The revenue from the LNG sales covers the payments of the charter hire for the ships (if a delivered sale), the operating costs of the LNG plant, the feedgas, and the servicing of any debt used to finance the project, taxes and royalties to the host government, and hopefully the profits to the project shareholders.

The project shareholders are usually most interested in their netback—that is, the value of the gas at the wellhead, which determines their profitability and also generates tax and royalties for the host government. The netback, of course, depends on the costs to bring the gas from the wellhead to the market.

Cost and cost reduction along the LNG chain

Over the 40-year history of the LNG business, increasing skills and experience in the technical and commercial aspects of the industry have resulted in more cost-competitive and cost-effective infrastructure and services. The LNG industry has shown itself to be subject to the experience curve and economies of scale.

LNG facility costs are estimated to have dropped 30%–50% across the LNG chain between the early 1980s and 2003. All stages have contributed to this—exploration and production, liquefaction, shipping, and regasification. However, this trend has reversed since 2003, as escalating raw material costs—combined with intensified worldwide competition for management, labor, key equipment items, and engineering resources—outweigh continued gains from improved technologies and economies of scale. Although all projects benefit from technological advances, these cannot entirely offset the problems faced by some projects disadvantaged by long shipping distances to main markets, high location-cost factors, or expensive production costs because of hostile or remote environments. The LNG industry has become a victim of its own success.

Lower LNG export facility costs bring benefits to LNG exporters and importers alike, particularly with expansions of existing projects. For a start, the LNG exporter may be more willing to incur a greater equity risk by committing to project construction without full-capacity sales. Indeed, this proved to be the case with Qatar's RasGas venture and Oman LNG. This in turn creates further benefits: first, the buyer (in both cases Kogas) did not have to wait for other buyers to be lined up before the export projects were committed; second, the projects were advantageously positioned to compete for subsequent sales with the additional capacity (Oman LNG to Japan's Osaka Gas and India's former Dabhol Power Company and RasGas to India's Petronet import consortium). Lower LNG costs also allowed LNG to compete in lower-priced markets, such as ALNG Train 1, which sold 60% of its output to the United States during a period when U.S. gas prices were seen as far too low to make LNG a viable supply option.

Exploration and production

As a result of major differences between gas reserves (in size, depth, complexity, and location), coupled with varying legal, fiscal, and royalty regimes, the economics of upstream gas production vary substantially among different projects. They can be further affected by the benefits of major condensate streams or the costs of dealing with undesirable constituents such as CO_2.

Upstream exploration and production costs have decreased substantially over recent years owing to the increasingly widespread use of three-dimensional seismic, horizontal drilling, and subsea completion technologies. Development can be successfully completed at far greater reservoir depths—and in the case of offshore development, far greater water depths—than was the case 20 years earlier. Unit costs for gas development can range between an effective rate of zero, when liquids can cover the entire upstream investment, up to $1.00/MMBtu in more complex reservoirs.

Liquefaction

The unit cost of a liquefaction plant decreased by about a third over the last 30 years of the 20th century because of increased scale, design efficiencies, improved project management, and increasing competition between engineering, procurement, and construction (EPC) contractors. Plant costs bottomed out below $200 per ton per annum (tpa) capacity in some cases. Hence, a large LNG plant of around 8 MMt/y costs between $1.5 and $2 billion. Operating costs are relatively low (5%–7% of capital costs). In addition, gas shrinkage through the liquefaction plant owing to fuel consumption and LPG production ranges from 7% to 15%, depending on the feedgas composition and the liquefaction process being used.

As an example, the three-train 6.6 MMt/y Malaysia LNG Satu plant was built in 1983. Capital costs were about $433/tpa of LNG capacity. By contrast, the two-train 6.6 MMt/y liquefaction plant at Oman was built in the year 2000. At the time of construction, the two 3.3 MMt/y trains were the largest in commercial operation. Capital cost of the Oman LNG facility works out to about $273/tpa—that is, a unit cost reduction of more than one-third.

The most recent EPC contract awards, however, have been in the range of $250–$350/tpa, indicating that the downward capital cost trend is at an end. Perhaps the clearest indication of this reversal came from Indonesia's 7.6 MMt/y (10.6 Bcm/y) Tangguh project, where an 18-month delay in the final investment decision between late 2003 and early 2005 led to its EPC cost increasing from $1.4 billion to $1.8 billion after the original EPC bid expired, necessitating a price renegotiation.

Rising liquefaction construction costs reflect, at least in part, the sharp cost increases experienced since 2003 for many raw materials and labor used in LNG projects. For example, steel prices increased by over 130% from the start of 2003 through December 2004 before retreating to around double their January 2003 levels. Similarly, prices for nickel—a critical component in the cryogenic and stainless steel grades required for LNG plant storage tanks and piping—rocketed from $7,000 per ton in early 2003 to above $17,000 per ton in mid-2005. Strong economic growth and domestic construction activity in countries such as Pakistan and India has also reduced the migrant worker pool available to Middle Eastern countries such as Qatar.

The limited pool of experienced EPC contractors available to meet escalating project demand has also played a part in driving up construction costs. The LNG industry's Big Three EPC contractors—Chiyoda, KBR/JGC, and Bechtel—completed on average one to two LNG trains per year until 2003. Now the number of trains to be completed each year has multiplied. For example, 10 new liquefaction trains are expected to be completed during 2009 alone—a vast increase from both historical and current construction rates. However, available project management, engineering, and construction resources have not entirely kept pace with the LNG industry's rapid growth. Although some additional contractors, such as Chicago Bridge & Iron (CB&I), Foster Wheeler, and Technip have begun to assume leading roles on some projects, doubts remain as to whether the pool of suitable EPC resources can expand to keep pace with demand. This might encourage qualified contractors to seek higher margins for their work, or it might increase the number of project delays.

Shipping

The cost of ships has varied considerably over time. Poten & Partners has estimated that shipyard prices for LNG vessels have declined by as much as $100 million over the past 10–15 years. During the 1980s, prices reached $260 million for 125,000–135,000 m^3 tankers. However, Korea's Daewoo Marine Engineering and Shipbuilding agreed in March 2000 to build a 138,000 m^3 tanker for Belgian shipping company Exmar at their Okpo shipyard for a price of under $145 million. Admittedly, this price represented an all-time record low for a large LNG newbuilding; ship prices have moderated and rebounded since then. Poten & Partners estimated that in 2006, yard prices for a large (138,000–145,000 m^3) LNG tanker were approximately $200–$210 million. Nevertheless, today's yard prices represent a significant savings compared to the asking price 10 years ago for an LNG tanker that had a smaller cargo capacity, slower speed, and higher boil-off rates.

The average cargo capacity of a typical LNG tanker on order today is greater than the ships built 10–15 years ago, even as average costs have fallen. For example, Australia's NWS project has a fleet of eight LNG tankers dedicated to fulfilling its supply obligations to Japan. Each ship has a capacity of about 125,000 m^3 and was delivered to NWS between 1989 and 1994. In May 2000, the NWS joint venture partners ordered a ninth LNG carrier to serve an expansion train. The 138,500 m^3 ship built at Korea's Daewoo is larger than the rest of the NWS fleet. Furthermore, shipowners ordering ships on speculation have opted to order larger ships as well. In 2004, the Greek shipowners Dynacom and Tsakos ordered ships with 150,000 m^3 carrying capacity. Also in 2004 and 2005, AP Möller ordered six 154,200 m^3 ships and later chose to increase the size to 165,500 m^3. This trend took a dramatic leap upward in 2006 when Qatar ordered a fleet of ships, the so-called Q-flex and Q-max vessels, with varying capacities of 209,000–266,000 m^3. While the size of these ships will significantly reduce Qatar's shipping costs, they are incompatible with many of the world's LNG terminals.

Cash operating costs include bunker fuel, crew costs, port charges, canal tolls, insurance, maintenance, regular dry-docking and insurance and are substantially lower than the capital costs charge included in the daily charter rates. In addition, the LNG shipper will incur the cost associated with the boil-off gas generated during the voyage. When gas was worth less than oil, boil-off was less of a concern, since it was simply substituted for bunker fuel in the ship's boilers—and even forced boil-off was used to increase the available gas fuel. In the past few years, improved cargo insulation systems have reduced daily boil-off rates from around 0.25% to 0.15% or even less. With newer ships using diesel propulsion, gas cannot always be substituted for fuel oil, so boil-off rates become more critical, and boil-off handling requires the addition of reliquefaction to the ship. Lower boil-off rates also mean the ship needs to retain less heel on board following discharge.

For each project, shipping costs are primarily a function of the distance between the sellers' and buyers' facilities, although route-specific variables, such as Suez Canal tolls or high port charges, make this less than a perfect linear relationship. As a result, shipping costs may be the single largest variable when comparing different overall project chain costs.

Regasification terminals

The costs of terminals varies considerably, depending on the local construction costs, the cost of land, the regasification technology and capacity, and the total amount of storage installed, which varies from 35,000 to over 2,000,000 cubic meters. The terminal owner decides on the required storage, baseload, and peak vaporization capacity, depending on the seasonality of the market and the degree of security of supply required. A conventional onshore terminal with 200,000–300,000 cubic meters of storage now typically costs at least $500 million, not including land and downstream pipeline costs. Operating, maintenance insurance, and security costs are typically on the order of 3%–4% of capital costs. A major variable between terminals arises from the choice of vaporization technologies. Most Far East terminals deploy open-rack vaporizers (ORVs), which use seawater as their heat transfer medium and only fuel gas for backup vaporization. By contrast, most U.S. terminals use gas-fired vaporizers, since U.S. environmental regulations make the use of ORVs impossible. While gas-fired vaporizers have a significantly lower cost and a smaller size than the ORVs, they also use about 1.5% of the terminal's LNG throughput for fuel, making this the single-largest expense in operating these facilities. U.S. terminals, especially in the Gulf of Mexico, are now experimenting with heat exchangers using ambient air for vaporization. Given these variables, terminal costs, including capital recovery, have a range that can vary between $0.35/MMBtu and $1.00/MMBtu.

Value generation along the LNG value chain

The aggregate costs associated with production, liquefaction, shipping, and regasification yield a total cost range of $2–$3.50/MMBtu, from wellhead through terminal. This makes LNG competitive in the market against oil products when crude oil prices are around $15–$22/bbl (fig. 3–2). Although the most recent capital cost increases have undoubtedly increased total chain costs, most LNG projects continue to be competitive at the level of long-range oil prices used by the oil companies to assess project feasibility and certainly generate significant economic rents to their owners at the $50–$75-oil-price environment in existence through 2005 and 2006.

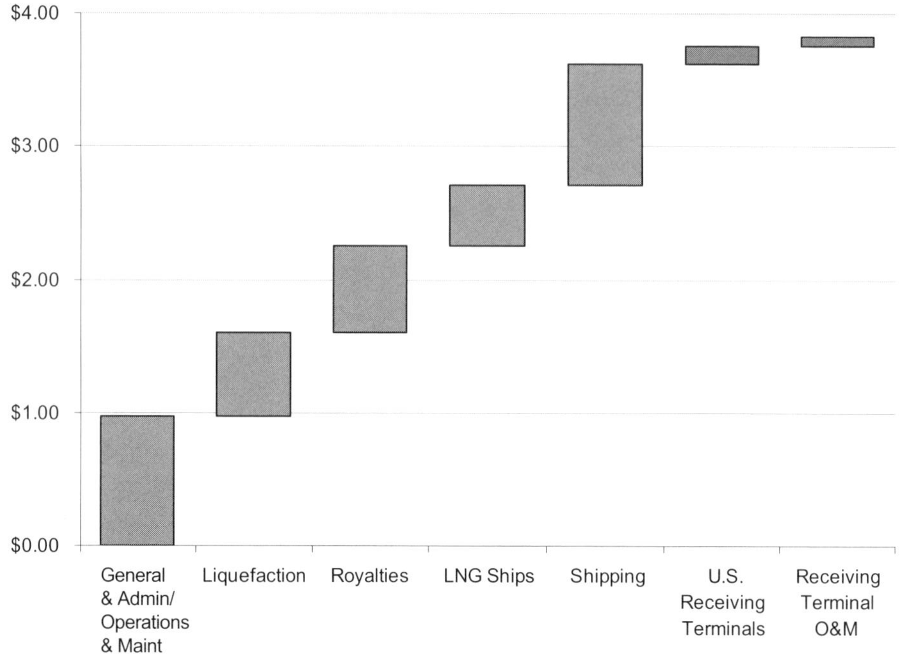

Fig. 3–2. Illustrative break-even costs for a greenfield LNG project 10,000 miles from the U.S. East Coast (Source: Poten & Partners)

The required values differ significantly between projects: As discussed previously, production costs vary because of the location, depth, and nature of the gas reserves; because of liquefaction costs, which differ by available plant location and equipment and manpower costs; and because of local taxes and duties. Shipping costs depend directly on distance to the market and will vary between $0.30/MMBtu for shipping across the Mediterranean or from Sakhalin to Japan, to more than $1.60/MMBtu for shipments from the Middle East to the United States. Middle Eastern LNG export projects can accommodate high shipping costs because of their low net gas costs, low construction costs, and economies of scale. Similarly, the Nigeria LNG project can live with relatively lower European gas prices because of medium shipping distances and low feedgas costs.

In view of the high up-front capital costs and because LNG is rarely, if ever, an energy price setter in any market—let alone one over which the project participants have much control, other than through the pricing formulas embedded in the LNG sales contracts—optimal project economics generally depend on maximization of sales volumes throughout the project's lifetime. Variable operating costs for the project chain are essentially zero, since the primary variable cost, the gas used for fuel along the chain, remains in the ground indefinitely with minimal value if not produced and sold. Labor, shipping, and other cash operating expenses are not truly variable unless plants or ships are mothballed for extended durations, which outside the United States has rarely happened. As a result, project participants will put a high premium on maintaining volumes even during periods of low prices. The opportunities created by the spot LNG market and by the increasing possibilities of cargo diversions and swaps are becoming more aggressively used by LNG sellers to maximize their sales volumes and by LNG buyers to manage their market fluctuations. Shipping to markets which have temporary gas shortages and are prepared to pay relatively high prices, even where this requires increased shipping distances, can create substantial additional values, which can be shared by the chain participants.

As a result, the LNG market is rapidly becoming more complex, with many types of commercial transactions new to the LNG industry but often borrowed from other segments of the energy industry. Both buyers and sellers are trying to carve out trading roles, moving away from the traditional point-to-point arrangements of the past. These changing conditions have facilitated—or induced—extensions of companies reach up and down the LNG chain.

Oil and gas majors, for example, are beginning to take positions in various downstream markets worldwide (fig. 3–3). Open or negotiated access to import terminal and pipeline capacity allows companies on both sides of the traditional buyer/seller relationship to buy LNG for their own account, acquire LNG terminal capacity, and compete for end-use sales. This trend has evolved quickly in Atlantic Basin gas markets. National oil companies, such as Sonatrach, Qatar Petroleum, and Petronas, have gained access to U.K. markets through capacity agreements with and/or direct investment in receiving terminals. Supermajors, such as ExxonMobil, Shell, and ConocoPhillips, are integrating downstream as well, securing access to and/or ownership in various North American and European LNG import terminals. In the Asia-Pacific region, there have been comparatively limited opportunities for international companies to participate in the downstream sector, as markets in Japan, Korea, Taiwan, and China are much slower than their European and U.S. counterparts in implementing energy market liberalization measures, although India has been more progressive in this respect. The move to forward integrate appears to be largely driven by producers seeking to secure long-term market access for their LNG production in an increasingly complex and competitive world.

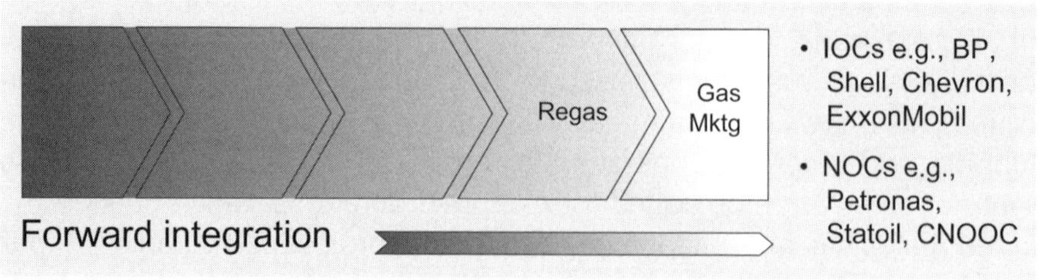

Fig. 3–3. Forward integration (Source: Poten & Partners)

By contrast, some utilities and other downstream companies have aggressively moved into the upstream and the liquefaction end of the chain (fig. 3–4). Osaka Gas, Tokyo Gas, Kogas, Union Fenosa, Gas Natural, and Gaz de France are all examples of companies moving into shipping, liquefaction, and exploration and production.

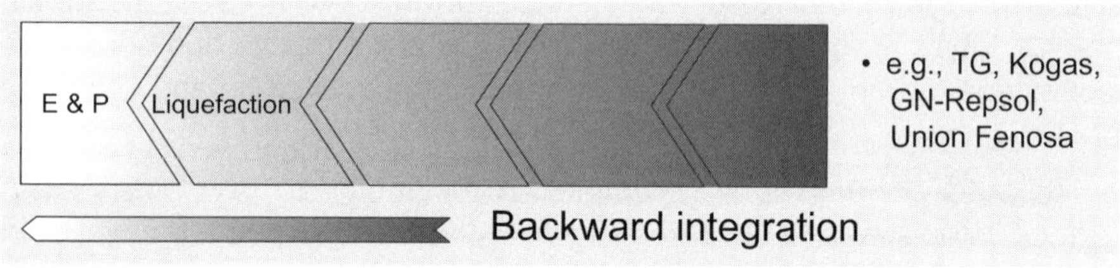

Fig. 3–4. Backward integration (Source: Poten & Partners)

By moving into additional segments of the LNG supply chain, downstream companies appear to be seeking to secure optimum pricing, volume flexibility, and some degree of LNG delivery control. Unlike the producers, these companies also appear to be seeking diversification opportunities to protect themselves from value erosion through competition in their home markets.

UPSTREAM NATURAL GAS 4

INTRODUCTION

Gas has historically been the poor relation of oil. The old joke goes that the geologist returns from the field with good news and bad news: the bad news is that he found no oil; the good news is that he found no gas either. In existing markets with domestic gas supplies, this has not been the case, and gas exploration has long been a target of development efforts in North America and Western Europe. However, the increase in worldwide gas consumption in recent years, along with the increasing difficulty and expense of accessing oil reserves, has led to a push to develop already-known gas deposits and to explore specifically for new gas fields.

Exploration for and production of natural gas is broadly similar to that of oil, and often the two hydrocarbons are found in association with one another. There are, however, some substantial differences. While the physical characteristics of natural gas can make transportation difficult (hence the need for LNG technology), its gaseous nature makes its extraction from the ground much easier than that of oil, which usually requires some sort of assisted recovery technique, especially as oil fields mature.

PHYSICAL AND CHEMICAL PROPERTIES OF NATURAL GAS

Hydrocarbons are so called because they are chain molecules composed of hydrogen and carbon atoms. Hydrocarbons are generally in the chemical form C_nH_{2n+2}. The higher n is, the heavier will be the molecule. The lighter hydrocarbons are gases at normal temperature and pressure—hence the term "natural gas." Natural gas is primarily methane, although heavier molecules can be found in the gas, depending on its source. A typical hydrocarbon composition of natural gas from the midcontinent United States is as follows:[1]

- Methane (CH_4): 88%
- Ethane (C_2H_6): 5%
- Propane (C_3H_8): 2%
- Butane (C_4H_{10}): 1%

In addition to these constituents, natural gas can contain water, carbon dioxide (acid gas), nitrogen, and less commonly, hydrogen sulfide. A large percentage of the world's helium production is derived from natural gas sourced from fields near Amarillo, Texas, although helium comprises a tiny fraction of the natural gas stream.[2] Methane is extremely volatile, with a boiling temperature of –161°C (–258°F) and a specific gravity of 0.6 (compared to a value for air of 1.0). The heavier constituents, propane and butane, can be liquefied at higher temperatures and lower pressures than methane and together are referred to as liquefied petroleum gas (LPG).

The composition of natural gas varies depending on its source. Heating values (i.e., the amount of heat produced by the combustion of a given quantity of fuel) for gas ranges from 900 to over 1,200 Btu/ft^3, with higher heat content being associated with greater proportions of heavier hydrocarbons.[3] Natural gas is colorless and odorless.

As noted in chapter 3, natural gas in a reservoir can occur as either associated gas, which is found in the same geological strata as crude oil, or nonassociated gas. Associated gas can exist either in solution within the oil or as a separate gas cap, distinct from the liquid phase. Because gas is lighter than oil and both are lighter than water, gas not in solution will occupy the highest sections of a reservoir.

A field developer has a number of choices when encountering associated gas. Flaring is one option—and is usually the cheapest and easiest way to dispose of a product that is only a nuisance in many circumstances. Given concerns over global warming and general environmental quality, flaring is viewed as an increasingly unacceptable solution to dealing with associated gas. In fact, the development of Nigeria's first (and thus far only) LNG project, Nigeria LNG, was in part driven by the government's desire to end associated gas flaring. Many oil field operators reinject gas into the oil and gas reservoir as it is produced, to maintain the formation pressure that drives the oil into the wells; the Prudhoe Bay field, on Alaska's North Slope, is a prime example of this process. Operators can also choose to monetize the gas in its own right, independent of oil production. However, not all reservoirs are susceptible to reinjection of the gas, nor can all resources be readily monetized, so flaring continues.

Non-associated gas occurs in a reservoir without significant oil or other heavy hydrocarbon liquids. Gas-condensate fields are gas accumulations in which the ambient pressure is so high that the heavier hydrocarbons remain in a gas phase, only to fall out of the gas stream in liquid form as they are brought to the surface during production. These liquids, known as condensate, generally comprise the C_5H_{12}, C_6H_{14}, and C_7H_{16} molecules and along with butane, propane, and ethane are often referred to as natural gas liquids (NGL), after being removed from the natural gas stream during processing.[4] Many of the stranded-gas reserves worldwide that are considered candidates to supply LNG projects are found in nonassociated gas fields.

NATURAL GAS RESERVES

The term "reserves" can have a variety of meanings and classifications. Generally, reserves refer to the volume of technically and commercially recoverable hydrocarbons in an oil and/or gas reservoir (as opposed to the total volume of oil or gas in place, much of which may not be recoverable using current technology and in current market conditions). There are three major classifications of reserves: proven, probable, and possible. The usage of these classifications varies with who is reporting, and the terms may be defined differently under various accounting standards used for purposes of financial reporting by public companies. To further confuse matters, the term "resources" is used to describe oil and gas that may be present even though there is no specific data supporting the estimate—for example, where conditions appear to be geologically favorable.

Generally, proven reserves are those reserves that are demonstrated to a high degree of certainty by the geological or geophysical delineation of the reservoir, the drilling of appraisal wells, and the testing of these wells' results. Their major characteristics (pressure, flow, composition, etc.)

have been analyzed. Information from producing reservoirs in the vicinity of the field being appraised may also be used in conducting the analysis. Designating reserves as probable or possible is more of a statistical exercise based on a wide variety of geological, physical, and economic criteria, but with much less information derived from actual drilling results. Usually reserves deemed to have a greater than 50% likelihood of being developed are considered probable, while those less likely to see development are described as possible.

The question of whether identified resources can be technically produced applies much less to gas than to oil, since oil reserves often require expensive, enhanced techniques to recover much of the oil in place, whereas gas reserves are more easily produced, because the driving mechanism that gets the gas to the surface is its own pressure. However, the commerciality test of proven oil reserves is more certain for oil than for gas, since it is much easier to demonstrate a market and price for potential future oil production than for gas production. Under U.S. accounting guidelines, companies are required to report their reserves on the basis of the price of the oil and gas that they are selling or planning to sell as of the last day of the year for which they are reporting (which can lead to some interesting reserve fluctuations if energy prices change dramatically between the successive years). U.S. companies cannot book gas reserves until they have demonstrated that the reserves are marketable—for example, by entering into a sales contract with a buyer. International companies generally have more latitude. This can result in anomalous disclosures, with a U.S. company classifying reserves from a field as probable or potential while a foreign company classifying them as proven (as happened in the Gorgon field in Australia, where in the absence of binding sales commitments, ExxonMobil did not count the reserves as proven, while Shell did, subsequently requiring Shell to revise its reserves figure).

Reserve estimates are constantly updated over the life of a reservoir, both to reflect the actual production of the oil and/or gas and as a result of a continuous reassessment of the remaining hydrocarbons in place and the likelihood of their recovery. As more wells are drilled and more seismic data are collected, the nature of a reservoir becomes increasingly clear. This will often lead to a reclassification of hydrocarbons from probable or possible to proven. Thus, even as oil and/or gas are removed from a reservoir during production, that reservoir's remaining proven reserves may increase.

Worldwide, the largest deposits of estimated natural gas reserves are found in Russia (table 4–1); recent estimates suggest that these reserves are nearly twice as large as those of the nearest rival, Iran. Qatar is currently estimated to have the world's third-largest gas reserves, virtually all in the giant North Field. Two other Arabian/Persian Gulf states—Saudi Arabia and the United Arab Emirates (UAE)—round out the top five. Together, these five nations contain over half of the world's current gas reserves. These estimates illustrate the difficulty of distinguishing between reserves and resources. For example, while the United States has *reserves* of 192 Tcf (5,441.3 Bcm), its *resources* are estimated to be 10 times this level. The United States has maintained its reserves around this level for years, even while producing in excess of 20 Tcf (566.8 Bcm) per year.

Table 4–1. Estimated proven reserves of the top 30 gas reserve holders, as of January 1, 2006 (*Source:* Oil and Gas Journal, December 19, 2005, pp. 24–25)

Country	Reserves (Tcf)
Russia	1,680,000
Iran	971,150
Qatar	910,520
Saudi Arabia	241,230
UAE (Abu Dhabi)	198,500
United States	192,513
Nigeria	184,660
Algeria	160,505
Venezuela	151,935
Iraq	111,950
Indonesia	97,786
Norway	84,260
Malaysia	75,000
Turkmenistan	71,000
Uzbekistan	66,200
Kazakhstan	65,000
Egypt	58,500
Canada	56,577
Kuwait	55,515
Libya	52,650
China	53,235
Netherlands	62,000
India	38,880
Azerbaijan	30,000
Ukraine	39,600
Oman	29,280
Trinidad and Tobago	25,880
Australia	27,640
Pakistan	28,153
Bolivia	24,000

The rankings in table 4–1 do not, however, reflect the overall gas production by country. Although Russia is the world's largest producer, in keeping with its reserve position, the next four largest producers are, in order from largest to smallest, the United States, Canada, the United Kingdom, and Algeria. Iran, the second-largest reserves holder, is ranked 9th in production, at approximately one-seventh of the Russian output. Qatar is 18th.

In terms of consumption, the United States is the clear leader, using about 23 Tcf (652 Bcm) of natural gas in 2004. The Russian Federation is second with 14.4 Tcf (408 Bcm), or 16% of world consumption. Germany, the United Kingdom, and Canada round out the top five, each consuming around 3 Tcf (85 Bcm) in 2001 and together accounting for just over 10% of global gas consumption.

Geology of natural gas

A hydrocarbon system is made up of four essential parts: a source rock, a migration route, a reservoir rock, and a trap (including a cap formation). The source rock is the organic-rich layer created by the prehistoric burial of plant and animal remains. Over time, the organic material is subject to great heat and pressure as it is buried under successive layers of new rock, a process known as maturation. This combination of heat and pressure essentially cooks this carbon-rich material until it forms hydrocarbon molecules.

Often this source layer takes the form of shale, a dark, carbon-rich rock comprising grains of sand or silt interspersed with relict organic material. Carbonate rocks (rich in calcium carbonate formed almost entirely from the remains of living organisms) and sandstones can also be source rocks. Shales, sandstones, and carbonates are all examples of sedimentary rocks—rocks that are composed of material derived from preexisting sources that has been transported to and deposited in a basin. Sedimentary is one of the three major rock classifications, the others being igneous (resulting from the cooling of liquid magma) and metamorphic (rocks, whether originally sedimentary or igneous, that have been altered by heat and/or pressure).

The organic material within a source rock can be of either plant or animal origin (including algae). The original biological form can have an impact on whether the hydrocarbon created is more likely to be oil or gas. A large amount of terrestrial, "woody" plant material will produce a dry gas (i.e., low in liquids content), while high proportions of relict algae in a source rock will produce more oil (all else being equal).

The depth of burial also plays a role. As the source rocks are buried deeper, they are subject to greater temperatures and pressures, which "crack" the hydrocarbon chains into smaller and smaller molecules. Eventually, these hydrocarbons can become methane (CH_4). Geologists often refer to windows: Beyond certain depths, source rocks are in the gas window, where they are capable of forming gas only. Above this depth is the oil window. Generally, the oil window occurs at depths of between 7,000 and 18,000 feet,[5] while the gas window is deeper than 18,000 feet. These windows represent a general rule of thumb, and their actual depths are dependent on a number of other geological factors.

Like any fluids, hydrocarbons tend to move from areas of higher pressure to areas of lower pressure. Therefore, they seek out migration routes, to move away from the high-pressure zones where they were created. Often this movement is aided by the migration of water, which is squeezed out of the source rock (and even out of individual minerals within the source rock) as pressure increases. As hydrocarbons are created, they can move through the source rock either via fractures and bedding planes or via pores between the grains making up the source rock. The ratio of pore space to a rock's total volume is known as porosity; as oil and gas are formed, the organic material from which they are formed shrinks, increasing the rock's porosity. The ability of fluids to move through a rock is a function of the rock's permeability.

Hydrocarbons move out of source rocks into reservoir rocks (often passing through carrier formations, which allow the passage of the fluids without actually trapping them). Reservoirs can be composed of a number of different rock types, the most common being sandstones. As the name suggests, sandstones consist of compacted grains of sand that have been eroded from terrestrial rocks, deposited (in deltas, beaches, channels, etc.), and, over time, buried. Sandstones often have high porosity and permeability (owing to the spaces between individual grains), making them ideal for both the transfer and trapping of hydrocarbons. Carbonates can also make good reservoir rocks, depending on how fractured or porous they are. A large proportion of Middle Eastern oil is trapped in carbonate reservoirs.[6]

Given the opportunity, hydrocarbons would continue to move through these sandstones or carbonates as long as they were driven by a pressure differential, until they reached the Earth's surface. Therefore, to form exploitable accumulations, the oil and gas must migrate into a trap. Traps come in a variety of forms; commonly, hydrocarbon-bearing sandstone is overlaid by an impermeable cap rock that prevents the fluids from migrating further. If the layers of sandstone and cap rock are folded as a result of movement of the Earth's crust, the oil and/or gas will accumulate in the highest sections of the reservoir rock and remain there (fig. 4–1). Faults can also form excellent traps (fig. 4–2), as can impermeable salt domes (fig. 4–3). Salt domes form a large proportion of oil and gas traps in the Gulf of Mexico. Traps can even be formed by gradual diminishment of the porosity and/or permeability of the reservoir rock.

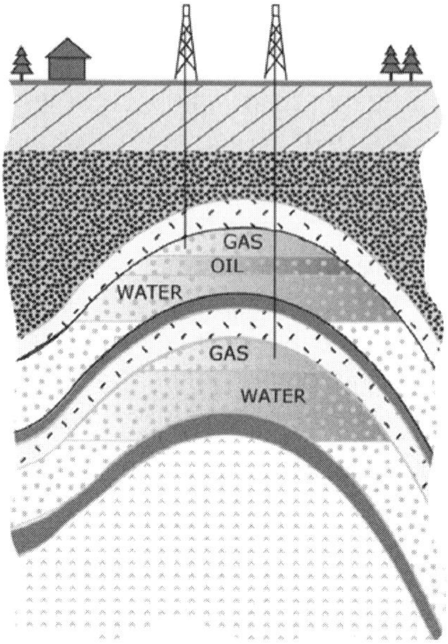

Fig. 4–1. Gas trap created by folding (Source: Poten & Partners)7

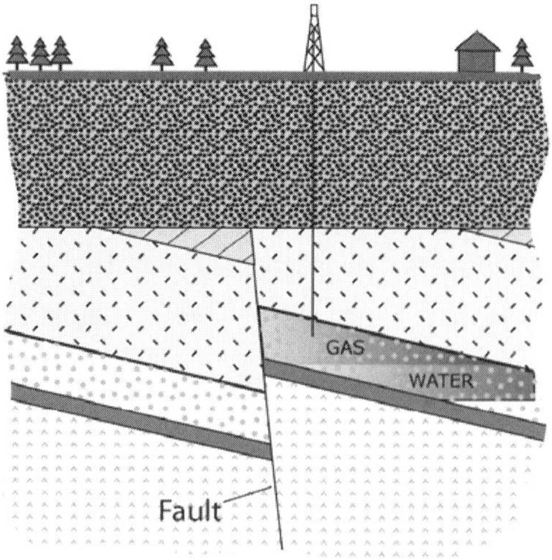

Fig. 4–2. Fault-bounded gas trap (Source: Poten & Partners)

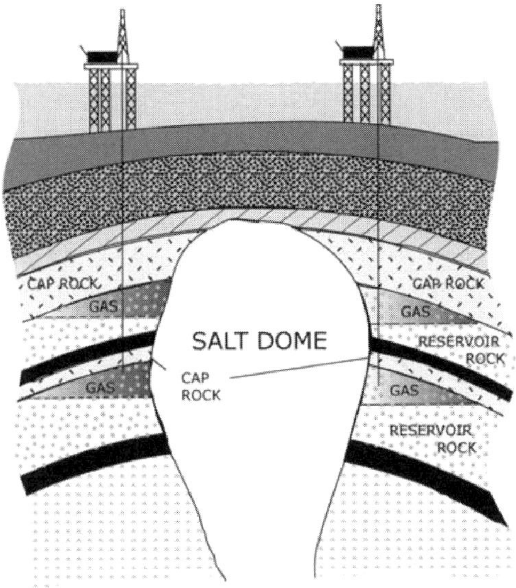

Fig. 4–3. Gas traps created by salt dome intrusion (Source: Poten & Partners)

Natural gas exploration

Nearly all methods of oil and gas exploration are indirect; that is, an explorationist or prospector is, at least initially, looking for signs of the possibility of hydrocarbons, instead of hydrocarbons themselves, and looking for indications of geological conditions that would be favorable to the presence of hydrocarbons. The oldest and least certain of these methods is direct geological investigation. Geologists use both contour maps of the Earth's surface, showing highs and lows of the topography, and the composition of outcrops (surficial exposures of underlying rock layers) to make informed guesses as to the likelihood of hydrocarbon traps in an area. Geologists also consider the prehistoric conditions of a region, such the presence of an ancient river delta where organic material would have been swept into concentrated accumulations and subsequently buried. Somewhat more directly, geochemical analyses, which examine the chemistry of plants and soils for the presence or effects of hydrocarbons seeping to the surface, can give an indication of buried oil or gas. The most effective method for hydrocarbon prospecting, though, is geophysics.

Geophysicists have three main types of tools at their disposal. Measurements of gravity and of the Earth's magnetic field can indicate anomalies, which give insight into the nature of the underlying rocks. Variations in gravity indicate a rock's density, and abrupt changes in density can indicate significant variations in rock types or the presence of salt domes pointing to potential hydrocarbon traps.

Magnetic surveys analyze the variations in different rock layers' magnetic fields, which are largely controlled by the presence or absence of magnetite, a magnetic mineral that is a common constituent of basement rocks (those rocks, usually igneous, that underlie the sedimentary layers that produce and contain oil and gas). Knowledge of the depth of the basement allows a geophysicist to quantify the thickness of a sedimentary layer within a basin, for estimating whether an area was conducive to the generation of hydrocarbons. Gravity and magnetic measurements are also useful in identifying salt deposits that may act as traps.

The primary tool of geophysicists in the search for oil and gas, however, is seismology, which uses sound waves propagating and reflecting through the Earth's crust to draw a picture of the underlying geology and expose stratigraphic traps that may hold hydrocarbons. These sound waves are emitted from a source that imparts a shock wave to the subsurface rocks (on land, the sources are often explosives, while at sea, air guns or electrical sparkers are used). These waves travel through the Earth's crust, and as they pass through a boundary or contact between different layers of rock, some of their energy is reflected back to the surface. These reflected waves are detected by carefully spaced arrays of detectors (referred to on land as geophones and at sea as hydrophones; see fig. 4–4).

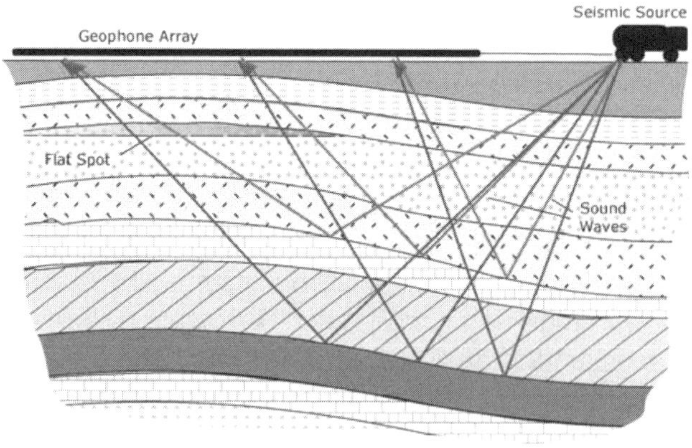

Fig. 4–4. Onshore seismic survey. Sound waves reflect off boundaries between rocks and are detected by the geophone array. (*Source:* Poten & Partners)

Analysis of the energy and the travel time of these reflected waves gives enormous insight into the nature of the subsurface, allowing scientists to paint a picture of the different layers of rock in a basin and the contacts between these layers. The amount of time it takes for a wave to travel to a contact plane and back to a detector gives an indication as to the depth of that layer. Strong differences in the amplitude and frequency of wave reflections can indicate abrupt changes in density between rock layers, which are often signs of gas-saturated reservoir rocks (gas is not dense, so sound waves travel at a much lower velocity through a sandstone rich in gas). Oil and gas can also be identified via seismic through the identification of flat spots, which are flat reflective layers within curved rock layers—the flat reflector is often not a rock contact at all, but a contact between oil, gas or water. The analysis process requires massive amounts of computer power to map the subsurface formations. The oil industry is the largest customer for supercomputers in the world.

By systematically setting a series of explosive charges along a line, geophysicists can map a cross section of the subsurface. Using arrays of geophones along a series of lines parallel to one another and a set distance apart allows an investigator to map a block of a basin, a process known as three-dimensional (3D) seismic. A relatively new technique is four-dimensional (4D) seismic, which entails taking a series of seismic readings in the same area over time, allowing one to track the evolution of a hydrocarbon field as it is produced. These advances in exploration techniques have dramatically improved geoscientists' knowledge of the subsurface. As a result, the predictive capability of the exploration process has increased, and better subsurface mapping allows more accurate prediction of reserves.

Seismic data have proven invaluable in the identification of potential prospects, which are areas that are shown to have all of the components necessary for an oil or gas field: a reservoir rock, a cap rock, and a trap that has a reasonable probability of containing commercial reserves of oil or gas. Independent contractors often gather seismic data and sell it to larger companies that have the capital and resources to fund further exploration. Improved computer techniques also allow for the reprocessing of vintage seismic data, which can be used to identify formations that were obscured during earlier analysis.

The only way to establish whether a prospective field contains oil or gas is by drilling. Operators begin with a wildcat, or exploratory, well, which will confirm (or refute) the presence of hydrocarbons estimated by the indirect exploration methods described previously. As the well is drilled, a series of measurements known as well logs are taken from the wellbore. Measurements are made via wireline, in which a recording device is lowered into a well, recording and extrapolating characteristics of the rock formation through which it passes; these logging devices can establish a formation's thickness, porosity, permeability, pressure, and electrical resistivity, all valuable factors in determining the potential productivity of a given formation. Wireline logs can also directly establish the presence of oil or gas. The drilling of successful wildcat wells is usually followed by the drilling of additional, appraisal wells in the same area.

Modern drilling is almost entirely done by rotary rigs (figs. 4–5 and 4–6, showing onshore and offshore structures, respectively). These drilling rigs support a long length of jointed steel pipe (the drill string), at the end of which is a drill bit. The drilling rig rotates the length of pipe, which in turn rotates the bit and causes it to dig through the rock, creating a wellbore (the actual hole of the well). Drill bits can be in a variety of configurations; the most common modern bit is a tricone bit, which comprises three separate toothed cones on the end of the bit that spin independently of one another, essentially chewing through the rock. Very hard rocks are often drilled using a diamond bit, a static bit covered in industrial diamonds. Bits are subjected to enormous pressures (generally between 3,000 and 10,000 psi, depending partially on the depth down hole and the weight of the drill string) and are usually changed every 40 to 60 hours of drilling.

Fig. 4–5. Onshore drilling rig (*Source:* img.tfd.com/thumb/7/72/Natural_gas_rig.jpg)

Fig. 4–6. Offshore drilling rig (*Source:* mits.doi.gov/quickfacts/index.cfm)

As wells are drilled, a heavy, viscous mixture of clay and water and/or oil, known as drilling mud, is injected down hole, through the drill string and the bit. This mud performs several functions. The injected mud is forced to the surface, carrying with it cuttings of rock. Analysis of material brought to the surface by drilling mud, known as mud logging, can give valuable insight into formation conditions. The mud also serves to lubricate the drill string. The weight of the mud regulates the borehole pressure and reduces the chances that pressurized hydrocarbons will blow out of the wellbore. As the well is drilled, steel tubing, known as casing, is periodically inserted into the wellbore and is cemented to the side, preventing the formation from collapsing on the drill string.

Actual drilling is undertaken by a drilling contractor, who owns and operates the drilling rig. The cost of drilling is largely determined by the location: Onshore drilling using a simple rotary rig is substantially less expensive than offshore drilling, the main difference being the type of rig platform used. For offshore fields, a number of different platform configurations are available, depending largely on the water depth.

In shallow water, rigs can be placed on drilling barges. Barges are especially useful in river delta regions, such as those in Nigeria or the Mississippi Delta. For somewhat deeper water, jack-up rigs provide a stable platform that can be moved if needed. Jack-ups consist of two distinct platforms: a hollow lower mat and an upper platform, on which sits the drilling equipment, connected by three vertical legs. The rig is towed to the drilling site, the mat is flooded and sinks to the bottom, and the upper platform is then jacked up the legs (in a manner similar that used by a common rack-and-pinion car jack) until it is well above the waterline.

For deeper water, semi-submersible platforms are towed to the drilling site and anchored into place. These platforms have flotation pontoons below the waterline, which keep them afloat while maintaining stability in rough seas. Semi-submersibles are relatively easy to move once drilling is complete. Drill ships are used for very deep seafloor drilling. These ships have a hole cut in the center of their hull (the moon pool) through which they can drill the seabed. This type of drilling relies heavily on Global Positioning System (GPS) technology: The ship's position relative to the wellbore is constantly monitored, and its position is maintained by a system of thrusters.

As with advances in seismic techniques, innovations in drilling technology have led to improvements in exploration technology. Wells can now be drilled deeper into formations going over 30,000 feet below the surface. Offshore rigs can operate in increasingly deeper water, often at depths exceeding 25,000 feet. Slimmer wellbores and improvements in muds, drill bits, and drill strings allow for faster and more accurate drilling. Even then, a deepwater exploration well can take months to drill and evaluate, often at costs exceeding $100 million. Horizontal drilling, a procedure in which the drill string is deflected from the vertical, allows drillers to penetrate much more of a reservoir layer than was traditionally possible. This also allows greater overall gas production from a given well.

Natural gas production

Once exploration drilling and appraisal drilling have been completed and it has been established that a prospect will produce commercial hydrocarbons, development drilling can begin. All wells, normally including the exploration and appraisal wells, are completed. Well completion entails setting casing strings, composed of connected lengths of casing pipe. These pipes, usually 25–35 feet long and up to 30 inches in diameter, are joined together and run down a well, providing a steel liner that prevents the adjacent rock from collapsing on the wellbore and allowing the drill string to reach ever greater depths. Casing diameters generally decrease with depth, with successive casing strings set within one another going deeper and deeper, so that a casing string looks somewhat like a telescope, with the narrowest portion in the producing formation (fig. 4–7). The space between the casing string and the wall of the drilled borehole or the previous casing string (the annulus) is filled with cement, the makeup of which depends on the conditions of the wellbore.

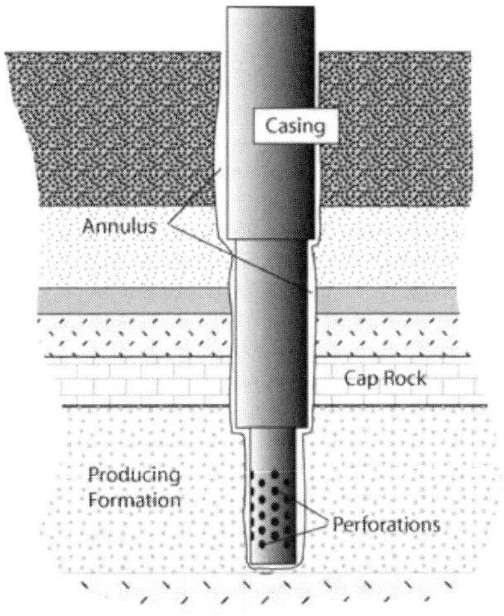

Fig. 4–7. Well casing, showing diminishing diameter of casing with depth (exaggerated) (*Source:* Poten & Partners)

Once the cement surrounding the casing is set, hydrocarbons can flow into the well in one of two ways. The simpler is to set the casing only to the top of the producing formation, then continue drilling, so that the borehole goes past the bottom of the casing, directly into the producing formation, allowing oil or gas to flow directly from the rock into the well. However, this allows very little control over the production process and runs the risk of subsequent collapse, so it is reserved for the simplest and most stable formations. In most wells, the casing is set through the producing formations, and the casing string is perforated through the same depths as the producing formations. These perforations are created by puncturing the casing string at the desired depths, often by shooting holes through the casing.

Unlike oil, which often requires the application of various recovery techniques to get it to the surface, gas is driven by its own pressure and therefore flows into the well and out of the ground of its own accord. Formations with especially low permeability (and, therefore, low gas flow) or fields that are reaching the end of viable pressure drive in their natural state can be stimulated to enhance their production in a number of ways. The introduction of large volumes of water or nitrogen-based foam at very high pressure into a well can cause the formation to fracture, opening up pathways in the rock, in a process known as fracing. The injected fluids are often impregnated with sand or other small substances that are carried into the newly created fractures and prevent their closing. With limestone (and some sandstone) reservoir rocks, the injection of acid through the well casing can also open up gas paths (limestone is especially vulnerable to acid). Gas reservoirs that need these initial forms of treatment, often tight sands or shales, are rarely candidates for supplying LNG projects because the costs of gas development and production are so high as to render the upstream uneconomical compared to other, more productive formations.

Once the wellbore has been completed, a string of hollow pipe, called production tubing, is run into the wellbore, and the oil or gas flows to the surface through this tubing. In wells with multiple formations, there may be more than one string of production tubing.

The surface completion of a gas well is usually simply a wellhead fitting with a series of valves, known as a Christmas tree (fig. 4–8).

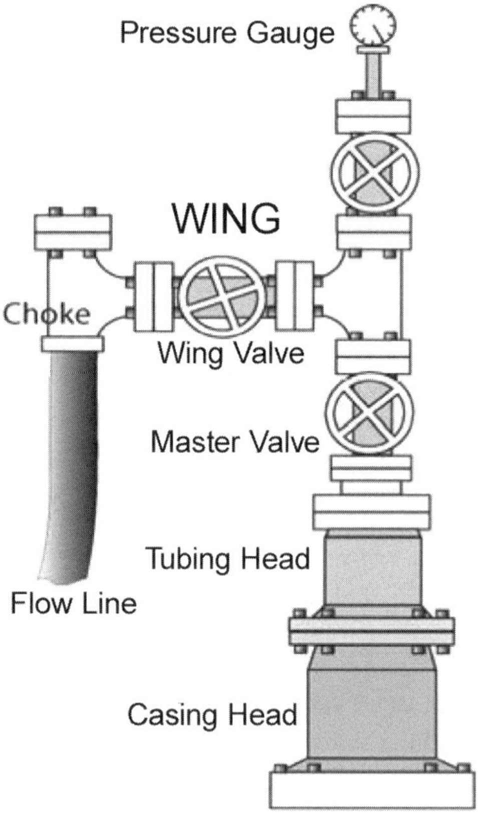

Fig. 4–8. Christmas tree (*Source:* Poten & Partners)

The Christmas tree is attached to the head of the casing string and the production tubing, with valves permitting the flow to be controlled within each string. Above the production valves is the wing, which connects the tree to a flow line or a gathering line (a pipeline connecting the tree to field treatment facilities) to move the gas into a pipeline for transportation. The wing valve and the choke regulate the flow of gas. Trees also incorporate pressure gauges to monitor the flow rate and pressure. Control of reservoir pressure is crucial in gas field development, not only to regulate the flow and maintain the pressure necessary to drive production but also to prevent heavier hydrocarbons from liquefying and dropping out of the gas stream while still in the reservoir, making recovery of these liquids much more difficult.

Large gas fields usually comprise a number of wellheads and associated Christmas trees. These are integrated by a field gathering system, essentially a series of flow lines that feed gas from each well into a central processing unit, where some of the initial liquids and other contaminants can be removed.

Onshore fields are easier to develop, as the wells can be spaced throughout the field, minimizing the amount of drilling that must be done to tap a given reservoir. Offshore is a different proposition. With an offshore field, the production phase must be managed from a specially built platform, which carries all the equipment that would be found in the onshore environment (fig. 4–9). These platforms are either fixed to the seabed or floating and anchored to the seabed. The development of an extensive gas field may require the installation of multiple platforms. As operators move into ever deeper water to access new gas fields, subsea completions allow development with more limited platform requirements. These well completions are essentially Christmas trees on the seafloor. Flow lines from each feed into a central manifold, which then feeds the gas into a pipeline leading either to a central platform or to shore. A number of new gas developments (including the giant Ormen Lange field in Norway and the Chevron-led Greater Gorgon LNG project in Australia) use or plan to use subsea completion configurations.

Fig. 4–9. Offshore gas production platform (*Source:* CSIRO)

In addition to the aforementioned trends in exploration drilling, development drilling has also seen other advances, especially in the area of horizontal drilling. Horizontal drilling begins in the same way as conventional drilling, but shortly after the drill bit penetrates the rock, the driller can begin steering the bit to create a wellbore that slopes away from the drilling rig, intersecting the producing formation at a near horizontal angle, then drilling for several thousand feet along the formation. By use of this technique, two benefits are realized: first, much more of the field can be covered from a single drilling point, keeping costs lower, especially in the offshore environment; second, because the bit is steered within the producing formation rock strata for extended distances, the wellbore will intersect a much greater proportion of the formation and should thus result in enhanced productivity.

The combination of improved seismology and enhanced drilling techniques has brought down the exploration and field development costs over the past decade, by as much as one-third, with a resulting improvement in field economics. Seismic technology alone has improved the success rates of exploration drilling from around 1 well in 10 in the 1970s to around 1 well in 3 today.

Natural gas field processing

Natural gas straight out of the well can contain various impurities that may need to be removed prior to injecting the gas into a pipeline. Quality specifications are dependent on the feedgas supply contract. For LNG production, further processing often takes place prior to liquefaction.

Hydrocarbons heavier than methane, whether liquid or gas, can be removed from the feedgas stream near the production field, depending on the configuration of the pipeline, through a process known as stripping. Condensates are the easiest to remove; they could cause the most problems if left in the pipeline, where they might drop out of the gas stream and block pipeline flows. NGLs can also be removed in the production area. Chilling the feedgas stream in a propane-cooled vessel can cause NGLs to drop out. Percolating the feedgas through a series of trays containing heavier, liquid hydrocarbons can also remove NGLs.

Gas needs to be dehydrated prior to being introduced into a pipeline, since water can form hydrates, which are methane molecules bonded in ice. These solid hydrates can form at temperatures up to 20°C, depending on pressure, and can block pipelines. Water is removed from the feedgas by passing the stream through a glycol bath. Glycol, a liquid desiccant, draws the water out of the feedgas.

Most pipeline contracts require the removal of carbon dioxide (referred to as acid gas) and hydrogen sulfide before transport, since both have a corrosive effect on pipeline steel. H_2S is also toxic as a gas, and combustion of the compound creates sulfur dioxide. Gas with high CO_2 and/or H_2S content is referred to as sour gas, as opposed to sweet gas. Both gases are removed by a sweetening process, which entails passing the feedgas through liquid amines (mono-, di-, and triethanolamines). Shell's patented Sulfinol process, which adds a physical solvent to the amines, is commonly used to extract acid gases. Increasingly, CO_2 is being considered for reinjection into reservoirs (i.e., sequestered), to prevent its introduction into the atmosphere.

Natural gas pipelines

Once gas has been processed to pipeline quality, it is sent via transmission pipeline to the LNG plant. Onshore gas transmission pipelines are made of sections of steel pipe, welded together and buried in trenches (fig. 4–10). Offshore pipelines can be positioned by large pipe-laying ships or barges, which carry lengths of continuous pipeline (up to about 26 inches in diameter) on enormous spools that pay out as the ship moves forward; alternatively, the pipe is welded and dropped to the seabed as it pays out over the stern of the ship or barge (fig. 4–11). Offshore lines are often laid directly on the seabed; where the seafloor is soft enough or close to shore, these lines may be trenched and buried. Offshore lines may be coated with concrete for added protection and to offset any buoyancy in the line.

Fig. 4–10. Onshore gas pipeline construction (Source: ZGG GmbH)

Fig. 4–11. Offshore gas pipeline construction (*Source:* www.offshore-technology.com/.../eca/eca3.html)

The pressure inherent in gas wells is usually sufficient to push gas through flow lines to the field's central processing facility, although gathering-system compression may be installed in cases of lower-pressure wells or later in the life of a field as natural pressures decline.

Downstream of the processing facilities, however, the larger pipeline diameters used for gas transmission require higher pressures. Diameters for the larger pipelines transporting gas long distances range up to 56 inches. For maintenance of pressure in these pipelines, compressor stations may be built along the route, giving the gas stream periodic boosts. The number and the power of these compressors are a function of the pipeline's total length and diameter and the volume being transported. For transmission lines linking gas fields to LNG plants, the objective is to keep the line as short as practicable and use as little compression as possible. Larger-diameter pipelines need less compression, but the initial installation is more expensive. For example, a 56-inch transmission line was laid across Trinidad to link gas fields off the east coast with the liquefaction plant on the west coast of the island.

Where it would be impractical or expensive to strip out all the liquid hydrocarbons in the gas stream, the field developer may utilize a multiphase pipeline, where the gas stream is specially handled to ensure that the liquids (oil, NGL, and/or water) move with the gas until the line reaches a treatment area. There are a number of different flow regimes that describe how the liquids and gas move through the pipeline—as a mist, as separate stratified layers, as gas and "slugs" of liquids, or as a liquid impregnated with gas bubbles. This type of line is most commonly used to move gas from offshore fields, where the cost of removing and exporting the liquids near the wells may be prohibitive.

The environment in which a pipeline will operate is a major determinant of its design. Pipelines designed for Arctic environments need to be able to operate at temperatures well below freezing, and in many cases are not buried at all, since burial in permafrost or in soil that is continuously freezing and thawing can have adverse effects on the pipe (the 800-mile Trans-Alaska Pipeline is the best known example). Onshore pipelines that cross rivers may require complex bridges or trestles. In rain forest environments, special attention must be paid to construction and restoration techniques to avoid permanent damage to the sensitive ecosystem. The stress of laying pipeline offshore is much greater than that of burying pipeline onshore, and the steel strength required should be chosen accordingly. Undersea pipelines are also much more susceptible to corrosion. Pipelines routes that cross over coral reefs near shore can require the use of directional drilling, to avoid laying pipe directly over sensitive coral. Globally, pipeline construction is attracting much more attention than ever, given the potential for serious environmental damage; Peru, Sakhalin, and Florida are among the regions where environmental concerns have complicated pipeline construction.

Once the gas has been produced, treated, and transported, it is ready to enter the liquefaction plant.

NOTES

[1] Hyne, Norman J. 1991. *Dictionary of Petroleum Exploration, Drilling & Production*. Tulsa: PennWell.

[2] Ibid.

[3] NGC+ Liquid Hydrocarbon Drop Out Task Group. Dec. 17, 2004. White paper on liquid hydrocarbon drop out in natural gas infrastructure.

[4] Ibid.

[5] Hyne, *Dictionary of Petroleum Exploration, Drilling & Production*.

[6] Jenyon, Malcolm K. 1990. *Oil and Gas Traps: Aspects of Their Seismostratigraphy, Morphology and Development*. New York: John Wiley & Sons.

[7] The graphics of figures 4–1 to 4–4 were created by John Malone with Adobe Illustrator during his time at Poten & Partners.

THE LIQUEFACTION PLANT 5

INTRODUCTION

The liquefaction process transforms natural gas into LNG by cooling it to –163°C, after which it is stored until it can be shipped on board LNG tankers (fig. 5–1). There are variations in liquefaction plant designs, but fundamentally the liquefaction processes are very similar and, setting aside the scale, quite straightforward. Liquefaction is nothing more than a giant refrigeration process, involving no application of chemical processes to the natural gas other than pretreatment for impurities.

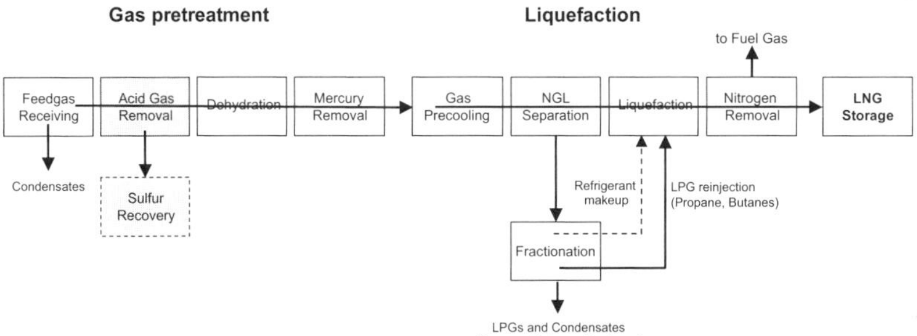

Fig. 5–1. Natural gas liquefaction flow diagram (*Source:* Poten & Partners)

SITING CONSIDERATIONS

The LNG plant is a large and complex industrial undertaking. It typically includes gas processing and purification, liquefaction, product storage and marine loading systems, utilities, control rooms, material and equipment warehousing, maintenance shops, and infrastructure facilities, often including housing for the operating staff.

Because the feedgas pipeline to the plant can be costly, sponsors generally seek to minimize the distance between the gas fields and the liquefaction plant. For example, a two-train 6.6 MMt/y (9.2 Bcm/y) LNG project requires more than 1 Bcf/d (10.3 Bcm/y) of feedgas. A 40-inch pipeline to transport this quantity of gas daily could cost around $2–$5 million per mile, depending on a variety of factors including whether the gas fields are onshore or offshore, the topography and complexity of the terrain (tropical jungle being more challenging than desert) between the fields and the plant, environmental considerations, the remoteness of the facilities, and the availability of pipe-laying equipment.[1] By contrast, the cost to construct liquid-loading lines and harbor infrastructure is so high that there are clear advantages to locating close to deepwater. These are examples of the trade-offs that play a major role in site selection.

Other issues relate to the environmental and physical aspects of the site. Factors such as water depths, tides, currents, and wave activity have a direct impact on the marine facilities. For plants located in the Northern Hemisphere, the potential for ice buildup in the harbor is a factor to be considered. Onshore soil and seismic conditions also influence the design of storage and other structures.

The need to build roads, airstrips, construction docks for material and equipment delivery, utilities, and housing for employees can raise the overall cost of liquefaction projects substantially. In remote or challenging areas, the cost of labor also increases as employees receive higher compensation for tougher work conditions; the costs associated with transportation and employee care are also much higher. In this respect, the various Qatar LNG projects now hold an advantage, since they are ideally located close to the gas field and have access to infrastructure developed for earlier projects. Indonesian projects at Arun and Tangguh, by contrast, are far more remote and consequently incur much higher costs. Australia's NWS project encountered high costs as a result of its remote location, extreme heat, and the cost of dealing with Australian labor unions. Russia's Sakhalin Island, with its below-freezing temperatures, tundralike conditions, and ice-prone waters, represents the most remote and tough project environment to date, as well as one of the costliest. The two-train Sakhalin II LNG facility in the

Russian Far East entails the construction of offshore oil and gas production facilities, costs associated with construction in extreme cold weather, a pair of 500-mile oil and gas pipelines to bring the production to a nearly ice-free port, and substantial support infrastructure. Theoretically, these disadvantages are balanced by Sakhalin's proximity to its target markets of Japan, Korea, and Mexico.

Political risk considerations also have to be factored in before choosing a potential location. Some locations are more vulnerable to disruptions, including sabotage, kidnappings, and threats of terrorism.

LIQUEFACTION PROCESS: TECHNOLOGY OVERVIEW

Feedgas purification and pretreatment

The natural gas entering a liquefaction facility will often contain several contaminants that must first be reduced to acceptable levels to ensure satisfactory liquefaction plant performance or to meet LNG sales specifications or both. The level of each contaminant depends largely on the characteristics of the production field and the extent of upstream gas treatment. A description of the various pretreatment processes follows.

First, any hydrocarbon condensates still present in the incoming natural gas stream are separated, used as plant fuel, or resold. Acid gas removal comes next, reducing carbon dioxide levels to around 50 parts per million (ppm), to prevent freezing in the main cryogenic exchanger. Hydrogen sulfide levels are similarly reduced, to below 3 ppm, to meet normal sales gas specifications.[2] LNG facilities typically use either any of the many available amine-type systems or Sulfinol to meet these specifications. If the feedgas contains significant hydrogen sulfide, it may also be necessary to convert this compound to sulfur by running the separated acid gas effluent stream through a sulfur recovery unit.

Feedgas leaving the acid gas removal system is saturated with water vapor that must be removed to prevent freezing in the main liquefaction exchanger. This dehydration is achieved in two steps. First, the gas is cooled using air or water and a precooling refrigerant to condense much of the water out of the gas stream. Second, the gas is passed through a molecular sieve to reduce residual water vapor to very low levels (below 0.1 ppm).

The feedgas may also contain mercury. This contaminant must be removed down to the smallest detectable amount, about 0.1 microgram per normal cubic meter (Nm^3), because even trace quantities of mercury can cause corrosion of aluminum heat exchanger equipment.[3] Mercury removal is typically achieved by passing the feedgas through a sulfur-impregnated carbon bed, where the mercury reacts with the sulfur to form mercuric sulfide.

Finally, any remaining heavier-hydrocarbon components, such as pentanes, hexanes, and aromatics (e.g., benzene), must be separated to prevent freezing in the main cryogenic exchanger. These heavy hydrocarbons are removed by condensing the liquids using a precooling refrigeration process ahead of the main liquefaction process. The separated liquids are typically fed into a fractionation system involving a succession of distillation columns, typically a de-ethanizer, de-propanizer, and de-butanizer in sequence, with each column stripping out one component from the liquid mix. Any recovered lighter hydrocarbons from this fractionation process, such as ethane, propane, or butane, are either used as refrigerant makeup, reinjected into the liquefaction feedgas (up to the gas specification limits), used for plant fuel, or sold as separate NGL products.

Liquefaction processes

Several proprietary processes are marketed today for large-scale baseload natural gas liquefaction plants. These processes fall into the following broad categories:

- Pure-refrigerant cascade process
- Propane-precooled mixed-refrigerant processes
- Propane-precooled mixed-refrigerant, with back-end nitrogen expander cycle
- Other mixed-refrigerant processes
- Nitrogen expander-based processes

Table 5–1 shows the processes used in liquefaction facilities. All these liquefaction process designs are proprietary. The choice of an initial design is critical since all future trains will certainly utilize the same design. Expansion licenses are generally negotiated at the front end of each EPC contract for development of a new plant.

Table 5–1. Liquefaction processes at LNG export plants worldwide, as of 2006 (*Source:* Poten & Partners)

Project	Start-up Date	Process
Algeria, Arzew/Bethioua	1964	Technip Cascade
Alaska, Kenai	1969	Phillips Optimized Cascade
Libya Marsa El Brega	1970	APCI MCR
Brunei LNG	1972	Mixed-Refrigerant Process
Algeria, Skikda	1973	Mixed-Refrigerant Process
Abu Dhabi, ADGAS	1977	APCI MCR
Indonesia, Arun	1977	APCI MCR
Indonesia, Bontang	1978	APCI MCR
Malaysia, MLNG Satu and Dua	1983 and 1994	APCI MCR
Australia, NWS	1989	APCI MCR
Qatar, Qatargas	1997	APCI MCR
Qatar, RasGas	1999	APCI MCR
Trinidad, ALNG	1999	Phillips Optimized Cascade
Nigeria LNG	1999	APCI MCR
Oman LNG	2000	APCI MCR
Malaysia, MLNG Tiga	2003	APCI MCR
Egypt, Damietta	2004 (proj.)	APCI MCR
Egypt, Idku	2005 (proj.)	Phillips Optimized Cascade
Norway, Snøhvit	2006	Mixed-Fluid Cascade

Pure-refrigerant Cascade process. The Cascade process is currently used or specified for five LNG projects worldwide: Kenai, in Alaska; the ALNG facility in Trinidad and Tobago; Egyptian LNG, in Idku; Australia's Darwin LNG; and Equatorial Guinea LNG. The last four plants use an improved and more efficient version of the basic Cascade process, developed by Phillips, called the Optimized Cascade process. Phillips and Bechtel have an alliance agreement for design and construction of liquefaction plants incorporating this process.

The process consists of three separate pure-component refrigerant cycles that provide cooling at progressively lower temperatures to liquefy natural gas. As shown in fig. 5–2, each refrigerant cycle consists of a compressor, a condenser, an expansion valve, and an evaporator.

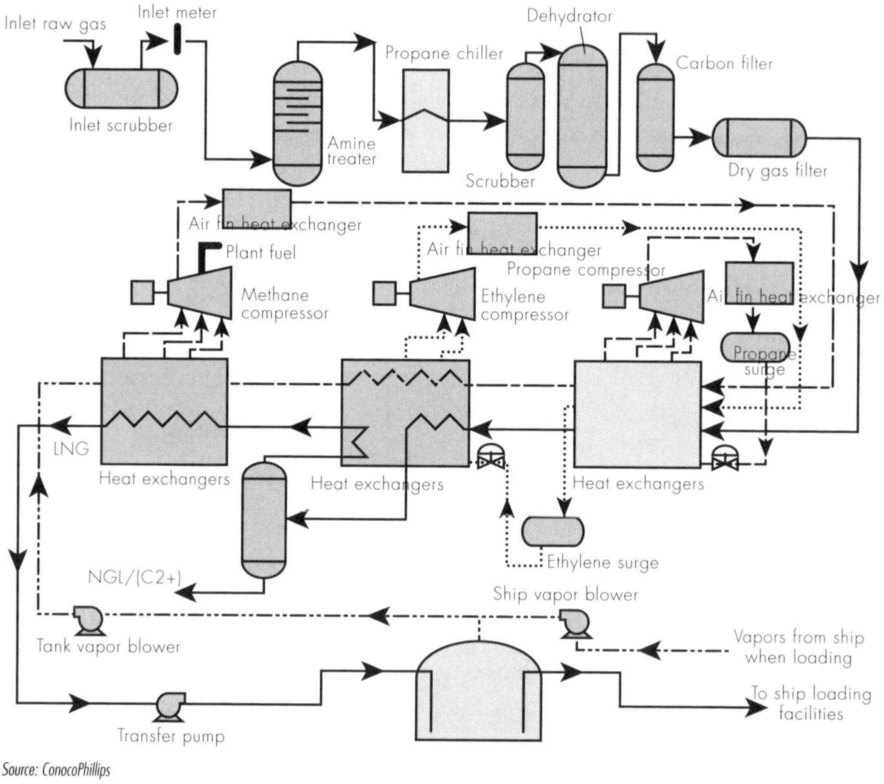

Fig. 5–2. Phillips Optimized Cascade process—ALNG Train 4 (*Source:* ConocoPhillips)

After feedgas pretreatment, high-pressure feedgas is cooled to a temperature of around –30°C through a propane refrigeration cycle. In this cycle, the propane refrigerant is condensed at high pressure, using either air or water cooling. The condensed liquid is then expanded by subjecting it to a series of lower pressures and temperatures through a throttling valve and is completely vaporized to cool feedgas and methane refrigerant flows, as well as to condense the ethylene refrigerant used in the subsequent refrigeration cycle. Vaporized propane is then compressed back up to its initial high pressure to complete the refrigeration cycle.

The cooled feedgas then goes through the remaining two cycles in much the same way. In the second cycle, the feedgas is further cooled, to around –100°C, through an ethylene refrigerant cycle that is also used to condense the methane refrigerant employed in the third refrigeration cycle. Finally, the expansion of high-pressure methane refrigerant in the third cycle cools the gas to the liquefaction temperature, around –163°C.

The major advantage of the Cascade process is its simplicity of operation and control owing to its use of pure-component refrigeration systems. The Optimized Cascade process can also result in lowered capital costs by doubling up the methane refrigerant compressor as a fuel gas compressor, using nonproprietary brazed aluminum plate-fin heat exchangers for liquefaction service and importing makeup refrigerants, rather than producing and blending these on site.

However, pure-component refrigeration processes have somewhat lower thermodynamic efficiencies than precooled mixed-refrigerant processes, increasing the compression power and fuel gas consumption needed for natural gas liquefaction. Process efficiencies can be improved by using additional refrigerant steps, but this increases the complexity of the equipment and piping needed, increasing plant investment costs. The unequal distribution of horsepower load among the three refrigeration services (propane, ethylene, and methane) also complicates compressor/driver selection and maintenance requirements. Finally, importing the refrigerant makeup—in particular, ethylene—increases the operating costs.

Propane-precooled mixed-refrigerant (C3-MR) cycle. This process—the work horse of today's LNG industry—is used in over 80% of the world's completed trains, including projects in Algeria, Abu Dhabi, Brunei, Indonesia, Malaysia, Qatar, Australia, Nigeria, and Egypt (Damietta). Each C3-MR project has unique features depending on the technology available at the time of design and construction and local environmental characteristics, but the fundamental concept is the same. New projects being constructed or developed also use variants of this process.

The C3-MR system uses a multi-component refrigerant—usually nitrogen, methane, ethane, propane, butane, and pentane—to condense and evaporate natural gas in one cycle over a wide range of temperatures. The mixed refrigerant used is Air Products & Chemicals, Inc.'s (APCI) proprietary Multi-Component Refrigerant (MCR).

Dry, treated gas is first precooled to around –30°C by using propane refrigerant. The precooling step condenses any remaining heavy hydrocarbons and some LPG in a scrub column. These liquids are separated into their components in a fractionation train and then are used as refrigerant makeup, are reinjected into the liquefaction feedgas (up to the gas specification limits), or are sold as separate NGL products. The precooled (–30°C) feedgas is then sent to the main cryogenic heat exchanger (MCHE), where it is condensed and then subcooled at elevated pressures. The subcooled liquid natural gas (i.e., LNG) leaving the MCHE is then flashed to near storage tank pressure, cooling the LNG to approximately –161°C and ejecting a nitrogen-rich stream that can be used for fuel gas.

The APCI MCHE consists of thousands of small-diameter spiral-wound tubes extending the entire length of the heat exchanger. The precooled natural gas and MCR flow upward through these tubes, in which they are cooled and condensed. As the MCR emerges at two levels, it is passed through pressure-reducing throttling valves and passes into the shell of the MCHE, where it flows downward over the outside of the tubes, vaporizing to provide refrigeration to the tube-side fluids. The low-pressure MCR vapor leaves the bottom of the MCHE at about –30°C and is then recompressed to about 650 psi in a multistage compressor, with water or air cooling provided between each compression stage. The MCR flow is then further precooled using the propane-precooling refrigerant before reentering the tube side of the MCHE (fig. 5–3).

The main advantages of the C3-MR process are its proven technology and high efficiency. C3-MR liquefaction systems have been widely used for nearly 30 years in a wide variety of process and environmental settings. Start-up and operation of these facilities have generally been free of major problems, and plants have generally exceeded design throughputs on a continuous basis.[4] The C3-MR process also achieves high efficiencies by adding the propane precooling stage for both feedgas and the mixed-refrigerant loop, allowing the MCR vaporization temperature curve to closely match the natural gas liquefaction curve. This, of course, comes at an extra equipment cost, but the operational gains have proven this additional investment to be justified.

A disadvantage of the MCR process is limited flexibility to shift refrigeration load between the propane and mixed-refrigerant cooling circuits, but to some degree, this problem has been alleviated by more-recent designs having both propane and MCR compression stages on a single turbine driver, to better balance the available turbine power.

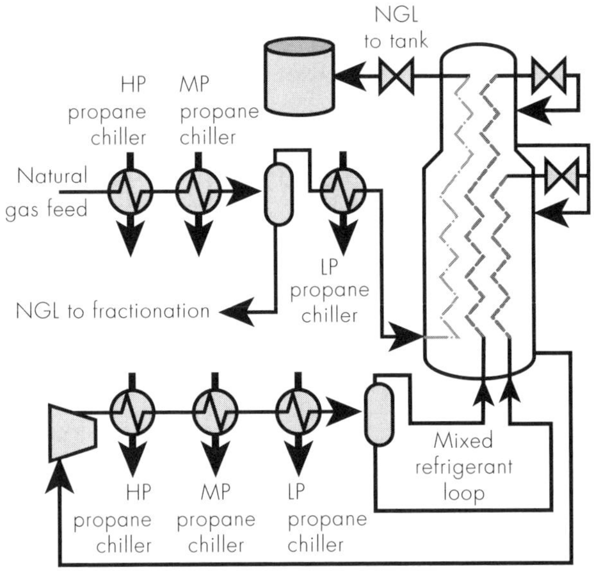

Fig. 5–3. Propane-precooled mixed-refrigerant (C3-MR) process. LP = low pressure; MP = medium pressure; HP = high pressure. (*Source:* Air Products)

The APCI AP-X process. The drive toward increased liquefaction economies of scale led APCI to develop a variant of their C3-MR process that increases the liquefaction train capacity from 5 to 8 MMt/y (7 to 11.2 Bcm/y) while still utilizing established MCHE designs and compressor configurations. This new AP-X process, introduced in 2001, adds a third cycle of nitrogen expander (N_2) refrigeration to the back end of the C3-MR process's propane (C3) mixed-refrigerant (MCR) cycles (fig. 5–4). This N_2 cycle takes the LNG subcooling duty off the MCR cycle, increasing the natural gas capacity and reducing the refrigeration loads on the first two cycles. While N_2 cycles are new to baseload LNG, they have been widely applied in air separation applications and peakshaving LNG facilities. Six 7.8 MMt/y AP-X trains are currently under construction in Qatar—for the Qatargas II (two trains), RasGas III (two trains), Qatargas III (one train), and Qatargas IV (one train) projects.

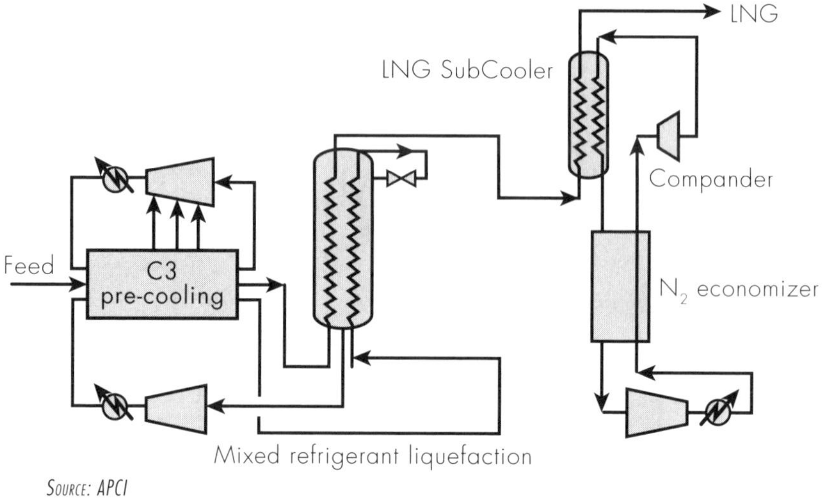

Fig. 5–4. APCI AP-X process (*Source:* APCI)

Other mixed-refrigerant processes. The efficiency and reliability of the C3-MR process has led to the development of several other mixed-refrigerant processes. These variations aim to eke out additional process efficiencies by using mixed refrigerants, rather than propane, for the precooling stage and also introduce a wider variety of heat exchanger equipment, compressor, and driver configurations, to reduce equipment costs, increase vendor competition, and in some cases, reduce carbon dioxide emissions.

Shell dual mixed-refrigerant (DMR) *process.* Shell has introduced both propane-precooled and mixed-refrigerant–precooled variations on the APCI C3-MR process that are not dependent on APCI's proprietary spiral-wound MCHE technology. The propane-precooled design is being used for trains 4 and 5 at Australia's NWS LNG project, while the DMR process has been specified for Russia's Sakhalin II project and Australia's Gorgon venture.

Axens Liquefin DMR *process.* The Axens process liquefies natural gas in plate-fin heat exchangers (PFHEs) using a two-stage DMR process (fig. 5–5). Using PFHEs rather than spiral-wound exchangers makes the process more expandable, increases the number of available exchanger suppliers, and eliminates the need to separate refrigerant phases in the exchanger, thereby reducing equipment costs. The DMR design enables refrigeration loads to be readily balanced across the two similar refrigerant compressors, reducing overall power requirements, increasing the applicable range for the more robust centrifugal compressor designs and reducing spares costs. No baseload Liquefin facilities have been built to date, although front-end engineering designs (FEEDs) incorporating this process have been drafted for several potential projects.

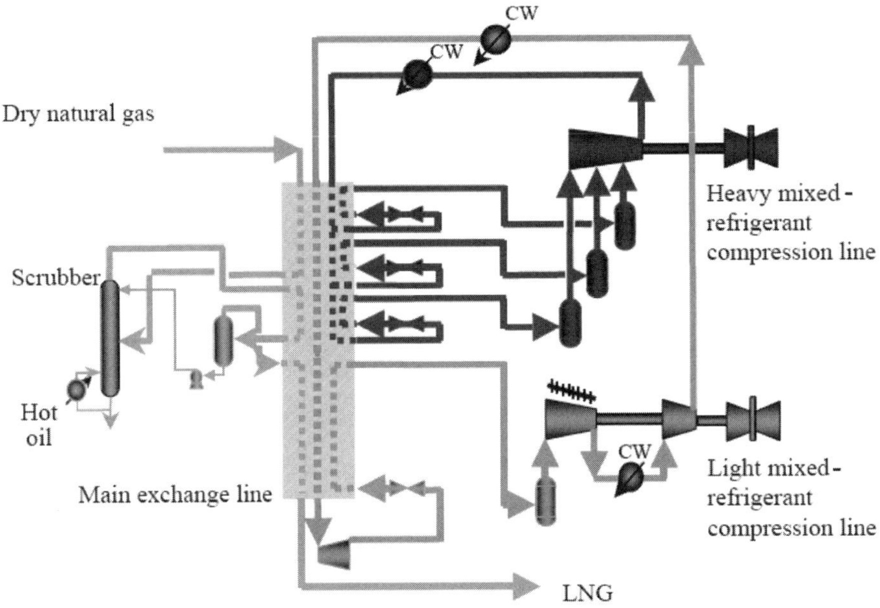

Fig. 5–5. Axens Liquefin dual mixed-refrigerant (DMR) process (*Source:* Axens, BP)

Statoil-Linde mixed-fluid cascade (MFC) *process*. The Statoil-Linde process liquefies LNG by using three mixed-refrigerant cycles (fig. 5–6). The first, precooling cycle uses a mixture of ethane and propane refrigerants in a plate-fin heat exchanger, while the intermediate stage, liquefaction, and the final, subcooling stage take place in Linde's spiral-wound aluminum heat exchangers. Refrigeration power can come from three turbines or from large electric motors. An MFC liquefaction train is currently under construction at Norway's 4.3 MMt/y (6 Bcm/y) Snøhvit project.

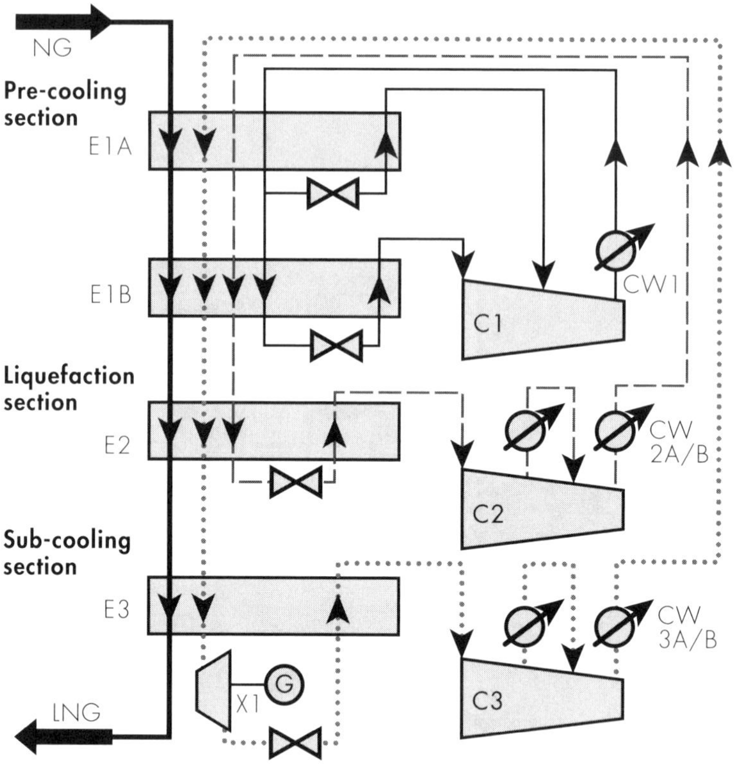

Fig. 5–6. Statoil-Linde mixed-fluid cascade (MFC) process (*Source:* Linde)

Nitrogen expander–based processes. The APCI AP-X process is not the only design incorporating a nitrogen expander–based refrigeration process. Several nitrogen expander–based designs are available from process vendors such as BHP and ABB Lummus that perform the entire liquefaction process. Although these processes are not as scalable as their Cascade and mixed-refrigerant alternatives, they are appropriate for small baseload, offshore, and peakshaving applications owing to their simple, robust, and compact designs.

High-pressure nitrogen vapor from a nitrogen compressor is cooled against water and is then further cooled and expanded in a series of expanders and heat exchangers to provide refrigerant flow at the required temperatures and pressures. After cooling and liquefying the natural gas flow, the low-pressure nitrogen is partially compressed using energy from the expanders, reducing the power required in order to return the circulating gas to high pressure in the main nitrogen compressor.

Driver technology

The choice of drivers for the refrigeration compressors has for several years been a source of ongoing debate, which seems likely to continue. The very earliest plants used steam turbines to drive the compressors, with the notable exception of the Kenai project, which used gas turbines (more efficient at Alaska's colder ambient temperatures). Steam turbines offered the advantage of reliability, although the need for vast amounts of treated cooling water was a major drawback. By the late 1980s, as industrial gas turbines became more broadly accepted in a variety of applications, especially in power generation, these became the drivers of choice. However, there are several differing approaches: ALNG uses multiple, smaller gas turbines in a very flexible arrangement, while the Nigerian and Qatari projects use much larger turbines coupled to multiple compressors. A further variation is the use of electric drive compressors with the electric power provided from gas turbines operating as power generators. Air cooling has generally replaced water cooling. While air cooling has a much larger footprint, the technology appears more reliable and avoids the need for complex, maintenance-intensive water-cooling systems.

Utilities

As liquefaction plants are often located in remote regions, the provision of utilities may be a critical feature of the plant design. The plants usually have their own power generation facilities, with 100% redundancy to minimize operational interruptions. Water supply may also be a factor, especially if water-cooled equipment is being used in the process.

LNG STORAGE TANKS

Although not an integral part of the liquefaction process, LNG storage plays a critical role in project cost and scheduling. LNG tanks are large and expensive, with their costs potentially representing up to 10% of the total installed plant value. Tank construction is often on the project's critical path, but technological advances and decades of experience with established tank designs have helped shorten LNG storage tank construction schedules.

The required storage capacity for a particular facility is largely governed by planned LNG tanker size, while additional capacity is also required so as to allow LNG tanker scheduling flexibility and handle planned and unplanned plant outages. In addition, LNG tanks must provide for minor capacity allowances to maintain minimum liquid suction head requirements for the in-tank LNG pumps. The result typically is the installation of storage equivalent to twice the cargo capacity of the largest LNG tanker for the initial trains of the liquefaction plant; for instance, a project that uses 138,000 m^3 LNG tankers would typically include approximately 275,000 cubic meters of storage. Individual storage tank sizes have increased over the years, from 36,000 cubic meters at Alaska's Kenai facility to as large as 188,000 cubic meters for the recently commissioned Darwin LNG project. As expansion trains are added, LNG storage capacity tends to be added more slowly, at about half the rate used for the initial trains.

There are several types of LNG storage tanks. The choice of storage tank design is largely determined by safety and operational considerations, based on plant location, layout constraints, engineering design standards, and code requirements. The two broadest classifications are aboveground and belowground storage. In this section, we will focus entirely on the design of aboveground tanks, because they are more commonly used in liquefaction plants. Belowground storage tanks have been used only at some import terminals—in particular, in populous settings such as Tokyo Bay—for aesthetic reasons.

All LNG storage tanks have a double-walled design. Tank designs are typically classified as single containment, double containment, or full containment.

Single-containment tanks

Single containment refers to a freestanding, open-top inner tank made of 9% nickel steel, with a carbon steel outer tank. A layer of several feet of perlite insulation is sandwiched between the two tanks. The base of the inner tank rests on rigid foam blocks for insulation, then on the foundation. The choice of foundation is dictated by site soil conditions and can have a ringwall, pile, or stone column design. The tank base usually includes a heater system to maintain the ground at a constant temperature and prevent tank disturbance due to frost heaves. The tank has a steel roof designed to contain gas vapor and support a suspended ceiling that insulates the top surface of the inner tank. The outer steel tank wall will not contain any LNG in the event of a breach in the inner tank, so this type of tank must have external secondary containment, usually a bermed area with sufficient capacity to contain the entire contents of the tank plus a margin of safety. This tank design is the least expensive. Single-containment tanks have operated worldwide without major incident for over 30 years in locations that have sufficient plot area for the secondary containment berms and to permit significant separation between the tank and adjacent process facilities and other tanks.

Double-containment tanks

Double-containment tanks are similar to single-containment systems, except that the outer tank is capable of containing liquid spills in the event of a breach in the inner tank wall. This tank design has a freestanding 9% nickel inner tank and an outer tank made of either prestressed reinforced concrete or poured-in-place reinforced concrete strengthened by an earthen or rock embankment. Double-containment tanks require less plot area than single-containment designs because of their concrete outer wall. However, the roof is still constructed of steel and will not contain vapor produced by failure of an inner tank. The approximate cost for a double-containment tank is 40% higher than for a single-containment design. Recent steel cost increases have raised prices for this tank design nearer to the cost of the all-concrete full-containment design. This is a subject of discussion in the next section.

Full-containment tanks

Full-containment tank designs add a concrete roof to the double-containment tank's concrete outer walls (fig. 5–7). This roof can withstand higher pressures and lower temperatures than the steel tank design, providing containment for any vapor produced by a breach in the inner tank. Full-containment tanks provide the greatest design integrity and allow the closest spacing between tanks and process equipment when land area is constrained. However, this is the most expensive aboveground tank design, with a cost about 50% higher than for a single-containment design.

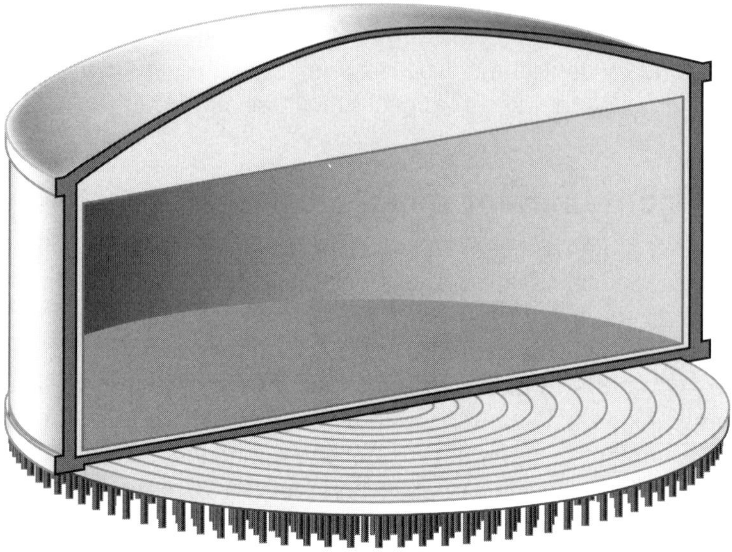

Fig. 5–7. Full-containment LNG storage tank (*Source:* Korea Gas)

Membrane tank

Membrane tanks are similar to the designs found in membrane containment LNG tankers. Primary LNG containment is provided by a flexible stainless steel membrane, supported by a layer of insulation mounted on an outer prestressed concrete wall. This outer concrete wall and roof can contain both the liquid and vapor from a leak in the primary membrane. Membrane tanks have similar or slightly higher costs than freestanding full-containment designs. Very few membrane tanks are in service, as they are perceived to be less durable than other tank designs.

LNG LOADING JETTY

LNG jetty facilities are designed to berth and load the LNG tankers. An LNG tanker mooring is typically accomplished with the assistance of three or four tugboats. Once the LNG tanker is moored and the loading arms on the jetty are connected, loading pumps in the facility's storage tanks transfer LNG into the LNG tanker's cargo tanks through a cryogenic piping system supported by the loading jetty. Product loading typically takes between 12 and 13 hours for a 138,000 m^3 LNG tanker. However, an additional 12 hours is usually required for berthing, loading arm connection/disconnection, cargo measurements, and where required, LNG tanker cooldown.

LNG tankers that are entering service or have been waiting for extended periods to load cargoes will arrive with LNG cargo tanks at temperatures higher than the LNG to be loaded. To load the LNG tanker, the cargo tanks must first be cooled down, a process that must be performed at very low loading rates, taking up to 12 hours and generating large quantities of boil-off gas. Boil-off gas or vapor generated during loading is returned to the shore facilities and reliquefied.

The practical limit for jetty utilization at a loading port is around 60%, accounting for scheduling variances, weather, and regulatory restrictions. This results in a limit of about 210–220 loadings a year per jetty, the equivalent of about 13 MMt/y (18 Bcm/y) of throughput if larger LNG tankers are used.

PROJECT DEVELOPMENT AND EXECUTION

LNG liquefaction projects require substantial capital investment, a high degree of technical expertise, and significant project management skills. Complicating the endeavor is the need for coordination between the development of the LNG liquefaction facility and the production facilities, the shipping, and where necessary, the regasification terminal. This makes the construction of a baseload liquefaction facility the domain of major engineering/construction firms that can perform such complex projects in remote locations worldwide. A phased approach is typically used in developing the facility (fig. 5–8).

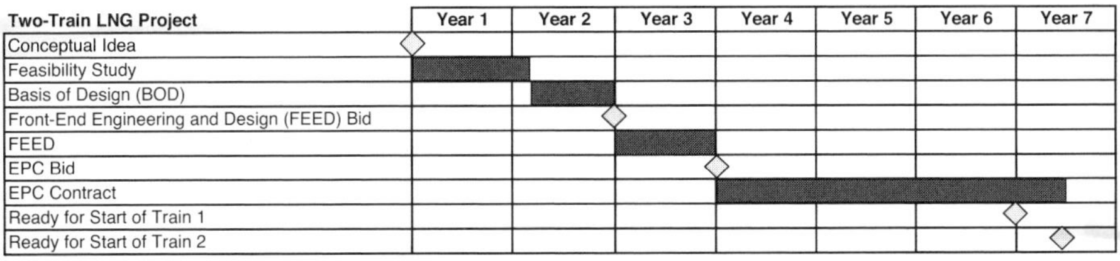

Fig. 5–8. LNG export facility development phases (*Source:* Poten & Partners)

The process of developing a project starts after the identification and confirmation of sufficient gas reserves, through a broad-based feasibility study that determines the conceptual design and identifies potential plant locations. This study typically includes a preliminary economic analysis to guide sponsors in deciding whether to pursue development. It also addresses adequacy of gas reserves, environmental issues, and potential obstacles.

The steps involved in project development are as follows:

- Basis of design (BOD) follows the feasibility study. At this stage, the conceptual design is finalized, and the fundamental engineering parameters are identified. A more rigorous analysis is performed on expected feedgas quality, LNG supply parameters, storage, marine facilities, utilities, modules spacing, and safety. Contractors may be asked to use their own engineering design standards or adopt the standards of the sponsors. The BOD is a necessary step before issuing a formal front end engineering design (FEED) request to potential contractors.
- The FEED is intended to further develop design, including detailed specifications and layout, to get a more accurate cost estimate as a deliverable to the EPC bidding stage. The FEED identifies equipment and provides a detailed design of the facility. Depending on the contractual philosophy, critical items could be preordered at this stage to accelerate the schedule. The FEED contractor usually prepares engineering documents and bid packages to a sufficient level of detail to be used in the EPC bidding. The FEED deliverables can greatly influence the overall cost of the project, as the liquefaction process and storage capacity are determined during this phase. Historical data suggest that the largest cost-saving opportunities are captured during the FEED phase. FEEDs are funded by the project sponsors. There is evidence that funding multiple FEEDs may result in more competitive bidding and improved plant designs, but this approach will place additional demands on the sponsors' project management team.
- EPC bidding generally takes several months and culminates with the selection of the contractor through either bidding negotiation or a combination. The EPC contractor is responsible for bringing a project to completion and start-up of the operation according to the sponsors' design and specifications. The EPC award is followed by the process of detailed engineering and procurement. This colossal effort requires substantial experience and can take over two years, overlapping construction. Procurement of proprietary heat exchangers, turbine drivers, and process compressors is particularly important, as vendors for these specialty items can require lead times in excess of two years, creating scheduling and

cost problems. Shell, a company involved in over a half-dozen LNG projects, has pushed for standardization in an effort to substitute large proprietary equipment items with smaller standard ones, to promote competition and shorten the overall schedule (for further discussion, see "Standardization and use of offsite fabricated modules," under the section "Recent Trends").

- The EPC contractor will lead construction by supervising a number of subcontractors and suppliers and will manage a construction workforce that could be as large as 10,000 people.[5] Knowledge of local resources, regulations, and culture can help immensely in navigating a potentially treacherous construction period.
- Transfer of the project risk from the EPC contractor to the project sponsors occurs at the final-acceptance stage. Delays can have a detrimental effect on the overall LNG chain, since the plant construction is designed to be coordinated with upstream development, LNG tanker construction, regasification construction, and commencement of contractual obligations under the SPA. Delays in one part of the chain can potentially wreak havoc on the entire development plan by delaying shipment of LNG and the flow of revenues. The transfer from construction to operation status takes on greater significance in a project finance environment, where it signals transition from recourse to nonrecourse financing for the sponsor.
- The importance of a timely finish has induced project sponsors to incorporate liquidated damages (LDs) as well as early completion and performance bonus provisions into construction contracts. LDs are compensation that the contractor has to pay to the sponsors in case of an unexcused failure to meet critical milestones, primarily the in-service date, or the failure of the plant to meet its design output and operating performance. The LDs are usually designed to cover interest, loss of revenues, and overhead expenses incurred by the sponsors during the delay period or during periods of below-design performance. Construction budgets usually include contingency amounts (5%–15%), and the EPC contract generally has provisions for either a proportion of payments to be held back to cover such risks or other forms of security.[6] LDs do not cover delays due to events of force majeure, which stem from circumstances beyond the contractor's control. Force majeure is best mitigated through insurance. The design and placing of appropriate insurances covering all aspects of the project construction is another area requiring detailed and expert review and negotiation.

- Reflecting the importance of the finish-construction milestone, the EPC contract incorporates detailed completion and testing procedures. Typically, mechanical completion occurs on completion of construction. It is followed by operational completion, which integrates punch-list items and commissioning activities. Final acceptance follows a successful completion of sustained testing and signals final transfer of responsibility to the project sponsors. Warranties will start on the achievement of this milestone.
- After the plant is operating, maintenance and debottlenecking activities have a great impact on future production. After gaining operating experience, plant debottlenecking typically adds 5%–10% capacity by upgrading or modifying critical equipment items that limit production. Debottlenecking efforts are typically fairly easy to justify, as the costs are relatively small (on the order of $20–$50 million) compared to the revenues from the incremental production.[7] Earlier plants, with their more conservative designs, offered much greater opportunities for debottlenecking, but as designs have improved, many of these gains have been built into the initial plants and debottlenecking opportunities have lessened.
- Sponsors can also take advantage of economies of scale by leveraging existing infrastructure through expansions. The cost to expand liquefaction plants is based on the original project development plan. If surplus capacity is built into the initial design and construction of major components (storage tanks, marine facilities, gas supply pipelines, and utility systems), then these facilities may not need to be replicated for an expansion train, providing significant economies. Before expansions can be fully considered, additional proven gas reserves must be available to the project; however, it is not unusual for the expansion process to be started before the initial trains are operational, thereby avoiding the cost of demobilizing and remobilizing the EPC contractor and the sponsors' project management team.

RECENT TRENDS

Larger trains

Economies of scale as a result of bigger individual trains and larger venture production capacity have enhanced the competitiveness of LNG in international energy markets. A decade ago, the largest LNG production train was about 2.5 MMt/y (3.5 Bcm/y). By the mid-to-late 1990s, 3 MMt/y (4.2 Bcm/y) became the benchmark, rising to 4–5 MMt/y (5.6–7 Bcm/y) by the turn of the century. The latest LNG mega-trains in Qatar have nameplate capacities of 7.8 MMt/y (10.9 Bcm/y). This progression in liquefaction train size is illustrated in figure 5–9.

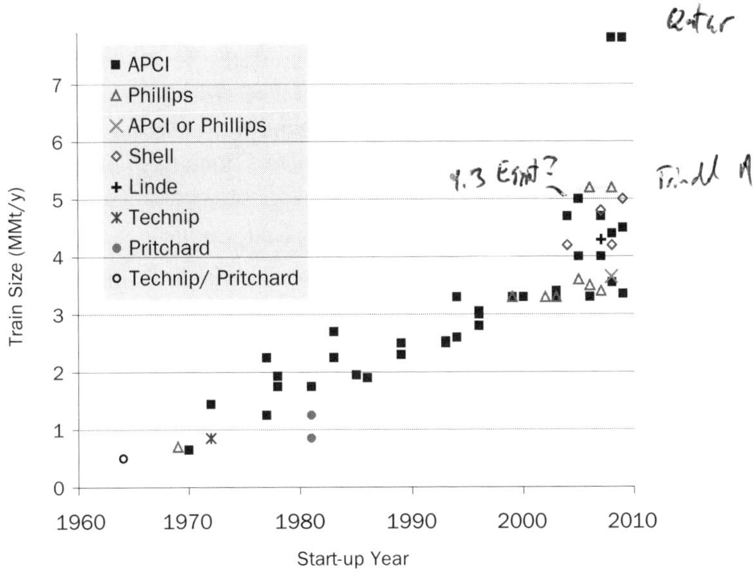

Fig. 5–9. LNG train size growth (*Source:* Poten & Partners)

One limitation to train size has been the feasibility of manufacturing larger heat exchangers and transporting them from the manufacturing site to the field. For the spiral-wound heat exchangers used by APCI, the transportation restrictions from the company's manufacturing location to the shipping port have constrained the feasible exchanger diameters to 18–20 feet. However, APCI overcame this constraint with the AP-X mega-train process—not by increasing the length and diameter of the exchanger, but by adding an additional refrigeration cycle in a separate process unit that reduced the refrigeration duty of the existing exchanger design. As a result, the AP-X process can produce 7.8 MMt/y (10.9 Bcm/y) of LNG by using spiral-wound exchangers similar to those found in their 5.0 MMt/y (7 Bcm/y) C3-MR train designs.

LNG plants have progressively employed ever-larger gas turbine drivers to power refrigerant compressors as train sizes have increased. Earlier gas turbine-driven LNG plants used smaller, GE Frame 5 (or equivalent) dual-shaft gas turbines as compressor drivers. LNG train capacities were then increased to 3.3 MMt/y (4.6 Bcm/y) or more for the C3-MR liquefaction process by stepping up to GE Frame 6 gas turbine drivers for the propane-precooling refrigeration cycle compressor and GE Frame 7 gas turbine drivers for the mixed-refrigerant compressor. This was followed by the use of GE Frame 7 gas turbine drivers for both the propane and mixed-refrigerant cycles, taking individual train capacity up to 4–5 MMt/y (5.6–7 Bcm/y). The upcoming Qatari mega-trains have taken this trend further, using GE Frame 9 gas turbine drivers for the propane, MCR, and nitrogen cycles. Large electric motors are being used as compression drivers on Norway's Snøhvit project, but their widespread use will require designers to overcome start-up, operating flexibility, and cost issues associated with these motors.

While mega-trains are demonstrably technically feasible, establishing their commercial viability is a far more complex issue. Although mega-train projects do provide economies of scale, they require a larger reserve base than typical projects and place more capital at risk. Finding sales outlets for mega-trains also constitutes a greater challenge than for traditional projects, as volumes are substantially greater. Only a few buyers may be willing to make large purchase commitments from single trains, as LNG buyers typically seek multiple smaller LNG contracts to diversify their supply sources and match the requirements of newly liberalizing and competitive LNG markets. Thus, the trend with the Qatari mega-trains has been to have the sponsors emerge as the buyers for the entire train production and assume the risk of placing the LNG in the market.

Reversal of cost reduction trends

The industry has grown rapidly in the past decade. At the end of 2005, there were 17 operating projects, 5 expansions, and 4 greenfield projects under construction, compared with only 11 plants operating in 1995. One major reason for the industry growth rate has been the substantial drop in liquefaction unit costs, with the resulting increase in cost competitiveness for LNG relative to other fuels and pipeline gas. According to the International Energy Agency (IEA), the average unit investment for a liquefaction plant in 2003 was under $200 tpa, compared with $350 tpa in the 1970s and 1980s (fig. 5–10).[8]

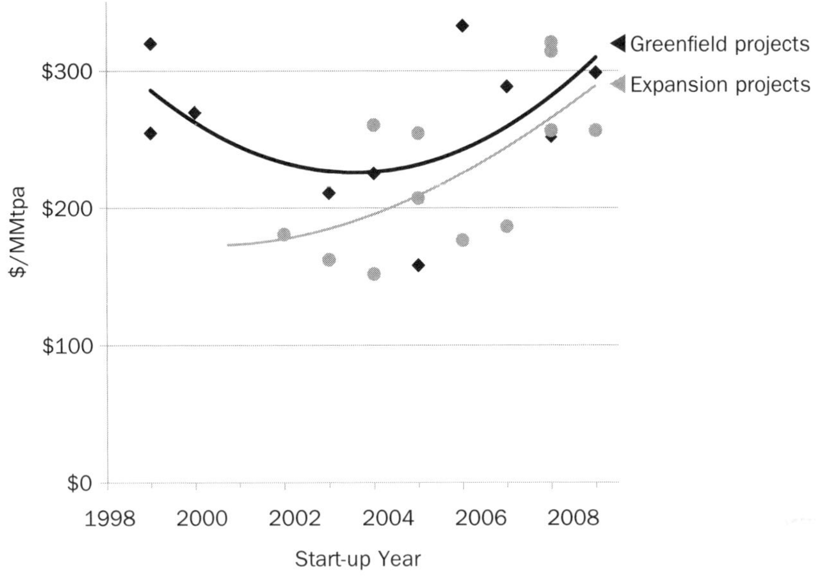

Fig. 5–10. LNG plant unit costs (*Source:* Poten & Partners)

The cost reductions observed until 2003 were due to many factors. An early move away from steam turbines (used in Algeria, Indonesia, and Brunei) toward gas turbines (as in Australia's NWS and Malaysia's LNG Dua and all subsequent projects) increased train capacities and brought costs down, as gas turbines are generally cheaper than steam turbines, which typically require boilers, boiler feed water makeup facilities, and steam condensers. The transition from water cooling (Brunei) to air cooling (at NWS) also allowed further cost reductions. In LNG storage, the use of larger-sized storage tanks helped bring down costs. Early tank designs were typically smaller than 40,000 cubic meters. In the 1990s, tank volume rose to 150,000 cubic meters, and today, tanks with capacities of 188,000 cubic meters have been built. Finally, increased engineering experience, tighter design margins, a competitive FEED and EPC bidding environment, and increased application of larger turbine drivers to reap economies of scale allowed less conservative designs to emerge and costs to fall further.

However, recent cost increases across several key raw materials—such as carbon and stainless steel, nickel, and concrete—combined with strong demand for qualified engineering contractors, project personnel, and skilled labor have combined to reverse this cost trend. EPC costs for projects committed during 2005 rose to between $250 and $350 tpa and cost escalation did not slow during 2006. Project management has been strained, with several projects experiencing serious cost overruns and delays in their projected start- up dates.

The effect that rising costs will have on LNG project feasibility remains to be seen. While LNG facility costs have risen sharply, the accompanying increase in oil prices and a seller's market for LNG make it more likely that constrained personnel, equipment and construction resources, rather than pure cost concerns, may dictate any potential slowdown in the rate of LNG growth.

Standardization and use of off-site fabricated modules

The critical path for construction of an LNG plant is usually driven by the delivery of long-lead items, such as heat exchangers, compressors, large turbines, and LNG storage tanks. Manufacturing delays thus can have dire consequences for completion schedules. Substitution of large pieces of proprietary equipment with smaller, more standardized ones can benefit both schedule and cost by introducing more competition between suppliers. When the vendor base is larger and the equipment is less specialized and complex, the costs are generally lower, and the delivery time is shorter. This rationale was one of the drivers for implementation of Shell's DMR process, and Shell has continued to drive these standardization initiatives.[9]

This concept is almost opposite to the mega-train concept, by which economies of scale are achieved through pushing critical pieces of equipment to their design limits. Standardization allows for repeat design and ease of operation, as equipment is not pushed to its limits but operates well within proven technical parameters. Design is engineered around selected standard equipment, rather than engineering equipment specifically to accommodate a particular design strategy.

Standardization has already left a positive mark on the LNG construction industry. LNG storage tanks, for which design and construction has been largely standardized and the use of prefabricated post-tensioned panels is very common, have experienced a significant reduction in cost. Shell hopes to push this concept further by prefabricating pipe and preassembling skid-mounted units for compressors and pumps, and even barge-mounting entire liquefaction plants. Some of these modular fabrication techniques have been applied to Train 5 at Australia's NWS project. Statoil has taken this concept even further at Norway's Snøhvit liquefaction plant, building many of the process units on barges and towing the completed units to the site. However, much of the motivation in this last case was to minimize the effect of Arctic conditions on the construction schedule, rather than to provide a broadly applicable construction approach. Ironically, part of the delay in the Snøhvit project came as a result of delays in shipyard fabrication of the liquefaction modules, illustrating the risks associated with innovative engineering and construction techniques.

One drawback to extensive off-site modularization is that most LNG-exporting countries do not have the strong manufacturing and fabricating industry that is needed. On the contrary, these countries would rather see old-fashioned in-place construction techniques, which tend to generate more construction jobs.

Offshore liquefaction facilities

The increased demand for LNG early this decade led to the conceptual development of several new fixed or floating technologies aimed at exploiting offshore stranded-gas reserves either too small or too remote for conventional land-based liquefaction facilities. However, the higher construction costs associated with these concepts, together with the continued advancement of large conventional and mega-train projects, have stalled many of these proposals.

The gravity-based structure (GBS) concept, intended for shallow waters, provides an artificial offshore island for LNG production and storage. The concept involves prefabricating massive concrete structures at an onshore location and then floating and towing the finished facilities to the installation location, where they are flooded and sunk to rest on the seafloor. GBS designs allow for sufficient height above water level to provide sufficient freeboard for expected sea conditions at the facility location.

GBS technology for building offshore oil and production facilities has been proven and applied to a multitude of projects worldwide, particularly in the North Sea. The challenge remains to apply these technologies cost-effectively to the LNG liquefaction process. Compared to oil and gas GBS production structures, LNG facilities will require much larger footprints and will be feasible in a much narrower range of water depths.

In the designs for floating LNG (FLNG) and GBS, the LNG storage tanks must be enclosed within the structure. The liquefaction modules that rest on top of the structure must be adequately spaced to ensure safe operations (fig. 5–11). However, technological risks remain high, and further breakthroughs are still needed for design to become reality. The berthing and loading of LNG tankers has to be feasible in a wide range of sea conditions, with higher relative motion between the LNG tanker and the liquefaction structure than is the case with onshore terminals. This could be a major technological challenge, particularly for floating production, storage, and offloading vessel (FPSO) designs, as no concept has yet been proven reliable for flexible cryogenic connections between LNG tanker and floater. Several concepts are currently being developed, but none has yet been applied.

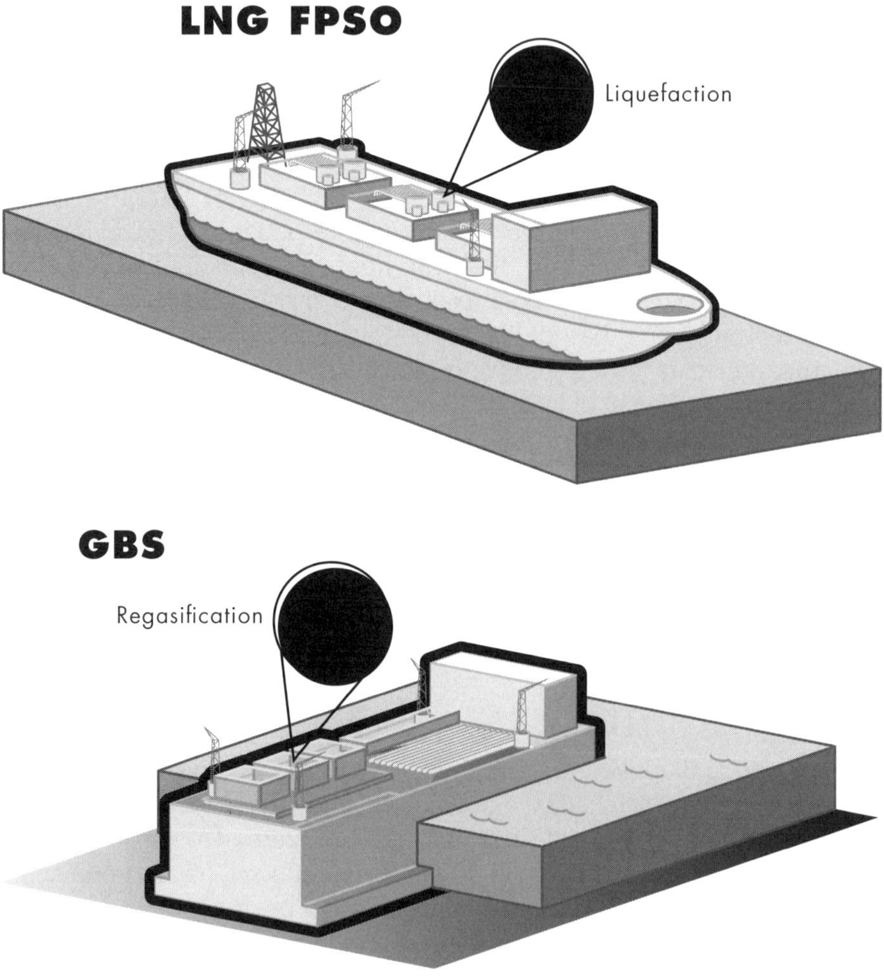

Fig. 5–11. GBS/FPSO (*Source:* Bouygues-Technigaz)

Notwithstanding the elegance and creativity of these conceptual designs, they face the almost insurmountable problem in that the world has access to plenty of gas reserves which can be liquefied at a lower cost in onshore facilitie, using tried and true methods. For the time being, offshore LNG production is a solution in search of a problem.

NOTES

[1] Poten & Partners and Merlin Associates. 2004. LNG *Cost & Competition*. New York: Poten & Partners and Merlin Associates, pp. 172–74.

[2] Peebles, Malcolm W. H. 1992. *Natural Gas Fundamentals*. London: Shell International Gas Limited.

[3] Poten & Partners and Merlin Associates, LNG *Cost & Competition*.

[4] Ibid.

[5] Ibid.

[6] Ruster, Jeff. 1996. Mitigating commercial risks in project finance. *Public Policy for the Private Sector*. February. Note 69.

[7] Poten & Partners and Merlin Associates, LNG *Cost & Competition*.

[8] Cornot-Gandolphe, Sylvie, and Ralf Dickel. 2002. *Flexibility in Natural Gas Supply and Demand: Supply and Demand*. OECD.

[9] Groothuis, Cas, Dave Fletcher, and Rob Klein Nagelvoort. 2001. *Changing the* LNG *Game*. Paper presented at the 13th International Conference & Exhibition on Liquefied Natural Gas. Seoul, May 14–17.

LNG TANKERS 6

INTRODUCTION

The idea of transporting liquid methane, or LNG, was conceived by Godfrey L. Cabot, who received a patent in 1915 for transporting liquid gas by river barge. It was not until 1951 that William Wood Prince, chairman of the Union Stock Yards of Chicago, put the concept to use. Prince had the idea of liquefying and storing gas produced in Louisiana in riverside tanks and then transporting it by barge up the Mississippi River to Chicago. Here it would be unloaded, regasified, and consumed by the Union Stock Yards. Prince commissioned Willard S. Morrison, a consulting cryogenic engineer, to lead the project.

This first effort failed to materialize because the American Bureau of Shipping (ABS), a classification society, refused to class the barge, claiming that the project had taken insufficient security measures. Later, a number of gas companies and shipowners came together to develop the concept, with the aim of economically transporting the gas over long distances. These pioneers of oceangoing methane transportation included Continental Oil Company (Conoco), the Union Stock Yards of Chicago, Shell, Arthur D. Little, Lorentzen, and a large consortium of French companies. The industrial progress was to a large extent led by the British Gas Board and Gaz de France. Their interest came from converting customers from town gas to natural gas. They were also breaking new technological grounds in developing insulated containment systems for maritime gas transportation. Competition was fierce and research and development were taking place on both sides of the Atlantic without much collaboration or sharing of technology.

THE PROTOTYPE LNG SHIPS

The first oceangoing LNG vessel was created by the conversion of a U.S. war surplus cargo ship, the *Normati* (built in 1945 and owned at the time by Norgulf), into a 5,000 m^3 LNG tanker named *Methane Pioneer.* This prototype was a joint effort by a company called Constock International Methane, a partnership of Conoco and Union Stock Yards, and was funded by the British Gas Council. In 1959, the owning company became Conch International Methane Limited; the partners were Conoco (40%), Union Stock Yards (20%), and Shell (40%). The *Normati* was converted to an LNG tanker at the Alabama Dry Dock shipyard in Mobile and was delivered in October 1958. The cargo containment consisted of five aluminum self-supporting prismatic cargo tanks, with balsa insulation panels and a secondary barrier for protection in the event of an LNG leak.

The *Methane Pioneer* started its maiden voyage with a full cargo of LNG on January 25, 1959, from Constock's LNG storage facility near Lake Charles, Louisiana. After a 27-day trans-Atlantic voyage, it reached Canvey Island, on the River Thames, in England, on February 20, 1959.

A second prototype was the *Beauvais*. It began its life as a wartime Liberty vessel, the *John Lawson*, which at the time of conversion was owned by the Compagnie Générale Maritime. The conversion was undertaken by a group of companies operating as the Methane Transport Company. It was led by member Gaz de France, working closely with French shipyards, which at the time were studying LNG as a new business activity. This vessel had a capacity of 640 m^3, contained in three different tank and insulation designs. Each was built by a different yard, testing slightly different technologies.

The *Phytagore*, a third experimental ship, built in 1965 with 610 m^3 capacity, used the Technigaz membrane cargo containment system. This ship was later converted into a fish carrier. In 1994, Technigaz merged with Gaz Transport, which had also patented a competing membrane containment system. Today, Gaz Transport & Technigaz (GT&T) is owned by Gaz de France (40%), Total (30%), and the Saipem-owned Bouygues Offshore (30%).

THE FIRST PURPOSE-BUILT COMMERCIAL SHIPS

The *Methane Princess* and the *Methane Progress* were two sister ships (the industry term for ships constructed to the same specifications) built in 1964 by British shipyards—Vickers Armstrong in Northwest England and Harland & Wolff in Northern Ireland, respectively. These tankers were owned by Conch International Methane. Each had nine prismatic cargo tanks of the Conch design with a capacity of 27,400 m^3 per tanker. They served the Algeria-to-Canvey Island LNG trade on behalf of British Gas. The *Methane Progress* enjoyed a service life of 22 years, while the *Methane Princess* operated for 28 years.

The *Jules Verne*, a 25,840 m^3 tanker with a cylindrical cargo containment system, was built by the Ateliers et Chantiers de la Seine Maritime and was owned by the Société Gaz-Marine. She began operating in January 1965, serving the Algeria-to-France trade, and later operated between Algeria and Spain until 2004, under different management and with a new name, the *Cinderella*. The ship was sold to Taiwan Maritime Transport Company in 2004 and has since then been used for training purposes.

After 1970, LNG tanker technology and size underwent considerable development, and an increasing number of shipyards began building LNG tankers according to specific project requirements. In 1971, Gazocean ordered a 50,000 m^3 LNG tanker from Chantiers de l'Atlantique that used the Technigaz membrane concept. This tanker, the *Descartes*, is still operating in the Mediterranean basin in the Gaz de France pool of ships.

LNG SHIP CONTAINMENT AND HANDLING SYSTEMS

The containment system has to serve several important functions. It has to seal the LNG in a gas-tight compartment to ensure no admixture with air, insulate the LNG from influx of heat and thus minimize boil-off, and prevent the very low temperature of the cargo from reaching the vessel's hull, where it would cause steel brittleness.

In the early years of LNG containment development, many experimental designs were worked on, including variations of membrane, prismatic, and spherical tanks. Most received patents. Some experimental designs include the following:

- Pittsburgh des Moines & Gaz Transport
- Hitachi Zosen & Chicago Bridge and Iron
- Sener Sphere Concept
- Lorentzen's Concept
- Burness, Corlett Solution
- Contranstor Proposal
- Rockwell International Design
- Owen-Corning Design
- McDonnell Douglas Design
- The Dytam Concrete LNG Design
- Ocean Transport Pressure System
- McMullen System
- The Bridgestone System
- LGA-Zellentank System
- Linde Wall Tank System
- Verolme Vertical Cylindrical Design

The industry quickly rationalized and chose two containment systems, the self-supporting independent and membrane types, both of which have been extensively developed. They are expensive to build since they require cryogenic materials.[1] These designs can be further broken down into subcategories (table 6–1).

Table 6–1. Main LNG ship containment tank designs (*Source*: Poten & Partners)

Category	Self-supporting Independent Tank Designs	Membrane Tank Designs
Particularity	Cargo tanks are constructed independent of the hull structure	The ship's inner hull provides the structural strength of the cargo tank
Containments	Kvaerner Moss spherical tanks IHI-SPB* prismatic containment Others: Conch and Esso (utilized on small ships built in the 1960s)	Technigaz tanks (TGZ Mark I and III) Gaz Transport design (GT'96) CS-1** containment

* Ishikawajima-Harima Heavy Industries developed this design. The SPB acronym is derived from the description of the tank: Self-supporting, prismatic, independent type B tank. This tank design, a direct descendant of the earlier Conch system, was used in two 89,900-cubic-meter ships (the Arctic Sun and the Polar Eagle) completed in 1993 by Japan's IHI for Phillips-Marathon's Alaska LNG export project to Japan. Recently, FLEX LNG has ordered two 90,000 cubic meter SPB vessels for delivery in 2010–2011.

** The Combined System—1, as its name indicates, is a hybrid of the Mark III and the GT'96 containments. CS-1 combines the advantages of both systems, using existing technology and proven materials. The first LNG ship to install this containment system was delivered in 2004 by the Chantiers de l'Atlantique in France for the account of Gaz de France.

Self-supporting, independent tanks

These are heavy, rigid structures built to withstand the weight of the liquids. These tanks are spherical (the familiar Moss Rosenberg design) or box shaped, and the tankers' hull is designed to support the rigid tank structure.[2]

Membrane tanks

These tanks are box shaped, and made of light, flexible metals that require a rigid load-bearing insulation system over the entire tank surface to allow the transfer of loads from the tank to the tanker's hull. The tanker's hull provides the structural rigidity to the tanks. The insulation system must provide rigid support over the whole membrane surface while allowing it to contract and expand as necessary.[3]

Each containment system has its own technological and commercial advantages and drawbacks. Commercial and operational issues are summarized in figure 6–1.

Containment Sections and Profiles	Commercial and Operational Implications
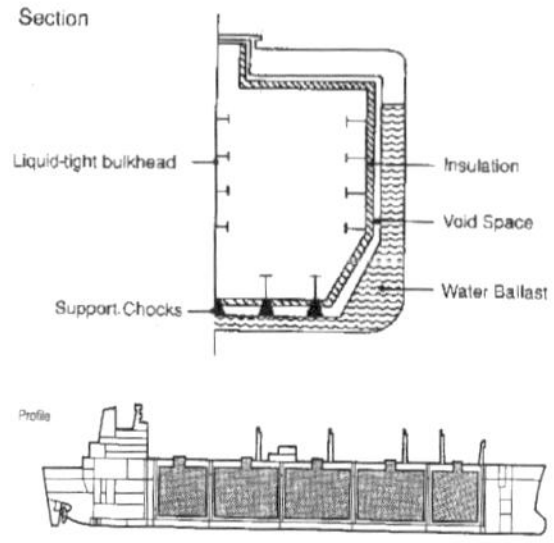	***IHI-SPB Prismatic*** Lower fuel consumption than Moss No tank-filling restrictions (no potential slosh damage) Smaller ship dimensions than spherical tanks Good maneuverability Low wheelhouse and cargo control room air drafts Unrestricted navigation visibility (flat continuous deck) Good access to inside and outside tanks Almost all welding is automatic (85%) Excellent safety in case of groundings Long cool down and warm-up times due to high thermal mass of tank and insulation Only 2 ships were built using the IHI-SPB technology
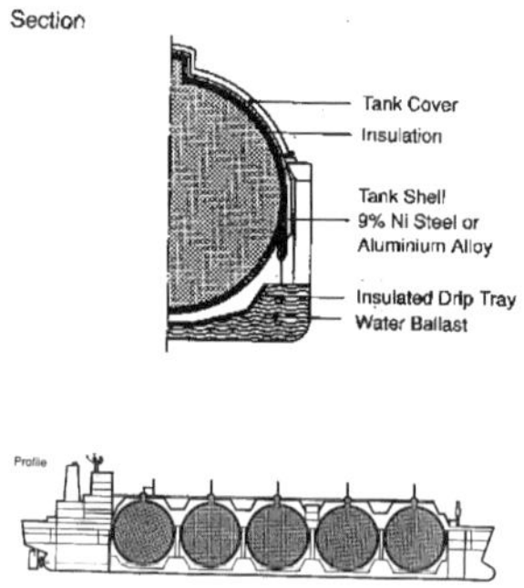	***Kvaerner Moss*** Most proven of all second-generation containments Excellent operating history No tank-filling restrictions No slosh damage potential 95% of welding is automatic (reducing defects probability during construction) Larger-dimensional ships (for the same carrying capacity than the others) Less maneuverability (high wind area) More affected by weather and poor navigation visibility Higher canal charges (40% higher gross tonnage than for membrane ships) Slightly higher fuel consumption Most difficult deck access and maintenance
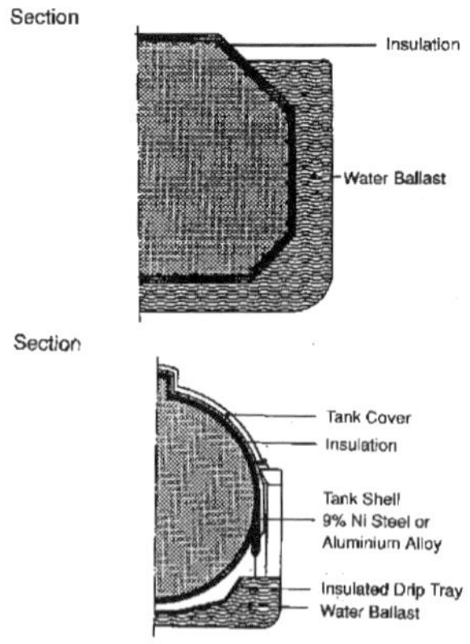	***Membrane Tanks (GT'96 and TGZ Mark III)*** Lower fuel consumption than for Moss Lower canal charges (smaller gross tonnage) Maximum usage of hold's volume for cargo Primary barrier has first-class history Unrestricted navigation visibility (flat continuous deck) Good maneuverability Low wheelhouse and cargo control room air drafts Potential slosh damage problems due to cargo tanks Membrane fatigue life is difficult to measure Difficult accessibility to containment system Labor intensive during construction—increased probability of defects

Fig. 6–1. Overview of LNG ship containment systems (diagrams from Malcolm W. H. Peebles, *Natural Gas Fundamentals*, London: Shell International Gas Limited, 1992)

Over the past 30 years, the technology used to build LNG ship cargo containment systems has changed very little. Indeed, many of the technologies in use today are the same as in the 1970s. The only new development thus far this decade is the GT&T CS-1 membrane ordered on the Gaz de France tankers for delivery in 2006; this is a combination of GT&T's existing systems.

In May 2006, the LNG fleet consisted of 199 tankers. Of these, 45% had Moss-type cargo tanks, 51% had Gaz Transport (GT) or Technigaz (TGZ) membranes, and 4% had other types of containment systems. The market share of the two leading technologies will change by the second half of the decade, as more than 80% of the ships on order employ GT&T membrane technology.

Cargo-handling systems

In addition to having safe containment systems, LNG tankers must be able to load, discharge, measure, and monitor their cargoes. This requires a whole range of cryogenic pumps compressors, temperature sensors, and cryogenic liquid level gauges. Much of the cryogenic equipment was developed as an offshoot of the American project to land a man on the moon before 1970. The availability of this developed and tested special equipment helped the industry establish a reputation for safe and reliable operation.

LNG shipbuilding

Today, two continents have shipyards capable of building LNG vessels: Europe and Asia. Figure 6–2 illustrates the movement of the LNG shipbuilding industry from the West to the East. Since the same swing took place in the LNG trade (i.e., it originated in the Atlantic Basin, which was outpaced by growth in Asia starting in the early 1980s), it clearly accelerated the shift in the LNG shipbuilding industry. Since the main LNG-consuming countries, notably Japan and Korea, were industrialized nations, they wanted a piece of the LNG transportation pie—a path later followed by China. At the same time, the industry's technology became increasingly reliable, and commercially viable projects developed in other locations. LNG tanker sizes naturally increased to satisfy demand.

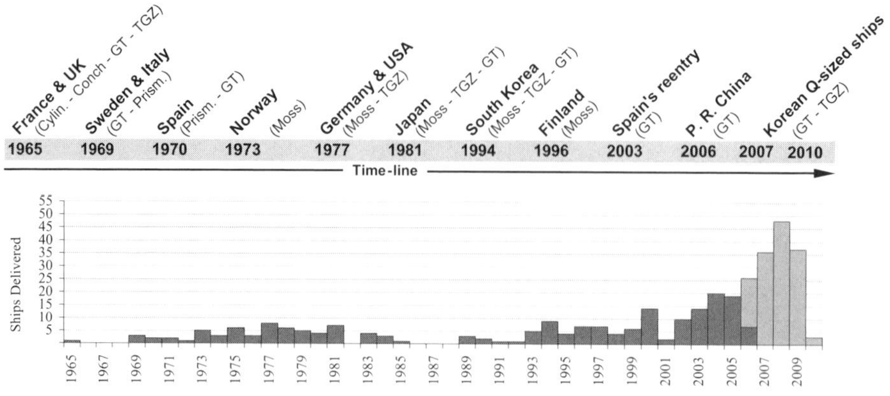

Q-sized ships refer to ships ordered for the Qatari projects. These Korean-built ships are sized between 209,000 and 266,000 cubic meters. The first Q-sized ships are planned for delivery late 2007.

Fig. 6–2. Countries' entry into the LNG shipbuilding sector. (*Source*: Poten & Partners)

As figure 6–2 shows, LNG tanker orders and deliveries went through a trough in the 1980s, revived in the 1990s, and showed little signs of slowing down at the beginning of this decade. Currently, the LNG shipbuilding industry is experiencing activity of unprecedented proportions.

EVOLUTION OF LNG SHIPBUILDING

In the early years, European naval architects and LNG tank designers played a key role in developing and building these highly specialized ships. Hence, European yards controlled LNG shipbuilding for some time, before containment system licenses and technology transfer arrangements were negotiated with shipbuilders in Asia. To this day, Southeast Asian LNG shipyards dominate the shipbuilding industry, although Korea has surpassed Japan, as the world's foremost LNG shipbuilder. As the LNG trade has expanded to accommodate more and more buyers and sellers, so too has the world's LNG ship delivery capability. By the end of 2002, total worldwide LNG shipbuilding capacity was estimated between 37 and 41 ships per year, mostly in the Far East. In 2006, the world's annual LNG shipbuilding capacity was up to about 70 tankers.

Europe. At first, European shipyards received a number of orders from LNG start-up projects in both the Atlantic and the Pacific markets. The largest ship order of the early 1970s was placed by Shell Tankers in the United Kingdom, which selected three French shipyards to build seven LNG tankers of 75,000 m³, using two membrane technologies, GT and TGZ. These were followed by a series of orders in French shipyards by French and Algerian owners for membrane vessels of 125,000–130,000 m³ and by the Malaysia International Shipping Corporation (now known as MISC Berhad), which ordered five 130,000 m³ tankers. Meanwhile, in Norway, Moss Rosenberg Verft used their own Moss technology to build two 87,000 m³ tankers, the *Norman Lady* and the P&O *Challenger* (now the *Höegh Galleon*). They were soon followed by the *Hilli* and the *Gimi*, the first large spherical tank LNG tankers, with a cargo-carrying capacity of 126,000 m³. HDW in Germany delivered two large LNG tankers in 1977 that used the Moss design, the *Höegh Gandria* and the *Golar Freeze*,[4] both 125,800 m³.

Some 33 years after building the *Laieta* in 1970, Spain reentered the LNG shipbuilding scene. The major Spanish gas importer, Enagás, placed an order in the summer of 2000 for four LNG newbuildings at their domestic yard, Izar.[5] Today, there are only two European shipyards with LNG shipbuilding abilities (table 6–2). Generally, European yards find it very difficult to compete with their Southeast Asian (namely Korean) counterparts because of much higher labor costs.

Table 6–2. Europe: Active LNG shipyards (*Source*: Poten & Partners)

Shipyard	LNG Shipbuilding Capacity*	Containment Experience
Chantiers de l'Atlantique (France)	3	GT, TGZ, and CS-1
Izar (Spain)	3	GT

* The capacities are estimates based on each yard's maximum annual delivery capabilities. A shipyard's maximum capacity may differ from actual potential building capacity in any given year owing to exposure to other markets and their ordering cycles (bulk, tankers, containers, etc.), which may distract attention from another type of carrier or a later order.

United States. General Dynamics and Newport News built 13 large LNG ships between 1977 and 1980, using the Moss and TGZ technologies, respectively. Eight tankers were built for Burmah Gas Transport to serve trades from Indonesia to Japan and South Korea. Three were built for the ill-fated El Paso project to bring Algerian LNG to the U.S. East Coast, and two were built to trade into Lake Charles. Two of those tankers are now owned by Bonny Gas Transport (a fully owned subsidiary of Nigeria LNG) and serve Nigeria's gas exports; two are owned and operated by Shell; and a fifth, the *Suez Matthew*, trades from Trinidad to the United States under the French-owned company Suez.

Avondale built three LNG tankers, also for the El Paso project, using a polyurethane foam (PUF) combined containment and insulation system. The system failed to receive classification certification, and the vessels were not permitted to load LNG. All three subsequently became the subject of a large insurance claim. Two of the vessels were later converted into coal carriers, which also burned coal as fuel. The United States currently has no viable LNG shipbuilding capacity.

Asia. Japan and later South Korea became world leaders in the general shipbuilding industry. Their competitive advantage was achieved through large investments in automation, coupled with low labor and material costs relative to western shipbuilders. These advantages were somewhat mitigated by other factors. Construction of the cargo containment systems was not easy to automate and required considerable new investment. Most of the cryogenic equipment and materials required were available only from the United States and Europe.

Japanese ship repair yards were able to secure almost exclusive dry-docking and maintenance contracts for the first generation of U.S.- and European-built LNG vessels trading into Japan. The repair facilities were all associated with the major shipbuilders; thus, the builders were able to acquire much knowledge and information to facilitate their entry into the building market. Japan entered the LNG shipbuilding arena at the end of 1981 with an order by Gotaas Larsen for a Moss spherical containment tanker, the *Golar Spirit*, placed with Kawasaki Heavy Industries. Spurred by orders from domestic owners supported by domestic charters, Japan rapidly built up their LNG shipbuilding market share, focusing almost exclusively on the Moss containment system. They achieved the dominant position throughout most of the 1990s and currently have an annual LNG shipbuilding capacity of about 11 tankers from five shipyards; however, capacity for 2010 deliveries has further increased to about 15 tankers annually. In 2004, the Japanese shipyards Imabari and Universal shipbuilding entered the LNG shipbuilding business by winning orders from a Shoei Kisen/K-Line partnership and Sonatrach, respectively. Japanese LNG shipyards are summarized in table 6–3.

Table 6–3. Japan: Active LNG shipyards (*Source*: Poten & Partners)

Shipyard*	LNG Shipbuilding Capacity**	Containment Experience
Kawasaki Heavy Industries	3	Moss
Mitsubishi Heavy Industries	5	Moss and GT
Mitsui Engineering & Shipbuilding	2	Moss and GT
Universal Shipbuilding	2	TGZ and CS1
Imabari Shipbuilding	3	TGZ, GT, and CS1

*IHI is not currently building LNG ships, although the yard is capable and is currently seeking a reentry into LNG shipbuilding.

**The capacities are estimates based on each yard's maximum annual delivery capabilities for 2010 delivery. A shipyard's maximum capacity may differ from actual potential building capacity in any given year owing to exposure to other markets and their ordering cycles (bulk, tankers, containers, etc.), which may distract attention from another type of carrier or later orders.

It was not until the mid-1990s that South Korea began LNG tanker construction. To protect their lucrative shipbuilding market, Japanese shipbuilders were reluctant to share the steam turbine propulsion technology that Korea lacked. Support was not forthcoming from European shipbuilders either. Foreign shipowners were hesitant at placing orders for such specialized tankers in shipyards with no LNG experience. Korea therefore faced an uphill task and, like Japan, obtained an initial niche through domestic orders.

Hyundai Heavy Industries delivered the country's first LNG tanker in 1994, the *Hyundai Utopia*, to transport Kogas's LNG imports. The 125,000 m^3 Moss four-tank vessel was based very closely on a Japanese design and included much Japanese equipment (agreement having been reached on technology transfer). Kogas not only had a monopoly for all gas imports but was also the second-largest LNG importer in the world. When Kogas signed new LNG supply contracts on an FOB basis, it prompted Korean shipowners to become involved and to collaborate with major South Korean yards. In late 1999, Hyundai Heavy Industries secured its first export order from a non-Korean owner when Nigeria LNG's Bonny Gas Transport ordered two 137,300 m^3 LNG tankers.

South Korean yards seized the initiative from the Japanese yards, offering owners more competitive LNG shipbuilding terms, together with attractive price tags, and winning the lion's share of the newbuilding orders from 1999 onward.[6] In May 2006, about 75% of tanker orders were placed with South Korean shipyards; at the same time, Japan had 19% of the order book, and the remaining 6% was with Chinese and European yards. The four major South Korean yards enjoy an LNG shipbuilding capacity of approximately

50 ships per year for 2010 delivery. Although Hanjin Heavy Industries and Construction has not delivered any LNG ships since 2000, they have taken two orders from STX Pan Ocean in 2005 and early 2006. South Korean LNG shipyards are summarized in table 6–4.

Table 6–4. South Korea: Active LNG shipyards (*Source:* Poten & Partners)

Shipyard	LNG Shipbuilding Capacity*	Containment Experience
Daewoo Shipbuilding & Marine Eng.	15	GT
Hanjin Heavy Industries & Construction	2	GT
Hyundai Heavy Industries	17	Moss and TGZ
Samsung Heavy Industries	16	TGZ
STX Shipbuilding	2	GT and TGZ

* The capacities are estimates based on each yard's maximum annual delivery capabilities for 2010 delivery. A shipyard's maximum capacity may differ from actual potential building capacity in any given year owing to exposure to other markets and their ordering cycles (bulk, tankers, containers, etc.), which may distract attention from another type of carrier or a later order.

China. China, which became an LNG importer in 2006, followed the Japanese and Korean examples. Guangdong LNG Transportation Group[7] ordered five LNG tankers at the Hudong-Zhonghua yard to provide transportation for Australian LNG that will supply the terminal at Guangdong (table 6–5). There is also an option for a sixth tanker, with a 2009 delivery date. All of these LNG ships will use membrane technology transferred from France through a collaboration agreement.

Table 6–5. China: Active LNG shipyard (*Source*: Poten & Partners)

Shipyard	LNG Shipbuilding Capacity*	Containment Experience
Hudong-Zhonghua Shipbuilding Group (and others)	5	GT

* The capacities are estimates based on yards maximum annual delivery capabilities for 2010 delivery. China will deliver its first LNG ship at the end of 2006 and its second in the first half of 2007. A shipyard's maximum capacity may differ from actual potential building capacity in any given year owing to exposure to other markets and their ordering cycles (bulk, tankers, containers, etc.), which may distract attention from another type of carrier or later order.

Other Chinese shipyards are gearing up to build LNG tankers for the Chinese trade. The Dalian New Shipyard, Nantong (NACS), and the Jiangnan Shipbuilding Group are keen to win new orders; they hold licenses for both Moss and membrane containment systems, which has resulted in their acquiring licenses for both. In addition, Shanghai Waigaogio Shipbuilding has acquired a license to build membrane LNG tankers.

Patents and licenses

The developers of containment technologies patented their work to ensure the exclusive right to build and license their inventions. At least 500 patents have been registered for marine transportation containments. However, as the market rationalized and two designs became dominant, the licensing of the patent rights has been focused on these systems.

Moss containment technology. Moss Rosenberg Verft patented the Moss containment technology. When the shipyard closed down, the Moss Maritime engineering company[8] retained independent ownership of the design. The Kvaerner Masa[9] yard of Finland obtained a license to build the design and gained the rights to market the product on behalf of Moss Maritime, although it was not until 1996 that the Finnish yard received newbuilding orders. In July 2001, Saipem, the offshore engineering subsidiary of Italy's Eni Group, purchased Moss Maritime and with it the Moss containment patent.

Sensing that the market was shifting to the more competitive Asian shipyards, Moss Maritime and Kvaerner Masa extensively promoted the technology and sold licenses to a large number of yards. Japan dominated the shipbuilding market from the early 1980s to the late '90s; since three out of five Japanese yards capable of building LNG tankers have Moss experience (although some later constructed membrane ships), by the end of the 1990s, the Moss spherical containment LNG tankers were the most popular type, and their total capacity outsized all other containments combined.[10]

Membrane containment technology. Until the mid-1980s, Gaz Transport and Technigaz each received many contracts for LNG ships ordered and constructed in France. After that time, Gaz Transport began to struggle financially as shipbuilding moved to Japan, which had primarily adopted the Moss system. Technigaz, however, was more secure, as it was not solely focused on ship containments but also sold technology for onshore LNG storage tanks.

The two groups had been slow to market their membrane licenses to foreign yards in fear of losing business at French yards. After Gaz Transport and Technigaz merged in 1994, to become GT&T, they continued to market and license their patented technologies on an individual basis. GT&T was more successful in Korea, where membrane technology established itself as the market leader. The French shipyard Chantiers de l'Atlantique also recognized that marketing its LNG know-how would be more profitable than trying to compete for contracts against Asian shipyards, and it also provided membrane ship technology to Korea.

While China was seeking assistance to build its first series of LNG ships, GT&T and Chantiers de l'Atlantique agreed to provide the necessary technical support. A similar strategy was adopted when Spain's Izar received an LNG tanker order from Enagás in 2000.

Saipem of Italy not only owns Moss Maritime but also purchased Bouygues Offshore (France) in September 2002. Bouygues Offshore has a 30% ownership of GT&T (GT, TGZ, and CS-1) through its 100% ownership of Technigaz.

TYPICAL LNG SHIPBUILDING PROJECT

Some familiarity with LNG shipbuilding costs is important for an understanding of the financial implications of proceeding with a newbuilding order.

LNG tankers are the world's second most costly merchant vessels after large cruise ships. In 1990, a new 125,000 m^3 LNG tanker was priced around $260 million. Korea's decisive entry[11] into the business significantly reduced the price structures imposed by Japanese shipyards (which were still more competitive than European shipbuilders). Earlier this decade, the most competitive yards were delivering 138,000 m^3 LNG tankers for prices in the region of $160 million.[12] This forced less competitive yards to revise their cost structures. Since 2000, shipbuilding prices have slowly increased, together with tanker sizes. In the first quarter of 2006, shipyards were pricing conventional 145,000 m^3 tankers with steam turbine propulsion in the region of $210 million and 155,000 m^3 tankers with dual-fuel diesel/electric propulsion for an additional $10–$15 million (above the equivalent steam turbine LNG tanker). The much larger LNG tankers ordered by the Qataris, specifically the 209,000–216,200 m^3 ships (Q-flex) and the 262,000–266,000 m^3 vessels (Q-max), carried reported price tags of between $250–255 million and $280–285 million per ship, respectively, at the time of contracting.

Before contract signing

A shipowner must take into account a number of issues before ordering an LNG tanker. Aside from the project's financing structure and shipyards' quoted prices, the owner must evaluate which cargo containment system and specifications are best suited to his commercial and quality needs and the requirements of the specific project that the tanker will serve.

After reviewing the design with classification societies, shipyards, and equipment/machine makers, the owner selects a yard. The selection process can take several forms, but the most common means of selection is to award a contract after a competitive tender and short-listing procedure or to choose a yard on the basis of personal preference (whether it be a close historical link with the yard, a known first-class builder, or a predilection toward the builder's specifications, terms, and conditions). Only then will the final proposal be submitted to all the concerned parties and approved, prior to the contract signing, shipbuilding, and delivery.

Project scheduling

As an increasing number of ships are ordered, yards strive to become more efficient. Today, however complex a ship's agreed specification, a yard is capable of providing an exact delivery date more than two years into the future.

Construction of LNG ships, as with other specialized ships, requires major infrastructure, highly sophisticated machinery, a professional workforce, well-structured project scheduling, and strict production management. Figure 6–3 illustrates the course of actions taken during a typical LNG shipbuilding project. In general, for a 145,000 m^3 membrane tanker, the project takes around 30 months from contract signing to completion and delivery. Actual construction time is roughly 18 months from steel cutting to delivery.

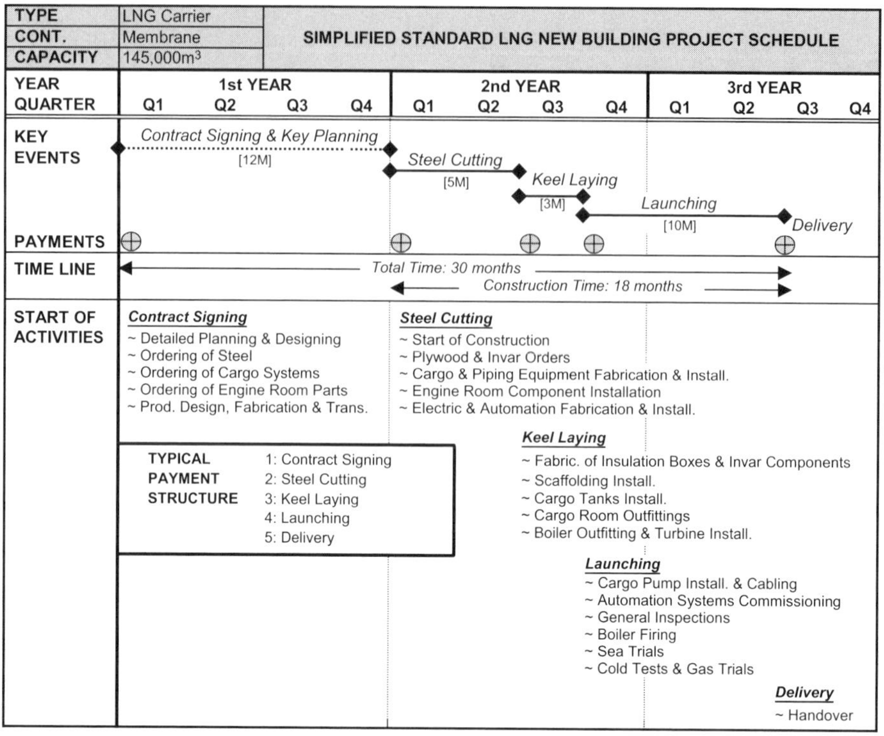

Note: The timeframe given is only indicative, as each yard has a slightly different building practice—fabrication and installation of cargo containment systems are different and alter the critical path procedures; the building period also varies in accordance with the ship specifications required by the owner or project.

Fig. 6–3. Representative LNG membrane vessel newbuilding project schedule. (*Source*: Poten & Partners)

During the construction process, the shipowner generally sends a supervision team, which consists of naval architects/engineers and steel, cryogenic, and paint inspectors representing the owner's interest (either internal employees or independent contractors). Many site teams also include an owner's health, safety, and environment (HSE) advisor, especially if a series of sister vessels are being constructed and work is being performed in several locations. The team resides on-site throughout the entire construction period, although the composition of the team may change as work progresses. Among other responsibilities, their role is to review the day-to-day activity, perform frequent inspections, and closely monitor building progress to ensure that the vessel is being built according to the agreed specifications.

The time frame for acquisition of a membrane containment vessel in the previous example applies equally well to a Moss vessel. This, however, very much depends on the individual yard's capacity, LNG shipbuilding experience, and order book for other merchant ships. Both membrane and Moss ships have different critical paths during the building process, as they differ in technical and physical details. For example, in a membrane ship, construction of the tanks is carried out within the hull and cannot commence until the hull is substantially complete. The spheres for a Moss ship, by contrast, can be built separately in parallel with the hull, then inserted into the openings on deck. However, this does not necessarily save time. On a Moss vessel, the piping systems and structure on deck can be mounted only after the installation of the spheres. For a membrane ship, the construction of the tanks is done through openings in the side of the ship's hull, so that the deck and all its piping structure can be installed at the same time. Another example is welding the containment system. For Moss spheres, 90% of the welding is automated. The same is more or less true for the GT'96 membranes, but it is much less so for the TGZ Mark III, which requires more manual welding of the corrugated stainless steel membranes.

Standards of construction

In 1976, the IMO, a United Nations agency, published the International Gas Carrier Code (IGC Code) to provide an international standard of construction. The code's requirements include design criteria of the cargo tanks, accepted construction material, location of tanks, piping arrangements, boil-off and cargo-handling requirements, and safety arrangements. Today, government bodies and classification societies of every major maritime country administer and enforce the code.

The unmatched safety record of LNG carriers gives testament to the value of the IGC Code and its enforcement, especially at a time when the number of LNG carriers is expanding rapidly.

TYPICAL PARAMETERS OF LNG SHIPS

LNG ships have increased in capacity and capabilities over the past 35 years. Today's ships are more than five times the size of the first two *Methane* sister ships, and the Q-max ships being built will be almost ten times as large. Table 6–6 provides a general example of LNG tanker specifications. In the crude oil tanker market of the 1970s, following the closure of the Suez Canal, longer trade routes and larger ships meant economies of scale and lower dollar-per-ton-per-mile costs. The same principle was applied to

LNG tankers. Distances between the LNG sources and destinations were becoming longer,[13] and the appetite for LNG was growing at a hefty pace.

Table 6–6. Main LNG tanker specifications, categorized by size (*Source*: Poten & Partners)

	LNG Vessel Size Category (Membrane & Moss Combined)					
	18,000–50,000 m^3	65,000–90,000 m^3	120,000–135,000 m^3	137,000–145,000 m^3	216,000 m^{3*}	264,000 m^{3*}
DWT (Metric tons)	10,000–22,000	50,000–60,000	67,500–73,000	68,600–76,200	101,100	122,200
LOA (Meters)	130.0–207.0	216.0–250.0	280.5–293.5	276.0–290.0	315.	345.0
Beam (Meters)	26.0–29.5	34.0–40.0	41.5–43.5	42.5–46.6	50.0	55.0
Draft (Meters)	7.0–9.5	9.5–10.5	11.0–12.0	11.0–12.0	12.0	12.0
Speed (Knots)	14.5–16.5	17.5	18.5	18.5–19.5	19.0	19.0
Boil-off (% per day)	0.26–0.24	0.21–0.18	0.25–0.15	~0.15	–	–
Manning requirements	16–22	~27	28–34	28–34	~34	~34

Note: The figures are generalizations. Each shipyard offers slightly different specifications, and it also changes according to the containment type.
* Q-Flex and Q-Max ships will have onboard reliquefaction capabilities and therefore have no boil-off indicated.

The larger a vessel's capacity, the greater are the main dimensions, most significantly the beam. Recent decreases in boil-off are not specifically related to size but rather to technological advances in the cargo insulation systems. There is also a slight difference between Moss and membrane vessel sizes. For the same cargo-carrying capacity, a Moss vessel is physically larger because of the inefficient use of the hull cargo space, which is occupied by spherical tanks.

Table 6–7 illustrates the status of the LNG fleet as it stood in the first quarter of 2006. The breakdown in the first two categories (size and age) does not include ships on order. With 199 tankers currently trading at sea, the fleet will total about 340 ships in early 2010 after the current newbuildings are delivered.[14]

Table 6–7. LNG ships: Size range, age profile, and trade allocation (*Source*: Poten & Partners)

LNG Vessels: Some Facts (2006)					
Size Breakdown $(m)^3$		Age Profile (years)		Fleet Allocation (ships)	
< – 49,000	8.0%	<–10	55.0%	Pacific fleet	103
50,000–99,000	8.0%	11–20	12.5%	Atlantic fleet	74
> –100,000	84.0%	21–30	21.0%	Unspecified	22
		31–40	11.5%	Existing fleet	199
				New–buildings	143
				Total Fleet	342

The majority of the fleet is larger than 100,000 m^3, and more than half the tankers are less than 10 years old. LNG shipping is indeed a new and emerging marine transport industry. However, as many as 45 tankers (31% of the existing fleet) were built between the early 1970s and early '80s, to serve the original LNG projects, including Algerian exports to Europe and the United States and Japanese imports from Alaska, Brunei, Indonesia, Malaysia, and Abu Dhabi.

THE LNG FLEET

Drivers of growth

As mentioned previously, the LNG trade counted 199 tankers in early 2006, and a staggering 143 tankers are on order at the yards, with delivery schedules between 2006 and 2010. It is also expected that more orders for 2010 delivery will be exercised during 2006 and 2007 (fig. 6–4).

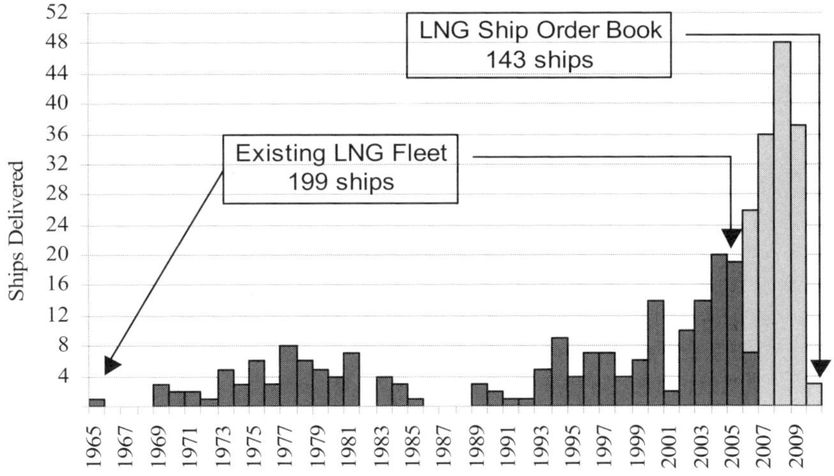

Fig. 6–4. LNG ship deliveries by year (*Source*: Poten & Partners)

Between 1969 and 1999, the industry saw 116 tankers delivered to their owners, an average pace of 4 deliveries each year. Within a nine-year span (2000–2009), as many as 226 tankers will have been delivered—on average about 25 tankers per year. Why has the industry experienced such a boom in LNG tanker orders this decade? What have been the main drivers for such a growth? The answer to the first question is the amalgamation of a number of dynamic market factors, which includes the following drivers:

- The expansion of the LNG industry, and the development of new and expanding export and import projects, require expanded LNG shipbuilding.
- The Asian crisis and the addition of Korea as a major LNG shipbuilder have heavily influenced the shipbuilding industry and have driven the price of newbuildings to an all-time low.
- Natural gas prices in the United States skyrocketed in the winter of 2000–2001 and reached a peak of $9.16/MMBtu (Henry Hub spot price) in January 2001. Many LNG suppliers had spare production capacity and immediately sought to sell LNG cargoes into one of the two existing and operational U.S. LNG terminals.[15] European LNG buyers also arranged trans-Atlantic cargo swaps to take advantage of these gas prices. This had important ramifications for shipping:
  - The new trades, especially to the U.S. Gulf Coast, called for much longer shipping distances, and required more shipping capacity.
  - Owing to the traditional nature of the industry, spare shipping capacity was in short supply. Shipping was a bottleneck and therefore rapidly became a very valuable asset, even if they lacked full employment for the ship. Short-term and spot charter hire rates reached unprecedented peaks.
  - Midstream (and downstream) participants perceived the control of tankers as a highly prized trading asset.
  - Independent shipowners, some of whom had never been in the LNG transportation business, seeing attractive newbuilding prices, ordered on speculation, resulting in a surge in demand for LNG tankers.
  - Project participants and supermajors BP and Shell also took notice of the price situation and ordered tankers to serve their own trading activities. These companies participate in LNG projects worldwide and are securing access to markets around the globe. Trading flexibility demands that shipping capacity must be provided above baseload project requirements.
- Thus, the huge LNG carrier order book reflects the importance that the industry assigns to the control of shipping. While some orders are dedicated to specific trades (the traditional formula), many are nontraditional orders, and these are becoming key in the evolution of the LNG shipping model. The intended uses of newbuildings on order range from purely speculative to owners acquiring a strategic asset for trading purposes.

LNG tanker ownership

Aside from a few constructions in the early years, LNG tanker ownership takes essentially one of three forms:

1. The fleet is owned by an independent shipowner and is chartered to a seller or buyer under a long-term lease agreement.
2. The fleet is owned directly by the LNG seller or indirectly, by a separate entity established and owned by the seller (a special-purpose vehicle [SPV]).
3. The fleet is owned by the LNG buyer or the buyer's SPV.

It is important at this stage to differentiate between tanker ownership, management, and control. In many cases, the owners of tankers are separate shipping entities or consortia[16] serving their national or home country companies and chartering the ships to the seller or the buyer, depending on the terms of the LNG sale (FOB, CIF, or ex-ship). Therefore, control of the tankers is not through the actual shipowner, but rather through the buyer or the seller (known as a disponent owner or time-chartered owner, since this is not the owner with whom the ship is registered). Similarly, the management of the tanker can also vary. Depending on the size of the dedicated fleet and the charterer's in-house ship management resources, fleet management is either administered by the actual shipowner, the LNG seller or buyer, or an independent tanker management company contracted to provide first-class personnel and operations management.

To a great extent, these ownership structures still dominate the LNG shipping market today. However, as the industry has grown and gained a proven track record, ownership and control of LNG tankers has become much more diversified, with each arrangement customized to a particular project. Furthermore, when the price of newbuildings drastically fell in 1999, by about 40% from a decade earlier, independent shipowners, as well as emerging LNG buyers, sought a piece of the pie. The lowering of the price barrier encouraged a number of shipowners to enter the lucrative LNG shipping market, and at the same time, a number of speculative tankers were built. Large shipowners, such as Bergesen dy ASA (now known as BW Gas ASA), Golar LNG, and Exmar, ordered series of tankers without confirmed back-to-back term charters, thus making these orders somewhat speculative. Other owners, such as Leif Hoëgh, Naviera Tapias, and Knutsen and Marpetrol, ordered new tankers only after a confirmed term-charter agreement. None of these independent shipping firms has upstream or downstream gas market interests.[17] Even oil and gas majors like Shell and BP and established joint venture projects[18] took the opportunity to order lower-priced LNG ships without a firm dedication.

As of early 2006, many of the so-called speculative tankers have been tied up to charterers on their delivery, either with expanding export projects or with buyers adding to or diversifying their portfolio of LNG purchases. As to the other undedicated speculative vessels, it is uncertain what will happen on their delivery; whether a true spot market is triggered remains to be seen. Nonetheless, owners of ships with yard prices of up to $160 million seek to secure long-term business for their tankers to ensure regular revenues and bank loan payments. A few months of unemployment for a new tanker can be financially painful to an independent shipowner, not to mention what could happen if the owner had a fleet of unemployed ships! Will this be a repeat of the El Paso history? (Twenty-two years after their first ship mortgage default, the company again got into LNG and chartered several tankers from Exmar that they couldn't fully utilize.)

SHIP OPERATIONS

Cooldown

Regardless of the containment system, the ship's tanks must be cooled down prior to the loading of cargo. This will minimize vaporization of the cargo and will enable the tanks to avoid thermal shock. Traditionally, a small volume of LNG is purchased at the load port and is used to gradually cool down the containment system until there is liquid at the bottom of all tanks. Once the tanks are cooled down, it is normal to keep them in the cold condition throughout a vessel's trading period. They are warmed up again only for the next scheduled refit or if earlier access is required for essential maintenance. At each cargo discharge, the pumps are stopped before the tanks are completely empty, the retained cargo being called LNG heel. The quantity of heel is calculated to maintain the tanks in cryogenic condition until arrival at the next load port; boil-off from the heel also provides a portion of the fuel required for propulsion on the ballast voyage. This procedure avoids the time and cost associated with cooling the tanks down before each and every loading and avoids repeated thermal cycles (warm to cold to warm) which stress the containment system.

Boil-off

LNG cargo is carried as a boiling liquid at slightly higher than atmospheric pressure. Any influx of heat causes the cargo to boil and returns its surface to a gaseous state. This boil-off gas is used as fuel in the boilers of steam turbine-powered vessels, and can be used to power today's newer dual-fuel marine diesel engines.

Even with today's advanced technology, insulation of the tanks is not perfect, although it is very close to it. The temperature inside the tanks increases very slightly during the sea passage and therefore causes small quantities of LNG to boil off. The rate of boil-off can increase during a storm, while the cargo is sloshing around inside the ship. Typically, the daily boil-off gas represents 0.1%–0.25% of the ship's cargo-carrying capacity. New ships have lower boil-off ratios than older ships owing to improved insulation systems. Boil-off exerts increased pressure in the tanks. If nothing is done to relieve this pressure, it eventually causes the tank relief valves to open, venting cargo into the atmosphere. Since onboard LNG reliquefaction facilities are expensive to construct and operate, it has thus far proven to be uneconomical to re-liquefy the gas on board.[19] However, the Q-sized (209,000–266,000 m^3) ships for the Qatari projects can justify the costs and are being built with reliquefaction units.

Pioneers of LNG shipping found an elegant alternative. The cargo tanks are maintained at a stable pressure by using the boil-off gas as fuel for driving their steam turbine propulsion systems. Until recently, almost all LNG vessels have had steam turbine propulsion. Hence, the use of boil-off as fuel is standard practice. It greatly reduces the ship's bunker fuel requirements and fuel bill,[20] provides an environmentally clean fuel for the boiler, and reduces boiler maintenance costs.

Cargo loading/discharge

Cargo operations have been well described by Malcolm W. H. Peebles, in his book *Natural Gas Fundamentals*:

> During loading any excess of boil-off generated on the ship is returned to the shore by compressors installed either on the ship or shore, where it may be used as fuel in the shore power plant or re-liquefied and returned to the shore storage. The vapor return flow rate will normally be the highest during the initial stages of loading when the pipelines and receiving tanks are relatively warm. During this phase the loading rate will be restricted so that the vapor return flow rate is limited to the available capacity of the compressors. As the loading system temperature stabilizes the vapor flow rate will reduce and the LNG loading rate increase. Loading systems using dedicated ships are usually designed to allow a loading operation of a large LNG ship to be completed within fourteen hours.[21] Discharging operations are essentially the reverse of loading and take approximately the same time.

LNG SHIP SAFETY AND ACCIDENT RECORDS

To date, LNG shipping boasts an exemplary safety record. This reflects the industry's professionalism, the value of the IGC Code, and the success of bodies such as the Society of International Gas Tanker and Terminal Operators (SIGTTO), which advocate the highest standards in all safety aspects, including design, construction, operation, crewing, and maintenance. Although accidents have occurred, very few serious incidents have been recorded, and none has resulted in serious breakdown of the cargo containment system.[22]

A case in point is BG's October 2005 discovery of problems with one of the storage tanks aboard the 145,000 m^3 *Methane Kari Elin*. There was an increased nitrogen migration that exceeded manufacturer specifications across the secondary barrier on one of the newly built LNG ship's tanks. Subsequently it was determined that the secondary barrier was leaking slightly as a result of a problem with an epoxy adhesive (glue) administered to the triplex layer between the primary and secondary barriers. However, no LNG ever escaped the tank. The tanker underwent repairs in Korea and resumed service in the summer of 2006. Other LNG tanker operating incidents include a collision, groundings, small liquid spills during cargo transfer, and mechanical breakdowns.

MAINTENANCE AND LIFE EXTENSION (SHIP LONGEVITY)

The industry has demonstrated that the useful service lives of properly maintained LNG tankers are well in excess of the 20-year life normally associated with conventional oil tankers and originally assumed for many LNG projects. For example, Japanese buyers, who are extremely concerned about safety, commissioned an extensive study of a Pacific basin fleet's condition and life expectancy and agreed to accept the tankers for continued service for another 20 years following an already completed 20-year LNG supply contract. Industry leaders now expect an LNG vessel's service life to be around 40 years, given the completion of a comprehensive life extension program. The longevity of a tanker is largely due to continuous investment in and adherence to sound maintenance policies.

Older tankers provide a valuable cost advantage to the owner, which in turn can make shorter-term trades attractive.

LNG MARITIME INDUSTRY TRENDS

LNG shipping will probably retain a traditional structure for most of the long-term fixed trades in which vessels are ordered and built to meet specific requirements. Since LNG SPAs often require that tankers make regular round-trip voyages on a fixed schedule and usually at even intervals, the dedicated tankers have little idle or uncommitted time. Some LNG SPAs require that tankers be dedicated to fulfilling the shipping requirements of a specific contract. Thus, it is difficult to use any operational spare capacity beyond a specific project's transportation requirements.

Nonetheless, the advent of short-term trades and the drive to lower transport costs are transforming the industry at the margin. A surprising number of new tankers were ordered without long-term charter commitments. A key to short-term trading is the control of shipping capacity and the right to exercise delivery, to support merchant trading activities. Buyers and sellers alike are increasingly seeing value in control over tankers.

The issue of controlling tankers—and the resulting flexibility it can provide to the owner or charterer—is tied to the issue of simultaneous operational logistics at the LNG export and import terminals. In the traditional LNG project model, tankers were designated for specific trades with a regular and predictable schedule of loadings and discharges. The introduction of several buyers who control their own tonnage, perhaps of various sizes and specifications, and expect to load at different outlets can present difficult operational problems at the LNG export terminal.

The terminal operator will be presented with similar challenges at the import terminal, due to multiple suppliers and firm gas throughput obligations. The problem increases with third-party terminal owners, serving multiple capacity holders that supply the terminal with LNG from different countries. These problems can become acute as operations at these facilities approach their respective capacities. Alleviation of these logistical problems may require additional investments in facilities in order to create buffer capacity or restrictions on the very flexibilities that the buyers are seeking.

A solution opted for within the industry is careful scheduling and cooperation between shippers of LNG. However, as more and more trades are added to the global matrix and complexity increases, this relatively smooth cooperation may no longer suffice, since buyers and sellers may no longer share common goals.

TECHNOLOGY DEVELOPMENTS

Engines and propulsion

The LNG shipping industry has historically been reluctant to adopt new technologies and designs. Steam turbine engines are a well-proven technology, being highly reliable, having low maintenance costs, and permitting the safe and easy disposal of boil-off gas. However, steam propulsion has relatively low fuel efficiency. Moreover, as diesel engines become standard in merchant shipping, suitably qualified oceangoing steam engineers are in short supply. It was not until early 2002 that Gaz de France broke from this pattern and ordered a small LNG carrier using new technologies for both containment and propulsion: the new CS-1 membrane tank and a low-pressure dual-fuel diesel/electric propulsion system. Gaz de France worked with GT&T and Alstom (Chantiers de l'Atlantique) on the containment system, while Finland's Wärtsilä provided the propulsion technology. Today, several commercially available alternative ship propulsion systems are being evaluated. Changing the propulsion system of the tanker will affect the overall ship design, as the different engine types vary structurally, in size and shape, thereby influencing the cargo-carrying capacity. Different methods of dealing with boil-off gas will also affect the transportation economics.

Larger LNG ship sizes

Larger LNG tanker designs are on the drawing board, with several under construction at shipyards[23]. The latest series of tanker orders have cargo-carrying capacities up to 266,000 m^3—a step increase of over 80% in tanker's cargo-carrying capacity from the conventional 145,000 m^3 ships. Such large tankers offer larger economies of scale (i.e., a reduced ton-per-mile cost of transporting the LNG), as well as larger LNG deliveries. These larger tankers will require appropriate accommodation at the loading and unloading facilities. Until recently, the industry's standard was for tankers in the 125,000–155,000 m^3 range. These capacities were dictated by size restrictions of the existing terminals in the Tokyo Bay area, since Japan is the world's largest LNG importer.

Building much larger ships implies that they will be dedicated to specific new "point-to-point" projects. No terminals today can accommodate these large LNG ships, although new terminals in construction will be able to do so. Unless existing LNG importers reconfigure and reinforce their terminals' berthing facilities, the next generation of LNG tankers will be tied to new projects in development and to being limited to calling at a small universe of terminals.

NOTES

[1] Peebles, Malcolm W. H. 1992. *Natural Gas Fundamentals*. London: Shell International Gas Limited.

[2] Ibid.

[3] Ibid.

[4] Gotaas Larsen was bought by Osprey Maritime in 1997 and was subsequently taken over by Golar LNG in 2001.

[5] Spain's leading shipbuilder, Izar, was created after a merger between Bazan and Astilleros Españoles shipyards.

[6] The Asian financial crisis of the late 1990s is one of the factors responsible for the LNG shipbuilding market. The crisis hit Korea's economy with particular intensity, and the value of the Korean currency, the won, declined by more than 50%. This gave a tremendous boost to the competitiveness of Korean shipyards, which saw their labor costs in U.S. dollars decline significantly.

[7] The structure of the consortium is as follows: China Ocean Shipping Company (25.5%), China Merchants (25.5%), NWS project participants (30.0%), Energy Transportation Group (3.0%), Shenzhen Marine (8.0%), and Guangdong Yeudian (8.0%).

[8] Moss Maritime is a leader in marine technology. Their expertise lies within the fields of special-purpose vessels, platforms, and floaters for the offshore industry.

[9] Today, the Kvaerner Masa yard is owned by AKER Kvaerner ASA.

[10] There are other reasons why Japanese yards opted for Moss licenses. There is a lot more automation involved in building Moss vessels, and this containment system has proven to be safer and stronger than membrane ships. (Safety is a big concern for LNG ships calling and operating in the Tokyo Bay area.)

[11] The Asian crisis in 1999 had an adverse impact on the Korean economy, slowing the nation's LNG demand and Kogas's demand for new LNG term supplies. Korea's LNG shipbuilding industry came to a halt after years spent gearing up their yards to accommodate all of South Korea's LNG imports. This standstill of domestic orders motivated the local shipyards to expand their marketing horizons and penetrate the international LNG shipbuilding scene full steam ahead.

[12] The shipyard price is $160 million. The owner will incur additional costs throughout the building process: during the construction, the cost of finance (i.e., interest), which varies according to the financial package, yet is typically between $10 million and $15 million; and toward the end, the deck and outfitting costs, in the region of $6–$7 million.

[13] The original trade route was about 1,500 nautical miles, from Algeria to England. Today a standard trip from the Middle East to Japan is about 6,400 nautical miles.

[14] As of the first quarter of 2006.

[15] Of the five mainland LNG terminals in the United States, only two were in operation at the time: the Distrigas LNG receiving terminal, in Boston, and the Trunkline LNG receiving terminal at Lake Charles, Louisiana. The two mothballed terminals were Cove Point, Maryland, and Elba Island, Georgia. The fifth—Excelerate Energy's Gulf Gateway offshore facility, off Louisiana—did not yet exist.

[16] The consortium that has the largest LNG fleet in the world in terms of cubic capacity is the MOL (Mitsui OSK Line), NYK (Nippon Yusen Kaisha Line), and K-Line (Kawasaki Kisen Kaisha Line) Consortium, also known as the J3 (Japanese Three).

[17] Golar LNG intends to provide a floating storage and regasification unit for the proposed Offshore Floating LNG Terminal Toscana (OLT) in Italy. It also has a preliminary agreement for capacity at TORP Terminal LP's proposed Bienville Offshore Energy Terminal in the U.S. Gulf of Mexico.

[18] The cost of ships ordered for specific projects fall into a different category, since they are generally considered as sunk costs. Indeed, LNG vessels are integral in such arrangements, in which projects are characterized by large capital costs, relatively long lead times, and long-term contracts between buyers and sellers.

[19] The only ship with an onboard reliquefaction facility currently trading is the 135,000 m^3 LNG *Jamal*, delivered in 2000 by Mitsubishi Heavy Industries and trading between Oman and Japan.

[20] The cost of the calorific value (in MMBtu) of boil-off has historically been less than that of fuel oil. The method of valuing boil-off has always been disputed. Some will argue that since it would otherwise be lost, there is no value, merely a savings on fuel costs. Others impose a fixed or variable cost based on LNG's FOB value or based on the resale value of the cargo at its destination.

[21] Peebles, *Natural Gas Fundamentals*.

[22] The closest the industry has come to the breach of a cargo containment system was in 1978, when the fully laden El Paso *Paul Kayser* grounded near Gibraltar, causing serious damage to the bottom plating. However, the membrane containment system remained intact, and no cargo was lost.

[23] As of December 2005, the Qatar Gas Transportation Company (Nakilat) was the only entity assembling fleets of larger LNG ships for Qatari export projects aimed at northern Europe, the United Kingdom, and the United States.

LNG IMPORT TERMINALS 7

INTRODUCTION

The LNG receiving or import terminal is the final link in the LNG chain and the point of connection to the consumers. While liquefaction plants act as enormous refrigerators to convert natural gas into a liquid, LNG receiving terminals turn the liquid back into gas by warming it up, then sending it into the pipeline system.

The regasification and sendout processes are relatively straightforward. The marine infrastructure and storage tanks of an LNG import terminal and a liquefaction plant are essentially identical. However, while all LNG import terminals generally have the same components, their specific design and layout varies, depending on such factors as the nearby pipeline takeaway capacity; the size of LNG tankers expected to use the terminal; proximity to deep water; the topography, geotechnical characteristics, and surroundings of the site; the applicable regulatory regime; and the choice of vaporization technology.

STORAGE AND SENDOUT CAPACITY

A terminal's storage and sendout capacity is a function of many variables. Storage size will be dictated by available land area, LNG tanker sizes, sales profiles (including seasonality, interruptibility, and access to alternative gas supplies), regulatory considerations, and commercial drivers for the terminal owner. Vaporization capacity and technology have similar variables to consider. For example, if the terminal is located near existing gas pipelines, the terminal's ultimate capacity will be a function of the takeaway capacity of the nearby pipelines and the ability to expand that capacity. If the market is highly localized, the capacity becomes a function of the local market.

For example, the LNG receiving terminals on the U.S. Gulf Coast feature large storage and sendout capacities of up to 4.0 Bcf/d (41 Bcm/y), given their location in a primary gas supply area and their resulting proximity to large-capacity gas transmission lines.[1] The Caribbean terminals, in Puerto Rico and the Dominican Republic, are quite small, as they are limited to serving attached modestly sized power-generating plants. An example of a midsized terminal is Suez's facility in the Northeast, at Everett, Massachusetts, which has 4.35 Bcf (165,000 cubic meters) of storage available for tanker discharge and an average regasified LNG sendout capacity of 0.5 Bcf/d (5 Bcm/y), with peak capacity in excess of 0.7 Bcf/d (7 Bcm/y). The Everett terminal is located in the gas market area, where the transmission lines are smaller than they would be in the Gulf of Mexico, but Everett is also connected to a 1,600 MW power plant, which expands its capacity quite significantly.

LNG import terminals can be expanded relatively easily. The simplest and most cost-effective way is by adding more vaporizers. However, if a significant quantity of new vaporization capacity is added, the LNG terminal developer may be faced with the expense of building one or more new storage tanks. This will not be a major problem as long as there is enough space on the terminal site for the new tank. However, LNG storage tanks take a comparatively long time to build and are the most expensive component of a facility. An LNG terminal owner may also need to build more unloading facilities to handle increases in LNG tanker traffic. Before doing so, the owner must seek the consent of the relevant port authority and must ensure that the increase in LNG tanker traffic does not interfere with existing port operations.

The Everett, Massachusetts, terminal again illustrates the incremental expansion approach. As originally designed and permitted, the terminal's vaporization capacity was limited, and the throughput was around 0.125 Bcf/d (1.3 Bcm/y). By the addition of more vaporization, pipeline connections, and the adjacent power plant, the terminal's throughput capacity was expanded by almost five times. Everett now boasts a baseload sendout capacity of over 0.5 Bcf/d (5 Bcm/y), and a peak capacity of about 1 Bcf/d (10.7 Bcm/y)—all with no increase in storage volume.

An onshore LNG import terminal is depicted in figure 7–1.

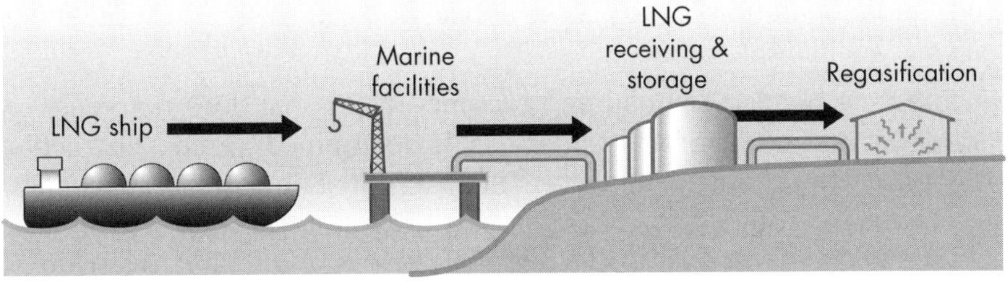

Fig. 7–1. An onshore baseload LNG receiving facility (*Source*: https://www.piersystem.com/clients/crisis_569/ImportTerminal.jpg)

DESIGN AND CONSTRUCTION

A company that intends to develop an LNG import terminal has several hurdles to face before breaking ground at the preferred site. It must ensure that the proposed location is consistent with local, state, and national environmental and safety guidelines and must go through an often rigorous licensing and permitting process (for details, see chapter 17). The sponsor must decide on the proposed facility's design and operational parameters. In the case of utilities developing LNG terminals, the decision to add a facility or expand an existing one may also be subject to an economic review by the regulatory authorities, who will determine whether the facility is necessary for the utility to meet its customers' requirements and if so, will then permit the utility to include the terminal in its rate base and allow the recovery of the corresponding costs and investment returns. The same approach also holds for third-party open-access terminals, although the standard of customer need is often achieved simply by showing contracts with parties who wish to make use of the facility to unload and process their LNG.

Generally, after an initial feasibility study, the sponsor hires a recognized engineering firm to perform detailed FEED work, to create a design for an LNG terminal that fits their requirements and provides sufficient detail for regulatory review and approval. Once the design has been agreed on and the requisite licenses have been obtained from the regulatory agencies, the sponsor commissions an EPC contractor to build the marine facilities, vaporization system, and LNG storage tanks. The permitting and licensing schedule can vary between countries and within the same country, depending on the degree of central versus regional involvement, political support or opposition, and the complexity of the site. Licensing can take between one year and five years following formal application submittal, and the feasibility study and preparation of the license application can easily add another one to two years in front of that.

The time needed to build an LNG import terminal does not generally vary with the size of the facility. Rather, it is determined by the construction schedule for the storage tanks, which are a terminal's most time-consuming and expensive component. Aboveground LNG storage tanks usually take between two and three years to build, while belowground tanks may take up to five years to construct.

Large gas and electric utility companies, especially in Japan, were instrumental in developing many of the concepts of LNG import terminal design. Their resulting design philosophy reflects several factors: the generally conservative nature of these utility companies, the critical role that LNG plays in the company's and the country's energy supply, and the magnitude of the downstream investments in gas distribution systems and power generation facilities. This design philosophy emphasized the importance of large storage capacities relative to throughput rates and duplication of critical components, aimed at ensuring the availability of 100% of the terminal's design throughput except under very unusual circumstances. However, in places where LNG plays a less critical role in the overall energy supply picture, such as Europe and the United States, the needs for maximum redundancy and excess storage capacity have been less valued and have led to the adoption of a less conservative design philosophy. In all cases, safety and security of the facilities are an important consideration and usually result in the installation of multiple (redundant) safety systems.

The design parameters for an onshore baseload LNG import terminal must accommodate two modes of operation: vaporization, in which LNG is pumped from storage and then vaporized, treated, and distributed to off-site customers based on market demand; and LNG tanker unloading, during which the contents of an LNG tanker are off-loaded into terminal storage while normal vaporization and sendout rates are maintained. LNG tanker unloading typically takes between 24 and 36 hours; maximum LNG boil-off vapors are generated during this operation. This in turn establishes the design of the terminal vapor recovery system. The sizing of individual equipment components and the degree of redundancy and operating flexibility depend primarily on how the regasified LNG is utilized, as well as on variations in the daily and seasonal load demand pattern, the size and frequency of the LNG tankers calling at the terminal, downstream gas quality considerations, regulatory requirements, and the physical location of the terminal.

A growing number of LNG import terminals supply regasified LNG for power generation. In these projects, regasified LNG-fired CCGT power plants are located adjacent to the receiving terminal, thereby providing an anchor market for the LNG receiving facility itself. Depending on the specific economics and operating rules of the power market, these plants often operate in the midrange supply segment, running at 50%–70% load factors.[2]

Even if the power plant is used for baseload supply, regasified LNG demand is subject to seasonal and daily demand variations. Adequate LNG storage must be provided to balance average annual import supply with short-term changes in demand. Vaporization equipment must also have sufficient capacity to meet peak load demand.

COST

More than 60% of the cost of an LNG receiving terminal is associated with the construction of LNG storage tanks, marine and off-loading facilities, and safety systems. Although the cost of these facilities is essentially fixed, regardless of annual capacity, it is difficult to give a meaningful figure for the cost of an LNG terminal. That is because factors unique to the location of the facility play a disproportionate role in determining the final construction costs, including the following:

- Local geologic considerations (e.g., soil stability and seismic activity) and the need to tailor infrastructure to them. For example, LNG import terminal sponsors that plan to build a facility in an earthquake-prone area may want the LNG storage tanks to be buried. This would lead to significant extra costs, as additional civil work[3] must be done to isolate the tanks from the surrounding soil and especially from the incursion of water.[4]
- The cost of real estate. In Japan, where waterfront space is tight, terminals are often built on filled land, which is not only expensive but also subject to additional engineering considerations.
- Site layout, regulatory, and safety considerations. These will dictate the number and size of storage tanks and choice of single-containment, full-containment, or below ground tanks, which can result in cost variances of up to five times for the same overall storage capacity.
- Local and regional labor and construction costs. For example, labor costs are generally higher in the United States or the United Kingdom than in China or India.

- The choice of vaporization technology. Open-rack vaporizers are more expensive than gas-fired vaporizers but cost much less to operate.
- The use of local power supplies, or the development of dedicated power generation within the terminal facility.
- The need for downstream facilities to tie into the pipeline grid, including pipelines and gas treatment and odorization equipment.
- The marine environment. For instance, the need to dredge the site's marine facilities to accommodate LNG tankers and dispose of the dredge material can impose significant costs; also, the need to place the berth at an extended distance, away from the storage tanks, can result in much higher costs.

Additional project costs could be incurred by licensing and permitting activities needed to accommodate local residential/environmental concerns about the project. Upgrading or building infrastructure—such as roads, pipelines, or electric transmission—at the designated site could also add to the project cost.

MAIN COMPONENTS OF LNG IMPORT TERMINALS

All baseload onshore LNG import facilities, regardless of terminal sponsor or design contractor, basically work the same way and feature the same components, as follows:

- Tanker berthing and unloading facilities
- Storage tanks
- Regasification system
- Facilities to handle vapor and boil-off gas
- High-pressure LNG pumps
- Metering and pressure regulation station
- Gas delivery infrastructure
- Gas odorization, calorific value control (some terminals, mainly in Japan, are equipped with LPG unloading, storage, and vaporization facilities enabling LPG blending to raise the heating value of the vaporized LNG; in other regions, nitrogen or air injection equipment is used to achieve the opposite effect), and LNG truck loading facilities (at some terminals)

A schematic of an LNG import terminal is presented in figure 7–2.

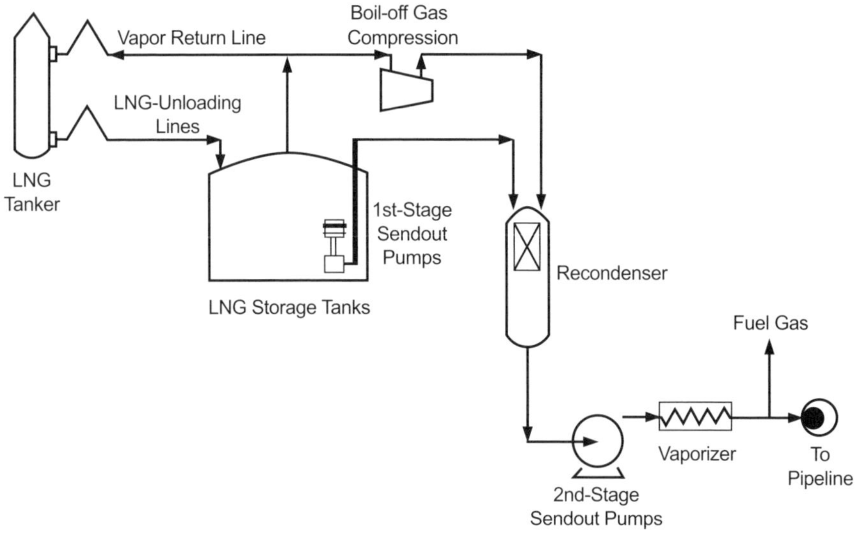

Fig. 7–2. LNG import terminal gas flow (*Source:* M.W. Kellogg)

Marine facilities

An LNG import terminal must have good port access to locate the dedicated facilities to unload LNG carriers. Typically, one or more berths will be built alongside the LNG import terminal, provided that sufficient water depth is available (or can be dredged) to receive and unload the LNG tankers. Alternatively, a jetty is built to connect the berth to the shore. The water depth required at the berth is 12 meters for a 130,000 m^3 LNG tanker. Deeper water is needed to accommodate larger LNG tankers, which have a bigger loaded draft; for example, a 265,000 m^3 LNG tanker would need a water depth of at least 13 meters.

Each unloading berth is equipped with several unloading arms that connect the LNG tanker's manifolds with the unloading line. They incorporate articulated joints to allow for different sizes of LNG tankers and for the LNG tanker's movements as the tide rises and falls. The arms are often equipped with automatic emergency release couplings, which ensure rapid disconnection in the event of an emergency situation. Unloading line(s) run from the arms to the storage tanks, where the LNG is stored until it is needed for vaporization. These dedicated lines are usually made of stainless steel or some other material, such as aluminum, that can safely withstand the extremely low temperatures of LNG. They are insulated to reduce heat transfer from the atmosphere to the LNG as much as possible. Unloading lines also include expansion loops, which permit the lines to expand and contract as they warm up and cool down without overstressing the lines.

Most terminals have more than one unloading line, so that the lines can be kept cold between cargo deliveries by continuously circulating LNG through the unloading lines from storage to the berth and back again. If only one unloading line is installed, then a separate circulation line is required to feed LNG into the unloading line to keep it cold. LNG vapor is carried back to the LNG tanker's cargo system by separate vapor return line(s), to ensure that the vapor pressure in both the shore and the LNG tanker's storage tanks is maintained within the design operating parameters for these tanks. The marine facilities may include a vapor return blower to maintain the pressure in the LNG tanker's cargo tanks. LNG is unloaded from the LNG tankers into the storage tanks by using the LNG pumps installed in the LNG tanker's cargo tanks. Where the unloading line is very long, additional booster pumps may be installed between the LNG tanker and the shore tanks to assist in the cargo-pumping operation.

LNG off-loading typically requires 24 hours. While the actual cargo-pumping operations may require only 12–16 hours, the mooring of the LNG tanker, the connection of the unloading arms, and the disconnection and unmooring prior to departure all add to the time involved. To this can be added the time needed to conform to harbor and port restrictions at LNG import terminals, where LNG tankers compete with other established, often high-density, port traffic. For example, countries such as Japan impose a nighttime transit ban on tankers carrying hazardous cargoes. All such tankers arriving at the discharge port in the evening must wait outside the bay or harbor channel before traveling to their discharge ports in a convoy—with the requisite safety and security distance between each LNG tanker in the convoy. Consequently, port transit restrictions can add several hours to the LNG tanker's overall off-loading time.

Storage tanks

The purpose of an LNG storage tank is to maintain the liquid at –163°C before it is vaporized and delivered into the local gas market. The tanks at an import terminal are exactly the same as those at a liquefaction plant (for details, see chapter 5). An LNG import terminal developer is faced with two important decisions related to storage: how much to build and the type of storage tank required. Because an LNG import terminal is often the sole or primary source of gas supply for a region, it is essential for its sponsors to thoroughly assess the facility's storage requirements to enable it to meet unexpected surges in demand, as well as such unforeseen events as a delay in a cargo delivery. The selection of a tank design and the associated foundation design will be influenced by several factors, especially the geology, topography, and soil conditions of the site; seismic concerns; the quantity of land available; regional safety regulations, especially with regard to vapor dispersion and exclusion zone requirements;[5] and, of course, aesthetic considerations.

Design. When it comes to choosing a design for their LNG import terminal's storage facilities, owners face two main decisions. First, they must decide whether to build storage tanks that are aboveground or that are partially or fully buried. Second, they must decide whether to build single- or full-containment storage tanks.

Buried (in-ground) tanks are usually membrane tanks and consist of a pre-stressed concrete outer wall and an inner layer constructed of load-bearing foam, usually made of polyurethane and polyvinyl chloride (PVC), over which is laid a thin, cryogenic steel membrane, which is in contact with the LNG. The insulation system allows transfer of the membrane loads to the outer wall. A slurry wall is first installed to prevent influx of underground water; the main tank is built inside it. Examples of this design are found in Japan.

In-pit tanks are similar to full-containment aboveground tanks but are constructed belowground in a concrete-lined pit. The inner tank is constructed of 9% nickel/steel, and the outer tank is constructed of pre-stressed concrete. This design is particularly applicable to locations subject to high seismic activity, since it can essentially be a freestanding structure, while retaining the safety benefits of an in-ground installation. Tanks of this design have been constructed in Belgium, Greece, and Japan.

In-ground tanks are considerably more expensive than aboveground tanks, with soil conditions, seismic considerations, and other environmental factors having a great effect on the cost. If the LNG terminal is relatively close to populated areas (which is true of many Asian LNG receiving facilities), addressing the nearby community's aesthetic sensibilities may also factor into a decision to bury the tanks. Ironically, in-ground tanks may offer a lower measure of protection to their surroundings since a full tank fire, which might result from a total roof failure (often the worst case assumed by the regulatory authorities), has a greater thermal impact with an in-ground tank than an aboveground tank.

Where land is at a premium, the developer may opt for a full-containment storage tank, thereby eliminating the need to build an impoundment and berm around the tank. As a rule, this impoundment will be capable of containing the contents of one full tank plus a reserve margin in case of a leak or spill involving the entire contents of the tank. Full-containment tanks reduce the tank's footprint and, consequently, the amount of land needed to build the terminal. However, recent changes to U.S. regulatory policy now requires the use of an impoundment around full-containment tanks as an additional safety measure. While full-containment tanks are considerably more expensive than single-containment tanks, they are generally considered to be safer, have much smaller thermal and vapor exclusion zones than other tanks, and can be placed on smaller sites.

Safety. For aboveground tanks, secondary containment is built around each tank, to contain the whole tank's contents if it fails for any reason (the inner tank being the primary containment). These walls are capable of withstanding extremely low temperatures. In the case of a full-containment tank, the outer, pre-stressed concrete wall fulfills this function; for a single-containment tank, the outer steel wall cannot withstand the cryogenic temperatures, and a surrounding impoundment area and berm act as the containment. For obvious reasons, retaining walls are not necessary for tanks that are totally in-ground. All types of tank must be surrounded by gas and fire detectors.

Tank foundations are designed on the basis of local earthquake criteria and soil conditions to avoid tank failures in earthquakes. All tanks are equipped with temperature monitors to ensure that any failure of the insulation can be measured and rectified. Tank foundations are equipped with heaters to ensure that the ground remains at a constant temperature and to avoid frost heaves, which could damage the bottom insulation or foundations. Tanks are also equipped with level devices that detect any shifts or uneven settlement of soils that could also threaten the tank's integrity.

Capacity. More conservative utility companies favor large margins in LNG storage volume relative to annual throughput. As a rule, however, LNG receiving terminals must have sufficient storage capacity to accept a full cargo of LNG from the largest LNG tanker expected to call at the terminal, plus a margin to allow for delays in shipping schedules. If there is a large variation in sendout rates between summer and winter and the LNG supply portfolio does not accommodate this fluctuation, then the terminal may require additional storage capacity in order to cope with seasonal demands, including extreme cold weather.[6] In addition, the terminal's storage capacity must be sufficient to deal with short term fluctuations between cargo deliveries and sendout rates.

Also, consideration may be given for adding storage capacity to allow for an early cargo delivery or to accommodate a lower-than-expected sendout rate. The tank must also be sized to hold a heel—that is, the level of LNG that is needed to maintain the operation of the tank's primary pumps, which are set in wells in the floor of the tank. Beyond the level of storage capacity to accommodate LNG tanker sizes, seasonal storage rates, and heels, the choice of maximum storage capacity becomes less of a science and more of an exercise of judgment and commercial objectives. In a world where LNG may become a more readily traded commodity, LNG storage could take on additional value for opportunistic reasons and trading considerations, and may justify the addition of more storage. Conversely, the traded-LNG world might afford Asian utilities the opportunity to meet seasonal LNG demands with less storage than has been the case.

Low-pressure LNG pumps are installed inside or close to the LNG storage tanks. LNG delivered by these pumps is circulated through the unloading lines to maintain cryogenic temperatures when no LNG tankers are unloading. However, the primary function of these pumps is to feed LNG to the high-pressure pumps, which raise the pressure of the liquid to a little above the desired gas sendout pressure before sending the liquid to the vaporizers. Because the capital and operating costs of LNG pumps are much lower than those of gas compressors, LNG is pumped at high pressure, typically 50–80 bars, into the vaporizers. The gas then needs no further compression before it is sent into the region's pipeline grid or fed to

Quality concerns. Variations in LNG quality in the storage tank may occur as a result of weathering (changes in LNG composition within the tank due to the preferential boil-off of light components, e.g., nitrogen and methane, when the LNG sits for extended periods of time without withdrawal) or off-loading LNG of a different quality (density) than the LNG in the terminal storage tank (known as the tank heel). This is usually the result of receiving LNG from different supply sources.

If LNG cargoes of different densities are stored in the same tank and are not adequately mixed, stratification (separation into distinct layers of different densities) may occur. If it does, it creates an opportunity for tank rollover—the sudden mixing of the two layers as their densities equalize because of heat input from outside and tank dynamics. Rollover is a safety concern because a large amount of boil-off gas is generated rapidly and may cause structural damage to the tank.[7] Several LNG buyers, mainly in Japan, avoid this problem by segregating LNG storage according to supply source. In other words, they dedicate storage tanks to specific suppliers—Brunei, Indonesia, Malaysia, and so on—thereby obviating the possibility of mixing LNG supplies with different physical characteristics. However, not every LNG terminal owner has the economic means or sufficient space at the facility to do this. LNG import terminal owners with only limited storage at their disposal can fill their tank(s) from either the top or the bottom and can use the in-tank pumps to promote mixing, thus ensuring that stratification does not occur.

Vaporizers

The vaporizers at an LNG receiving facility transform LNG back into its gaseous state by warming the liquid so that the gas is at or above 5°C (41°F). There are several types of vaporizers in common use, but they all employ the same general principle—extracting heat from water to warm the LNG.

Open-rack vaporizers (ORVs). ORVs take seawater from the adjacent body of water and flow it down the outside of hollow panels,0 and heating the LNG that is flowing up through the interior of the panels in the opposite direction to the water flow (fig. 7–3).[8] The seawater and the vaporization systems must be treated with chemicals to avoid the fouling of the vaporizers with marine growth, and the resulting water discharges carry the treatment chemicals back to the ocean with potential adverse environmental impacts. The discharge of cold seawater into the sea may also cause environmental concerns, since water temperature fluctuations may adversely impact marine flora and fauna. To mitigate this, the seawater is sometimes warmed by an intermediate fluid before being discharged. ORVs are commonly found in Asian terminals but are not used in U.S. terminals owing to the difficulty of permitting the discharges under U.S. environmental regulations. ORVs are usually much larger and more expensive than gas-fired vaporizers, since the lower ambient temperature of the seawater requires a much larger surface area to warm the LNG.

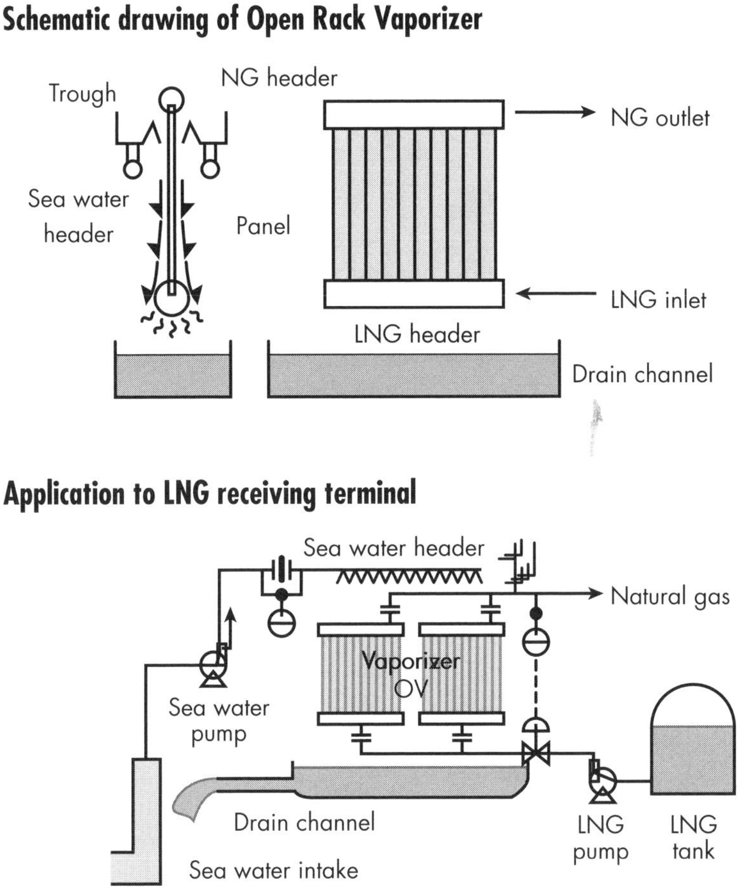

Fig. 7–3. ORV (*Source:* Kobe Steel)

Submerged combustion vaporizers (SCVs). SCVs typically use natural gas to heat the LNG (fig. 7–4). They operate by flowing the products of combustion into a bath of water in which the LNG flows through an immersed bundle of tubes and is converted into gas. In this design, the LNG and the heat flow in the same direction. SCVs use more energy than do ORVs and thus are more expensive to operate, but they create no water discharges. However, gas-fired vaporizers do create air emissions, which can raise other environmental and permitting issues. Typically, gas-fired vaporizers will consume 1.5%–2.5% of their throughput as fuel.[9]

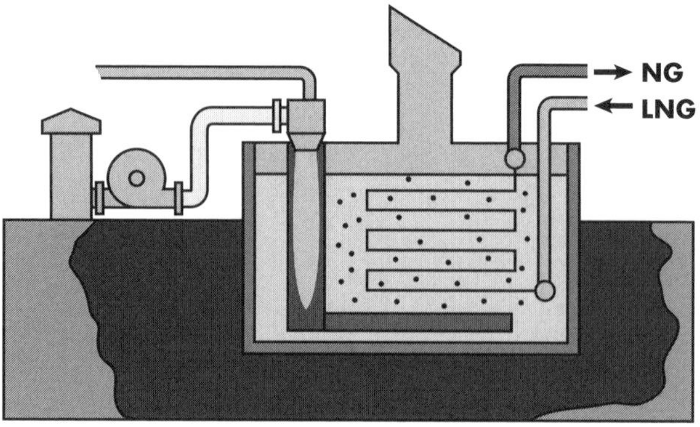

Fig. 7–4. SCV (*Source:* China Petroleum Corporation)

Shell and tube vaporizers (STVs). STVs are generally smaller in size and are cost competitive with SCV systems, but they require the provision of an external heat source (fig. 7–5). Heat is supplied to the LNG vaporizer by a closed circuit with a suitable heat transfer medium, typically a water/glycol mix that is heated in a conventional boiler. These vaporizer systems usually require a stable LNG flow at design and turndown conditions, with provisions to prevent freeze-up within the vaporizer at low flow rates. In import terminals, variable flow rates can be achieved by using multiple STVs. STVs are now being used for specialized applications, particularly where an alternative source of heat is available, such as from a power plant or a cold energy utilization process.[10] In these applications, an intermediate fluid between the heat source and the vaporizer will be used. STVs have similar fuel consumption requirements as SCVs, but their air emissions are easier to control.

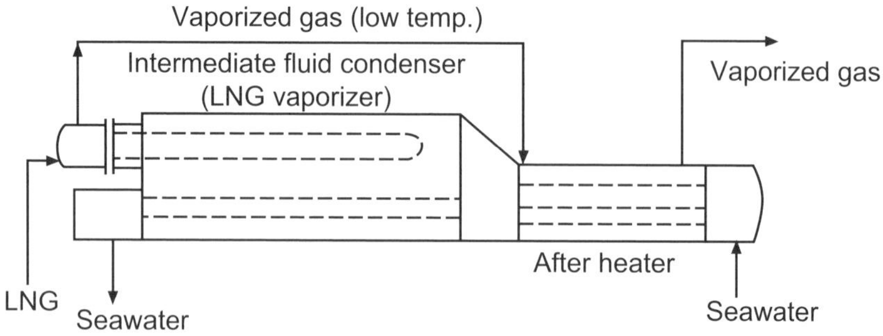

Fig. 7–5. STV (*Source:* Janusz Tarlowski and John Sheffield, M.W. Kellogg, and Charles Durr, David Coyle, and Himanshu Patel, KBR, "LNG Import Terminals—Recent Developments," p. 10)

Ambient air–heated vaporizers. These utilize ambient air, in either a natural draft mode or a forced draft mode, to vaporize LNG. Such vaporizers are suitable for service in warm climates and where plot space is available. They are manufactured by conventional air-cooler manufacturers and have been used at the Petronet LNG terminal, at Dahej, India. They require large sites, as the equipment footprint is also large. The advantage of these vaporizers is that they have the least environmental impact of any design, with no air or water discharges.

Combined heat and power (CHP) unit with gas-fired vaporizers. To decrease the gas consumption of gas-fired vaporizers, as well as to increase the efficiency and economics of the entire regasification process, the receiving terminal can be modified to use a cogeneration concept that offers energy savings and environmental advantages. This has been implemented at Belgium's Zeebrugge LNG terminal cogeneration project. The heart of the CHP facility is a gas turbine that generates electric power. The hot exhaust gases from the turbine pass through a heat recovery tower and transfer their heat to raise the temperature of a closed hot water circuit. This hot water will then be circulated and injected in the water bath of the vaporizers and will transfer its heat to regasify the LNG.[11] This applies to both SCVs and STVs.

Most terminals equipped with ORVs also have installed SCVs. The combination and number of vaporizers are a function of the facility's expected sendout profile, the quality and temperature of the available seawater, regulatory limitations, gas prices, and other factors. For example, an LNG import terminal may use energy-efficient seawater vaporizers for the baseload component of terminal sendout and install a gas-fired vaporizer to meet short-term demand fluctuations and act as backup to enhance system reliability.

Boil-off gas facilities

Because LNG is a cryogenic liquid, a significant amount of insulation is required for all components of an LNG terminal, especially the storage tanks and liquid lines. Generally, boil-off is about 0.05% per day of tank volume or less. All LNG terminals are equipped with systems that either capture the boil-off gas and send it into a reabsorber downstream of the LNG pumps or compress the gas and export it from the plant. During LNG tanker unloading, boil-off rates are elevated by the energy transferred by the pumping process, and a portion of the excess vapor must be returned to the LNG tanker to maintain the appropriate operating pressures in the cargo tanks and shore tanks. If a terminal has a gas-fired power generator, the residual gas may be used to fuel the plant's own needs. Many terminals are provided with heated vents on the storage tanks or a remote flare stack to dispose of boil-off in case of an equipment failure or if the rate of boil-off exceeds the capacity of the terminal's boil-off recovery system.[12]

Gas quality and treatment

The quality of the gas that comes from an LNG import terminal must be consistent with the requirements of downstream gas customers or meet the specifications of the interconnected gas transmission lines, which vary by region and by country. For example, receiving facilities located close to producing regions may be permitted to accept LNG with wide-ranging and fairly high calorific values. For example, the Lake Charles, Louisiana, receiving terminal can import lean LNG from places such as Trinidad, as well as rich LNG from Australia and Qatar. This is because the regasified LNG immediately mingles downstream from the terminal with gas production from the Gulf of Mexico and is often treated in NGL-processing plants before being sent on to market. But LNG import terminals that are located in market areas or that serve buyers with specific gas quality restrictions must closely monitor and, where necessary, adjust the quality of the regasified LNG that is delivered into the local grid.

The tariff specifications of the transporting pipelines, in accordance with the requirements of the downstream gas market and the availability of air or nitrogen injection at the terminal, will dictate the range of acceptable calorific (or heating) value of the LNG unloaded (see tables 7–1 and 7–2). For example, the terminal at Cove Point, Maryland, has a tariff requirement that limits unloaded LNG to a Btu content of less than 1,138 Btu per standard cubic foot (scf) (table 7–1), while regasified LNG must have a quality specification not to exceed 1,100 Btu/scf when it enters the pipeline. Therefore, capacity holders at Cove Point must ensure that the LNG they import into and send out from the facility meets these established parameters. These limits can restrict the capacity holders' LNG supply options.

Table 7–1. Maximum calorific values at onshore U.S. regasification facilities (*Source:* FERC, company Web sites)

Regasification Facility	Calorific Value (Btu/scf)
Cove Point, Maryland	1,138
Elba Island, Georgia	1,075
Everett, Massachusetts	1,175
Lake Charles, Louisiana	1,200

Table 7–2. Examples of average heating values by country (*Source:* EIA/DOE)

Examples of Average Heating Values by Exporter	
Country	**Heating Value (Btu/scf)**
Algeria	1,078–1,118
Trinidad	1,045

To ensure that the calorific value of the gas supplied to end users falls within the prescribed parameters, it may be necessary to dilute or enrich the vaporized LNG before it leaves the terminal. For example, the owner of the Cove Point, Maryland, terminal installed Btu-stabilization equipment that uses nitrogen injection to reduce the regasified LNG's Btu level. The additional cost of this treatment is billed to the capacity holders. The pipelines located downstream from Cove Point impose a nitrogen limit of 4% on gas received by their systems. The Everett, Massachusetts, terminal similarly treats regasified LNG but uses air, rather than nitrogen, as a result of the tariff requirements of the downstream pipelines.

U.S. and European authorities are making considerable progress towards developing uniform standards for gas interchangeability—the ability to replace a given gas supply with another gas without affecting end-use performance—within their respective markets. The issue is becoming ever more important as the two markets face the prospect of large and diverse gas and LNG import requirements. Despite differences, the changes are widening the range of acceptable supplies for LNG exporters selling into Atlantic Basin markets. While the quality situation in the Atlantic Basin is becoming increasingly standardized, the same cannot be said for the Pacific. Asian producers must balance the needs of the region's traditional rich gas market specifications against the lean gas market opportunities emerging in North America, particularly California.

In the United States, FERC (which has taken the lead in dealing with the gas quality issue) is widely expected to turn the recommendations published in the Natural Gas Council's (NGC) February 2005 "White Paper on Interchangeability" into a three-year interim industry standard. The central recommendation of the NGC paper is the proposal to use the Wobbe index—a more widely accepted measure of gas quality and predictor of burner performance, using both the composition of the gas stream and its specific gravity to compute the quality—to measure gas interchangeability.[13] As proposed by the NGC, gas quality would be limited to a range of plus or minus 4% from the historical Wobbe number in the local market, with a maximum Wobbe number of 1,400 corresponding to a limit of 1,110 Btu/scf (all based on calculations of higher heating value [HHV]).

In Europe, the industry group EASEE-Gas published a "Common Business Practice" (CBP) in January 2005, in an attempt to harmonize the various national gas quality standards, providing the basis for a more uniform pan-European standard for gas imports and cross-border trade. The EASEE-Gas CBP recommended a Wobbe index range of 13.60–15.81 kWh/m^3 (a Wobbe number of about 1,250 to 1,450). A 13.76 kWh/m^3 lower limit will be used initially, until further work on safety consequences of a 13.60 kWh/m^3 limit is completed. This band encompasses most of the existing national standards and is wider than the proposed U.S. limits. The European group has concluded, however, that full implementation will not be feasible before October 1, 2010. The changes will require a combination of national legislation, appliance management, maintenance practices, and blending that differs between the various national gas systems. The question of who will pay for gas quality adjustments also remains open.

Metering and pressure regulation station

Before leaving the terminal, the regasified LNG passes through a pressure-regulating and metering station to measure the gas. The gas may be odorized (e.g., with mercaptan, a sulfur-based additive) to aid in the detection of any leaks in the gas transportation system or customer appliances.

SAFETY AND SECURITY

The safety and security guidelines that govern the operation of LNG import terminals are very important, especially since the facilities are often located in or close to major urban areas. This became an even more sensitive issue after September 11, 2001. When what constitutes a terrorist target was reassessed, energy producing, transportation, and delivery infrastructure were all near the top of the list. As far as the LNG industry overall is concerned the threat of a terrorist attack on an LNG import terminal may represent a new *risk* to the safety and security of the surrounding communities, the terminal staff, and the facility, but the *hazards* and associated *consequences* remain very much the same as those of an accident.[14]

The design of the terminal, the equipment and materials used, and the operational procedures are geared toward risk reduction. This is achieved through prevention of spills of LNG and leaks of regasified LNG and, in the unlikely event that they would occur, through the management of the consequences (i.e., ensuring that any spills are contained and dispersed safely).

Safety systems are designed to be both active and passive. Examples of active systems include gas, fire, and smoke detectors, shut-down systems, and firefighting systems. Passive systems include the installation of spill control channels leading to sumps, where LNG can be contained and its boil-off rate (and resulting vapor production) can be reduced to low levels.

The locations of and distances between the tanks, vaporizers, liquid and vapor lines, and other facilities are determined by local regulations and/or by recognized international codes of practice. Distances to the nearest property lines and to populations off site are also assessed and controlled. In the event of a spill or fire at the terminal, having an adequate distance between the terminal and the surrounding area ensures that the gas vapor will have dispersed to below flammable limits before it leaves the facility property; it also ensures that any fire will be far enough away so that the public would have time to move to a safe distance and avoid the risk of being burned in such an incident. In the U.S. regulatory system, the safety of the terminal is managed by the imposition of exclusion zones for vapor and thermal risks that are calculated on the basis of the specific design of the terminal and its site and within which certain activities are prohibited. In Europe, regulatory authorities generally require that each facility be subject to a specific hazard analysis developed just for that facility, and there are fewer prescribed standards.

All LNG terminals have security systems to ensure that unauthorized people do not have access to the facility or the LNG tankers berthed there. The arrival, departure, and berthing of LNG tankers will normally be controlled by the local harbor authority or by the operating company, as appropriate, and each port will impose differing levels of safety and security for the LNG tankers. Since 9/11, there has been increased public and political attention focused on the safety and security of LNG terminals and the associated shipping, and regulators have responded by increasing safety and security assessments and requirements.

The result of this focus on safety has been an impressive operating record, with no incidents at LNG terminals ever resulting in any injury to the public or to adjacent property since the Cleveland accident in 1944. Fatalities and injuries to terminal staff have been few and far between and rarely have had anything to do with the LNG itself. The same has also been the case for the LNG tankers in the adjacent port and waterways.

PEAKSHAVING LNG PLANTS

All import terminals are designed to send out gas throughout the year in baseload service, although daily sendout rates can vary significantly. A peakshaving facility sends out gas only for a few months, weeks, or even days of the year. Some LNG import terminals have facilities for loading trucks to deliver LNG to smaller, satellite storage and regasification plants in the market area. Whereas LNG terminals must be sited on or close to the coast, peakshaving plants are located strategically from a market standpoint, usually near critical areas of gas distribution infrastructure and in regions that experience extreme demand peaks, such as the northern United States. While most peakshaving plants are generally smaller than their import terminal counterparts, they employ essentially the same design and technology concepts, with the exception of the marine unloading infrastructure.

FUTURE TRENDS

Onshore baseload LNG receiving facilities represent the vast majority of the world's LNG import capacity. In recent years, however, there has been great interest in building offshore LNG import infrastructure. Environmental awareness is increasing, and some communities near proposed LNG import terminals have objected to proposals on environmental or safety grounds. Furthermore, the move to offshore siting gained significant support in the United States after 9/11, largely because of widespread fears that LNG tankers and terminals could be potential terrorist targets. Consequently, there were about two dozen proposed offshore import terminal projects worldwide as of mid-2006. The sponsors of these terminals elected to focus development efforts offshore owing to a combination of the following factors:

- "Not in my back yard" (NIMBY). Several companies maintain that reduced proximity to the public would make siting and permitting an offshore LNG terminal less challenging than an onshore project.
- A perceived shortage of suitable onshore sites. As rising gas prices (and in the case of the United States, an eroding domestic supply base) have spurred LNG project development, the large number of potential developers have scrambled for a limited supply of suitable locations for LNG import and regasification facilities. In particular, this has been the case for developers pursuing the regional gas markets available on the densely populated U.S. East and West Coasts.
- Onshore port logistics. Potential issues with port congestion and weather conditions (e.g., fog on the U.S. Gulf Coast) have led

developers to promote reduced shipping voyage times, LNG tanker delay avoidance, and improved terminal availability as potential advantages for offshore LNG import facilities.

- LNG supply chain flexibility and costs. The LNG chain's high capital investment needs and evolving supply patterns have encouraged new supply chain models designed to reduce investment requirements and/or increase operational flexibility (enabling terminal operators to pursue seasonal demands and opportunistic price premiums at multiple locations).
- Regulatory considerations. From the mid-1980s, the U.S. had required onshore terminals to operate on an open-access basis, and this represented a potential obstacle to upstream project sponsors, who sought assured terminal access for their projects' LNG supply. There was also a concern that the U.S. would not license new onshore terminals in a post-9/11 world. In 2002, the U.S amended the Deepwater Port Act to allow for the development of offshore LNG terminals on a proprietary (closed-access) basis, spurring interest in offshore development. Some of that momentum evaporated once FERC began licensing new onshore terminals and allowing them to operate on a proprietary basis (the Hackberry decision, later written into the Energy Policy Act of 2005).

The various offshore LNG import terminals under consideration as of 2006 utilized a diverse range of technologies, mostly drawn from the offshore oil and gas producing industry. Offshore facilities must be designed to accommodate factors such as water depth, characteristics of the ocean floor, and wind and wave conditions. Offshore-terminal solutions include shipboard regasification, floating storage and regasification units (FSRUs), HiLoad, fitting existing offshore platforms with LNG off-loading and regasification equipment, gravity based systems (GBS, which are almost identical to the liquefaction structures described in chapter 5, but with different equipment on the structure), and the Bishop Process.

Shipboard regasification

LNG shipboard regasification vessels typically rely on Advanced Production and Loading's (APL) Submerged Turret Loading (STL) system (fig. 7–6). The STL buoy is connected to a pipeline at the seabed by a flexible riser and floats submerged at a depth of approximately 30 meters. When ready to discharge, the vessel connects to the terminal by pulling the STL buoy into a compartment of the LNG vessel, where it is connected to the STL vessel system.

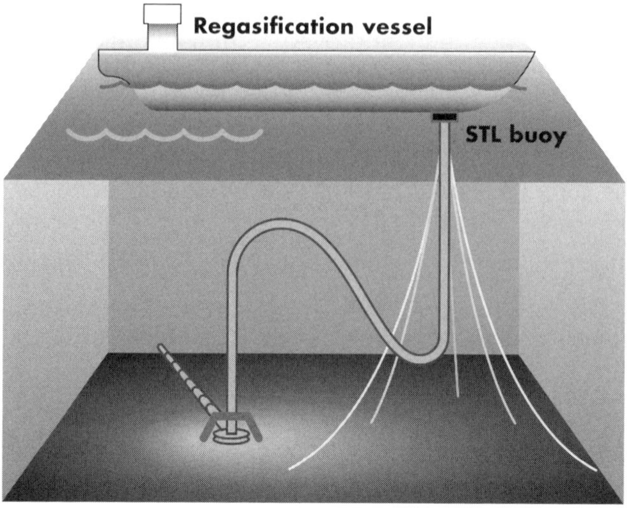

Fig. 7–6. Excelerate's Energy Bridge, an LNG regasification vessel (*Source:* Exmar)

The LNG is regasified on board the vessel, using seawater or a closed-loop freshwater circulation system. Vaporization with seawater takes place in shell and tube exchanges on the vessel deck. The recirculating loop for the STVs is heated using steam from the LNG tanker's boilers. The vaporized gas then passes through the STL system and the riser to a subsea pipeline and then to the onshore gas markets. The first application of the shipboard regasification concept, at Excelerate's Gulf Gateway terminal (fig. 7–6), also required construction of a separate metering platform, as the system ties in to two separate offshore gas gathering systems. Capacity of the shipboard regasification system is 0.4–0.7 Bcf/d (4–7 Bcm/y). Gulf Gateway also represents the first application of the STL buoy system to intermittent high-pressure gas service and is specifically designed for spot trading of LNG cargoes.

The trade-offs of the regasification system, however, include the need for a dedicated fleet of LNG vessels all with turret connections and vaporization equipment. The project owner must factor in additional tonnage for a given trade, as each vessel must remain moored for several days to vaporize its LNG cargo. To maintain an LNG vessel with shipboard regasification in baseload service requires the equivalent of more than one vessel to be attached to the offshore facilities at all times.

Concerns linger around the potential for sloshing damage to partially emptied membrane tanks due to the prolonged mooring periods required in order to discharge a vessel with a shipboard regasification system. (Sloshing would not be a concern for vessels that employ a Moss-type containment system.) The potential for sloshing damage is greatest for membrane tanks between 30% and 70% full; an unloading vessel with a regasification system will spend about three days with tanks in this range. In a variation of this approach, Excelerate has developed a hybrid terminal in Teesport, in northern England, where the shipboard regasification vessel connects to a shoreside manifold and discharges vapor from the vessel into the pipeline system nearby.

While shipboard regasification vessels can make deliveries to existing onshore terminals, only these specially equipped vessels can deliver to the offshore terminals, raising concerns about reliability in the event that a problem should arise with one or more of the shipboard regasification vessels in a given trade.

FSRUs

Floating Storage and Regasification Units (FSRUs) (fig. 7–7) can take two forms: a custom-built vessel or a converted LNG tanker permanently moored at the designated site. Converted LNG tankers use their cargo tanks as storage and are fitted with onboard regasification equipment, just like LNG shipboard regasification vessels. FSRUs generally require a minimum water depth of 150 feet for economic mooring (the FSRU may have one or two mooring points) and riser design. The FSRUs under consideration today will employ either a yoke or a turret system (a towerlike revolving structure) to allow the structure to weather-vane (rotate) around a fixed point, depending on the prevailing water and wind currents. An LNG vessel would unload to the FSRU by using either a side-by-side or an end-to-end connection. The LNG would be stored in the FSRU's tanks before being vaporized on board the structure and piped to shore via subsea gas pipeline.

Fig. 7–7. Moss-type FSRU (*Source:* BHPBilliton)

Custom-built FSRUs to be constructed of steel or reinforced concrete are in the planning stages. However, FSRU LNG import terminal proposals to date call for a steel hull; concrete so far appears to be favored for LNG floating *production* units, rather than *receiving* units. Unlike GBS systems and their concrete FSRU cousins, which are built at a graving dock that is then flooded to permit the units to be floated and towed to their site, steel-hulled FSRUs may be constructed at conventional shipyards. As a result, their construction is expected to be less expensive and less environmentally intrusive than for a GBS. Unlike a GBS, both concrete and steel FSRUs may also be readily moved to another location.

FSRU terminals present certain design and operational issues. One of the biggest is the LNG tanker-berthing process, which will result in motion between the LNG tanker and the FSRU during cargo discharge operations, unlike the rigid mooring arrangements of an onshore terminal. While off-loading through a loading arm or some other special system for the transfer of cryogenic liquid between the LNG tanker and the terminal, the stresses on the transfer system would be significant. Throughput capacities of FSRUs can be similar to onshore terminals, based on the size of the vaporization systems installed on the vessel.

The HiLoad offshore LNG-unloading solution

HiLoad (fig. 7–8) was initially developed as a deepwater tanker-loading system by Houston-based Remora Technology (a subsidiary of Norway's HiTecVision AS) with funding from ConocoPhillips. The HiLoad structure would attach itself to conventional LNG tankers and vaporize the unloaded LNG, injecting the warmed gas directly into pipelines supplying onshore gas markets at rates of 0.4–2.0 Bcf/d (4–21 Bcm/y). This approach eliminates the need for extensive aboveground storage tanks or large, barge-based marine structures for berthing and processing. The technology also eliminates the need for a dedicated LNG fleet, as the system can attach to any conventional LNG tanker of up to 250,000 m^3 capacity. However, HiLoad works best in warm water conditions; water temperatures below 54°F (12°C) would require external sources of heat or yield much reduced sendout rates.

Fig. 7–8. HiLoad offshore LNG import terminal

Adaptation of existing infrastructure

Unlike more traditional offshore LNG terminal solutions, which entail the construction of a custom-designed GBS or FSRU, existing offshore production platforms may offer project sponsors the option of utilizing some existing offshore infrastructure. Depending on the final project configuration, this could significantly reduce the project's capital costs. There is no single blueprint for converting an existing platform into an LNG tanker discharge facility, and the two projects that exist today differ greatly in scope: The proposed Main Pass Energy Hub (fig. 7–9) in the U.S. Gulf of Mexico calls for the development of significant LNG and gas storage infrastructure through the use of facilities originally installed for sulfur mining, while the proposed Clearwater Port, which is located on an offshore gas platform off California, has no storage at all.

Fig. 7–9. Main Pass Energy Hub

GBS systems

Gravity-based structures (GBS) (fig. 7–10) have been employed in offshore oil and gas production for several decades but have yet to be applied to an LNG facility. The chief proponents for this technology have been the supermajors, each of whom has at least one gravity-based project in development. ExxonMobil is the furthest along the development path: together with joint venture partners Qatar Petroleum and Edison Gas, it plans to commission in 2008 its Isola di Porto Levante GBS terminal on the Italian coast near Venice.

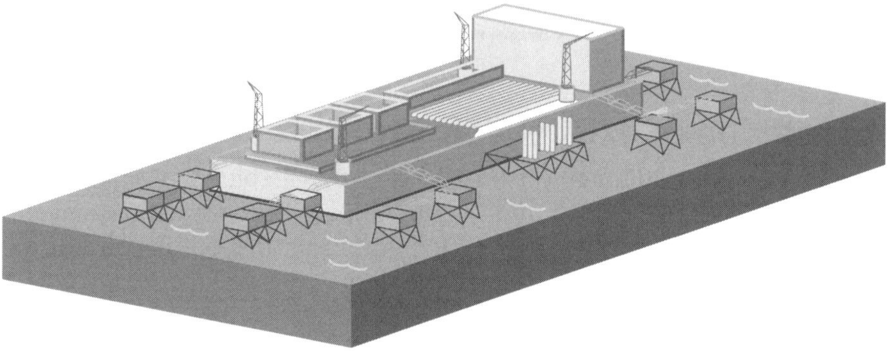

Fig. 7–10. GBS LNG facility (*Source:* ExxonMobil)

GBS units are massive, concrete structures that are prefabricated in a graving dock located onshore. The structures are then floated and towed to the installation location, where their ballast tanks are flooded and the structure is sunk to rest on the sea floor. The deck of the GBS unit is located at an elevation above the sea surface that provides sufficient freeboard for the sea conditions expected at the location. Their use is limited to areas with suitable substrates (i.e., relatively flat, sandy seabed) and water depths ranging from 60 to 85 feet. Because GBS units sit securely on the seafloor, terminal operators would not have to worry about LNG sloshing in the unit's storage tanks during rough weather. Nonetheless, offshore facilities will be highly exposed to the effects of meteorological and oceanographic forces from high winds, waves, and currents. Their fixed design means that LNG tankers cannot weather-vane to account for the prevailing wind and current conditions during docking and unloading, and the docking LNG tankers must also deal with wave interaction (coupling) owing to close proximity to the solid stationary platform. The LNG transfer system (i.e., unloading arms) must also compensate for the relative motion between the terminal and the LNG tanker during the unloading operation.

The Bishop Process

The Bishop Process entails unloading LNG, vaporizing it immediately, and sending the dense-phase gas to underground salt caverns, cryogenic LNG storage tanks—typically the most expensive element in an LNG receiving facility—with less expensive and easily scalable salt cavern gas storage. Salt caverns also offer greater storage capability owing to their bigger size, as well as their increased sendout flexibility. Salt caverns can be formed within salt dome structures by injecting the salt dome with water, to leach the cavern shape, and removing the resultant brine.

Fig. 7–11. Gas processing by use of the Bishop Process Exchanger (*Source:* Conversion Gas Imports)

LNG would be unloaded from the LNG tanker via a floating weather-vaning unloading platform—such as Bluewater's Big Sweep technology. The unloaded LNG is transferred through an undersea cryogenic line to a separate processing platform, where it is pumped directly to either pipeline pressure (nominally 1,000 psig) to meet onshore gas demand, or to the salt cavern storage pressure (between 900 and 2,000 psig, depending on the capacity of the caverns). LNG is converted to a dense phase gas by warming then injected into the salt domes. The Bishop process uses CGI's proprietary Bishop Process Exchanger (fig. 7–11), a robust pipe-in-pipe design that warms the LNG against seawater in a bank of long, parallel rack-mounted exchangers.

Offshore facilities—not the way forward after all?

While offshore LNG terminals offer certain attractions, they are not a simple answer to the challenges of siting onshore infrastructure. Assumptions about the comparative ease of siting and permitting an offshore facility have proven to be false. Although offshore LNG import terminals may seem less visible to the public, they receive the same degree of scrutiny from government regulators and organized interest groups as their onshore counterparts.

Moreover, offshore U.S. LNG terminals have encountered fierce opposition not only from local communities but also from various commercial and recreational fishing interests and the marine authorities on the grounds that their ORVs will harm marine flora and fauna. Terminals proposed for the East and West Coasts as a way of circumventing the apparently impossible task of siting onshore terminals in those regions have encountered opposition every bit as fierce as their onshore counterparts. Offshore facilities are also not immune to concerns from coastal communities on security grounds—namely, that infrastructure will be an attractive target to terrorists. Coastal residents have expressed fears that an explosion resulting from a terrorist attack or an accident at an offshore facility will result in a fireball engulfing coastal settlements. In the final analysis, offshore LNG import terminals face similar siting and permitting challenges as their onshore counterparts.

Offshore terminal developers must also overcome the LNG industry's inherent technical and commercial conservatism. Offshore LNG projects lack a proven operational track record and often call for the combination of multiple novel technologies. There is no assurance that an offshore facility will operate safely and consistently and prove to be commercially viable. Many offshore terminal designs are vulnerable to supply disruptions in heavy weather, in which the LNG tankers may be unable to berth in open water, raising questions as to their viability in sustained baseload service. Excelerate Energy's Gulf Gateway LNG terminal, which opened in March 2005, has not operated long enough for the industry to draw definitive conclusions about the terminal's safety, reliability, or commercial success. Offshore facilities will continue to face scrutiny and skepticism until projects have been up and running for an extended period of time.

Finally, offshore terminals appear to be more costly than their onshore equivalents, just as other offshore oil and gas installations usually are. Increasing opposition to the use of ORVs has effectively eliminated one of the only cost advantages that these terminals enjoyed. Offshore terminals incur the cost of offshore pipelines to deliver their gas to the same market where their onshore competitors are located, especially in areas outside the Gulf of Mexico. The regulatory rationale was lost when the United States began permitting onshore terminals on a proprietary-access basis. Unsurprisingly, many of the early proposals have been dropped entirely or are moving forward very slowly.

NOTES

[1] Multiple new terminals were under construction as of the time of writing, but plans were already in place to significantly expand these facilities. For example, Cheniere is expanding its Sabine Pass terminal from 2.6 Bcf/d to 4 Bcf/d. This would also entail a doubling of storage capacity, for a total of 960,000 cubic meters.

[2] Poten & Partners. C&C *Sourcebook*. New York: Poten & Partners, p. 59.

[3] Jobs that fall under the category of civil work include earthwork, the installation of lighting grounding and underground electrical work and equipment pads, the laying of fabric and the spreading of gravel, the installation of fencing, and the procurement and installation of all electrical equipment (working with an electrical contractor).

[4] M.W. Kellogg. 1992. *Northern Adriatic LNG Receiving Terminal Pre-Feasibility Study, Part I of II*. Prepared for INA—Industrija Nafte SPO, Zagreb, Yugoslavia, p. 4.

[5] In the United States, vapor and thermal exclusion zone requirements are specified in 49 *Code of Federal Regulations* 193. Natural gas/LNG is only combustible at a concentration of 5%–15% when mixed with air—and only if an ignition source is present. Regulatory authorities require that LNG terminal developers calculate how far an LNG cloud can travel (e.g., from a leak or a spill) before its concentrations in the air are considered to be safe and will not result in a fire; these calculations define the vapor exclusion zones. Thermal exclusion zones are calculated on the basis of a fire which could affect the entire LNG storage tank, and are designed to limit the thermal radiation risk outside the LNG terminal site. Importantly, certain buildings, infrastructure, and activities are prohibited in these zones, since there could be injury loss of life if an accident occurs.

[6] For example, Korea's TongYeong receiving terminal (which unloaded its first cargo in September 2002) was built specifically to handle the country's particularly high demand for LNG in the winter. The terminal has a total storage capacity of 980,000 kiloliters, with 7 tanks each holding 140,000 kiloliters. However, there

is room for more than 11 tanks at the site. See Kogas TongYeong terminal. http://www.kogas.or.kr/english/lng/Tongyeong-Terminal.pdf (accessed May 24, 2006), p. 4.

[7] For example, an accident attributed to rollover took place in 1971 at the La Spezia receiving terminal in Italy. The import terminal operator stored LNG with different densities and heat content, which formed two layers of LNG. The sudden mixing of these two layers (i.e., rollover) results in the release of large volumes of vapor. In this case, about 2,000 tons of LNG vapor discharged from the tank safety valves and vents over a period of a few hours, damaging the roof of the tank. See California Energy Commission. LNG safety. http://www.energy.ca.gov/lng/safety.html (accessed May 24, 2006).

[8] Poten & Partners. 1999. LNG technology contracting and cost trends. In LNG *Cost & Competition: Sourcebook*. New York: Poten & Partners, p. 62.

[9] Ibid.

[10] Ibid.

[11] Yang, C. C., and Zupeng Huang. 2004. Lower emission LNG vaporization. LNG *Journal*. November/December, pp. 24–26.

[12] Ibid.

[13] On April 11, 2006, FERC administrative judge, Presiding Judge Herbert Grossman, issued a ruling in a hotly contested case between AES Ocean Express LNG and the Florida Gas Transmission (FGT). The two parties were in disagreement about the quality of regasified LNG potentially flowing into FGT's system from AES's proposed LNG import terminal in the Bahamas. The initial decision established the Wobbe index range for LNG imports and set a precedent for taking a regional approach to gas quality standards. The ruling set the acceptable range of the Wobbe index for regasified LNG at 1,340–1,396. This places the maximum Wobbe number slightly below the 1,400 cap suggested by the supplier's coalition. The recommended specifications also set the gross heating value range for regasified LNG entering the FGT system at 1,025–1,110 Btu/scf, the upper limit of which is in line with the Natural Gas Council Plus working group's interim guidelines, submitted to FERC in February 2005. The FERC clarified and affirmed the initial ruling in April 2007. FERC further affirmed the judge's decision to reject a cost-recovery mechanism in FGT's proposed tariff. This would ahve recovered outlays related to testing, remediation, and repair costs associated with LNG delivered into FGT's system, even if it met the proscribed gas quality specification. See FERC, "Initial Decision: AES Ocean Express LLC v Florida Gas Transmission Company," April 11, 2006, Docket No. RP04-249-001.

[14] Quillen, D. 2002. LNG safety myths and legends: Investment in a healthy U.S. energy future." Presentation. Houston, May 14–15.

THE EVOLUTION OF THE LNG INDUSTRY 8

INTRODUCTION

The LNG industry has exhibited impressive growth over its history, nearly doubling in size each decade between 1970 and 2000. By 2005, worldwide volumes were over 195.4 Bcm (139.6 MMt), a 6% increase from the previous year. Although the international pipeline trade has also shown robust growth, LNG has managed to increase its share of the global gas market substantially. In 1975, LNG represented just 10% of total cross-border trade.[1] By 2005, LNG represented more than a quarter of international gas flows.

This growth has been driven by declining capital costs along the LNG chain, strong global gas demand, abundant natural gas reserves located in remote areas, a proven industry record of safety and reliability, and solid financial returns. In recent years, these factors have led to a spate of announcements of liquefaction and regasification projects, coupled with a surge in orders for new LNG tankers. Even though some of these projects will never reach the construction stage, total liquefaction capacity is expected to triple between 2000 and 2015, with corresponding growth in receiving terminal and shipping capacity (figs. 8–1 and 8–2).

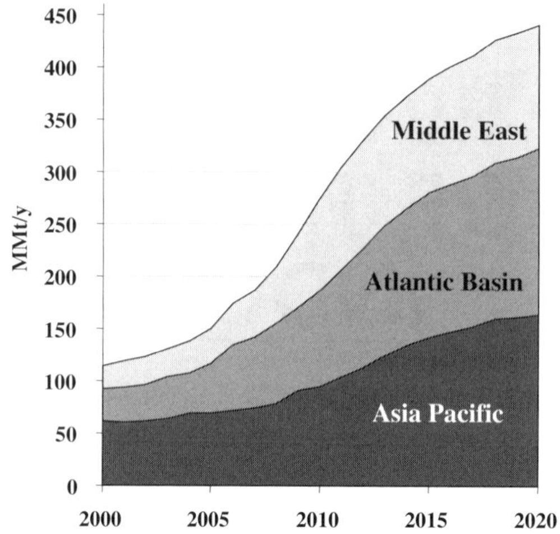

Fig. 8–1. Global LNG supply forecast to 2015 (*Source:* Poten & Partners)

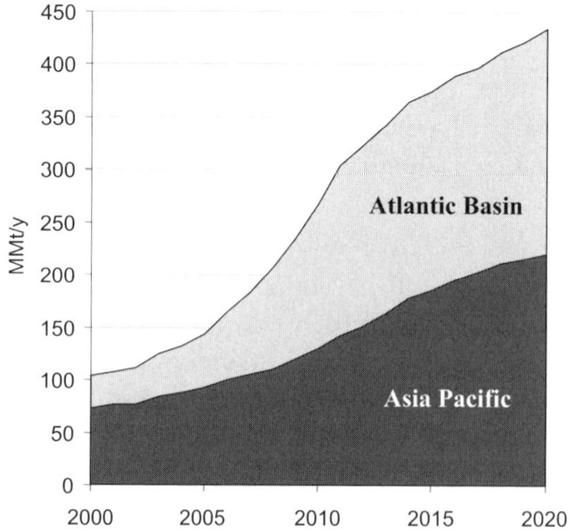

Fig. 8–2. Global LNG demand forecast to 2015 (*Source:* Poten & Partners)

In 2005, LNG was transported to 14 importing countries from 13 exporting countries.[2] Since 1970, Japan has been the anchor market for LNG. Although growth rates have moderated in the region, Asia-Pacific markets, now including India and China, still account for the majority of LNG traded—around two-thirds in 2005. Meanwhile, European and U.S. LNG imports have increased substantially because of declining growth in domestic production and pipeline deliveries and rising consumption (figs. 8–3 and 8–4).

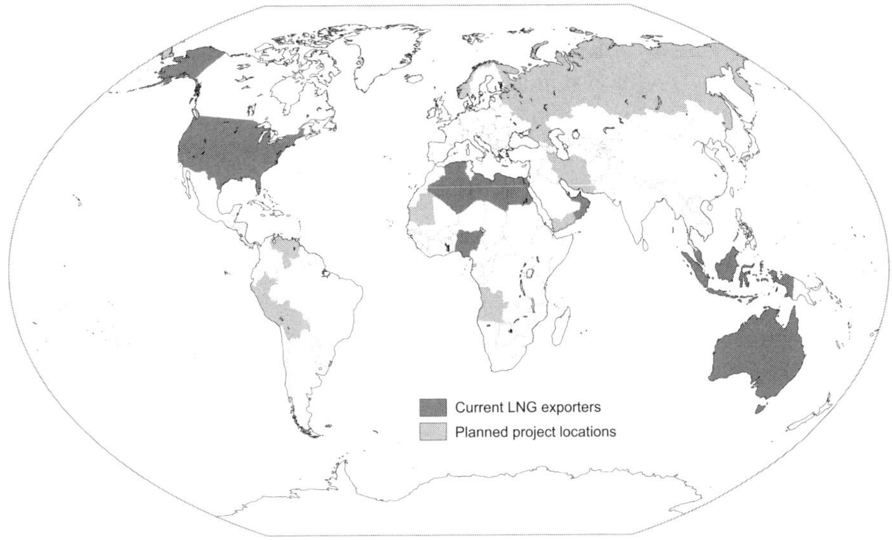

Fig. 8–3. LNG-exporting and -importing countries in 2005 (*Source:* Poten & Partners)

Importers / Exporters	Abu Dhabi	Algeria	Australia	Brunei	Egypt	Indonesia	Libya	Malaysia	Nigeria	Oman	Qatar	Spain	Trinidad	USA	Importer Totals	% Change from 2004
Belgium		2.0													2.0	[illegible]%
[illegible]ran[illegible]e		[illegible]			0.2				[illegible].0	0.[illegible]					[illegible].0	[illegible]%
[illegible]ree[illegible]e		0.[illegible]			0.[illegible]										0.4	[illegible]0%
India			0.1							0.1	4.1				4.2	+142%
Italy		1.9										0.2			2.0	+18%
Japan	5.1		10.2	6.3		14.3		13.6		1.0	6.3			1.2	58.0	+2%
Portugal		0.1							1.1						1.2	+15%
Puerto Rico													0.4		0.4	-16%
South Korea	0.1		0.8	0.6	0.3	5.6		4.7		4.4	6.2				22.6	+2%
Spain	0.2	4.2			2.7		0.6	0.1	3.6	1.6	3.4	-0.2	0.4		16.6	+22%
Taiwan			0.3			3.6		3.0		0.2					7.1	+4%
Turkey		3.0							0.8						3.7	+26%
United Kingdom		0.4													0.4	N/A
USA		2.0			1.5			0.2	0.2	0.1	0.1		9.2		13.1	-2%
Exporter Totals	5.4	19.7	11.4	6.9	4.7	23.4	0.6	21.6	8.5	7.3	20.1	0.0	10.1	1.2	139.6	+6%
% Change from 2004	-7%	+5%	+29%	-2%	N/A	-6%	+1%	+7%	-8%	+8%	+13%	N/A	-2%	+2%	+6%	

Fig. 8–4. Global LNG trade matrix, 2005 (*Source:* Poten & Partners' LNGAS.com Web site)

WHO IMPORTS LNG?

Europe

Europe was the world's first LNG market. The first LNG deliveries came from Algeria—to the United Kingdom in 1964 and to France the following year. In the early 1970s, Spain and Italy started importing LNG from Libya. Belgium followed a decade later with imports, again from Algeria. Turkey began importing LNG in 1994, followed by Greece in 2000 and Portugal in 2003.

The discovery of natural gas in the North Sea eliminated the United Kingdom's need for LNG imports, and the terminal at Canvey Island was subsequently dismantled. However, the decline of North Sea reserves led to a revival of LNG imports. In 2005, a new terminal on the Isle of Grain began operations, and two more terminals are under construction. Meanwhile, new terminals are also being built in Spain, Italy, and France, and proposals for import capacity have been made in countries as diverse as Cyprus, Germany, the Netherlands, and Poland.

Asia

Although the LNG trade began in the Atlantic Basin, the focus soon moved to Asia, as Japanese utilities emerged as the dominant buyers of LNG. In 1969, the first Asian trade started between Alaska and Japan. Over time, Brunei, Abu Dhabi, Indonesia, Malaysia, Qatar, and Australia joined Alaska as exporters to Japan. Japan remains the world's largest importing country, accounting for 42% of the world total in 2005, down from more than 50% in 2000. South Korea entered the market in 1986 and is now the world's second-largest importer: its 2005 import level of 33.6 Bcm (24.3 MMt) accounted for 16.2% of the world's LNG purchases. Taiwan also imports LNG.

Because these three countries have few indigenous resources and little access to pipelines, they rely almost solely on LNG for their natural gas supply. Given the difficulties of displacing oil as a transportation fuel, to create a diversified energy supply mix, these countries have been keen to move away from oil in power generation markets, spurring growth in consumption of gas and other fuels. Although imports continue to grow in these three countries, a long economic slowdown in Japan moderated growth in that market, while Korean gas demand continued to rise at very rapid rates.[3]

China and India are now emerging as LNG importers. India received its first cargo in 2004, and at the end of 2005, two terminals were operating.

China unloaded its first cargo in the spring of 2006 at the newly completed Guangdong LNG import terminal, and a second facility, in Fujian, should be up and running by 2008. Both countries could grow into significant buyers in this region. Other potential importers include Chile, Hong Kong, New Zealand, Pakistan, the Philippines, Singapore, and Thailand.

The Americas

The United States began importing LNG from Algeria in the early 1970s, into the Distrigas import terminal, in Everett, Massachusetts. In the decade that followed, three more import terminals were built, at Cove Point, Maryland; Elba Island, Georgia; and Lake Charles, Louisiana. However, the removal of price controls from domestic natural gas production beginning in 1978, coupled with FERC Order 380 in 1984, made LNG uncompetitive, and the Cove Point, Elba Island, and Lake Charles terminals were shut down. The Everett and Lake Charles terminals were able to renegotiate their contracts and import LNG from Algeria at more competitive rates beginning in 1987.

With the steady growth of natural gas demand in the 1990s, LNG made a comeback, and the remaining two mothballed facilities, at Cove Point and Elba Island, were recommissioned for use in 2003 and 2001, respectively. A fifth terminal, Excelerate's offshore Gulf Gateway, in the Gulf of Mexico, began operating in 2005. By 2002, expansions were underway at each of the onshore terminals. U.S. LNG imports reached just over 18.2 Bcm (13.2 MMt) in 2005, making the United States the world's fourth-largest LNG importer.

In this supply-constrained market, LNG is expected to play a major role in meeting future gas demand. By early 2007, construction had started on four new terminals in the United States, and 12 more had received authorization from FERC to proceed. The United States has become the target market for many proposed liquefaction facilities around the world.

Elsewhere in the Americas, Puerto Rico began importing LNG in July 2000, and the Dominican Republic opened a small terminal in early 2003; in both cases, the LNG was dedicated to gas-fired electric power plants. Mexico has also witnessed a stream of LNG import proposals, also primarily to feed increased demand for gas-fired power generation, and the country commissioned its first LNG receiving facility in 2006, with one to follow in 2008. Canada has approved two terminals in the Canadian Maritimes. One is under construction, the second has been mothballed. Several others are in the permitting stages on both coasts. Chile is also considering importing LNG, with two or three proposals in various stages of development. Finally, Brazil, Honduras, and Jamaica have also proposed import facilities.

THE EVOLUTION OF THE LNG BUSINESS MODEL

The traditional LNG business

The risks, both technical and commercial, involved in developing the early LNG business resulted in a conservative approach during the first 40 years. Nearly all the LNG produced was sold under an integrated project model, directly to creditworthy gas or electric utility buyers in countries with high credit ratings. The utilities' credit was underpinned by their captive end-use customers, and the full cost of obtaining the gas was recovered in regulated tariffs.

During this period, there were relatively few import and export facilities, and those were tightly controlled, often with significant host country government involvement. In the absence of a contractual commitment between buyers and sellers, projects failed to materialize as liquefaction plants, terminals, or ships could have sat idle because there was no assurance of LNG supply or market. Speculative development was not a viable option for the participants or financiers, since project economics depend on uninterrupted delivery of most of each project's volumes. Consequently, long-term contracts that committed most or all of a facility's capacity to known markets always lay at the heart of the LNG business. Indeed, financial institutions backing a proposed liquefaction project insisted on buyer commitments before consenting to project lending.

Multiyear SPAs (typically for 20 years) minimized project investors' risks by guaranteeing the project's ability to repay its borrowings while giving the project shareholders a reasonable return on their investments. Historically, contract terms were inflexible and did not accommodate changes in volume that arose from shifts in market demand. Virtually all long-term SPAs contain what are called take-or-pay provisions. As the name indicates, if the buyer failed to take the contracted gas volumes, it would have to pay for the LNG anyway. There was generally limited off-take flexibility (less than 10% of annual quantities) and no destination flexibility. This meant that the contracted volumes had to be delivered to the specified import terminal(s). Prices were largely set with reference to crude oil or petroleum products, and there was limited opportunity to review and reopen these pricing provisions.

The commercial agreements embedded in the SPAs also reflected an iterative process of facility development coordination between buyers and sellers, and the SPAs were executed before construction started. Tankers were ordered and built for specific trade routes. The number of ships and their sizes were customized to accommodate the specific distance and volumes involved in each trade. Similarly, receiving terminals were built to accommodate the ships and the quality specifications of the natural gas that they would be receiving. Conservatism in design endowed each component of the infrastructure with built-in redundancy to ensure that volumes would be unaffected by routine maintenance or breakdowns.

The model that developed was conceptually similar to a floating pipeline. In the floating-pipeline model, gas is transported continuously from one end of the pipeline (the liquefaction facility and loading terminal) to the other end (the import terminal) by the dedicated shipping fleet. The traditional model of a floating pipeline guaranteed a steady, dependable trade.

Barriers to flexibility in traditional contracts

The traditional model had inherent limitations that made it difficult to deviate from the long-term point-to-point trade model. Even if the economics favored diversion of contracted volumes, this could be prevented by interference from the following factors:

Dedicated shipping. SPAs contained restrictions on changing the ships dedicated to a long-term SPA, a particular concern if the proposed new outlet involved longer shipping distances and therefore could disturb the scheduling of the overall fleet. Adding new ships to an existing trade or trading dedicated ships into a new plant or terminal required consultation and approval from all participants in the existing and proposed trades, a time-consuming process at best.

Buyer needs. Utility buyers' main concern was security of supply. These buyers insisted on high levels of redundancy to ensure security, which was paid for through their contracts. Their high credit ratings underwrote the project. If a ship was diverted from a long-term trade, the redundancy was reduced, and the risk of shortfall was increased. Buyers had no economic incentive to consent to such arrangements since under the utility cost pass-through model they could not reap any economic benefit from additional value created by such short-term opportunities; instead, they had to pass this on to their customers. Further, if the utility came up short of adequate supply, the consequences could be severe, both economically and in terms of relationships with regulators overseeing and approving the utility's investments and rates of return.

Liquefaction commitments. Project owners did not intentionally build surplus liquefaction capacity for use outside long-term commitments. Although liquefaction trains were designed with some excess capacity, it was intended to ensure that the facility could meet its obligations. However, as time passed and operations became more efficient, some liquefaction plants experienced significant spare capacity, as much as 40% of design levels, which was available for sale. Again, the terms of the SPAs intervened. Even when other markets beckoned, the LNG supplier generally had to offer the existing customers the right of first refusal for additional short- and long-term volumes. These spare volumes were often committed under new or expanded long-term contracts with the original buyers, and the short-term quantities were used by the existing buyers to improve volume flexibility.

Lack of transparency and liquidity. Lack of competition in gas markets meant that there was no transparency and liquidity. There were no reliable price signals to let buyers and sellers know if a given transaction made any sense. Moreover, natural gas markets entirely based on long-term contracts from the wellhead to the utility left little opportunity for finding buyers to take short-term volumes, especially with all LNG terminals operating on a proprietary-access model. This lack of competitive markets helped entrench the long-term traditional model.

LNG "club rules." The LNG community was held together by long-standing relationships between a limited number of counterparties. High costs of entry and the need for de facto government approvals on the buyer and seller sides limited the number of international companies that could participate. The result was a small, semiclosed club of participants that included state-owned national oil companies and utilities and energy supermajors.

Besides these obstacles, the need for consent between buyer and seller to anything that represented a deviation from the basic SPA created another obstacle to changing the model. The consequences of something going wrong so outweighed the benefits of everything going right that essentially nothing happened. There was also the unspoken concern that once one party proposed reopening the SPA for new commercial considerations, the other party would also have the right to review the provisions of the agreement that they might wish to have changed. The lack of market transparency made the transaction hard to value, and often created an underlying fear that the party proposing the transaction would disproportionately benefit from the new commercial arrangements. Ronald Reagan's words "trust but verify" succinctly described a difficult hurdle for the industry to overcome.

Historical attempts to change the model

As long as each new LNG project required mutual long-term commitment—and the SPAs essentially gave the buyers veto rights over sales to other parties—there was no uncommitted capacity in the LNG chain to permit the development of an LNG commodity market via short-term or spot trading of LNG cargoes and transportation. This does not mean, however, that there were no early attempts to inject commercial innovation into the LNG business. Companies seeking to increase liquidity saw the shipping sector as the optimal entry point. In the early days of the industry, several shipowners placed orders for LNG vessels without having first committed to a dedicated trade. In some cases, the owners of these so-called speculative ships were able to find stable employment for their vessels. Others, though, met with financial disaster.

For example, the *Gastor* and the *Nestor*, built for an Anglo-Dutch group in 1976 and 1977, respectively, were a speculative investment. The vessels were delivered into a shrinking market and remained idle until purchased by Nigeria LNG's Bonny Gas Transport in 1990, at a significant discount from their original construction cost, and were renamed the LNG *Lagos* and LNG *Port Harcourt*, respectively. Two ships built in Sweden in 1981 and 1984 represented a last-ditch effort by the Swedish government to find employment for the Kockums shipyard before it closed and suffered a similar fate. Bonny Gas Transport subsequently acquired these vessels in 1991, and they are now known as the LNG *Bonny* and the LNG *Finima*.[4]

The U.S. experience was even more painful. El Paso, among the largest U.S. pipeline companies, undertook a project to import LNG from Algeria to the United States in a fleet of nine dedicated vessels, selling the LNG to the owners of the Cove Point and Elba Island terminals. However, a dispute arose between El Paso and Sonatrach over the price of the LNG. Following the oil price increases after the Iranian Revolution of 1979, Sonatrach had sought to gain price parity for its LNG sales from all its customers. El Paso asked the DOE to intervene in the pricing dispute, which quickly escalated to a government-to-government level. The DOE refused to accept a price increase four or five times higher than the previous price of $1.30/MMBtu.[5] The United States had just reached an agreement with Canada on a price for Canadian imports lower than that sought by Sonatrach, and did not want to upset that precedent. El Paso's import plans were aborted, and LNG shipments stopped in April 1980.

In February 1981, El Paso announced that it was writing off its investment in LNG and barely avoided a bankruptcy filing. To make matters worse, three of the LNG tankers ordered by El Paso never passed their sea trials. A new insulation technology failed under the cryogenic temperatures, and the vessels never entered LNG service. Three of El Paso's vessels were scrapped outright. Three ships were repossessed by the U.S. Maritime Administration (MARAD), which had provided financing on which El Paso defaulted. They were mothballed before being sold in 1990. MARAD took the biggest write-off in its history in association with the El Paso financings.

Combined with the other idle speculative LNG ships ordered by hopeful LNG shipping players, the laid-up fleet exceeded 20 LNG vessels by the mid-1980s. (Trunkline's LNG tankers followed El Paso's into MARAD repossession when the trade to Lake Charles was suspended in 1981.) The venture proved to be difficult and extremely expensive for El Paso and the speculative shipowners. The end result convinced participants in the LNG industry that the traditional business model should not be tampered with. This mind-set continued to dominate the LNG industry for the next decade.

The door to new types of trade was opened during the early 1990s, when surplus LNG production in Indonesia led state-owned oil and gas company Pertamina to come up with innovative sales deals to sell excess LNG to its Japanese buyers. These deals were known unofficially as the superdeals. The superdeals introduced flexibility into individual buyer off-take obligations and used surplus shipping capacity within the Indonesian fleet. Each deal was time and volume limited and thus was distinct from the existing long-term supply contracts. Contracts had no take-or-pay provisions, volumes varied from year to year but were subject to a total number of cargoes to be taken over the life of the contract, and price incentives maximized off-take. The superdeals involved additional sales only to existing contract holders and required buyers' commitments ahead of the contract year to schedule cargoes. Nonetheless, they represented the first substantial break from traditional contractual arrangements and set the stage for further innovations.

Later in the decade, a series of interlinked events reinforced the growth in nontraditional trades. The Asian financial crisis dampened regional demand at the same time that new liquefaction projects came on line to serve Asian markets. During this period, European countries were supply constrained because of their growing demand and production problems at the Algerian liquefaction facilities. In an unprecedented move, the market responded to these market imbalances by redirecting some of the LNG from new projects to Europe and the United States.[6] In December 1986, a cargo of LNG made its way from Bontang, Indonesia, to Boston in one of the first true spot LNG transactions ever undertaken.

TRANSFORMATION OF THE INDUSTRY

For three decades, the conventional model dominated LNG transactions. However, in recent years, the natural gas and electric power industries have been transformed by liberalization, and the LNG business has been forced to react, at least to serve those markets that have gone furthest toward wholesale competition. The single largest effect has been an increase in the number of shorter-term contracts that offer more flexibility in off-take volumes, delivery points, and timing. This has led to the creation of a growing spot market for LNG.

This transformation was the result of a confluence of multiple factors, described in the following sections.

Gas and power market liberalization in the United States and Europe

The traditional downstream gas industry had as its primary objective the need to ensure adequate supplies for consumers; gas transmission companies and utilities made money by receiving a regulated return on their investments in assets while the cost of gas and operating expenses were simply passed through to consumers. This system did not give incentives to buyers to get the best prices or structure the most efficient contracts; any additional profits the buyers made were simply returned to the consumers. Under the prevailing model of wholesale gas market deregulation, the transmission companies either exit or separate their merchant roles (i.e., gas buying and selling) and turn into pure transporters of the commodity, using an open-access approach by which they let other companies gain access to their systems on a nondiscriminatory basis. The transporters become sellers of throughput capacity. Multiple companies bid on this capacity; when they are not using it themselves, they resell it. As a consequence, multiple companies may be sending gas through a pipeline at the same time.

By unbundling these functions, the regulators hope to create an active wholesale market, where gas is freely traded throughout the pipeline grid. As a result, natural gas is an actively traded commodity in North America and, to a lesser extent, in Europe. Active trading seems a more remote possibility in established Asian LNG markets, where the isolated markets that characterize the region's gas industry make privatization and liberalization in Japan and South Korea's industries a work in (glacial) progress. Wholesale electric markets have followed a similar pattern and have a "knock-on" effect on the gas markets, since gas is typically the marginal fuel in most competitive wholesale power markets.

In countries that are moving to competitive markets, the method of pricing natural gas is changing with the growth of gas-on-gas competition and the resulting decoupling of gas and oil prices. Regional benchmark prices are created, and futures, swaps, and basis[7] markets emerge, along with cross-commodity (electricity vs. gas) trading opportunities. Although a true global price for gas may not exist, these benchmarks facilitate price transparency, helping LNG buyers and sellers to optimize deliveries between the three key LNG-importing regions of North America, Europe, and Asia. The emergence of a single, world price for LNG is unlikely; instead, several strongly correlated regional prices will probably interact in the same way that benchmark crudes (Brent in Europe, West Texas Intermediate [WTI] in the United States, and Dubai in Asia) do on the oil market.[8] Since LNG is significantly more expensive to transport than oil, the LNG price correlation will be weaker, and until North American West Coast markets are open to LNG suppliers, the Pacific will remain more insulated from these trends than the Atlantic.

Opening wholesale natural gas markets to competition turns the risk-reward equation on its head. No longer is there a capped regulated return per unit of gas. Instead of more stable regulated prices, gas prices can become highly volatile, fluctuating widely with swings in demand. There is plenty of opportunity to make and lose vast sums of money very quickly. Indeed, over the past decade, gas and electricity markets in North America have shown the most volatile pricing of any traded commodity using industry standard measurements. These attributes drove the rise of the merchant energy traders (Enron, Dynegy, Mirant, and Calpine), often not even owning assets but living (and subsequently dying) on their ability to trade just the wholesale commodity. These markets also gave rise to the scandals associated with the Enron collapse, the California energy crisis, and the demise or crippling of many merchant companies. Increasingly, commercial and investment banks and hedge funds are active in the gas trading markets, seeking to profit from proprietary trading strategies in largely financial products.

Decreases in capital costs

The impact of the cost decreases discussed in chapter 5 cannot be overstated. They have enabled LNG to become a preferred method of commercialization for gas reserves. Technological innovations and increased competition from contractors have contributed to the decreases in capital costs. Concordant with rising costs and falling reserves in the main markets, LNG can now compete on purely economical terms across a much wider swath of the world's gas markets.

Lower-cost financing

With maturing technology, established reliability, and broader market and supply access, the LNG industry is also experiencing a drop in its financing costs. LNG projects and facilities offer lenders a very attractive opportunity to underwrite long-term loans, reducing debt service costs. At the same time, competition throughout the LNG chain is forcing equity investors (and service providers) to reduce their returns in order to secure their investments and future growth. This has been particularly prevalent in LNG shipping, where charter rates have fallen based on lower costs of capital, and in the upstream and downstream, where host countries are forcing competitive tenders for reserve development rights and LNG supply opportunities. More competition reduces returns and, ultimately, costs.

Expansion of the LNG "club"

Throughout the 1980s, only three or four major energy companies appeared to possess the project management capabilities, technical skills and financial resources to develop a large new LNG project. Now there are at least 15 international and national energy companies with such aspirations. The pool of potential EPC contractors has similarly expanded. The dispersion of technological know-how among energy companies, EPC contractors, and equipment manufacturers has helped level the playing field by allowing companies new to LNG to gain access to what was perceived as proprietary technology and knowledge. Also, many exporting countries want to reduce their reliance on supermajors by working with companies that may have less ability to dictate terms. On the market side, simpler technology and the relatively smaller scale of import terminals have opened that business segment to many more participants.

Changing upstream strategies

Energy companies have found it increasingly difficult to find world-scale gas reserves in their domestic markets. Access to international oil prospects has also become far more competitive and more difficult in a high-oil-price world. This combination of factors has driven producers to explore for gas in areas increasingly far away from traditional markets.

Meanwhile, financial disclosure regulations are pressuring upstream companies to reevaluate reserves not under commercial agreement for exploitation. As a consequence, producers are shifting expenditures from exploration to developments connecting known reserves to markets, making

LNG an increasingly favored option. For instance, 95% of ExxonMobil's worldwide gas reserve additions in 2005 were associated with LNG projects in Qatar.[9]

Critical and diversified mass

The steady growth in the global LNG trade gives participants increasing confidence that they will be able to find a buyer or seller within a reasonable period of time should anything happen either to upset the initial commercial arrangements or to permit a project to go to construction without all its output sold or supplies contracted. Examples include the swift redirection of volumes that had been destined for the Dabhol power project in India and several U.S. import terminals that are proceeding to construction with less than 100% of their capacity under firm commitments. In some Asian markets, rules determining the level of redundancy and security required for LNG import terminal construction have been somewhat relaxed, reflecting the positive safety history of LNG projects and confidence in the availability of adequate supply.

What does all this mean for the LNG industry? On the one hand, it may be more difficult for LNG importers to lock in downstream buyers to traditional long-term contracts, because their buyers will be increasingly unwilling to take on the long-term risk entailed by an inflexible contract. On the other hand, in a liquid and large gas market, finding long-term buyers may not be necessary and may even be undesirable given recent U.S. experiences with merchant energy companies as potential LNG or gas buyers. With the entry of many diverse participants, including aspiring LNG traders, finding creditworthy LNG and downstream buyers is another challenge. At the same time, the increase in the number of suppliers and buyers is allowing industry participants to shift their attention from security of supply to price. Buyers and sellers are now willing to consider a wider range of pricing terms and mechanisms, destination flexibility, and less rigid off-take and supply conditions. Competitive market forces, diverging corporate strategies, and sheer project scale are causing the club to suffer some severe stress and certainly to become less gentlemanly. Commercial innovation is gradually supplanting technical knowledge as a competitive advantage for the industry.

NEW BUSINESS STRATEGIES

LNG participants have been forced to rethink their business and asset strategies to adapt to industry changes. Three major trends represent departures from the historic model:

- Committing to an LNG project before 100% of the liquefaction capacity is sold
- Downstream integration by LNG producers and upstream integration by LNG buyers
- Ordering ships that are not dedicated to specific trades or projects

Uncommitted liquefaction

It is still unusual to deliberately build a project with uncommitted capacity, although the industry appears to be heading in this direction.[10] As train sizes increase—units with 7.8 MMt/y of capacity are being built in Qatar, while Australia (Browse), Nigeria (Nigeria LNG), and Russia (Shtokman) are also considering the construction of mega-sized liquefaction units—it has not been easy to find firm buyers for the entire capacity before construction starts. Few, if any, buyers can commit to such a scale of purchase, even in consortia. This is even truer for the traditional Japanese buyers, whose incremental supply needs are getting smaller as the market growth slows down. In the race to get into liquefaction, some projects are moving forward with a financial commitment before all the off-take capacity is committed. This is a revolutionary development, even though by the time some of these facilities are completed, they will be fully committed. In other cases, the upstream owners of the gas plan to take control of the LNG supply through the terminals and into the wholesale gas markets of North America and Europe.

Integration along the LNG chain

Despite the growth in the number of shorter-term contracts, securing external financing for a project still requires finding a long-term market for the gas. An emerging strategy by liquefaction participants has been to contract for import terminal capacity or to build import terminals to use as a primary sales channel. Such integration helps ensure access to a market, mitigates some of the risk of excess liquefaction capacity, and allows the LNG seller to take advantage of price arbitrage opportunities across different markets.

North America and Europe are seen as the preferred destinations for this LNG. Both have extremely large integrated gas markets that can absorb significant volumes. Although Japan and Korea are by far the largest LNG buyers, their natural gas markets are relatively small, and access is problematic. Most uncommitted liquefaction projects are therefore targeting Atlantic (and mainly U.S.) markets.

In the absence of a solid buyer, ensuring market access through import terminals is an important issue. LNG developers trying to market their own LNG must secure enough import capacity to deliver all the LNG from their planned liquefaction trains. There are currently two ways of gaining import terminal access in the Atlantic.

As markets in the United States and Europe liberalize, many existing LNG import facilities have allowed third parties (including arms length affiliates of the terminal owner) to have access to regasification capacity rights for a fee approved by the regulatory oversight body. Virtually no Atlantic Basin terminals continue to be exclusively owned by and operated for the sole benefit of a single entity, usually the local utility. For new terminals, the decision as to whether a terminal owner may have proprietary access depends on decisions by regulators and legislators. These in turn are based on the requests of facility developers and perceptions of market need.

Where regasification terminals are treated like pipelines, open access to the throughput capacity of the facility is made available to third parties under various bidding or allocation schemes, with the owner charging a regulated rate for the facility's use. Facilities that operate in this fashion include the Cove Point, Elba Island, and Lake Charles terminals in the United States, all the Enagás-owned Spanish terminals, and the Fluxys terminal in Belgium. Access to other European terminals has proven difficult, and at times, regulatory intervention has been required in order to force the owners to make capacity available to third parties.

If import facilities are viewed as an extension of the upstream supply assets that help introduce the gas into the pipeline network and regulators accept this argument, access is proprietary (limited to the terminal owner) or negotiated (the capacity holders reach negotiated agreements with the terminal owners on whatever terms they see fit), similar to the way in which production assets such as processing plants or gathering pipelines are used. In these cases, the capacity at the terminals is not subject to regulated rates or open-access requirements.

For LNG producers integrating downstream, it may be desirable to be able to build proprietary import terminals instead of being forced to bid for capacity in an open market. Arguments for proprietary terminals include the following:[11]

- Securing a sufficiently large market for new liquefaction facilities. As liquefaction trains grow larger, a new train could easily supply the entire capacity of a large (1 Bcf/d [10 Bcm/y]) import facility. Builders of new liquefaction capacities want a guarantee that they will be able to place all or most of their LNG before they can build the liquefaction plant, and a classic open-access regime could force them to share the throughput rights with unrelated third parties through a bidding process, thereby causing them to come up short of the needed capacity for the train output. In some cases, liquefaction owners will be forced to bid for capacity multiple times at different facilities, as Shell did in the United States, introducing additional logistical challenges. Conversely, capacity at open-access or negotiated-access terminals may be shared among many participants bringing supplies from multiple liquefaction plants on differing sizes of vessels, making coordination between the capacity holders challenging and likely resulting in a less efficient use of the terminal owing to irresolvable logistical conflicts between the parties.
- Coordinating construction timing to ensure that terminals are not left idle. Construction of the liquefaction facility and the regasification terminal should be completed so that they are both on line at the same time. Otherwise, one of the facilities will be left idle, forcing the owner to try to find outlets for the LNG or buyers for the excess terminal capacity; such a situation reduces project optimization. However, since the import terminal is generally subject to more regulatory oversight, delays, and challenges than the export facility, it is not always possible to synchronize these projects exactly. The complexity associated with constructing the liquefaction plants in increasingly challenging environments has led them to slip behind terminal schedules in certain instances.
- Scheduling cargoes. Shipping logistics become much more complicated when an LNG supplier is delivering to multiple terminals where access is shared; LNG deliveries may not occur optimally, nor are tankers always deployed efficiently.

How this evolves in open markets will vary from terminal to terminal. In some cases, there may be a combination of proprietary access for the terminal owner(s) with some capacity kept available (sometimes on a mandatory basis) for third-party access.

Controlling access at import terminals is the first step in reaching markets. In liquid markets, imported LNG is sold into the pipeline grid at market-based rates. Finding creditworthy buyers for these LNG imports can be difficult. Buyers who meet credit requirements often cannot absorb significant amounts of gas at one time. Moreover, steady imports of LNG may overwhelm local market requirements, depressing local market prices and requiring additional investment in downstream pipeline capacity to sell the gas farther away from the facility at a higher price.

Some of the larger LNG players are developing portfolio approaches to LNG. Through LNG project participation, they have contracted for their own dedicated LNG supplies. They have ordered their own ships and are gaining access to markets through SPAs that allow them to supply LNG from different locations, and/or they are finding dedicated regasification capacity in multiple markets. Examples of companies pursuing this approach include Shell, BP, and BG. Others such as ExxonMobil appear to be following an approach closer to the floating-pipeline concept.

Although the trend has been integration downstream from the liquefaction facility, some import terminal owners are integrating upstream and acquiring shares of liquefaction projects. Now that markets are becoming competitive, importers who are integrated into shipping and liquefaction can hedge their price risk when increasingly volatile gas markets spike. However, most downstream companies take modest shares in liquefaction facilities; this is because, as utilities, they do not have the risk appetite to invest heavily in overseas ventures, and history suggests that such investments by utilities have very mixed financial results. The financial markets do not like to see utilities diversifying into such business, preferring the stability and assured dividends from classic utility investments.

Shipping

Destination flexibility and spare shipping capacity are increasingly being prized by buyers and sellers alike. If LNG buyers accept rigid off-take obligations in the face of increased domestic market uncertainty, they must have control of shipping and flexible destination rights to manage their supply-demand balance through merchant trading activities. Conversely, if sellers grant flexible off-take obligations, they must have access to shipping to move discretionary volumes to alternative markets. Both approaches will likely require that the parties have access to spare shipping capacity, to maximize their opportunities in very diverse markets. In contrast, the spare shipping capacity typical of the classic early project models was maintained solely as a means of ensuring very high reliability in delivery schedules and volume assurance.

The advent of flexible, short-term trades is transforming the LNG shipping industry. For the most part, new LNG ships are still being ordered in response to specific requirements arising from long-term SPAs, and they will represent the majority of the LNG fleet. However, a surprising number of newbuildings have been ordered without long-term charter arrangements. With wide divergence in gas prices between geographically disparate markets, charter rates and utilization for uncommitted ships have varied widely, from as low as $25,000 per day to over $120,000 per day. At times, up to 20 ships have been idled, waiting for cargoes to appear.

The logistics of simultaneous operations at export plants and import terminals create new issues. In the traditional LNG project model, ships were committed to specific trades with a predictable schedule of loadings and discharges. However, once there are several buyers each controlling their own ships—often of different cargo capacities and with the potential to discharge at different terminals on short notice—the scheduling process becomes more complex and can cause a loss of LNG production.

These logistical challenges may also be duplicated at the LNG import terminal. After all, it is becoming more usual for receiving facilities to have two or more capacity holders whose separate LNG supply and shipping arrangements will inevitably conflict. Given that the LNG importer may have entered into downstream pipeline commitments and/or strict gas sales agreements with end users at the terminal's tailgate, the terminal operator must carefully schedule each ship's arrival and the sendout of LNG. The conflict between different users' cargo discharge and sendout objectives invariably requires complex contractual undertakings and almost inevitably results in a diminution of the terminal's effective throughput capacity. The situation becomes even more complex if the original capacity holders then assign or sell their terminal's capacity rights to third parties.

Effect of the transformation of the industry

For those companies electing to pursue it, the shift from the floating-pipeline model to a model of an integrated network with highly flexible trading arrangements is often characterized as an improvement. Optimization of assets is commonly cited as a positive aspect of the new model, but this depends on what part of the chain is being optimized. Although liquefaction may be more effectively used in the new model, since excess LNG can be sold in multiple locations, such optimization has costs. It requires flexibility in shipping and import terminals, which means that there needs to be excess capacity in both, and this may not represent the most efficient utilization of these assets. The true value of the trading model may not be realized until there is a larger critical mass of assets along all segments of the chain, as is the case in the oil industry. The tanker fleet in the crude oil industry is about 4,225 ships globally, while the LNG fleet numbered around 200 vessels as of mid-2006.[12]

THE SHORT-TERM AND SPOT LNG MARKET

The rise of short-term trades

Figure 8–5 shows the rapid growth of short-term LNG trades since the early 1990s. By 2005, short-term LNG trades exceeded 26.6 Bcm and accounted for almost 14% of total LNG traded.

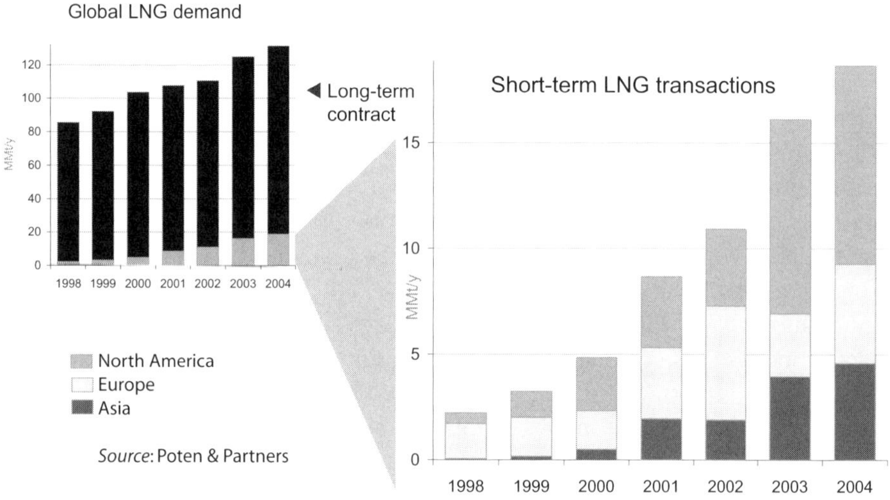

Fig. 8–5. Emergence of spot and short-term LNG trades

Although the term "spot trade" is frequently used, it has a different connotation in the LNG markets. Normally, spot trading refers to a cash sale and immediate delivery of a commodity, without restrictions on subsequent sales. In most markets, spot sales are the dominant commercial transactions. However, because of the planning required, the lack of a globally liquid market with transparent prices, and the limited number and scale of the assets in the industry, arrangement of immediate delivery of an LNG cargo is rare. Furthermore, spot LNG trades often refer to the delivery of multiple cargoes over an extended period, including cargoes delivered or re-directed under long-term contract provisions. Accordingly, the terms "spot" and "short-term" are often used interchangeably. Here, we will simply use the term "spot" for either type of trade.

Why has there been such a focus on spot trades? Because of the economic nature of the business, with high fixed costs, marginal volumes (which generally manifest as spot trades) represent virtually pure profit to be allocated among the participants in these trades.

Potential sources of surplus capacity

Given the dominance of long-term contracts, with their usually inflexible volume requirements, the sources of spot LNG cargoes need to be recognized in advance, since they are going to be volumes left over from long-term contractual commitments and may be subject to buyers' and/or sellers' rights under these contracts. In developing SPAs, the parties often address these spot volumes. Increasingly, even volumes under long-term contracts that embed flexible destination rights are taking on the appearance of spot cargoes—making even more elusive the distinction between spot and term quantities.

Wedge volumes. This is capacity created when a new liquefaction train is brought on line and LNG is available for sale before buyers achieve their long-term contract volume off-takes. A liquefaction train requires very little buildup time before reaching full capacity, whereas SPAs very often include a buildup period—sometimes lasting for years—before the contract plateau level is reached. This is designed to allow the buyers time to build market demand that usually materializes at a more modest pace. LNG contracts also usually factor in extra time between the start of the plant and the start of firm contractual deliveries, to provide a buffer in the event of construction delays. During this period, the buyers are rarely obliged to take these early volumes. The dramatic increase in train sizes and output, along with improved EPC execution, which has seen early delivery of liquefaction plants, has lengthened the duration of the ramp-up period, leaving significant excess capacity available for spot sales. By contrast, for projects targeting the U.S. market, there is no need for a buildup period in the SPAs, since LNG represents such a small component of the overall supply picture and pricing is set by the market; in such projects, buyers and sellers are equally motivated to move as much volume as quickly as possible, especially in the early years of a project when debt repayment is usually at its highest.

Expiration of long-term contracts. Historically, before a long-term contract ended, the original buyer and seller renegotiated the terms and extended and often expanded the volumes under contract, maintaining the volume flow without interruption. This is no longer always the case. The increased number of buyers and sellers, regulatory changes, declining reserves and production behind liquefaction plants, and evolving corporate strategies result in the reduction—or nonrenewal—of volumes under term contracts.

Buyer overcommitment. Projecting long-term supply needs is not an exact science, and buyers may overcontract for supplies because of both conservative and aggressive tactics. A buyer who has contracts far exceeding demand and adequate storage inventories will seek to sell contracted LNG volumes elsewhere. Buyers' overcommitment will contribute ever-larger volumes to spot trades.[13]

Conservative liquefaction plant design. A focus on the reliability of deliveries versus project costs led to the overdesign of liquefaction trains, with the result that actual plant capacity is often well above design capacity (as much as 40% in some early LNG projects). Debottlenecking efforts that improve plant production also create extra volumes. The surplus volumes can be made available for spot trades. Once the higher capacity is established, it is often added to the existing long-term contracts, reducing quantities for spot sales. As the plant designs become more stable, contractors are also reducing the conservatism in design, further eliminating spot sales volumes.

Contract and operational flexibility. Spot capacity can arise when a buyer in a long-term contract exercises whatever volume flexibility is permitted under the terms of these contracts. Even though these flexibilities may be limited to 5% or less, they nevertheless represent a source of spot volumes. Spot volumes will also arise as LNG suppliers offer seasonal deliveries to temperature-sensitive markets, as has been the case in recent term purchases by Korea's Kogas. The off-peak volumes can be marketed elsewhere. Liquefaction plants can often ramp up production for short term durations for a variety of reasons. For example, the ALNG plant, in Trinidad, can increase production by as much as 5% during rainy periods!

Contract failure. In some cases, unforeseen circumstances will lead to the failure and early termination of an SPA. In one well-known example, India's Dabhol project, which was never completed because of a pricing dispute, reneged on its SPAs with Oman and Qatar, leaving these suppliers to find new markets. However, in contrast to Sonatrach in the 1980s, which was left with a surplus of gas when deals with the United States fell through, the sellers were able to sell into the spot market while looking for long-term buyers.

Spot trades in the United States and Europe—driven by price

The emergence of actively traded natural gas markets in the United States and parts of Europe means that decisions on when and where to import can be based solely on gas prices and terminal access. Forward markets, both exchange traded and private, further enhance this development. The price of LNG cargoes can be fixed months in advance by the buyer and/or the seller. These types of arrangements can be quickly unwound if better opportunities present themselves, often by financial settlement between the parties, recognizing the costs of unwinding forward sales positions; the potential incremental costs and savings to be shared among the parties; and the replacement of the LNG with other gas supplies.

Notwithstanding the high fixed costs of the industry, sellers often require a minimum market price before they will consider spot cargo deliveries. The minimum price level may not be profitable using financial accounting measures, reflecting capital cost recovery. Pricing will necessarily reflect the cost of transportation, especially when the distances between exporter and importer are long. In early trades, sellers were very concerned that spot sales, especially those made to the United States in the low price environment of the 1990s, would undermine the pricing of their long-term contracts; conversely, today buyers worry that high marginal spot prices in U.S. and European markets could affect their long-term contract pricing. In practice, these concerns have not been realized, as the other conditions associated with short-term sales reflect commercial terms that may prove unacceptable in long-term contracts.

As spot market trading becomes more sophisticated and widespread, companies will use surplus capacity to arbitrage price disparities between different markets. However, simply because the price is higher in one market than another does not mean that it is high enough to justify selling the gas into the higher-priced market. For example, assume that a Middle Eastern supplier finds ready buyers in both the United States and Spain. A single ship traveling from the Middle East can deliver only two cargoes to the United States in the same amount of time it would take to deliver three cargoes to Spain. In these circumstances, the costs of acquiring incremental short-term shipping and the scheduling of the liquefaction production would be key factors in determining which market was the preferred destination.

Spot trading becomes even more complex when cargo diversions are taken into account. Most diversion arrangements call for the sharing of incremental profits between the buyer and the seller of the diverted cargo.

However, defining incremental revenues and costs is not always an easy matter, especially when the cargo is to be diverted to a market where pricing is not transparent or where each of the parties may have taken different financial hedging positions, which may require unwinding. Such considerations may explain why cargo swaps and exchanges, commonplace in the gas pipeline industry, rarely occur in the LNG industry. As complicated as it is to agree on value sharing between two counterparties to a cargo diversion, the idea of agreeing on value sharing between three or four parties to a swap creates an almost insurmountable obstacle; by the time any agreement might be reached, it is entirely possible that the opportunity will have disappeared. As a result, the industry still witnesses fully loaded LNG tankers passing eastbound and westbound in the Straits of Gibraltar (and northbound and southbound in the Suez Canal); given the very high cost of LNG shipping, the value capture available from rationalizing these trades is very high.

Asian spot markets—still driven largely by relationships

In Asia, the spot market is driven by physical requirements of the customers, given the lack of other sources of natural gas to create market liquidity. Because long-standing relationships are extremely important (driven by the potential for additional long-term sales), spot deliveries are often agreed to between existing sellers and buyers at the underlying term contract price. Only if such sales cannot be made will the parties turn outside their existing contractual arrangements. This is considered a part of the service for captive customers. Over the recent past, this practice has eroded somewhat, as buyers have used the spot market to obtain additional supplies on terms not readily matched by their existing relationships. Examples include spot purchases by Japanese electric utilities to cover nuclear power production problems, by Kogas to cover extreme winter seasonal requirements, and by Indonesia's Pertamina to cover shortfalls in its own LNG production levels. Where Pacific buyers seek spot LNG, price is not the primary concern. Assurance of delivery or flexibility are paramount, as even very-high-priced volumes will be averaged in with long-term contract purchases and passed on to the end customers.

Challenges of spot transactions

Reaching the negotiation stage for a spot LNG transaction requires finding a supplier with uncommitted capacity or finding potential buyers with available import capacity and locating a vessel. Negotiating for a spot cargo can be extremely time and resource intensive, and there are no guarantees that the deal will be pulled together. Arranging for a single cargo often takes as much time as arranging for a term trade. To address this, the industry is moving to more standardized master contracts, in which the majority of the terms and conditions are established in advance and individual term sheets are executed as cargoes become available.

Even with master contracts, these deals may be tricky to arrange. If a ship is required outside the seller's or buyer's fleet, it must be vetted and meet the requirements of the loading and unloading facilities. Scheduling additional cargo loadings and discharges at busy terminals can create further obstacles to successful transactions.

FUTURE POSSIBILITIES

Among the emerging topics of debate is whether LNG can facilitate a global marketplace for natural gas and when and how such a market will materialize.

As this book goes to print, there are no global benchmark prices for natural gas. As LNG increases its share of the global gas market and spot trades increase their share of the LNG market, the market will become more sophisticated in arbitraging price disparities between regions. This should increasingly link different regional prices together and move the natural gas industry toward global pricing benchmarks. The spot market will also drive gas-on-gas competition in markets where gas pricing has traditionally been linked to other fuels. Before these linkages can happen, spot markets must develop and mature. The lack of a physically liquid and price transparent market in Asia and a constrained one in Europe will continue to create barriers to a global gas market. When pure trading companies, controlling no long-term assets, become an established feature of the industry, gas as a global commodity may finally have arrived.

NOTES

[1] Cedigaz. 1999. World LNG Outlook. G. Maisonnier, Paris.

[2] The number of importers includes Puerto Rico as part of the United States.

[3] A forecast prepared by the Korea Energy Economics Institute in December 2005 highlights Korea's growing supply needs. According to the MOCIE think tank, demand will rise from 25.4 MMt in 2006 to 30 MMt/y by 2010. This is about 5 MMt higher in 2010 than the latest official projection from Kogas and MOCIE, which was put together in 2004 and is still used by the Koreans in their long-term planning. By law, this forecast has to be updated every two years, and a new version is scheduled for release later in 2006.

[4] They had never traded and had never been named before this purchase.

[5] The base purchase price stated in the LNG sales contract between El Paso and Sonatrach was $1.30/MMBtu, subject to semiannual escalation based on the New York Harbor prices of No. 2 and No. 6 fuel oils. See U.S. Energy Regulatory Administration. 1978. [El Paso Eastern Company, et al.] application to import LNG from Algeria. ERA Docket No. 77-006-LNG, December 21, 1978.

[6] Abu Dhabi's ADGAS signed short-term ex-ship deals with Gaz de France and Belgium's Distrigaz to help fill Algerian supply shortfalls in 1995 and during the first quarter of 1996. The sales to Gaz de France and Distrigaz were followed by a short-term FOB contract with Spain's Enagás after the successful sale of two trial cargoes in early 1995. This contract was progressively extended through the end of 1998.

[7] Basis is the difference in price between two locations and can be seen as a proxy for the market value of transportation between these locations, even when the transportation service is provided by pipelines under a regulated tariff.

[8] Maisonnier, Guy. 2005. The ties between natural gas and oil prices. *Panorama* 2006, November, p. 5.

[9] In 2005, 95% of ExxonMobil's worldwide gas reserve additions were associated with LNG projects in Qatar.

[10] Examples are Malaysia LNG Tiga and Australia's NWS Train 5. The owners of these separate projects gave the go-ahead for construction to begin (in 1999 and 2005, respectively), despite the fact that the ventures were not underpinned by even a single binding LNG SPA.

[11] Bainbridge, Phil. 2002. FERC Conference—LNG Panel. October 25.

[12] The world crude oil tanker fleet numbered 4,225 vessels as of July 2006. This refers to ships over 25,000 deadweight tons. This number will increase dramatically over the next three years, as there were 1,394 crude oil tankers on order at this time.

[13] An excellent example is Turkey, which has been keen to redirect its Algerian and Nigerian LNG cargoes to other markets. This is because Turkey has contracted for much more gas than it actually needs. Prior to Turkey's severe economic problems (plus price deregulation moves) in 2001, Turkish natural gas demand had been projected to increase very rapidly in coming years, with the prime consumers expected to be natural gas-fired electric power plants and industrial users. In the aftermath of that crisis, however, state natural gas and pipeline company Botas revised its natural gas demand growth projections sharply, from about 1.6 Tcf in 2005 to under 0.9 Tcf in that year, a 45% downward revision. However, Turkey was already contracted to buy far more gas than it actually required. To date, Turkey has signed deals for around 1.8 Tcf of natural gas imports in 2010, more than 25% above the Botas forecast for Turkish gas consumption (1.4 Tcf) in that year. Currently, about 1.1 Tcf of gas comes from Russia (0.7 Tcf), Iran (0.2 Tcf), and Algeria and Nigeria (0.2 Tcf) in the form of LNG. Consequently, it is believed that gas from pipelines such as the Blue Stream and new projects such as the Trans-Caspian Pipeline or Shah Deniz will be more than sufficient to meet Turkey's requirements for some years into the future; the viability of the latter two pipeline projects is questionable, given Turkey's actual sluggish gas demand growth. See EIA. 2005. *Country Analysis Brief*. July.

ORCHESTRATION AND FINANCING OF AN LNG PROJECT 9

INTRODUCTION

Every LNG project requires a chain of facilities, organizations, and contracts connecting the resource and the end user. The physical chain runs from gas exploration, production and processing, pipeline transportation, liquefaction, shipping, importation, regasification to distribution. Alongside this physical chain is a parallel chain of business ventures, governments, and contracts that bind the links of the gas and LNG chain, divide the revenues to support the financing of the facilities and operations, and allocate and assign risks. Assembling this chain is often described as project formation.

The decisive event in project formation is the commitment to funding by the equity sponsors and the lenders, called the final investment decision (FID). Usually, the upstream sponsors make the FID, since the liquefaction plant represents the dominant investment in the chain; sometimes the FID is used to describe the commitment to building an import terminal. This commitment requires an assured, long-term revenue stream from the LNG buyers sufficient to fund the capital investment and operating expenses. In turn, the LNG buyers seek an assured LNG supply that can be used to serve and build markets.

To provide these assurances, an entire web of intertwined and interdependent venture and fiscal agreements, resource and cost assessments, and construction agreements in the host country must be established. Shipping must be secured, as well as buyer commitments. All of these must be brought on stream on a closely coordinated schedule. Project formation—the implementation of the set of agreements leading up to and including the sales agreements and the FID—is a complex, costly, and sometimes lengthy process. When project financing is introduced, the complexity is further increased.

There are two keys to successful project formation. The first is the establishment of a supply project in which the participants bring both project management capabilities and an alignment of seller, buyer, host country, and buyer country interests. The second is a creditworthy revenue commitment from the sale of LNG, to secure the funding.

MONOPOLY UTILITIES AND THE PROJECT-CHAIN BUSINESS MODEL

Through the mid-1980s, natural gas and electricity markets were largely controlled by regulated, monopoly-franchised utilities. In Japan, these were gas or electric utilities. In Europe, Korea, and Taiwan, LNG buyers were national, monopoly-franchised gas transmission utilities. In the United States, most LNG buyers were gas transmission utilities.

These utilities bought LNG ex-ship or, if they controlled shipping, FOB. Each utility managed all the downstream logistics, operations, and commercial transactions in its own market, including importation and regasification, inland transportation, and demand aggregation. They either sold the natural gas wholesale to electric generation, industrial, and gas distribution companies or distributed gas or electricity directly to end users.

The natural commercial structure for an LNG project in this environment was the project-chain model, in which the LNG supply project was the seller and the utility was the buyer. To secure funding, the supply project required that utilities make a long-term off-take commitment and deliver the LNG through import terminals controlled by the utilities. The supply project committed to funding and construction only when its design capacity was sold. Utilities could afford such commitments because they could recover costs through regulated tariffs. Shipping was dedicated and controlled by either the seller (ex-ship sale) or the buyer (FOB sale), but since there was little opportunity for trading, the control of shipping was not a strategic issue. In the absence of competitive wholesale natural gas markets, LNG sales prices were indexed to energy alternatives—typically crude oil prices in Asian markets and oil products prices in Europe.

The LNG trade evolved as a layered sequence of bilaterally committed trades. Each new LNG project had to find markets in advance. This model supported the financing of LNG projects, but the rigid commercial structure carried costs. Buyers were precluded from managing the risk of mismatched supply and demand obligations through inflexible contract terms. Sellers were precluded from selling to markets that offered higher prices, except on rare occasions when there was alignment of uncommitted excess production and shipping capacity and access to an import market. An emphasis on reliability by the buyers (as a function of the regulatory bargain described in chapter 2) resulted in excess capacity being embedded along the chain. The inefficiency was costly, but the utility buyers had no economic motive to support more efficient and profitable commercial arrangements. Finally, the financing arrangements were often linked to the importing country's export credit agencies and restricted the project to using that country's EPC contractors and shipbuilders. Limited competition resulted in higher costs, but again there was no motive to break the cycle.

THE EMERGENCE OF LNG MERCHANTS

In the late 1990s, three convergent forces started changing markets, costs, and financing requirements for LNG supply projects:

- The commoditization and liberalization of North American wholesale natural gas and gas transportation markets, followed by the beginning of liberalization in Europe, weakened the monopoly-franchised utilities and their guaranteed tariffs, insofar as they related to gas importation, transmission, and wholesale gas sales. (Retail deregulation, or unbundling, has experienced a limited record of success.) As a result, the logistic and commercial functions they had provided—import and inland transportation and wholesale merchant gas sales—emerged as both problems and opportunities for LNG sellers.
- After experiencing steep drops at the onset of wholesale gas-on-gas competition (North America and the United Kingdom being the most dramatic examples), natural gas demand and prices began to rise in North America and Europe. Electric power sector liberalization in North America and Europe contributed to this trend as gas became the fuel of choice in new power plants. Again, the United States,

the United Kingdom (with its famous "dash for gas"), and Spain were dramatic examples. Finally, the widespread availability of LNG import terminal capacity made access to these markets easier. This excess capacity had been created in the United States as a result of the failure of the earlier LNG projects and in Europe as a result of conservative design in the LNG terminals.

- Driven by the opportunities and challenges of new markets, LNG costs throughout the chain dropped by nearly half in real terms owing to improved design, increasing scale, and more competitive procurement from EPC contractors, process vendors, and shipyards. Reliability became less of a concern than efficiency, and by this time, it was clear to many that the LNG chain was an inherently reliable model, no longer requiring (and more important, no longer rewarding) the earlier conservatism and redundancy.

However, the impacts and outcomes differed between the Atlantic and the Asia-Pacific markets.

Today, for projects looking to Asian markets, monopoly utility buyers still dominate, although this is less true in Korea and may not be the ultimate model for China or India. However, the Atlantic markets, liberalization has eroded monopoly franchises, have offered increased access to and within the markets, and in general has increased the level of competition. Nevertheless, to fully realize the benefits of competition, changes were and are needed in terms of the access to LNG terminals, domestic transportation capacity, and downstream demand aggregation and marketing. LNG project ventures are ill-suited to these functions and have a hard time adapting to these changes, largely designed to accommodate markets dominated by pipeline supplies. Security of access to markets, certainty of LNG price structures, and creditworthiness of buyers become more challenging in this new environment.

After 2000, a new class of LNG merchants emerged and began to step into the role classically filled by the utility buyers. The newly emergent market structure afforded opportunities for supply access, marketing, and short-term arbitrage opportunities on both ends of the LNG chain. For companies such as Shell, BP, BG, and Repsol, these new opportunities afforded a means to enhance their positions in supply projects by increasing their control of shipping, import terminal capacity, and marketing across diverse terminaling and liquefaction positions, often by acquiring capacity in open-access terminals and by acquiring ownership of their own, non-dedicated LNG tankers. ExxonMobil, Chevron, and ConocoPhillips formed trades with new large export projects targeted at proprietary import terminals in Europe and North America. In some cases, the energy majors and the national oil companies (NOCs) take or retain title to the LNG through the import terminal and assume direct market risk as merchants. On the other end of the chain, downstream players, such as Suez, Gaz de France, Gas Natural, and Union Fenosa, expanded their shipping, import terminal capacity, and marketing activities, while the last three companies acquired shares in LNG supply projects.

This environment has resulted in a change of the commercial structures for new LNG sales and purchases. FOB sales from Trinidad's first ALNG train provided its customers with considerable sales and destination flexibility. Consistent with EU policy, Nigeria LNG has followed Norway and Russia in abolishing destination restrictions, although for the early trains, Nigeria LNG retained control over the shipping. Algerian pipeline and LNG sales terms are expected to conform. However, the loosening of destination restrictions does not translate into complete freedom for buyer or seller, since the terms of sales still may require the consent of both parties to a given change in destination.

LNG supply project sponsors may now buy LNG from the project for merchant sale in direct competition with the classic utility customers. New liquefaction trains in Trinidad and Egypt are being structured as utility-like tolling facilities without any assured LNG sales role for their owners. Utilities are being required to segregate their merchant and transportation functions and in their role as downstream gas marketers are moving upstream by taking equity ownership positions in LNG supply projects.

With lower costs and growing prospects for short-term sales, supply project sponsors have been willing to commit to FID when only part of the design capacity was sold. Beginning in 1999, Qatar's Ras Laffan LNG, Oman LNG, Malaysian LNG Tiga, and Sakhalin II all moved forward with less than full capacity sold. Australia's NWS Train 4 was committed to an extended buildup period in its long-term SPAs with Japanese buyers. The resulting volumes—called wedge volumes because of the shape of the supply curve—were sold to Shell, an equity participant, for short-term trading.

In Japan, buyers are shortening contract durations while acquiring shipping capacity to match the very gradual liberalization of their domestic markets. This loosening of trade terms has also aided the electric utility buyers in managing shortfalls in nuclear power generation by expanding thermal generation in the face of operating and safety problems with nuclear plants. Kogas has been very active in short-term trading to cover the extreme seasonal demands in its market. New LNG buyers, such as Pohang Iron and Steel, have emerged in the Korean market, developing their own import terminals, and more customers—possibly power generation companies—could follow. Flexible trading will grow in Asia-Pacific markets and should be further facilitated by the opening of western North America to LNG imports. This new market will provide Asian producers and importers with access to a more flexible market with transparent price realization, given the much shorter shipping distances than for sales to Europe and along the North American east coast.

SUPPLY PROJECT STRUCTURE AND FORMATION

The growth of competitive markets in North America and Europe has seen increased liquidity, flexibility, and capacity throughout the chain. This increased capacity, arising from the addition of new ships and import terminal capacity, as well as the more efficient use of existing assets, is not reliably available on a long-term commercial basis, and access to shipping and import capacity for the majority of the LNG must still be guaranteed for a new LNG supply project to move forward.

Requirements for an LNG project

Every LNG project must have the following basic components:

- A host country environment that offers stable legal and fiscal structures for resource exploitation and business income and resource taxation
- Assurance of the quantity and expected production profile of the natural gas and condensate resource base[1]
- Commitments by experienced, credible producers, contractors, and process vendors to build the facilities for gas production and transportation to the liquefaction plant and, if necessary, the import terminal at a known cost, on a set schedule, and with an assured level of performance
- Ownership or contractual control of shipping, LNG import/regasification capacity, and inland market access by the seller and/or buyer
- Guarantee of sales revenues through a mix of long-term contracts incorporating assured volume off-take, market responsive prices, and reliable market access
- Regulatory and political regime in the end-use market country that protects the terms of purchase and market access

- Strong, credible, and creditworthy contracting parties, which may include joint ventures in many project roles, with experienced management and operating track records
- Access to adequate funds, including equity and debt funding, for project formation and construction financing in amounts sufficient to cover unanticipated up-front investment costs and potential adverse developments during operations, especially sustained low-energy-price environments

Project formation

The process of assembling and orchestrating these elements is called project formation. Much like a chamber music group, there are several key players but no single conductor directs the musicians, although often this role is assumed in part by the supply project venture, which has the largest investment.

Host country agreements. The first order of business for the new project venture is to conclude a set of host country agreements (if these are not already in place) that establish the fiscal, commercial, and regulatory environment for the project's construction and operation. These agreements include the commercial and natural resource exploitation laws of the host country and prior agreements relating to specific resource access development, participation, royalties, and taxation.

In addition to preexisting development terms and fiscal structures, issues to be resolved during the formation stage include the following:

- Specific targeted fiscal or other government incentives associated with the LNG project development
- Access to or acquisition of lands owned by the government
- Safety, design, and environmental standards
- The terms of importation of project equipment and material
- Targets for the use of local content; labor relations; maritime regulations
- Operating standards
- Financial and currency issues (including foreign currency borrowing and repayment, currency conversion, repatriation of dividends, withholding, and other taxes on financial transactions)
- Regulatory stability
- Dispute resolution and arbitration procedures

These can be provided through legislative or regulatory actions or through sovereign contracts when the existing legal regime is inadequate.

Adequacy of the resource and gas supply. Typically, the project aims to monetize a gas resource that is known but not fully delineated. Compared to oil, natural gas projects require greater up-front investments and have much longer payout periods. Traditionally, neither buyers nor sellers would commit to an LNG project until sufficient resources and reservoir performance were demonstrated and certified for the economic life of the project (which can run 20 years or more). This may be an easy task, as was the case with Qatar's 900 Tcf North Field, or a more difficult and costly undertaking, as with the increasingly challenging offshore prospects in Australia, Russia, and West Africa. In Egypt, the Spanish Egyptian Gas Company (SEGAS) is actually buying feedgas from an existing natural gas supply system until sufficient new reserves are proven.

Facilities construction. Construction of a project's major facilities is usually performed by an EPC contractor, acting alone or in a consortium. Separate contracts may be let for production, pipeline, liquefaction, and marine facilities. Marine facilities may be built and owned by the project or by the host country (with the government's investment recovered through port fees). Within the prime contract for the liquefaction project, subcontracts will be let for specialized facilities and equipment, such as cryogenic storage tanks, gas turbine and compressor strings, and the liquefaction process units.

In the early days, the design and management of the construction project was a formidable technical and managerial challenge. EPC contracts were negotiated on a cost-plus basis and required intense cooperation between the contractor and the owners, with independent engineering firms and/or one or more owners acting as technical advisers to the project venture.

Today, project management capability has become widespread, aided by a better understanding of the design and operating parameters of the liquefaction plants, and clear evidence of the overall robustness of the technology. In a practice initiated by ALNG, a project will often solicit and pay for multiple, detailed FEED proposals; EPC contractors then submit lump sum bids, for a turnkey, performance-guaranteed construction contract based on these designs (which they may have developed). There are now at least six EPC contractors who can bid on such contracts and a growing number of vendors of cryogenic heat exchangers and processes (see chapter 5). As project costs have fallen and EPC contractors have grown larger, the need for the contractors to form consortia to bid on these projects (as a way of risk sharing) is no longer as important, and more bids can be expected on any single project than was the case in the past.

Competition, improved design, better construction management, and growing scale halved the real unit costs of liquefaction in the 1990s. At the same time, costs in gas exploration, production, and pipelining were also falling steeply through the wide and rapid deployment of improved technology. LNG supply costs were reduced to the point that the construction of large projects could be started before the sale of all the capacity was completed, with the uncommitted volumes available at such low cost that they would clear the price in any market.

LNG SPAS

The basis of project funding is provided by the revenues generated through long-term SPAs. The principle provisions of the SPA establish the pricing of LNG sales and the commitments to quantity off-take and delivery. Like many long-term contracts in international trade, LNG SPAs also contain provisions for specifying the duration of the contract and for determining the responsibilities and obligations of the parties, the technical specifications of the LNG and the facilities, payment terms, dispute resolution, financial guarantees, and force majeure.

LNG pricing

Where there has been no reliable independent determination of gas prices—which is the case for most countries outside the United States and the United Kingdom—LNG prices are generally indexed to oil or oil product prices. These links are not always linear, as some contract price formulas dampen out the extreme swings in oil prices. As oil and gas are most readily substitutable for one another (except in transportation fuels), it makes sense to link the pricing. Even in markets characterized by gas-on-gas competition, such as the United States, there is evidence that oil and gas prices do reasonably correlate over the long term. Where there is no competitive gas market and where the gas price is passed on to the customer, there is much less pressure to try and set the price on competitive terms. The buyer has no economic incentive to achieve a lower price, and oil-indexed pricing has the advantage that it can be explained and rationalized to the regulators who oversee the utility's pricing. On the seller's side, pricing linked to oil makes the LNG project revenue stream look more like the revenue stream from an oil project, a concept with which the producers, their shareholders, and financiers are comfortable.

Oil indexation also has the advantage of being based on a market with liquid and transparent pricing, which prevents manipulation. However, while crude oil and oil products were a significant part of electricity sector inputs in the 1970s, natural gas increasingly competes with coal, not oil. A few sales of natural gas and LNG in Europe have included indexation to coal or electric prices, but these types of formulas often show major deviations from oil and other gas prices and are much harder for buyers and sellers to justify to one another or to their host governments. The industry structure does not tend to reward innovation with respect to energy pricing in regulated markets.

Except for deliveries from Indonesia, LNG sales to Japan are indexed to the Japan Customs Cleared price (JCC; also known as the Japan Crude Cocktail). The JCC is published monthly and is calculated as the total import revenue divided by the total volume (in bbl) of imported crude and semifinished oils, and then implemented with various lags. Indonesian LNG (and crude oil) sales are indexed to the Indonesian Crude Price (ICP), a basket of Asia-Pacific crudes priced at Singapore. Indonesian sales to other East Asian buyers follow this pattern. Some Indonesian contracts have a minimum price.

Some non-Indonesian contracts have an S-curve structure, in which the slope of the price response is dampened outside a central range. However, the 2002 sale to China from the Australian NWS project had a price structure that resulted in a significantly lower price, while a 2001 sale from RasGas II to India's Petronet LNG had the price frozen at a low level for the first five years. Subsequent surges in world crude oil prices, however, combined with a tightening LNG supply situation, have encouraged LNG sellers to demand—and receive—significantly higher prices from all customers in Asia and resulted in pricing along traditional lines.

Algerian LNG sales, which are made largely on an FOB basis to Europe, have been indexed to European oil product prices, similar to the pricing of Norwegian pipeline gas. New sales to Europe generally continue to mimic pipeline sale prices, except for the Nigeria LNG sale to Italy's ENEL, which included a large coal-based component. Sales to the United States are made on the basis of net backs from wholesale gas market prices, such as the Henry Hub, and the United Kingdom is likely to follow a similar pattern using the National Balancing Point (NBP).

Shipping has been handled in many different ways in the past, including being embedded in the price of LNG. Increasingly, shipping is seen as more of a utility function, with the costs largely transparent to sellers and buyers. Shipping costs are simply being incorporated as adjustments to FOB, CIF, or ex-ship prices, depending on whether the buyer or seller is providing shipping.

LNG off-take

In the absence of accessible alternative markets, the buyer's purchase obligation provides the revenue stream that sustains project funding. In the typical project-chain business model, the buyer commits to lift an annual contract quantity (ACQ). Since variation in supply flow requires increased capacity for production, storage, and shipping, volume flexibility is limited—often less than 10% of the annual volumes. Typically, the buyer is obligated to take or pay for a high percentage of the ACQ volumes, ensuring cash flow for the supplier. Failure to lift the ACQ can result in the buyer's paying for the volume shortfall, with limited ability to recover these volumes later through makeup rights. The seller and the buyer are obligated to ensure the availability of their facilities and to cooperate in the development of an annual delivery program for scheduling production, shipping, and delivery.

SHIPPING

In the traditional project-chain business model, ships are committed to the trade and are controlled or owned by the seller in an ex-ship trade or the buyer in an FOB trade. Ships are typically owned separately from the liquefaction and import facilities, and ship financing is increasingly highly leveraged with mortgage debt secured by charter payments.

As Korean shipyards entered the LNG shipbuilding business in the 1990s, increased competition drove down ship construction costs. While prices have risen again since 2002 in the wake of rising materials prices and labor costs, the prospective entry of Chinese shipyards should bring prices down once again (see chapter 6).

FUNDING

Project funding comprises sponsors' equity contributions and debt finance. In the first two decades of the LNG business, project technology, costs, and performance were uncertain, and the financial community was not sufficiently knowledgeable to engage in project financing, more accurately described as limited-recourse lending. Projects were financed through equity or loans advanced by buyers' banks, multilateral credit agencies, and export credit agencies (ECAs) and were often guaranteed by the sponsors' corporate credit.

Project finance, in which recourse for service of third-party debt is limited to the revenues and assets of the LNG project itself, began in earnest in the early 1990s with the financing of Indonesia's Bontang Train F and has been widely employed since then. Project finance typically consists of a mix of syndicated loans from ECAs, other multilateral agencies, public or private bond financing, and commercial bank debt. The ECAs provide credit for project procurement in their home countries and create credit enhancement for other lenders, as they carry attributes similar to sovereign lending, which tends to reduce the political risk of defaults or currency inconvertibility. Ras Laffan initiated the first successful capital market financing for an LNG project, with an oversubscribed $1.2 billion bond issue.

Project financing is costly, with steep up-front fees and higher interest rates than corporate borrowing. However, it can bring structural benefits to the project: it removes the project debt from the sponsors' corporate balance sheets and allows much higher borrowing leverage by the project; it provides third-party funding to support the NOC participation; it brings the discipline of third-party due diligence to the technical and commercial structure of the project; and it may enhance the alignment of incentives among the sponsors and host government. For all but the highest-credit-rated sponsors (e.g., ExxonMobil) project financing usually lowers the cost of capital associated with the LNG project financing.

EVOLVING PROJECT VENTURE STRUCTURES

This section reviews in more detail the types and the evolution of project venture structures and participation. The structure and the participation in these ventures vary depending on sponsors, host country, market, resource access, and technical conditions. Ownership of facilities for production, feedgas pipeline transportation, liquefaction, and the port may be integrated into a single venture (or legal entity) or may be distributed among several ventures. Shipping can be chartered either to the LNG seller or to the buyer but is typically owned and financed separately.

Project venture participation includes companies that have production rights in the resource. One or more major international oil companies (IOCs) may join, even if they were not originally involved in the resource discovery, bringing financial, technical, project management, marketing, and operating capabilities and usually purchasing an interest in the reserves. If the host country has an NOC, it typically has a significant equity share. Buyers may also make equity investments to ensure more security of supply, to access project information, and as an investment opportunity in exchange for their purchase commitment.

Types of project ventures

LNG supply project ventures may be classified into six structures:

State owned and financed. The existing Algerian and Libyan projects are state owned and were financed through sovereign-guaranteed debt.

Integrated project. The simplest structure in theory is the integrated joint venture, in which the ownership of the upstream, pipeline, and liquefaction segments of the LNG train are shared equally among all project participants. Examples are Australia's NWS, Qatar's Ras Laffan LNG, and Russia's Sakhalin II project. There is no transfer price between the upstream and liquefaction, so that all project segments are taxed as a single entity. Risks—price risk, production risk, and political risk—are shared equitably among all the project participants. Setting up an integrated joint venture, therefore, requires full agreement by the partners about the project's strategy and governance.

Norway's Snøhvit project is an example of a true integrated joint venture, since both the upstream and the liquefaction segments are owned by six project partners and the entire project is subject to a single fiscal structure. Snøhvit has been placed in a Norwegian upstream fiscal regime, which subjects it to high taxation but gives it a faster depreciation schedule. This demonstrates one of the benefits of the simplicity of a joint venture: Two of the project participants are taking their share of production as LNG, while the others are selling at the FOB point to buying partners.

Resource taxation is typically assessed on an imputed net back to feedgas production. Because of Australian fiscal regimes, the NWS is organized as an unincorporated joint venture, with each investor responsible for making parallel decisions; a sales contract with the NWS is in fact six separate but identical sales contracts with each of the six participants.

Split-revenue ventures. The upstream and downstream facilities are owned and operated by different ventures, and the LNG sales revenue is split, according to an agreed formula, between the liquefaction and production interests. This structure allows different shares in the upstream and downstream ventures. In some projects, buyer representatives and the NOC may participate only in one segment. Examples of split-revenue ventures are Brunei LNG, Malaysia LNG, ALNG Train 1, Nigeria LNG, and Snøhvit. In this structure, different fiscal regimes typically apply to the distinct segments of the project. Other variations include further subdivision of interests, as is the case in Trinidad, where the National Gas Company also provides gas transmission services between the gas-producing fields and the liquefaction plant.

Fixed-price feedgas. The term "fixed" is somewhat of a misnomer: In projects that specify a certain feedgas-pricing formula, the price is often not fixed but is some function of the LNG price. The formula used may set the feedgas price as a fixed percentage of the FOB or the ex-ship LNG price, in proportion to the project's annual revenue. Alternatively, the formula may set a per-unit payment for feedgas that increases over time. The defining characteristic of this type of project structure is that, as opposed to cost-recovery-based projects, the upstream shoulders very little of the risk and receives none (or very little) of the upside if the LNG prices increase.

In the cases where the upstream receives a fixed fraction of the LNG price, be it FOB or ex-ship, the upstream percentage is usually less than 25%. This limits the production risk; it would also limit the fiscal burden on the upstream, except that in many projects with this type of structure (e.g., Oman's first two trains, or Abu Dhabi's ADGAS project), the government owns the gas reserves and sells feedgas to the LNG project.

In Oman, the government owns the feedgas and farms out production responsibilities to a separate company with representatives from both the government and Shell, the largest commercial participant in Oman LNG. Feedgas is sold to the project at a set per-unit price that is stepped up over the life of the project. By comparison, the Abu Dhabi national oil company (ADNOC) controls the producing fields and operates them in consortia with commercial oil companies. The feedgas price is a function of the LNG project's annual revenue.

Some projects do away with the upstream segment altogether. Union Fenosa's LNG facility in Damietta, Egypt, buys at least some of its feedgas from Egyptian General Petroleum Company (EGPC) directly from the gas transmission grid. EGPC gets to choose which fields are sources for the LNG project.

In this structure, the feedgas is owned and produced by the government or a government-dominated enterprise. Examples are ADGAS, Qatargas, Oman LNG, and SEGAS. Feedgas payments may involve some LNG sales revenue sharing. For some projects, large condensate coproduction provides significant revenue.[2]

Cost-based liquefaction. In Indonesian projects, the liquefaction facility is owned by Pertamina and is debt financed, and the borrowings are repaid on a cost-recovery basis. LNG sales revenues are deposited in a trustee bank, which then allocates the revenue to debt service, liquefaction plant operating costs, and taxes, with the remainder going to the production-sharing contractors. This structure has the effect of pushing profits into the upstream, where they are subject to higher taxation.

Toll-based liquefaction. The emergence of merchant trading by major oil and gas companies has led to a new structure, in which the producers retain ownership of the gas through the liquefaction facility, which is owned by the producers, buyers, and NOCs on some negotiated basis (which may not reflect the share of upstream production or purchase rights). The gas producers pay a fee to the tolling venture and sell the LNG on their own terms without reference to each other. A commercial structure that treats the liquefaction segment of an LNG project as a tolling facility provides a steady income for liquefaction and pushes economic rent into the upstream.

In this scenario, the allowable rate of return (RoR) for the LNG trains is set (usually somewhere between 8% and 12%), so that the liquefaction part of the project receives a set amount of the project revenue to cover operating costs and investment returns. Feedgas price is based on a net back from the LNG sales price. Within this structure, the owners and the operators of the liquefaction venture are less exposed to price and production risk. Their share is essentially guaranteed as long as the project has an after-tax cash flow that is equal to or greater than the allowable RoR. However, there is usually no upside for the liquefaction segment. Any economic rent over and above the target RoR set for the project goes to the upstream. Nearly all of the risk on the project is therefore borne by the production segment.

Pushing rents upstream is a good way to remunerate the upstream participants for the risks that they have taken in exploration and development of the gas fields. However, this system exposes more revenue to upstream taxation, which is typically higher than for liquefaction. The tolling-facility model is best applied either where the liquefaction segment is controlled by a government entity or NOC that is not involved in the producing fields or where gas is sourced from a number of different fields with different owners, some of whom may not participate in liquefaction.

Trinidad's ALNG is a good example of a downstream tolling structure. Ownership of ALNG Trains 2 and 3 are split between three partners. The gas is sourced from different fields operating under different PSCs. The liquefaction segment operates on a cost-plus-return system, while the feedgas price is based on a net back from the FOB sales. A similar structure is used by the LNG facility in Idku, Egypt, where the partners have built a number of trains, each liquefying gas from different Egyptian sources on a toll basis.

The Atlantic Basin market and project development

Figure 9–1 summarizes the growth prospects for LNG in the Atlantic Basin, a term generally used to refer to Europe, the Mediterranean, and North America. This region accounted for over 35% of all LNG imports in 2005, or some 73.4 Bcm (53.2 MMt), and could almost triple in volume by 2015, to just over 183 Bcm (133 MMt). This represents a 13% average annual growth rate.

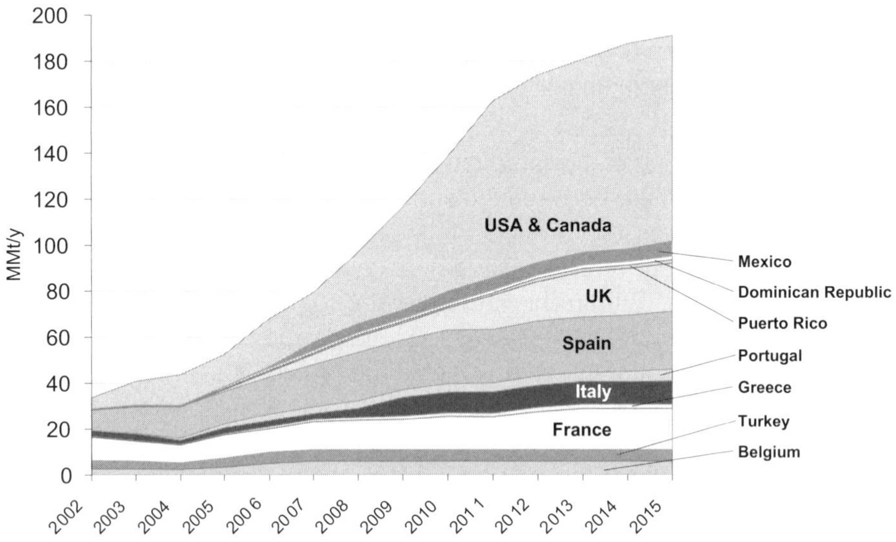

Fig. 9–1. Atlantic Basin LNG demand growth prospects (*Source:* Poten & Partners)

Sonatrach was the initial mover in the Atlantic Basin and was the unchallenged volume leader until 2005. Sonatrach controlled the entire LNG value chain from wellhead to loading port and in most instances also provided LNG shipping through its own fleet (although this fleet was initially owned by a separate Algerian state company subsequently acquired by Sonatrach). Sonatrach largely makes term sales in Europe, has been active in the U.S. spot market, and is venturing west of Suez with sales to India.

ALNG comprises BP, BG, and Repsol, as gas producers and off-takers, and Suez (originally Cabot LNG, then Tractebel), as an off-taker and owner of import terminal capacity in the United States. The National Gas Company of Trinidad not only participated as an investor but also provided gas transmission services to bring the gas to the plant. BP has access to import capacity in the United States and Spain; Repsol and Gas Natural have access to Spanish terminals but have sold large volumes of LNG to the United States; and BG has moved most of its volumes to the United States, although some cargoes have gone as far as the Pacific. Virtually all of Suez's volumes go to the Everett, Massachusetts, terminal.

The LNG export project in Nigeria had been under consideration since the early 1960s. When launched in the 1990s, the Nigeria LNG project brought together the Nigerian National Petroleum Corporation (NNPC) and three major energy companies—Shell, Eni, and Total—with significant oil production in the country. The project controls its own shipping and has largely made ex-ship sales to Europe. Nigeria LNG has become a significant spot LNG trader since its inception. In its later trains, Nigeria LNG held tenders to award LNG sales, on an FOB basis, to the highest bidders, who included Shell and BG. Shell has import capacity at the Cove Point, Maryland, and Elba Island, Georgia, facilities in the United States, and together with Total, equity in the Altamira receiving terminal in Mexico and Hazira in India. It is also developing import terminal projects elsewhere in North America and Europe. Total has access to North American, European, and Indian outlets, while Eni is seeking LNG capacity in the United States, as well as in Europe.

The Qatari LNG projects have made sales to Spain and will deliver LNG to a new terminal that is under construction in Italy. The BG-led Egyptian LNG project will ship LNG to a new terminal under construction in France, a proposed terminal in Italy, and BG-controlled capacity at Lake Charles and Elba Island. Union Fenosa of Spain joined with Italy's Eni to form the SEGAS LNG project in Egypt, which began supplying gas to a new import terminal in Spain in 2004; Union Fenosa is also a shareholder in Oman's Qalhat LNG, an expansion of the Oman LNG project, and is taking supply from this project.

A flood of new projects is being developed to serve new import terminals in Europe and North America. ExxonMobil and Qatar Petroleum are constructing two new large export projects that will supply large receiving terminals that they are building in the United Kingdom and the U.S. Gulf of Mexico, as well as import capacity at the terminal at Zeebrugge, Belgium. ConocoPhillips and Qatar Petroleum are developing another project in Qatar that will deliver LNG to the U.S. Gulf of Mexico, while Shell and Qatar Petroleum's project was originally targeted at Shell-controlled import capacity on the east coasts of the United States and Mexico. A significant aspect of all these developments is the emergence of NOCs, IOCs, and downstream utilities as LNG merchants participating through the chain to form new trades.

New African LNG export projects that were in the planning stage as of the end of 2006 include the following:

- Algeria's El Andalous LNG (Gassi Touil, Sonatrach, Repsol, and Gas Natural)
- Angola LNG (Chevron, Sonangol, BP, ENI, and Total)
- Equatorial Guinea (Marathon, Sonagas, Mitsui, and Marubeni)
- Libya (Shell)
- Brass LNG in Nigeria (ConocoPhillips, Eni, Total,[3] and NNPC)
- OK-LNG in Nigeria (ExxonMobil, Chevron, ConocoPhillips, BG, and NNPC)

In 2005, Russia's Gazprom was considering between Norsk Hydro, Statoil, ConocoPhillips, Chevron, and Total to co-develop the giant Shtokmanov field in Northern Russia for an export project at Murmansk, from which the gas would be destined for the United States and Canada. Gazprom was also linked to an LNG project near St. Petersburg being developed with PetroCanada and targeted at eastern Canadian markets. The Shtokman project appears to have gone into abeyance at the end of 2006, as Gazprom evaluated whether the reserves had more value supplying European pipeline markets.

The Asia-Pacific market and project development

Historically, Asia-Pacific markets and export projects have accounted for the largest share of the world's LNG trade. In 2005, nine countries exported 92 MMt (127 Bcm) of LNG to Japan, Korea, Taiwan, and India. Most of these deliveries came from Asia, the United States (Alaska), and the Middle East under long-term contracts, along with a few cargoes from North Africa. Asian sellers accounted for 49% of the world's exports, mainly shipped to Asian buyers but with a few spot cargos to Europe and the United States.

Starting with its first imports in 1969, Japan has always been the dominant buyer. Korea entered the market in 1986, Taiwan followed in 1990, India in 2004, and most recently, China in 2006.

Figure 9–2 shows historic and forecasted demand growth in future LNG import markets in the Asia-Pacific region (which covers Japan, Korea, and Taiwan, as well as India, China, and the west coast of North America). The first small project was developed in Kenai, Alaska, in 1969, at the behest of electric and gas utility buyers in the Tokyo Bay area. Subsequently, projects were developed in Brunei, Abu Dhabi, Indonesia, Malaysia, Australia, Qatar, Oman, and, prospectively, Russia and Iran.

The unique Indonesian structure previously discussed permitted Pertamina to own and finance the liquefaction project. Most projects have small but important participation from companies in buyer countries, to align interests with markets and funding.

The integrated ventures at Kenai, NWS, and Sakhalin II had no NOC presence when the projects were formed, although Gazprom has now entered Sakhalin after extreme pressure from the Russian government. The remaining projects have strong NOC participation in the liquefacton venture and share LNG sales revenue and market risk between the upstream and the downstream ventures.

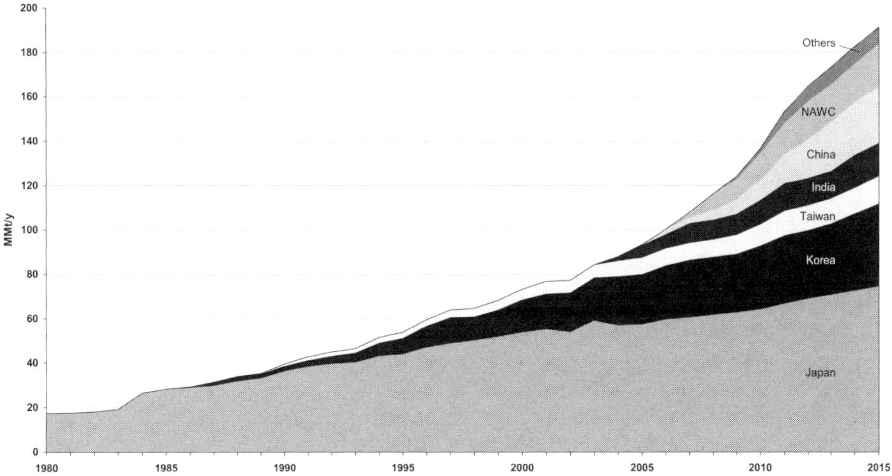

Fig. 9–2. Asia-Pacific region LNG demand growth prospects (*Source:* Poten & Partners)

South East Asian markets are still largely controlled by monopoly-franchised utilities, and these conventional structures will likely persist for some time. However, changes are occurring. In Japan, even though there is no enforced third-party access through LNG import terminals, domestic competition between electricity and gas utilities and independent power producers (IPPs) is emerging. When buyers renew their existing import contracts, they are calling for greater flexibility, shorter contract durations, and, in some cases, buyer control over shipping.

In Korea, although the unbundling and privatization of Korea Electric Power (Kepco) and Kogas has been stalled for a long time, independent LNG purchases are being made through limited open access to Kogas's terminals and the construction of independent import terminals.

The emergence of an LNG market on the west coast of North America will apparently be characterized by the development of import projects with the participation of LNG suppliers. An example is the merger of Shell's and Sempra's terminal projects in Baja California into a single terminal to receive LNG from the Sakhalin and Tangguh export projects. Woodside and Shell are developing both LNG export projects in Australia and import terminals on the west coast of North America.

LNG INDUSTRY TRENDS: THE EMERGENCE OF COMMERCIAL LNG

Changes in the structure of domestic natural gas markets have an impact on the commercial structure of the LNG supply business. When monopoly-franchised utilities dominated natural gas and electricity markets, they controlled the access to and downstream sales of a project's LNG. The project-chain business model certainly supported the financing of the supply project—but at a cost in lost value added through the efficient use of assets and trading.

In the Atlantic Basin, utilities' monopoly franchises have been heavily eroded at the wholesale level. In North America, pipelines have split their transportation services and merchant functions, resulting in competitive markets for both the natural gas commodity and its transportation. The United Kingdom has a single gas transmission provider, but the wholesale and retail markets are fully competitive. In continental Europe, a parallel process is under way, although national champions continue to play a much larger role, encouraged by their host governments (and former shareholders).[4] Where there is effective open access through import terminals and domestic transportation systems, the LNG seller may have to control access and transportation all the way to the electricity generators and gas companies or turn to independent energy merchants to fill this role.

Upstream of the import terminals, LNG merchants are emerging to take advantage of these opportunities and challenges. These are large companies capable of owning and managing a portfolio of diversified capacity positions throughout the chain: equity in supply projects, control over shipping, and import terminal capacity. They engage in commercial LNG—that is, a mix of long-term sales and purchases under increasingly flexible conditions, and short-term trading.

Shell, BP, and BG have augmented their upstream positions with diverse and flexible arrangements for shipping, downstream capacity, and wholesale marketing to their affiliates or third parties. ExxonMobil, Chevron, and ConocoPhillips are matching the development of new supply projects with new proprietary terminal projects, often with onward sales to their wholesale marketing affiliates. Conversely, Gas Natural and Gaz de France, who have major downstream positions, are moving upstream.

In this emerging structure, the role of the LNG project as a merchant seller recedes. In some projects, the LNG is sold to one or more of the sponsors, who assume the downstream merchant function. In others, the liquefaction plant is a tolling facility, and upstream gas producers retain title throughout the chain. There is no common pattern, and each project is developing individual commercial characteristics that reflect its shareholder makeup, financing requirements, and target markets.

In the Taiwanese and Chinese markets, utility buyers still dominate, given the need to aggregate customers in small or emerging markets. However, the very gradual growth of domestic competition in Japan, limited open access in Korea, and domestic merchant buyers in India are enhancing LNG competition and the value of flexible trading. The opportunity to arbitrage North American and Asian gas and electricity market values is proving irresistible. Commercial LNG is emerging in this region as well. Both buyers and sellers are taking on LNG merchant functions and are acquiring positions throughout the chain, to develop new trades and merchant trading.

The expected role of merchant trading is such that the industry is now seeing entrants who fit none of the classic roles of the club. Statoil took capacity at Cove Point and began trading through the terminal before it had even begun construction of the Snøhvit project. Mitsubishi has taken capacity in a Gulf of Mexico terminal. Merrill Lynch and Morgan Stanley are looking to add LNG to their commodity-trading operations.[5] Gazprom, expecting to become an LNG supplier, has entered into LNG trading through gas and LNG swaps in the Atlantic and Pacific basins. In all cases, these new participants own no liquefaction, ships, or import terminals.

PROJECT FINANCE

As described earlier, there are many models for the commercial and legal structure of the LNG chain components. However, the most common structure is a joint venture between the participants in the liquefaction plant, representing arguably the most critical and certainly the most capital-intensive component of the chain.

The joint venture structure accommodates equity participation by a variety of shareholders—typically IOCs, NOCs, buyers, and other entities (e.g., the Japanese trading houses) that may have some original stake in the resource or bring marketing and financial expertise. The joint venture structure often lends itself most readily to limited-recourse debt financing secured by the revenue and assets of the venture.

A joint venture has an independent financial structure. Initial funding during the project feasibility and development stage comes from equity provided by the sponsors. Ultimately, the project venture may contract for debt financing from some combination of commercial banks, ECAs, multilateral agencies (e.g., the World Bank or the Inter-American Development Bank), and bonds floated in the capital markets.

The term "project finance" usually refers to debt that is ultimately secured solely by the revenues and assets of the joint venture and with only limited recourse to the equity sponsors. This financing is generally put in place before construction of the project begins, and the loans are drawn down and equity is contributed as construction proceeds. In such a structure, the lenders will not take project completion risk, and the equity sponsors will guarantee debt service until completion and performance testing are demonstrated to previously agreed standards—hence the term "limited recourse."

In most projects, the sponsors require that EPC contractors assume a measure of completion risk and performance guarantees, along with bonuses for early completion and performance above design standards, through lump sum, turnkey EPC contracts. This form of risk allocation reduces the sponsors' completion risk but clearly requires EPC contractors with strong balance sheets of their own. Where other EPC contract structures are used, the sponsors may need to assume a much greater degree of completion risk.

History and motivation

Project finance in LNG is a relatively recent development. It requires sophisticated lenders and borrowers and entails a complex project formation process to secure and allocate the cash flow and contingency obligations among the participants. Project finance lenders also require specific analysis and oversight of technical and commercial viability of the project through the loan syndication process (where the loans are shared among many banks).

In the early history of the LNG business, the liquefaction plants were financed through sponsors' equity or sponsor-corporate loans. With the exceptions of Algeria, Libya and Nigeria, NOCs were rarely directly involved in the upstream projects, which were equity financed and operated by the gas producers. This was the case with projects in Alaska, Brunei, and Abu Dhabi and with Malaysia LNG Satu. In Indonesia, the liquefaction plants are owned by Pertamina. The first five trains of both the Arun and Bontang projects were financed through Japanese loans. The sixth Arun train was financed by a loan from Mobil, the upstream producer.

One of the earliest limited-recourse loan in the LNG business was made for Woodside Petroleum's participation in the NWS project. Since the project was unincorporated to permit the pass-through of early tax losses, the loan was secured on a limited-recourse basis by Woodside's one-sixth interest in the project. Subsequently, project finance was used for Indonesia's Bontang Train F; Malaysia LNG Dua; the upstream and downstream ventures of Qatargas; Trinidad's ALNG Trains 1, 2, and 3; Oman LNG; and the integrated Ras Laffan project, which floated the industry's first capital market bond issue.

Typically, projects considering or seeking project financing will retain a financial adviser in the early stages of the project, to support the financial analysis and provide the lenders with a degree of assurance that the project has been well structured and is expected to provide financially attractive returns to the shareholders during its life. Advisers typically are units of commercial banks, such as Citigroup and the Royal Bank of Scotland (RBS), or investment banks, such as Credit Suisse and Goldman Sachs. The advisers also play a key role by identifying the most optimal borrowing structure and sources of funds and negotiating with the lenders.

Advantages of project finance

Project finance is expensive, typically requiring millions of dollars in up-front fees and carrying a higher interest rate than other forms of debt finance. Nevertheless, it brings several advantages:

- Project finance does not appear on the participating sponsor's corporate balance sheet. Projects are usually financed with much higher leverage than corporations with strong projects able to borrow in the range of 70%–80% of their capital requirements. Only the sponsors' share of the equity investment in the project is reflected on their balance sheets. Project finance allows a sponsor to maintain a stronger balance sheet (lower debt-to-equity ratio) and gives the sponsor improved corporate financial flexibility, especially where the share of the project would represent a very significant investment exposure for the sponsor. During construction and acceptance testing, when lenders still have recourse, total investment and funding may require disclosure in the sponsors' financial statements, although to the extent the completion risk has been shifted to the EPC contractors, this disclosure may not be needed.

- NOCs and smaller IOCs may be hard-pressed to provide equity funding. Project finance may support larger, politically required participation by the host NOC and may avoid delays or other complexity arising from the need for NOC funding. Project finance can help align the interests of sponsors who have very diverse objectives and financial capabilities.
- The need for third-party due diligence, which lenders require for the entire project chain, provides checks and balances in the project structure and can help uncover and correct issues that could later prove problematic. It is often more politically acceptable for NOCs to accept funding with commercial and legal conditions laid down by independent lenders than to accept such terms from IOCs, who are the partners of NOCs in upstream investments.
- The participation of multilateral institutions, commercial banks, and ECAs may deter host countries from expropriation or other significant legal or regulatory changes, such as taxation or currency convertibility, after start-up.

Risk mitigation

Key risks that lenders will seek to minimize include the following:

- Effective management of construction and operations—especially the risk of cost overruns or misestimation. This includes the responsibility for future capital investments to maintain the plant or comply with legal or regulatory mandates, as well as local labor agreements with no-strike provisions.
- Experience and reputation of the borrowers/sponsors and the other counterparties to the major commercial agreements.

- Legal rights to the gas resources and to the land where the plant is to be built.
- Technical performance of the gas fields and pipelines.
- Fiscal, regulatory, and commercial frameworks of the host country.
- Market revenue risk—both price and volume.
- Contract rights that can lead to termination or suspension of key agreements and halt LNG sales or operations. This includes mismatches between the terms of key agreements in the supply chain that could give rise to claims by parties in the future.
- Appropriateness of insurance coverage, at each stage of the project development and commercial operation, with the lenders' interests secured for loss of assets or business interruption.
- Diminution of lenders' rights after financial closing, such as during subsequent plant expansions, which could access the secured assets or impinge on them.
- Project-on-project risk, such as when a third party is required to provide shipping or import terminal capacity, which in turn may be contingent on their own commercial, legal, financing, and funding agreements.

The lenders make their financial commitment after all the elements of project formation are put in place. Among the agreements and undertakings the lenders will require are the following:

- Joint venture formation agreements defining participation, funding obligations, shareholder rights, decision making, corporate governance, future expansion rights, rights to acquire and dispose of assets.
- Host country fiscal, regulatory, and operating agreements, including any necessary licenses, rights-of-way, and title to property required for the plant.
- Reserves delineation and certification, as well as confirmation of expected upstream development plans and production forecasts by independent petroleum engineers.
- Binding agreements for the supply of gas, the provision of shipping, and the sale and purchase of LNG.
- An EPC contract that provides appropriate assurance that the construction will be completed on time, within budget, and to the specified level of performance.
- Independent verification of the estimates of future gas prices and buyers' market development.

- Assurance of the availability of sufficient shipping and import terminal capacity to secure the project's LNG off-take.
- An appropriate package of insurance coverages, including commitments to maintain agreed coverages during the project's construction and operation.

As discussed in chapter 1, the lenders will seek to understand that the project represents a financially viable undertaking for all parties, not just the sponsors. An LNG SPA that proves uneconomical for the buyer will not likely survive the full term, as past history has demonstrated. Venture participation must include one or more companies with credible technical, financial, and management capabilities to form, construct, and operate the project. Significant participation by the NOC, where present, should align sovereign incentives with the project.

Recent years have seen a proliferation of competent and competitive EPC contractors, process vendors, shipyards, and lenders. This reduces costs and uncertainty in the formation and financing process. The annual scheduling of production, storage, shipping, and off-take ensures operational feasibility.

Revenue security is enhanced by the SPA terms, which allocate market pricing and volume risks between the seller and the buyer. Recent developments in destination flexibility should reduce buyers' and sellers' volume exposure; still, these may not receive full credit from the lenders, as they are not as of yet time tested. In many projects, buyers' payments for LNG are made to a third-party bank, which disburses funds for operating expenses, debt service, upstream gas suppliers, and taxes and, finally, to the shareholders in accordance with an agreed process.

Structure and participants

Typically, the package of bank loans to a project may have a tenor (term) of 8–12 years post-completion, with an initial debt service grace period of several months. Up to six months of reserves are initially set aside in escrow to cover debt repayments in the event of an unexpected interruption or diminution of the project's cash flow. Considerable attention is paid to structuring the priority of claims on project cash flow. Innovations in recent project financings include enhanced credit support from the sponsors to protect against low prices at RasGas and subordination of feedgas payments by Oman LNG.

The principal sources of project finance have been the major international commercial banks, including ABN Amro, Bank Paribas, Barclay's, Citigroup, Crédit Lyonnaise, JPMorgan Chase, Schroeder's, and Société

Générale. Large Japanese banks, such as the Industrial Bank of Japan and the Bank of Tokyo, have traditionally participated in LNG project finance.

Multilateral development banks—such as the Inter-American Development Bank, the Asian Development Bank, and the African Development Bank—may also participate. These banks are often focused on financing social infrastructure development tied to the export project.

Export credit will usually be provided by export-import (ExIm) banks, for hardware procurement in the lending country. Prominent examples are the U.S. Export-Import Bank, the Japan Export-Import Bank, the United Kingdom's Export Credit Guarantee Department, France's Compagnie Francaise d'Assurance pour le Commerce Exterieur (COFACE), and Italy's Servizi Assicurativi del Commercio Estero (SACE). In addition to lending on commercial terms to enhance exports, these agencies will insure exporters on commercial terms against short-term nonpayment risks, principally involving trade with other OECD countries. Such risks include the insolvency of private buyers, unfavorable currency fluctuations, and political risks. ExIm banks historically lent only on a recourse basis but have moved heavily into project financing since the mid-1990s.

Credit enhancement in the form of sovereign risk insurance is provided by official credit enhancement agencies, such as the U.S. Overseas Private Investment Corporation (OPIC), who may also act as lenders in their own right. Commercial banks are increasingly using political risk insurance, including coverage against currency inconvertibility or nontransferability, expropriation of assets, stock or bank accounts, and political violence, including war, terrorism, and civil strife.

PERFORMANCE

For the most part, LNG projects have performed extremely well from a financial point of view. Sustained high double-digit returns on equity are not uncommon, and the scale of the projects can have a meaningful impact on even a major company's financial performance. During the mid-1980s, the Arun project accounted for as much as 40% of Mobil Corporation's worldwide after-tax income, and Shell is believed to have sustained after-tax returns in excess of 20% on its LNG investments over the past 30 years.

All trades to East Asian buyers have proceeded without financial interruption or distress, although contractual shortfalls from the Bontang project since 2005 somewhat undermine this record. The fixed pricing terms for the early Alaska and Brunei projects were renegotiated in the mid-1970s price shock era. Difficult restructuring of pricing and off-take terms between buyers and sellers were completed without service interruption through the turbulent price and market conditions of the 1980s.

There have been two significant commercial and financial interruptions. The Algerian-U.S. trades were interrupted by regulatory changes and political considerations that exacerbated the commercial failure of the underlying SPAs in the face of high international oil prices and collapsing U.S. gas prices. The Dabhol project in India was never economically viable under the price of the project's electricity, which made the power unmarketable, and it stalled completely when sovereign support underpinning the power purchase agreements was withdrawn.

The lesson—that project financial viability depends on the underlying economic viability—may have been learned.

NOTES

[1] That is, assurances that the feedgas will flow readily to the liquefaction plant. A commercial case in point is Nigeria LNG Train 6, where NNPC was dragging its feet about actually providing its share of feedgas to the plant. Another (technical) example is Indonesia's Badak plant, where Total experienced difficulties in early 2002 in piping feedgas from the Mahakam permit owing to corroded pipelines (and a general lack of maintenance) and a well blowout.

[2] Condensate, or liquids, credits represent income accrued to the project from the production of associated condensate, LPGs, or (in some cases) crude oil. These credits essentially lower the per-MMBtu cost of producing LNG.

[3] Chevron withdrew from Brass LNG in early 2006. Total formally confirmed its acquisition of Chevron's 17% project equity in August 2006.

[4] This is despite EU gas and power sector liberalization measures. For example, in the spring of 2006, the European Commission raided the offices of 20 gas firms across five countries as part of an inquiry into anti-competition practices. Germany's RWE, France's Gaz de France, Austria's OMV, and Belgium's Fluxys said they were raided. Reports said firms in Italy and Belgium were also involved. The Commission said it was an initial step in "investigations into suspected anticompetitive practices." Separately, the Commission said it also raided power companies in Hungary. The EU has recently expressed concern about the need for more competition in energy markets across Europe, after a cold winter in which political problems led to disruption of supplies. The Commission was particularly worried about the way in which firms granted or restricted access to pipelines. See EU probes 20 European gas firms. 2006. BBC *News*, May 17.

[5] In March 2006, Sempra LNG executed a terminal use agreement with Merrill Lynch Commodities, Inc., a subsidiary of Merrill Lynch & Company, Inc., for capacity

at the Cameron LNG import terminal in Louisiana. The 15-year full-service capacity agreement provides Merrill Lynch Commodities with the capability to import 0.5 Bcf/d (5 Bcm/y). The agreement is contingent on Merrill Lynch Commodities' finalization of its LNG supply arrangements. Depending on the timing of Merrill Lynch Commodities' arrangements, Sempra LNG would have the flexibility to serve the capacity agreement from either the first phase of Cameron LNG's development, to be completed in 2008, or its proposed expansion, which could be completed in 2010.

GLOBAL LIQUEFACTION PROJECTS 10

INTRODUCTION

An LNG project consists of an integrated chain of facilities and contracts from the upstream to the downstream; however, the word "project" is often used to refer to just the liquefaction facility to which the upstream and shipping components are connected. This chapter contains a brief description of all the liquefaction facilities, by country, that were operating or under construction at the end of 2006. Developers have announced or considered greenfield plants in many other countries, including Angola, Iran, Papua New Guinea, and Venezuela.

It is impossible to predict which projects will ultimately be completed, since circumstances constantly change. Projects that were once considered unlikely have moved to the forefront, while seemingly more likely projects are continually delayed.

THE ATLANTIC/ MEDITERRANEAN REGION

The Atlantic/Mediterranean region, sometimes referred to as the Atlantic Basin, is home to the world's oldest LNG project, in Algeria. At the end of 2006, five countries were exporting from seven projects: two production centers in Algeria, two in Egypt, and one each in Libya, Nigeria, and Trinidad.

In the 1980s, the Atlantic Basin's growth in liquefaction capacity lagged behind that of the Asia-Pacific region. Although Algeria continued to expand with additional liquefaction projects during the late 1970s, after the Libyan liquefaction facility came on line in 1970, no Atlantic Basin countries developed export projects until 1999, when Nigeria and Trinidad both started production. Oversupply in European and U.S. markets was the main cause of this inactivity. However, declines in mature regional pipeline supplies have led to a rebirth of LNG in this area, and new capacity is being added. Two projects in Egypt went on line in 2005; two projects are under construction in Equatorial Guinea and Norway, and many additional projects have been proposed.

Algeria

Algeria was the first commercial exporter of LNG, starting with shipments to the United Kingdom in 1964. Algeria thus pioneered the LNG trade and dominated the Atlantic Basin for more than three decades, until competing export ventures started up in Nigeria, Trinidad, Egypt, and elsewhere in the Middle East. Algeria's greatest advantage is its proximity to European markets. Besides LNG, Algeria is a leading exporter of pipeline gas to Europe.

Algeria currently has two liquefaction centers—one located in Arzew/Bethouia and one in Skikda—comprising 18 trains (table 10–1). Both complexes are 100% owned by Sonatrach, the state-owned energy company. The trains were built over an 18-year period, and the oldest, GL4Z (Camel), at Arzew, has a capacity of 1.5 MMt/y (2.1 Bcm/y). At Bethioua, the 6 trains of GL1Z and the 6 trains of GL2Z have been refurbished/upgraded to a total capacity of 21 MMt/y (29.4 Bcm/y). At Skikda, there were 6 trains with an aggregate capacity of 5.9 MMt/y (8.3 Bcm/y) until January 2004, when 3 trains were damaged or destroyed by an accident.

Algerian production capacity is projected to increase with the construction of a replacement train at Skikda. In addition, Gas Natural and Repsol have been awarded the El Andalous (Gassi Touil) project and envision construction of a new one-train liquefaction plant with a prospective second train (table 10–2). The LNG projects at Arzew and Skikda are largely supplied by the giant Hassi R'Mel gas field, which contains an estimated 100 Tcf (2,834 Bcm) of gas. *Oil & Gas Journal* (OGJ), BP, and Cedigaz assess Algeria's total gas reserves at 160 Tcf (4,534.4 Bcm).

Table 10–1. Algeria: Existing LNG export projects[1]

Project	Start Year	Capacity (MMt/y)	Capacity (Bcf/d)	Train Capacities (MMt/y)	Shareholding
Arzew GL4Z	1964	1.5	0.2	3 × 0.5	Sonatrach 100%
Bethioua GL1Z	1978	10.5	1.4	6 × 1.75	Sonatrach 100%
Bethioua GL2Z	19811	0.5	1.4	6 × 1.75	Sonatrach 100%
Skikda GL1K	1972	0.85*	0.12*	1 × 0.85*	Sonatrach 100%
Skikda GL2K	1981	2.50*	0.34*	2 × 1.25*	Sonatrach 100%
Total		20.65*	2.85*		

* Capacity net of Skikda Trains 20, 30, and 40.

Table 10–2. Algeria: Planned LNG projects

Project	Sponsor Start Year	Capacity (MMt/y)	Capacity (Bcf/d)	Train Capacities (MMt/y)
Skikda rebuild	2011	4.5	0.6	1 × 4.5
Gassi Touil	2012	4	0.55	1 × 4.0
Total		8	1.1	

Algeria exports LNG to more countries under long-term contracts than any other supplier. It sells LNG to buyers in Belgium, France, Greece, Italy, Spain, Turkey, and has also supplied the United States (table 10–3). Sonatrach intends to continue boosting its exports, mostly through pipeline expansions and new pipeline projects but also by building new LNG export capacity. Sonatrach plans to build a replacement train at Skikda, which will replace the 2.6 MMt/y (3.6 Bcm/y) lost in the 2004 fire with a new 4.5 MMt/y (6.3 Bcm/y) liquefaction train. In addition, Gas Natural and Repsol plan to co-develop the El Andalous LNG export project with Sonatrach. This single-train project may be expanded at a later date. El Andalous is being developed as the first Algerian LNG project with foreign participation.

Table 10–3. Algeria: Contracted LNG volumes

Buyer*	Terms	Start	End	MMt/y	Bcf/d
Gaz de France	FOB	1992	2013	1.3	0.17
Gaz de France	FOB	1976	2013	3.7	0.48
Gaz de France	FOB	1972	2013	2.5	0.32
DEPA	Ex-ship	1998	2013	0.5	0.07
Eni Gas & Power	FOB	1996	2016	1.3	0.17
ENEL	FOB	1999	2010	1.2	0.15
Iberdrola	Ex-ship	2002	2017	0.8	0.1
Botas	Ex-ship	1994	2014	3	0.39

* Sonatrach also has a master agreement to supply Cepsa Gas (a Cepsa/Total/Sonatrach joint venture). Under this agreement, 2003 volumes were ~0.11 Bcf/d.

** No shipments currently taking place — in arbitration.

Sonatrach has also stated its intent to participate in the downstream sector by acquiring LNG import capacity in the Atlantic Basin. As of mid-2007, the firm was involved in LNG import ventures in Spain (as a shareholder in Regasificadora del Noroeste SA, which received its first cargo in May of 2007), the United Kingdom (as a capacity holder at Grain LNG), and possibly the United States (as a potential capacity holder in Cameron LNG and the Ingleside Energy Center).

Egypt

Egypt is starting to aggressively capitalize on its gas resource base of around 67 Tcf (1,900 Bcm), having inaugurated two LNG export projects in recent years (table 10–4). The first liquefaction complex is located at Damietta, which started operations in 2004. The second project, located at Idku, commenced operations in May 2005 (table 10–5). Combined, the two projects are estimated to produce more than 12 MMt/y (16.8 Bcm/y). Both Egyptian projects are located in the Nile Delta and have provisions to toll third-party gas going through their facilities. There is also potential for further expansions pending commitment of reserves. Indeed, overall Egyptian reserves amply support the country's ambition for expansions at both Idku and Damietta. Egyptian officials put the volume of gas reserves remaining to be discovered at close to 100 Tcf (2,800 Bcm), based on the results of studies performed by international companies.

Table 10–4. Egypt: Existing LNG export projects

Project	Sponsor Start Year	Capacity (MMt/y)	Capacity (Bcf/d)	Train Capacities (MMt/y)
Egyptian LNG T1 (Idku)	May 05	3.6	0.5	1 × 3.6
Egyptian LNG T2 (Idku)	4Q2005	3.6	0.5	1 × 3.6
SEGAS (Damietta)	2005	5	0.69	1 × 5.0
Total		12.2	1.69	

Table 10–5. Egypt: Existing LNG project shareholdings

Project	Company	Shareholding Upstream	Shareholding Liquefaction
Egyptian LNG T1 (Idku)	BG	25%	35.50%
	Petronas	25%	35.50%
	EGAS	-	12.00%
	EGPC	50%	12.00%
	Gaz de France	-	5.00%
Egyptian LNG T2 (Idku)	BG	25%	38.00%
	Petronas	25%	38.00%
	EGAS	-	12.00%
	EGPC	50%	12.00%
SEGAS (Damietta)	EGP	*	10.00%
	EGAS	*	10.00%
	Union Fenosa Gas	*	80.00%

* SEGAS is a tolling facility for upstream gas.

LNG from Damietta is sold to buyers with sales outlets in Spain, the United Kingdom, and the United States (tables 10–6 and 10–7). Volumes from Idku are shipped to buyers with import terminal capacity in France, the United States, and possibly Italy.

Table 10–6. Egypt: Contracted Idku volumes

Buyers	Terms	Start	End	MMt/y	Bcf/d
Gaz de France	FOB	2005	2025	3.6	0.47
BG — Lake Charles	FOB	2006	2026	3.6	0.47
BG — Brindisi	FOB	2007	2026	3.6	0.47

Table 10–7. Egypt: SEGAS (Damietta) allocations, 2005–2010

	2005	2006	2007	2008	2009	2010
BG/Petronas	1.61	1.61	1.61	1.61	1.06	-
BP	1.06	1.06	1.06	1.06	1.06	1.06
Union Fenosa	2.33	2.33	2.33	2.33	2.88	2.88
Undecided	-	-	-	-	-	1.06

Equatorial Guinea

Marathon and Sonagas made a final investment decision in 2004 to proceed with the single-train project (table 10–8). The two partners also formed a joint venture called Equatorial Guinea LNG Holdings Limited (EGLNG) to own and operate the greenfield facility, which produces 3.7 MMt/y of LNG. In June 2005, Marathon and the government of Equatorial Guinea announced that agreements have been entered into under which Mitsui and Marubeni acquired 8.5% and 6.5% interests, respectively, in EGLNG, which exported its first cargo in May 2007.

Table 10–8. Equatorial Guinea: LNG plant under construction

Project	Sponsor Start Year	Capacity (MMt/y)	Capacity (Bcf/d)	Train Capacities (MMt/y)	Upstream Shareholders	Downstream Shareholders
EGLNG	2007	3.7	0.49	1 × 3.7	Marathon 63.2%, Noble Energy 33.8%, GEPetrol 3%	Marathon 60%, Sonagas 25%, Mitsui 8.5%, Marubeni 6.5%

The EGLNG plant is fed by the 5 Tcf (141.7 Bcm) Alba gas and condensate field, which is the largest in Equatorial Guinea. Field operator and main LNG project sponsor Marathon has also suggested that Bioko Island could serve as a regional LNG hub, liquefying gas from neighboring countries' reserves; nearby Cameroon has approximately 3.3 Tcf (94 Bcm) of gas in the area, and southern Nigeria has more than 20 Tcf (570 Bcm).[2]

During 2004, Marathon announced a natural gas and condensate discovery on the Alba Block. The well was drilled to a total measured depth of 15,497 feet and encountered 270 feet of net gas/condensate pay. The Deep Luba discovery reinforces the additional resource potential of the Alba field, and if proven, these reserves could support further LNG expansions beyond Train 1. In August 2006, Marathon announced that EGLNG had signed a FEED contract for a second train with a planned capacity of 4.4 MMt/y. Neighboring countries Nigeria and Cameroon have each expressed interest in supplying feedgas to train-2.

Libya

The Libyan National Oil Company is the sole owner of a plant at Marsa el Brega, which was the world's second liquefaction facility (table 10–9). The original design capacity of the single-train plant was 2.3 MMt/y (3.2 Bcm/y). After the plant began operations in 1971, exports to its two customers, Spain and Italy, steadily increased for the next few years, reaching a peak of 2.6 MMt/y (3.6 Bcm/y) in 1977.

Table 10–9. Libya: Existing LNG export project

Project	Start Year	Capacity (MMt/y)	Capacity (Bcf/d)	Train Capacities (MMt/y)	Shareholding (Upstream and Downstream)
Marsa Brega	1970	2.3*	0.32*	3 × 0.77	NOC 100%
Total		2.3	0.32		

* Currently capable of producing only 0.8 MMt/y.

However, LNG exports from the Marsa El Brega plant have been reduced to about one-third of the plant's nameplate capacity. There are two reasons for this. When Libya nationalized the plant in 1980, the global price of LNG dramatically increased. At that point, Italy ceased to import contracted supplies. Instead, it opted to purchase cargoes on a spot basis, leaving Spain as Libya's only committed long-term customer. The second reason is a technical flaw in the plant design. This facility was designed to liquefy heavy NGL along with natural gas (methane), producing LNG with a very high Btu content. Few regasification terminals at that time were equipped to handle liquids extraction. In a 1990 refurbishment, Italy's sole terminal at La Spezia was modified, and consequently, it was rendered unable to accept Libyan LNG. Since then, Spain has been the only off-taker of Libyan gas. Moreover, the Marsa El Brega plant has also suffered as a result of years of economic sanctions that limited access to the outside technology and resources needed to maintain the facility.

Libya has an existing contract to supply 0.7 MMt/y (0.98 Bcm/y) of LNG to Spain until 2008. In 2004, Libya became an exporter of natural gas to Italy with the inauguration of the 8 Bcm/y (0.8 Bcf/d) Green Stream pipeline to Italy.

Libya has large unexplored areas that have been a strong focus of petroleum exploration efforts following the lifting of U.S. trade sanctions in 2003. Cedigaz and World Oil estimate that Libya holds 46 Tcf (1,300 Bcm) of gas, while OGJ and BP estimate the holdings at 52 Tcf (1,500 Bcm). Analysts agree that the country has substantial promise for new discoveries. The Libyan National Oil Company has estimated that the country has potential for up to 115 Tcf (3,300 Bcm). Combined with Libya's reentry into the world community, this puts Libya in a good position to compete for Atlantic Basin LNG market share in coming years.

This may occur sooner rather than later. In May 2005, Shell reached a comprehensive agreement for gas exploration and liquefaction with Libya's national oil company. Under the 30-year agreement, Shell will upgrade the Marsa El Brega plant. Output would increase from 0.8 to 3.2 MMt/y (from 0.97 to 4.4 Bcm/y). Shell has been given the mandate to develop five blocks in the Sirte basin, which are estimated to hold around 80% of Libya's gas reserves. Subject to gas availability, Shell will also undertake the joint development of a new LNG facility.

In addition, Woodside (45%), Repsol (35%), and Hellenic Petroleum (20%) recently signed a 30-year oil and gas exploration and production-sharing agreement with the National Oil Corporation of Libya. These companies may consider monetizing significant gas discoveries via LNG. Finally, U.S. companies such as Marathon, Amerada Hess, and ConocoPhillips have reclaimed their former Libya holdings, which may also hold the potential for future gas development.

Nigeria

Nigeria LNG is located on Bonny Island near the mouth of the Bonny River, in the Niger Delta region (table 10–10). The plant has five operating trains, with a capacity exceeding 17 MMt/y (23.4 Bcm/y). A sixth liquefaction unit is under construction, with planned start-up in 2008. Nigeria LNG is evaluating a further expansion of the Bonny facility, and in February 2007 signed a FEED contract for two supersized (8.5 MMt/y [12 Bcm/y]) trains, which would be the largest in the world.

Table 10–10. Nigeria: Existing LNG export project

Project	Start Year	Capacity (MMt/y)	Capacity (Bcf/d)	Train Capacities (MMt/y)
NLNG T1/2	1999	6.6	0.9	2 × 3.3
NLNG T3	2002	3.3	0.44	1 × 3.3
NLNG T4	2005	4	0.53	1 × 4.0
NLNG T5	2006	4	0.53	1 × 4.0
Total		17.9	2.4	

In addition to expansion of the existing Nigeria LNG plant, NNPC and international oil companies are at various stages of development and feasibility studies for the following LNG export plants (tables 10–11 and 10–12):

- Brass LNG commissioned a FEED contract in early 2004. Brass LNG is located in Brass River, Niger Delta, and was originally promoted by a joint venture comprising NNPC, Eni, ConocoPhillips, and Chevron. Chevron subsequently withdrew in mid-2006 and was replaced by Total.
- NNPC, BG, Chevron, and Shell have joined forces to develop a greenfield 22 MMt/y (30 Bcm/y) four-train project. This project, known as OK-LNG, would be located in Olokola, a free-zone port on the border between Ondo and Ogun states. Originally, BG, Chevron, and NNPC planned to build two 5 MMt/y (7 Bcm/y) trains. Shell later joined, doubling the capacity to 22 MMt/y (30 Bcm/y). Under a site-sharing scheme, ownership of the four trains would be split evenly between the original three partners and a joint venture comprising Shell and NNPC. The project would begin operations in 2012.

Table 10–11. Nigeria: LNG projects under construction or planned

Project	Sponsor Start Year	Capacity (MMt/y)	Capacity (Bcf/d)	Train Capacities (MMt/y)
NLNG T6	2007	4.1	0.55	1 × 4.1
NLNG T7/8	2012	14	2.13	2 × 7
Brass LNG	2011	10	1.34	2 × 5.0
OK-LNG	2012	22	2.94	4 × 5.5
Total		54.9	6.96	

Table 10–12. Nigeria: LNG project shareholdings (under construction and planned)

Project	Company	Shareholding
NLNG T6	NNPC	49.00%
	Shell	25.60%
	Total	15.00%
	Agip	10.40%
NLNG T7/8	NNPC	49.00%
	Shell	25.60%
	Total	15.00%
	Agip	10.40%
OK-LNG	NNPC	40.00%
	BG	14.25%
	Chevron	19.50%
	Shell	19.50%
	TBD	6.75%
Brass LNG	NNPC	49.00%
	ConocoPhillips	16.25%
	Eni	16.25%
	TBD	5.00%
	Total	13.50%

Although an LNG project in Nigeria had been discussed as early as the 1970s, Nigeria LNG was the first major natural gas project undertaken in the country. Credit and political risks had effectively barred the project from happening for decades. Eventually, so that the project could move forward, the first three trains were equity financed by the shareholders.

Nigeria has long been a producer of oil, and much of the country's natural gas reserves are associated with oil. One major impetus behind the Nigeria LNG project was to diversify the country's revenue base. Another, perhaps even greater driver was the need to reduce flaring of associated gas resources. Nigeria flares more gas than any other country, and this fact had long drawn criticism from international agencies, as well as Nigerian citizens affected by the local environmental impacts of flaring. At the project's outset, nonassociated gas fields were dedicated to supply the project to ensure reliability. Over time, the share of associated gas liquefied at the terminal is being greatly increased to reduce flaring.

Countrywide, Nigeria has an estimated 175 Tcf of gas (5,000 Bcm; according to OGJ, Cedigaz, BP, and World Oil). The Niger Delta area, where Nigeria LNG is located (and where Brass LNG is planned), is essentially a gas province and has sufficient reserves to support the planned expansions beyond Nigeria LNG Train 6. Feedgas is supplied to the Nigeria LNG plant from the onshore concession areas of the eastern part of the Niger Delta area, where about 50% of Nigeria's proven and probable gas reserves are located. Three upstream joint ventures, operated by Shell, Eni, and Total, have signed gas sales agreements with Nigeria LNG to underpin the plant's liquefaction trains. Feedgas for the proposed Brass LNG plant will likewise be sourced from the Eni-operated upstream joint venture.

The northwestern margin of the Niger Delta, which will host the OK-LNG project, is less explored, but the proposed LNG plant would be supplied from fields in the western Niger Delta, including the Escravos area, where ChevronTexaco has large upstream operations. The Escravos area has already been designated as an eventual supply source for Brass LNG Train 2; a new gas-to-liquids plant; the West African gas pipeline to Benin, Togo, and Ghana; and the domestic market.

Table 10–13. Nigeria: Contracted Nigeria LNG volumes[3]

Buyers	Terms	Start	End	MMt/y	Bcf/d
GDF	Ex-ship	1999	2021	0.38	0.05
ENEL	Ex-ship	1999	2021	2.80	0.34
Transgas	Ex-ship	1999	2021	0.32	0.04
Gas Natural	Ex-ship	1999	2021	1.21	0.16
Botas	Ex-ship	1999	2021	0.92	0.12
Transgas	Ex-ship	2003	2024	0.80	0.10
Gas Natural	Ex-ship	2003	2024	2.10	0.26
Eni	Ex-ship	2005	2028	1.20	0.15
Transgas	Ex-ship	2005	2028	1.52	0.19
Iberdrola	Ex-ship	2005	2028	0.40	0.05
BG Group	Ex-ship	2006	2025	2.50	0.32
Shell	Ex-ship	2005	2028	1.10	0.15
Endesa	Ex-ship	2006	2026	0.80	0.10
Total	Ex-ship	2005	2028	0.20	0.025
Total	Ex-ship	2008	2027	1.00	0.13
Shell	Ex-ship	2008	2027	3.00	0.39
BG	Ex-ship	2011	2031	1.67	0.22
BP	Ex-ship	2011	2031	1.67	0.22
ConocoPhillips	Ex-ship	2011	2031	1.67	0.22
ENI	Ex-ship	2011	2031	1.67	0.22
Suez	Ex-ship	2011	2031	1.67	0.22
Total	Ex-ship	2011	2031	1.67	0.22
BG	Ex-ship	2012	2032	2.25	0.30
ENI	Ex-ship	2012	2032	1.38	0.18
Occidental	Ex-ship	2012	2032	1.00	0.13
Shell	Ex-ship	2012	2032	2.00	0.27
Total	Ex-ship	2012	2032	1.38	0.18

Nigeria LNG currently sells LNG to France, Portugal, Spain, Turkey, and the United States (table 10–13). Mexico was added to the list of growing destinations for Nigerian LNG in August 2006, when the Altamira LNG import terminal was commissioned. North America is expected to be a major destination for LNG not only from Train 7 and beyond at Nigeria LNG but also from the grassroots projects currently under consideration.

Norway

Snøhvit will be the first European LNG export project when it starts operations in late 2007. The project is currently a one-train 4.1 MMt/y (6 Bcm/y) liquefaction facility located on Melkøya Island, in northern Norway (table 10–14). The country has an existing gas export industry through large pipeline trades to Europe. In 2004, Norway produced 78.5 Bcm of gas (7.6 Bcf/d), of which 75 Bcm was exported through pipelines to various European markets.

Table 10–14. Norway: LNG export project

Plant Name	Start Year	Capacity (MMt/y)	Plant Shareholders
Snøhvit	2007	4.1	Petoro 30%, Statoil 33.53%, Total 18.4%, GdF 12%, Amerada Hess 3.3% RWE-DEA 2.8%,

Countrywide, Norway holds an estimated 84.2 Tcf (2,400 Bcm) of natural gas reserves. The Snøhvit, Askeladd, and Albatross fields, which will provide feedgas to the Snøhvit LNG train, are estimated by Statoil to hold 6.5 Tcf (184 Bcm). This reserve base is sufficient to support the current project, but any expansion would be subject to further reserves certification.

Snøhvit's production is partially committed to buyers with import capacity in Spain (Iberdrola) and the United States (Statoil). Two of Snøhvit's owners, Gaz de France and Total, will lift equity-owned volumes from the project (table 10–15).

Table 10–15. Norway: Contracted LNG volumes

Importer	Buyers	Terms	Start	End	MMt/y	Bcf/d
France	Gaz de France	FOB	2006	2023	0.5	0.07
France	Total	FOB	2006	2023	0.8	0.1
Spain	Iberdrola	Ex-ship	2006	2026	1.2	0.16
US	Statoil	Ex-ship	2006	2025	1.8	0.22

Russia (including the Pacific Basin project)

As home to the world's largest gas reserves, Russia is now adding LNG as an alternative to develop its enormous resource base. Russia has well over a quadrillion cubic feet of gas. Russia has extensive pipeline infrastructure connecting the giant fields in Western Siberia to markets in Eastern and Western Europe (a total of 148.4 Bcm/y [14.4 Bcf/d]) of exports to Europe through pipelines).

LNG was not in Gazprom's gas development plans until after the year 2000. However, the Russian company is intending to go global and plans to utilize LNG to diversify its market reach to North America. Gazprom is already the largest gas producer in the world, with an output of 547.9 Bcm (19.3 Tcf) in 2005. The firm accounts for over 80% of Russia's total gas output and some 20% of worldwide natural gas production. However, this is all delivered by pipeline to customers in Russia, the former Soviet republics, and Western Europe. The Russian government and Gazprom are now pursuing LNG developments to diversify its markets, especially focusing on LNG sales to North America. To that end, Gazprom has begun discussions with numerous international oil and gas companies, targeting joint ventures for LNG development. Independent Russian players are also evaluating LNG plays, but it is unlikely that they will be able to proceed without the blessing—and ultimately, participation—of Gazprom itself.

Russia is developing three LNG export projects: one located along the Pacific Rim and two in the Atlantic Basin (table 10–16). The Sakhalin II venture in eastern Russia is the country's most advanced project. This entails the development of a two-train, 9.6 MMt/y (13.2 Bcm/y) liquefaction plant on Sakhalin Island. In July 2005, Gazprom signed a provisional agreement with project operator Shell to join the Sakhalin II consortium in exchange for granting Shell an interest in Western Siberian reserves. A few days after the signing of this agreement, Shell announced that the total cost for its integrated Sakhalin II project in Russia could hit $20 billion, nearly double the previous estimate. Start-up of the venture was also delayed by a year, to late-2008. Shortly after this announcement, the Russian government began applying enormous pressure to Shell and its partners with allegations of environmental damages caused by the project in what was seen as a thinly-veiled effort to allow Gazprom to force its way into the project. After months of very public wrangling, Gazprom acquired a 50% shareholding in the Sakhalin II consortium in 2007 for a payment of $7.45 billion, roughly the partners' cost, and the other shareholdings were reduced proportionately. The Russian government's position could be better understood when one considers that the development of the Sakhalin II project was carried out under a production sharing contract which allowed the project to recoup all its investment prior to paying any taxes or royalties to the government, effectively causing the government to subsidize the cost overruns.

Table 10–16. Russia: Planned LNG projects

Project	Sponsor Start Year	Capacity (MMt/y)	Train Capacities (MMt/y)	Shareholding
Sakhalin II	2008	9.6	2 × 4.8	Gazprom (50%) Shell (27.5%), Mitsui (12.5%), Mitsubishi (10%)
Shtokman	2015	14.8	2 × 7.4	TBD
Baltic LNG	2012	3.5	1 × 3.5	Gazprom (51%); TBD (49%)
Total		27.9		

The second Russian project under development is the Baltic LNG project, to be located near St. Petersburg. Feedgas for the liquefaction facility would come from the national pipeline grid. Gazprom is spearheading Baltic LNG's development, but it has not yet selected partners for the venture. Gazprom has been in discussions with PetroCanada to develop this project to supply markets in eastern Canada.

The third Russian LNG export play is the Shtokman project in the Barents Sea. This venture would be underpinned by the vast offshore Shtokmanov field, which according to Gazprom holds 113 Tcf (3,200 Bcm) of gas. The field also contains large amounts of condensates. Preliminary plans include a feedgas pipeline from the offshore production platform to a new plant located at an ice-free port near Murmansk, as well as a fleet of ships to transport LNG to the United States. A myriad of international oil and gas companies have voiced strong interest in joining Gazprom in developing this project. However, in late 2006, Gazprom announced it was suspending further negotiations with foreign investors, and was considering developing the reserves alone to meet the needs of its European pipeline customers.

A much less advanced Russian liquefaction venture is Yamal LNG, which is the brainchild of Tambeyneftegas. The Russian independent holds the production license for the South Tambey gas condensate field located in the northeast part of the Yamal Peninsula. Under phase I development,

Tambeyneftegas plans to expand condensate production at South Tambey from the current 2,500 barrels per day (bpd) to 8,000 bpd by 2008 and to lay a 165-kilometer pipeline to Cape Drovianoy, at the northeast edge of the Yamal Peninsula. Depending on feasibility studies, an LNG terminal, condensate separation plant, and a deepwater port would be built at Drovianoy.

To date, Russia has signed sales contracts for Sakhalin II volumes only (table 10–17). Taking into account the project's proximity to Japan, it is not surprising that the bulk of Sakhalin II's sales are to Japanese gas and power utility companies. However, project operator Shell has contracted for a portion of Sakhalin II volumes. These are destined for Mexico, where Shell has reserved LNG import capacity at the Energia Costa Azul terminal in the country's northwest.

Table 10–17. Russia: Contracted Sakhalin II volumes

Buyers	Terms	Start	End	MMt/y	Bcm/y
Tokyo Gas	FOB	2007	2031	1.1	1.5
Tokyo EP	FOB	2007	2029	1.5	2
Kyushu EP	Ex-ship	2009	2030	0.5	0.7
Toho Gas	Ex-ship	2009	2027	0.5	0.7
Tohoku	FOB	2010	2030	0.42	0.5
Hiroshima	FOB	2008	2028	0.21	0.3
KOGAS	FOB	2009	2029	2	2.7
Shell	Ex-ship	2008	2027	1.6	2.1

Trinidad and Tobago

The natural gas industry in Trinidad and Tobago is large and diversified. The successful addition of a variety of natural gas projects over the past two decades is due to the progressive attitude taken by the government, which has promoted a favorable investment environment and to the advantageous geographic position of Trinidad, close to large gas-consuming markets, such as North America and Europe. As an example of its open attitude, Trinidad and Tobago's government-owned gas company does not have a controlling share in the LNG project, which is a contrast to the way most other liquefaction facilities are owned.

The initial impetus of an LNG project in Trinidad came from a prospective buyer, Cabot LNG, which needed additional supplies for its Distrigas import terminal in Massachusetts and recognized the distance advantages Trinidad had over traditional U.S. LNG suppliers. The customer-driven project broke new ground on many fronts, setting in motion one of the fastest cycles from proposal to completion ever accomplished. By locking in customers (who were also project shareholders) early on, the project saved a lot of time that would have otherwise been required to market the LNG and secure long-term customers.

The company constrained the initial design and construction to a one-train facility geared toward the needs of those customers that had expressed interest. Because the company did not attempt to create a larger initial project, the timetable and the costs were dramatically lower than many earlier projects. ALNG loaded its first cargo from Train 1 on April 19, 1999, just six and a half years after a memorandum of understanding was signed with Cabot. Export capacity of Train 1 was designed at 3.0 MMt/y (4.1 Bcm/y); however, a two-step debottlenecking project raised its capacity to 3.3 MMt/y (4.6 Bcm/y). LNG from Train 1 is sent to the United States, Puerto Rico, and Spain.

Growing demand for Atlantic Basin LNG supplies, combined with the discovery of larger gas reserves than anticipated, encouraged ALNG to expand its project (tables 10–18 and 10–19). Trains 2 and 3 are each 3.3 MMt/y (4.6 Bcm/y) and came on line in 2002 and 2003, respectively. Although ALNG's original five partners had the right to participate in the expansion venture, shareholders Suez and Trinidad's National Gas Company (NGC) chose not to participate in the so-called Atlantic 2/3 project. This was because the financing was done through equity contributions, rather than through project financing. Moreover, the Train 2/3 plant was set up as a tolling facility with the rate of return on this segment of the project capped at approximately 9%, limiting NGC and Suez's incentive to invest. LNG from Atlantic 2/3 is sold to the United States and Spain (table 10–20).

Table 10–18. Trinidad: LNG projects existing or under construction

Project	Start Year	Capacity (MMt/y)	Capacity (Bcf/d)	Train Capacities (MMt/y)
ALNG T1	1999	3.3	0.4	1 × 3.3
ALNG T2/3	2002–03	6.6	0.87	2 × 3.3
ALNG T4	2006	5.2	0.68	1 × 5.2
Total		15.1	2.0	

Table 10–19. Trinidad: LNG project shareholdings (existing and under construction)

Project	Upstream Shareholdings	Plant Shareholdings
ALNG T1	BPTT* 100%	BP 34%, BG 26%, Repsol 20%, Suez Global LNG 10%, NGCTT 10%
ALNG T2/3	BP 62.5%, BG/North Coast Marine Area Partners 37.5%	BP 42.5%, BG 32.5%, Repsol 25%
ALNG T4	Tolling Facility	BP 37.8%, BG 28.9%, Repsol 22.2%, NGC 11.1%

* BP Trinidad & Tobago: BP (70%), Repsol.

Table 10–20. Trinidad: Contracted LNG volumes

Buyer	Terms	Start	End	MMt/y	Bcf/d
EcoElectrica	FOB	2000	2019	0.50	0.08
Gas Natural	FOB	1999	2019	1.20	0.16
Suez LNG NA	FOB	1999	2019	1.30	0.17
Gas Natural	FOB	2002	2022	0.70	0.10
Repsol	FOB	2002	2022	0.60	0.09
Gas de Euskadi	FOB	2003	2023	0.75	0.10
Repsol	FOB	2003	2023	1.40	0.19
BG	Ex-ship	2003	2019	2.40	0.34
Suez LNG NA	FOB	2003	2022	0.30	0.05
BP to Marathon	Ex-ship	2005	2009	1.20	0.16
Statoil	Ex-ship	2003	2006	0.75	0.10
Shell	Ex-ship	2004	2009	0.77	0.11
BG	FOB	2006	2026	1.50	0.20
BP	FOB	2006	2026	2.54	0.37
Repsol	FOB	2006	2026	1.16	0.14

* Puerto Rico supply originates at Atlantic LNG via a Suez LNG SPA.

** The supplier has flexibility of where to source the LNG. BP has Trinidad supplies available.

A fourth, 5.2 MMt/y (7.2 Bcm/y) Trinidadian liquefaction train shipped its first cargo in January 2006. By late 2005, planning for a fifth unit was underway, and the government of Trinidad and Tobago had gone public with plans to adopt a new shareholding structure for ALNG Train 5. The government now refers to this unit as Train X, to differentiate it from the plan's current ownership lineup, and is openly seeking a greater role for itself and other suppliers in the project. However, new gas reserves have not materialized as expected and the government is engaged in discussions with Venezuela in an attempt to bring gas from the Plataforma Deltana region to Trinidad for liquefaction. This has slowed down the plans for Train X.

THE MIDDLE EAST

The Middle East is home to the world's largest oil and gas reserves, but the region is farther from the major markets than any other region. The region is nearly 3,500 nautical miles to its closest markets in Europe, reached through the Suez Canal, and is over 6,000 nautical miles to existing Asian markets.

Despite distance disadvantages, the Middle East continues to expand its LNG export capabilities at a rapid pace. Natural advantages include an abundance of low-cost natural gas and the ability to swing supplies between the major markets to both diversify buyers in the long run and arbitrage price opportunities in the short run. Furthermore, as India grows into a major natural gas market, the Middle East will be well situated to serve it; Oman is less than 1,000 nautical miles from some proposed Indian terminals and is closer than any Asia-Pacific suppliers. There is definite interest on the part of other Middle Eastern countries, primarily Iran, to follow the lead of the existing suppliers into the LNG business.

Oman

Gas discoveries were made in 1989 that led to the Oman LNG project at Qalhat. The gas was far in excess of local demand and provided the opportunity for the government to diversify away from oil. The initial two-train project, which first exported gas in 2000, has an export capacity of 7.4 MMt/y (10 Bcm/y). A third, 3.7 MMt/y (5 Bcm/y) liquefaction train with a slightly different ownership structure, known as Qalhat LNG, was commissioned in November 2005 (table 10–21).

Table 10–21. Omani LNG export projects

Oman	Oman LNG	Qalhat LNG
Number of trains	2	1
LNG capacity (MMt/y)	7.4	3.7
Initial start-up	2000	2006
Business structure: Shareholdings in the LNG plant	**Oman LNG** Government of Oman 51% Shell 30% Total 5.54% Korea LNG 5% Mitsubishi 2.77% Mitsui 2.77% Itochu 0.92% Partex 2%	**Qalhat LNG** Government of Oman 46.84% Oman LNG 36.80% Union Fenosa 7.36% Osaka Gas 3% Mitsubishi 3% Itochu 3%
Entity responsible for marketing LNG	Oman LNG	Oman LNG

Natural gas resources for the project are 60% owned by the Government of Oman and operated by Petroleum Development Oman (PDO) with Shell, TFE, and Partex. Natural gas comes from the Barik, Saih Rawl, and Saih Nihayda non-associated gas fields. A 360-kilometer pipeline takes the gas from a gathering plant to Qalhat. The gas reserves that feed the plant are owned by the government; thus, feedgas delivered to the Oman LNG and Qalhat LNG plants is purchased from the government. Oman has limited natural gas reserves, making further expansion beyond the third train unlikely, and has experienced difficulty securing enough gas for the existing trains.

Oman LNG's two trains supply customers in Korea and Japan, while Qalhat LNG sells LNG to Spain and Japan (table 10–22). The Oman LNG venture is responsible for marketing LNG for both its own project and Qalhat LNG. Oman LNG had signed a deal to supply the Dabhol plant in India, but when that project could not take its gas, the company was able to market some of the gas to other customers under short-term deals until new long-term contracts could be secured.

Table 10–22. Omani LNG sales contracts

Buyer	Terms	Start	End	MMt/y
Qalhat LNG:				
Mitsubishi	FOB	2006	2021	0.8
Osaka Gas	FOB	2009	2026	0.9
Union Fenosa	Ex-ship	2006	2026	1.7
Oman LNG:				
Osaka Gas	FOB	2000	2024	0.7
Itochu	FOB	2006	2026	0.7
KOGAS	FOB	2000	2024	4.1
BP	Ex-ship	2004	2009	0.6
Shell	FOB	2002	2007	0.7
Union Fenosa	Ex-ship	2004	2005	0.8

Qatar

Qatar is home to two operating LNG export plants, both of which are being expanded through separate project companies (tables 10–23 and 10–24). Qatargas began operations in 1996 and as of 2006 sold about 9 MMt/y (12.4 Bcm/y) of LNG from a three-train plant to buyers in Japan and Spain. RasGas started operations in 1999 with two trains. The plant was expanded with the addition of a third liquefaction train in 2004, and a fourth train began operating in late 2005.

Table 10–23. Qatari LNG export facilities

Project	Start Year	Capacity (MMt/y)	Train Capacities (MMt/y)
Qatargas I (T1/2/3)	1996	9.9*	3 × 3.3
RasGas I (T1/2)	1999	6.6	2 × 3.3
RasGas 2 (T3/T4/T5)	2004	14.1	3 × 4.7
Total		30.6	

*Originally 7.7 MMt/y total nameplate capacity, this rose to 9.9 MMt/y following completion of debottlenecking.

Table 10–24. Existing Qatari LNG project shareholdings

Project	Company	Shareholding Upstream	Shareholding Liquefaction
Qatargas I (T1/2/3)	QP	65.0%	65.0%
	Total	20.0%	10.0%
	ExxonMobil	10.0%	10.0%
	Mitsui	2.5%	7.5%
	Marubeni	2.5%	7.5%
RasGas I (T1/2)	QP	68.0%	63.0%
	ExxonMobil	25.0%	25.0%
	Korea LNG	—	5.0%
	Itochu	4.0%	4.0%
	LNG Japan	3.0%	3.0%
RasGas 2 (T3)	QP	70.0%	
	ExxonMobil	30.0%	
RasGas 2 (T4)	QP	70.0%	
	ExxonMobil	30.0%	
RasGas 2 (T5)	QP	70.0%	
	ExxonMobil	30.0%	

Qatar plans to expand LNG exports based on its enormous gas reserves and room for expansion trains (table 10–25). The natural gas feedstock for both Qatari LNG projects (RasGas and Qatargas) comes from the world's largest nonassociated gas field, known as the North Field. Its recoverable reserves were revised sharply upward in 2002, from 500 to 900 Tcf (14,000 to 26,000 Bcm). All the LNG projects are located in Ras Laffan Industrial City and have LNG-loading jetties in the deepwater Ras Laffan port.

Table 10–25. Qatari LNG projects under construction

Project	Start Year	Capacity (MMt/y)	Train Capacities (MMt/y)
Qatargas 2 (T1/T2)	2008	15.6	2 × 7.8
Qatargas 3	2009	7.8	1 × 7.8
Qatargas 4	2010	7.8	1 × 7.8
RasGas 3 (T6/7)	2008, 2009	15.6	2 × 7.8
Total		46.8	

Qatar is focusing on expansion through large-scale developments. Because of large natural gas reserves, ample space at Ras Laffan for development of plant and loading facilities, and the availability of liquid and transparent markets in the Atlantic Basin, Qatar is taking advantage of economies of scale to develop up to six mega-trains, with capacities of around 7.8 MMt/y (10.8 Bcm/y) each.

Base Qatari LNG export ventures (Qatargas and RasGas) were conceived to supply LNG markets in the Far East. However, the subsequent increase in Atlantic LNG demand prospects encouraged both Qatargas and RasGas to seek sales west of Suez. Qatargas broke the mold first, signing medium-term SPAs with Spain's Gas Natural in 2001. Qatar's vast gas reserves, coupled with its greater distance from Atlantic Basin markets relative to traditional regional suppliers, encouraged Qatar to establish large-scale, integrated LNG export ventures dedicated to northern Europe and the United States, where economies of scale in all components of the liquefaction chain would enable Qatar to profitably deliver LNG to these growing demand centers. These mega-sized Qatari LNG projects are sponsored by Qatar Petroleum and international oil company partners (tables 10–26 and 10–27).

Table 10–26. Ownership of Qatari LNG projects under construction

Project	Company	Shareholding Upstream	Shareholding Liquefaction
Qatargas 2	QP/ExxonMobil	70/30%	70/30%
	QP/ExxonMobil/Total	70/30/0%	65/18.3/16.7%
Qatargas 3	QP	68.5%	
	ConocoPhillips	30%	
	Mitsui	1.5%	
Qatargas 4	QP	70%	
	Shell	30%	
RasGas 2 (T4)	QP	70%	
	ExxonMobil	30%	
RasGas 3 (T6/7)	QP	70%	
	ExxonMobil	30%	

Table 10–27. Qatari contracted LNG volumes

Importer	Buyer	Terms	Start	End	MMt/y	Bcf/d
Qatargas:						
Japan	Chubu Electric	Ex-ship	1997	2021	4.00	0.53
Japan	Chukogu Electric	Ex-ship	1998	2021	0.12	0.02
Japan	Kansai Electric	Ex-ship	1998	2021	0.29	0.04
Japan	TEPCO	Ex-ship	1998	2021	0.20	0.03
Japan	Tokyo Gas	Ex-ship	1998	2021	0.35	0.05
Japan	Osaka Gas	Ex-ship	1998	2021	0.35	0.05
Japan	Toho Gas	Ex-ship	1998	2021	0.17	0.02
Japan	Tohoku Electric	Ex-ship	1998	2021	0.52	0.07
Spain	Gas Natural	FOB	2001	2012	0.70	0.09
Spain	Gas Natural	Ex-ship	2002	2012	0.70	0.09
Spain	BP	FOB	2003	2007	0.75	0.10
Spain	Gas Natural	Ex-ship	2005	2025	1.50	0.20
Qatargas 2:						
Japan	Chubu Electric	Ex-ship	2008	2013	1.20	0.16
United Kingdom	ExxonMobil	Ex-ship	2008	2033	10.40	1.39
United Kingdom	Total	Ex-ship	2009	2034	1.50	0.20
France	Total	Ex-ship	2009	2034	1.85	0.25
USA	Total	Ex-ship	2009	2034	1.90	0.25
Qatargas 3:						
USA	ConocoPhillips	Ex-ship	2010	2035	7.80	1.04
Qatargas 4:						
USA	Shell	Ex-ship	2010	2035	7.80	1.04
Rasgas:						
South Korea	KOGAS	FOB	1999	2024	4.8	0.64
South Korea	KOGAS	Ex-ship	2004	2008	1.07	0.14
Rasgas 2:						
Spain	ENI	Ex-ship	2004	2022	0.75	0.10
India	Petronet LNG	FOB	2004	2028	5.00	0.67
Spain	Endesa	Ex-ship	2005	2025	0.80	0.11
Italy	Edison	Ex-ship	2007	2030	4.70	0.63
Belgium	Distrigas (BE)	Ex-ship	2007	2027	2.05	0.27
Belgium	QP + ExxonMobil	Ex-Ship	2007	2027	3.40	0.45
Taiwan	CPC	FOB	2008	2033	3.00	0.40
India	Petrnoet LNG	FOB	2009	2030	2.50	0.33
Rasgas 3:						
South Korea	KOGAS	Ex-ship	2007	2027	2.10	0.28
USA	ExxonMobil	Ex-ship	2008	2033	15.60	2.08

* No SPA, but fairly advanced integrated chain project.

** Assumed start date.

United Arab Emirates (UAE)

The Abu Dhabi Gas Liquefaction Company (ADGAS) became the first LNG supplier in the Middle East with the 1977 start-up of its two-train liquefaction facility located on Das Island. A third train was added in 1994, bringing the total design capacity to roughly 5.7 MMt/y (8 Bcm/y). The majority partner is the Abu Dhabi National Oil Company (ADNOC), which is also the sole shareholder in the upstream project (table 10–28).

Table 10–28. ADGAS LNG project ownership

Company	Ownership Upstream	Ownership Downstream
ADNOC	100%	70%
Mitsui		15%
BP		10%
Total		5%

The UAE is among the world's top five holders of natural gas reserves. The vast majority of this gas is in Abu Dhabi. The impetus for an LNG project stemmed from the desire to monetize these reserve holdings; in addition, during the 1970s, the country's oil reserves did not appear to be as large as those of some of its Middle Eastern neighbors (since then, proven oil reserves in the UAE have more than tripled). Feedgas for the liquefaction facility comes from Umm Shaif, Zakum, Abu al Buhkoosh, and El Bunduq offshore fields off Das Island.

The ADGAS project broke new ground with an SPA with TEPCO in Japan, creating what was then unequivocally the farthest long-term trade route between supplier and customer. Tokyo is over 6,000 nautical miles from Das Island, making the trade route at least 2,000 nautical miles farther than any previous contract. The contracted trade was considered extremely ambitious at the time; however, the relationship has worked. Throughout its history, TEPCO has remained the major customer for the LNG and LPG produced (table 10–29).

Table 10–29. ADGAS LNG sales contracts

Seller	Buyer	Terms	Start	End	MMt/y
AdGas	TEPCO	Ex-ship	1977	1994	2.30
AdGas	TEPCO	Ex-ship	1994	2019	4.70
AdGas	TEPCO	Ex-ship	2005	2006	0.60
AdGas	BP	FOB	2002	2005	0.75

ADGAS marketed volumes to customers in other areas of the globe under spot and short-term sales. However, owing to distance from markets and potential customers' financial problems, this project has faced challenges in securing other long-term contracts. A midterm deal with Korea was planned in the late 1990s but fell through when the Asian financial crisis hit. The company signed a 20-year contract for 0.5 MMt/y (0.7 Bcm/y) with Enron's Dabhol Power Company in India, but that contract fell apart when the import project collapsed, shortly before Enron's demise.

While the supplies exist for an expansion or another LNG project, the focus in Abu Dhabi has shifted toward satisfying domestic and regional gas demand.

Yemen

The two-train, 6.7 MMt/y (9 Bcm/y) Yemen LNG project has had a long gestation period, but the venture took off in early 2005, when the Yemen LNG consortium signed provisional sales agreements with two importers in the United States and Europe and with a third in Korea, for a combined 5.8 MMt/y (8 Bcm/y). YEMGAS, a joint venture between Technip, JGC, and KBR, was awarded the project's EPC contract in September 2005. The target date for Train 1 start-up is the end of 2008, with Train 2 coming on line approximately five months later (tables 10–30 and 10–31).

Table 10–30. Yemen: LNG project under development

Project	Sponsor Start Year	Capacity (MMt/y)	Capacity (Bcf/d)	Train Capacities (MMt/y)	Shareholding
Yemen LNG	2009	6.7	0.82	2 × 3.35	Total 39.62% Yemen Gas Co 16.73% Hunt Oil 17.22% 5K Corp 9.55% Hyundai 3%
Total:		6.2	0.82		GASSP 5%

Table 10–31. Yemen: Contracted LNG volumes

Buyers	Terms	Start	End	Max. MMt/y	Bcf/d
Total Gas & Power	Ex-ship	2009	2029	2	0.27
Suez Global LNG Trading	FOB	2009	2029	2.5	0.33
KOGAS	FOB	2008	2028	2	0.27

The Yemen LNG project will be underpinned by the Marib-area fields. The consortium has been granted exclusive access to these fields by the Yemeni government. The reserves currently dedicated to the project include 9.15 Tcf (260 Bcm) of proven reserves (sales gas) and 0.7 Tcf (20 Bcm) of probable reserves, with 1 Tcf (28 Bcm) allocated to the domestic market.

THE ASIA-PACIFIC REGION

The Asia-Pacific region supplies the most LNG of any region to the largest regional LNG market. Unlike the other regions, liquefaction in the Asia-Pacific region has steadily grown since the first export project, Alaska, began in 1969. Five countries have a total of nine export projects—two in Australia, three in Malaysia, two in Indonesia, and one project each in Brunei and the United States (Alaska). Five projects are concentrated on the island of Kalimantan (formerly known as Borneo), including all of Malaysia's projects in Sarawak State, the Brunei project, and the larger Indonesian project (Bontang, also known as Badak). Kalimantan has thus been informally dubbed the island of LNG.

Overall regional growth is inevitable. Although growth in the traditional markets of Japan and South Korea has somewhat moderated, the potential from China and India, both having major plans to add new energy infrastructure, is strong. The five current Asia-Pacific exporting countries have all considered adding additional export projects, with varying degrees of likeliness for completion. In addition, other countries in the region are in various stages of promoting export projects, including Russia and Papua New Guinea.

Australia

Darwin LNG. The ConocoPhillips-operated Darwin LNG project began operating in early 2006 (table 10–32). It is supplied from the Bayu-Undan field, located in the Timor Sea's Joint Petroleum Development Area, about 500 kilometers northwest of Darwin and 250 kilometers south of Suai, Timor-Leste. The Bayu-Undan field contains an estimated 3.4 Tcf (100 Bcm) of gas reserves. This low reserve level (by LNG project standards) has led to a somewhat unusual 17-year SPA that commits essentially 100% of the field's reserves and LNG production to TEPCO and Tokyo Gas.

Table 10–32. Australia: Darwin LNG sales agreements

Buyer	Terms	Start	End	MMt/y
Tokyo Electric	Ex-ship	2006	2024	2
Tokyo Gas	Ex-ship	2006	2024	1

Darwin LNG is currently a single-train, 3.3 MMt/y (4.6 Bcm/y) facility (table 10–33). The project has environmental approvals from the Australian authorities to expand up to 10 MMt/y (14 Bcm/y). There are not sufficient proven reserves to increase the plant capacity, but ConocoPhillips is an advocate for bringing gas from the nearby Greater Sunrise field to an expanded Darwin plant. However, Sunrise's final development has not been agreed, and the Greater Sunrise fields are the focus of some legal and fiscal uncertainty, owing to maritime border disputes between Australia and Timor-Leste. It remains to be seen whether there will be a realignment of equity interests in the integrated Darwin LNG project to accommodate the entry of a new feedgas source with a different ownership structure, or whether the owners of the field(s) will pay a fee to Darwin LNG for the privilege of using Wickham Point's infrastructure. Much will depend on whether Darwin LNG and any additional feedgas supply source have any common ownership.

Table 10–33. Australia: Business structure of the Darwin LNG project

Shareholdings	ConocoPhillips 56.72% Santos 10.64% Eni SpA 12.04% Inpex Corp. 10.53% Tokyo Electric/Tokyo Gas 10.08%
Project funding Project operator Entity responsible formarketing LNG	Equity financed ConocoPhillips ConocoPhillips

North West Shelf (NWS). At the time it started up in 1989, NWS was the first project in 20 years in which the major stakeholder was not a state-held entity (Alaska being the earlier example). Instead of direct participation, the government is remunerated through resource taxes, which have been levied at a higher level than on some of the other regional competitors.

NWS started with two trains in 1989 and a third train in 1992. After a relatively low-cost 1995 debottlenecking, each of these train's capacities was raised to 2.5 MMt/y (3.5 Bcm/y). A fourth, 4.2 MMt/y (5.9 Bcm/y) unit was added in 2005. After a fifth, 4.4 MMt/y (6.2 Bcm/y) train comes into service in late 2008, the project's total capacity (Trains 1–5) will be 16.3 MMt/y (23 Bcm/y), taking also into account not only the addition of the new train but also upgrades to existing infrastructure (table 10–34). The development of subsequent trains will be largely contingent not only on securing buyers but also on lining up the requisite feedgas.

Table 10–34. Australia: NWS LNG project export facilities

Project	Sponsor Start Year	Capacity (MMt/y)	Bcf/d
Train 1 and 2	1989	2 × 2.5	2 × 0.36
Train 3	1992	2.5	0.36
Train 4	2005	4.2	0.60
Train 5	2008	4.4	0.63

The NWS project is a true integrated joint venture, with the six project participants—BHP, BP, ChevronTexaco, Japan Australia LNG (MiMi, a joint venture between Mitsui and Mitsubishi), Shell, and Woodside—each owning an equal undivided interest in the entire project, from feedgas production to liquefaction facilities. A domestic gas pipeline project is owned by Woodside (50%), BP and ChevronTexaco (16.67% each), and BHP and Shell subsidiaries (8.33% each). Woodside Offshore Petroleum Limited, a subsidiary of Woodside, is the operator of the entire project. LNG-marketing efforts are the province of an organization known as North West Shelf Australia LNG, which again comprises the six members of the NWS venture itself.

Long-term contracts with Japanese utilities make Japan by far the largest market for Australian LNG (table 10–35). The company also makes short-term sales to Europe, the United States, and Korea. The project has some advantages over other suppliers looking to market in the Far East: it is closer to Asian markets than Middle Eastern projects; and compared to some projects, there is less political (thus operational) risk. These advantages contributed to the project's successful bid on a contract to supply the Guangdong import facility in China.

Table 10–35. Australia: Signed NWS LNG sales contracts

Importer	Buyers	Terms	Start	End	MMt/y	Bcm/y
Japan	Chubu Electric	Ex-ship	1989	2009	1.05	1.45
Japan	Chugoku Electric	Ex-ship	1989	2009	1.11	1.53
Japan	Kansai Electric	Ex-ship	1989	2009	1.13	1.56
Japan	Kyusu Electric	Ex-ship	1989	2009	1.05	1.45
Japan	Osaka Gas	Ex-ship	1989	2009	0.79	1.09
Japan	TEPCO	Ex-ship	1996	2009	1.18	1.63
Japan	Tokyo Gas	Ex-ship	1996	2009	0.79	1.09
Japan	Toho Gas	Ex-ship	1996	2009	0.23	0.32
South Korea	KOGAS	Ex-ship	2004	2010	0.50	0.69
Unspecified	Shell	FOB	2004	2009	0.74	1.02
Japan	Tokyo Gas	FOB	2004	2029	1.07	1.48
Japan	Osaka Gas	FOB	2004	2034	1.00	1.38
Japan	Toho Gas	FOB	2004	2029	0.30	0.41
Japan	Kyushu Electric	Ex-ship	2005	2025	0.52	0.72
Japan	Tohoku Electric	Ex-ship	2005	2020	0.40	0.55
Japan	Shizuoka Gas	Ex-ship	2005	2029	0.14	0.19
China	CNOOC	FOB	2006	2031	3.70	5.11
Japan	Chubu Electric	Ex-ship	2009	2016	0.47	0.65
Japan	Chugoku Electric	Ex-ship	2009	2021	1.40	1.93
Japan	Kansai Electric	Ex-ship	2009	2017	0.43	0.59
Japan	Kansai Electric	Ex-ship	2009	2014	0.50	0.69
South Korea	KOGAS	Ex-ship	2009	2016	0.50	1.69
Japan	Kyushu Electric	Ex-ship	2009	2017	1.40	1.01
Japan	TEPCO	Ex-ship	2009	2017	0.30	0.41
Japan	Tokyo Gas	Ex-ship	2009	2017	0.53	0.73
Japan	Osaka Gas	Ex-ship	2009	2015	0.50	0.69
Japan	Toho Gas	Ex-ship	2009	2019	0.76	1.05
Japan	Chubu Electric	Ex-ship	2009	2025	0.60	0.83
Japan	Tohuko Electric	Ex-ship	2010	2018	0.50	0.69
Japan	Kansai Electric	Ex-ship	2014	2023	0.93	0.69

The NWS joint venture invited its first Chinese customer, the China National Offshore Oil Company (CNOOC), to purchase an interest in NWS upstream reserves. This move was linked to Australia's successful bid to supply up to 3.7 MMt/y (5.2 Bcm/y) of LNG to the Guangdong facility starting in mid-2006. The NWS project established a joint venture company dubbed China LNG (CLNG) to own the natural gas to be processed and supplied under this contract. CNOOC has taken a 25% equity position in the new venture. CLNG pays a fee for the use of NWS infrastructure to process the feedgas dedicated to the Guangdong contract, but it does not own a share in the integrated NWS project itself.

Brunei

Brunei LNG Sendirian Berhad's (BLNG's) five-train liquefaction facility was the first large-scale liquefaction plant in Asia. Commissioned in 1972, it was also Shell's first foray into LNG. Shell has since significantly expanded its LNG portfolio and participates as a major shareholder in more than a half-dozen liquefaction projects.

The upstream and downstream components of the venture are separate (table 10–36). The State of Brunei and Shell own equal shares in Brunei Shell Petroleum SB, which produces feedgas in four offshore gas fields: Southwest Ampa, Fairley, Champion, and Gannet. Most production is sold to the Brunei LNG consortium for liquefaction and export at the Lumut plant.

Table 10–36. Brunei LNG project structure

Company	Ownership Upstream	Ownership Downstream
State of Brunei	50%	50%
Shell	50%	25%
Mitsubishi		25%

BLNG sent its first shipments to Japan in 1972. Japan continues to be the primary market, although Korean buyers began purchasing LNG under long-term contract in 1994 (table 10–37).

Table 10–37. Brunei LNG sales contracts

Buyer	Terms	Start	End	MMt/y
TEPCOEx-ship	1972	2013	4.03	
Tokyo Gas	Ex-ship	1972	2013	1.24
Osaka Gas	Ex-ship	1972	2013	0.74
KOGASEx-ship	1997	2013	0.7	

BLNG has also been working since the 1990s on a long-term project to upgrade the plant's existing trains. A five-year refurbishment of the trains ended in 1993, undertaken to reduce the amount of maintenance the plant would require going forward. The partners also wanted to reassure their current buyers that the plant could operate reliably beyond 2013 and through a third 20-year sales period.

BLNG has been mulling plans to add a sixth liquefaction unit for some time now, but Train 6 will likely remain in the conceptual stage until there is some certainty about existing buyers' renewal plans. Renewing the venture's existing sales agreements and finding new buyers for an additional train are not BLNG's only issues—the company must also procure sufficient reserves to support its production plans. Roughly 7.5 Tcf (210 Bcm) is required in order to maintain its existing 7.2 MMt/y (9.9 Bcm/y) production capacity during a third contract cycle, while some 4.2 Tcf (120 Bcm) is needed for a new 4 MMt/y (5.5 Bcm/y) train. If BLNG elects to adhere to recent trends and build an even larger train, these feedgas requirements would increase further.

Hopes to boost the venture's gas reserves rest with two deepwater offshore concessions—blocks J and K. These blocks were awarded in early 2002 to two separate consortia, led by Total and Shell, respectively. However, these very areas are at the heart of a maritime border dispute between Brunei and Malaysia. In early 2003, Petronas awarded deepwater blocks L and M to partners U.S.-based Murphy Oil and Petronas Carigali. However, the size and coordinates of Total's block J are almost the same as Murphy Oil's block I, while Murphy Oil's block M overlies the Shell-led consortium's block K. Malaysian officials have offered to devise a joint development zone with Brunei, but this would necessitate Brunei's redrawing its upstream contracts with the various oil companies. An agreement has so far eluded the neighboring governments.

Indonesia

Indonesia has long been the world's largest supplier of LNG, but it lost this position to Qatar in early 2007. Pertamina, the state oil and gas company, owns 100% of the Arun and Bontang LNG facilities, and separate operating companies manage each facility. These operating companies, PT Arun and PT Badak, are majority owned by Pertamina (55%) along with producers, lenders, and buyers. A third project, the Tangguh LNG venture, will begin operating in 2008. Tangguh is unique among Indonesian LNG export ventures because it is owned and operated solely by foreign companies. Pertamina plays no role whatsoever in the fully integrated Tangguh project.

Arun. Arun is located in the Aceh Province, in the northern part of the island of Sumatra. The Arun field was the first major natural gas discovery in Indonesia. Discovered in 1971, it was found to contain 17 Tcf (500 Bcm) of natural gas. The state owns all hydrocarbons in Indonesia, so Pertamina controls natural gas development through production-sharing contracts

(PSCs) with producers. ExxonMobil operates the natural gas field production for the Arun facility.

The first three trains were completed for the 1978 start-up. An additional two trains were added in 1984, and a final, sixth train was added in 1986 (table 10–38). Supply declines in the Arun field forced the early shutdown of two of the original six trains in April 2000, and the supply contracts were switched to Bontang. Until recently, most of the feedgas production has come from the Arun field, but ExxonMobil has added production from smaller fields to supplement declines. There are plans to shut down two additional trains by the end of 2009. The four trains in operation have a liquefaction capacity of around 8 MMt/y but have not been operating at capacity for some time. The plant may be shut down completely by 2015.

Table 10–38. Indonesia: Arun LNG export project

Project	Status	Startup	Capacity (MMt/y)	Number of Trains
Arun	Existing	1978	5.8	3
Arun Phase I Expansion	Existing	1985	3.9	2
Arun Phase II Expansion	Existing	1986	1.9	1

Political unrest from Islamic militants caused ExxonMobil to shut down the Arun plant from May through July 2001. This was due to rising violence between separatist rebels and the Indonesian military and attacks directed toward the facilities. While Pertamina was able to send excess supplies from Bontang to meet some of its contractual supply obligations, a few buyers were forced to seek supplies elsewhere. Repercussions from this episode were seen at other Indonesian LNG projects, as was evidenced when the first Chinese export project chose Australia as an LNG supplier over a new Indonesian plant, partially owing to reliability concerns. Moreover, there was some concern that the Bontang facility could be similarly targeted in the future.

Bontang (Badak). This facility is located in East Kalimantan, on the east coast of the island formerly known as Borneo. Soon after the Arun discovery, the Badak gas reservoirs were discovered, along with a series of nearby discoveries that were to underpin the Bontang LNG project.

Shipments began in 1977 with the first two trains, A and B. As new buyers were added, further trains were built. Trains C and D were added in 1983, Train E was added in 1990, Train F was added in 1993, Train G was added in 1997, and Train H was added in 1999. The eight trains have a combined liquefaction capacity of roughly 22 MMt/y (30.3 Bcm/y) (table 10–39). A ninth unit (Train I) is planned, but this cannot proceed until some clarification is obtained regarding the renewal of existing sales contracts. However, whether Bontang's buyers will renew their purchase deals has been a gray area for some time, since the Indonesian government appears keen to direct gas production to the domestic, rather than the export, market. Recently Bontang has failed to meet its production targets due to declining reservoir performance. Pertamina has been forced to purchase LNG from other suppliers to meet its sales commitments.

Table 10–39. Indonesia: Bontang LNG export project

Project	Status	Startup	Capacity (MMt/y)	Number of Trains
Bontang A,B	Existing	1977	4.5	2
Bontang C,D	Existing	1983	4.5	2
Bontang E	Existing	1989	2.3	1
Bontang F	Existing	1993	2.53	1
Bontang G	Existing	1996	2.8	1
Bontang H	Existing	1996	3	1

The majority of Arun and Bontang's LNG is exported to Japan, with smaller trades with South Korea and Taiwan (tables 10–40 and 10–41). Depending on the contract, shipping may be handled by either Pertamina or the buyer. Pertamina has chartered numerous vessels on both long-term and short-term arrangements to meet its shipping responsibilities.

Table 10–40. Indonesia: Arun LNG sales contracts

Buyer	Terms	Start	End	MMt/y
Tohoku EP	FOB	1983	2005	3.0
Tokyo EP	FOB	1983	2005	0.51
Tohoku EP	FOB	2005	2009	0.83
Tokyo EP	FOB	2005	2009	0.14
KOGAS	Ex-ship	1986	2014	2.0
KOGAS	Ex-ship	1992	2014	0.3
KOGAS	FOB	1994	2007	1.21

Table 10–41. Indonesia: Bontang LNG sales contracts

Buyer	Terms	Start	End	MMt/y
Chubu EP	Exship	1978	2010	2.15
Kansai EP	Exship	1978	2010	2.57
Kyushu EP	Exship	1978	2010	1.56
Osaka Gas	Exship	1978	2010	1.3
Toho Gas	Exship	1978	2010	0.25
Nippon Steel	Exship	1978	2010	0.62
Chubu EP	FOB	1983	2011	1.7
Kansai EP	FOB	1983	2011	0.91
Osaka Gas	FOB	1983	2011	0.45
Toho Gas	FOB	1983	2011	0.57
Osaka Gas	FOB	1994	2013	1.27
Tokyo Gas	FOB	1994	2013	0.92
Toho Gas	FOB	1994	2013	0.12
Hiroshima Gas	Exship	1996	2015	0.21
Nippon Gas	Exship	1996	2015	0.08
Osaka Gas	Exship	1996	2015	0.1
KOGAS	Exship	1992	2007	0.99
KOGAS	FOB	2008	2013	0.84
KOGAS	FOB	2014	2014	0.42
KOGAS	FOB	1998	2017	1.02
CPC	Exship	1990	2009	1.57
CPC	Exship	1998	2017	1.84

Tangguh. The fully integrated Tangguh project is located in the province of West Papua. Tangguh is operated by contractor BP Indonesia through a PSC with Indonesia's Executive Agency for Upstream Oil and Gas Activity (BPMIGAS). BP was also appointed by BPMIGAS as Tangguh's seller of record, meaning that it has the right to market LNG on behalf of the project. This is a departure from Indonesia's other two LNG export ventures, where Pertamina was solely responsible for marketing (table 10–42).

Table 10–42. Indonesia: Tangguh LNG project structure

Company	Ownership
BP	37.16%
CNOOC	16.96%
MI Berau B.V.	16.30%
Nippon Oil Exploration	12.23%
KG Berau/KG Wiriagar	10.00%
LNG Japan	7.35%

The two-train greenfield project is underpinned by gas reserves from the Vorwata, Wiriagar Deep, Roabiba, Ofaweri, Wos, and Ubadari fields (located in three PSCs). These fields have a combined proven and certified gas reserve base of 14.4 Tcf (400 Bcm). The 7.6 MMt/y (10.6 Bcm/y) project is fully committed to Korean, Chinese, and North American buyers (table 10–43). A joint venture comprising KBR, JGC, and PT Pertafenikki was selected as the EPC contractor, and the plant is scheduled to be operational by 2008. Tangguh has potential for further expansion and has adequate proven reserves within the three production areas that are committed to the project.

Table 10–43. Indonesia: Tangguh LNG project sales

Importer	Seller	Project	Buyer	Terms	Start	End	MMt/y
Korea	BP, on behalf of Tangguh Partners	Tangguh	K Power	Ex-ship	2005	2025	0.6
Korea	BP, on behalf of Tangguh Partners	Tangguh	POSCO	Ex-ship	2005	2025	0.55
China	BP, on behalf of Tangguh Partners	Tangguh	CNOOC	Ex-ship	2007	2032	2.6
Mexico	BP, on behalf of Tangguh Partners	Tangguh	Sempra	Ex-ship	2008	2028	3.7

Malaysia

As of the end of 2006, Malaysia was one of the world's largest exporters of LNG. There are three separate liquefaction facilities located at the port of Bintulu (table 10–44). Malaysia LNG (MLNG) Satu first shipped natural gas in 1983. MLNG Satu has three 2.7 MMt/y (3.8 Bcm/y) liquefaction trains (initially designed at 2.0 MMt/y, capacity was later boosted through debottlenecking). For many years, all the plant's output was sent to Japan, to Tokyo Electric and Tokyo Gas. MLNG Satu was initially owned by Petronas (65%), Shell and Mitsubishi (15% each), and the local Sarawak government (5%). In 2003, Petronas purchased Mitsubishi's and Shell's 15% equity stakes in MLNG Satu upon expiration of their 20-year joint venture agreement. However, Mitsubishi subsequently re-acquired a 5% stake in MLNG Satu, and the project's shareholding structure is now Petronas (90%), Sarawak state (5%), and Mitsubishi (5%).

Table 10–44. Malaysia: LNG export facilities

Project	Start-up	MMt/y	No. Trains
MLNG Satu	1983	8.25	3
MLNG Dua	1995	7.8	3
MLNG Tiga	2003	6.8	2

MLNG Dua became the second operational facility in 1995, when the first of three 2.6 MMt/y (3.6 Bcm/y) liquefaction trains came on line. The 6.8 MMt/y (9.5 Bcm/y) MLNG Tiga facility came on line in 2003. Although the latter facility currently has two trains, a third could be added later in the decade, if demand justifies it and if Petronas and its upstream joint venture partners can secure the additional feedgas quantities needed to underpin an expansion.

MLNG Satu and Dua supply customers in Japan, Korea, and Taiwan (table 10–45). MLNG began a first-of-its-kind arrangement with a buyer in 1996, when it agreed to deliver LNG from the same tanker to two different facilities in Japan as part of a regular trade arrangement. Shizuoka Gas wanted to purchase LNG and to take advantage of Petronas's shipping capability but could not accept the entire off-take from the large ships, so an extra stop was added en route to another buyer.

Table 10–45. Malaysia: Signed LNG sales contracts

Importer	Buyers	Terms	Start	End	MMt/y	Bcm/y
Japan	TEPCO	Ex-ship	1983	2003	4.00	5.52
Japan	Tokyo Gas	Ex-ship	1983	2003	2.00	2.76
Japan	TEPCO	Ex-ship	1991	2003	0.80	1.10
Japan	Tokyo Gas	Ex-ship	1991	2003	0.60	0.83
Japan	Saibu Gas	Ex-ship	1994	2013	0.36	0.50
Taiwan	CPC	Ex-ship	1995	2014	2.25	3.11
Japan	Kansai Electric	Ex-ship	1995	2015	0.42	0.58
South Korea	KOGAS	FOB	1995	2015	2.00	2.76
Japan	Tokyo Gas	Ex-ship	1995	2015	0.80	1.10
Japan	Osaka Gas	Ex-ship	1995	2015	0.60	0.83
Japan	Toho Gas	Ex-ship	1995	2015	0.28	0.39
Japan	Tohoku Gas	Ex-ship	1996	2016	0.50	0.69
Japan	Shizuoka Gas	Ex-ship	1996	2016	0.45	0.62
Japan	Sendai City Gas	Ex-ship	1997	2017	0.15	0.21
South Korea	KOGAS	Ex-ship	2003	2010	2.00	2.76
South Korea	KOGAS	FOB	2004	2008	0.79	1.09
Japan	TEPCO	Ex-ship	2004	2019	3.20	4.42
Japan	TEPCO	FOB	2004	2019	0.93	1.28
Japan	TEPCO	Ex-ship	2004	2020	0.40	0.55
Japan	TEPCO	FOB	2004	2020	0.27	0.37
Japan	Tokyo Gas	Ex-ship	2004	2024	0.22	0.30
Japan	Tokyo Gas	Ex-ship	2004	2019	1.60	2.21
Japan	Tokyo Gas	FOB	2004	2024	0.24	0.33
Japan	Tokyo Gas	Ex-ship	2004	2020	0.13	0.18
Japan	Tokyo Gas	FOB	2004	2019	0.47	0.65
Japan	Tokyo Gas	Ex-ship	2004	2020	0.40	0.55
Japan	Osaka Gas	FOB	2004	2024	0.16	0.22
Japan	Osaka Gas	Ex-ship	2004	2024	0.15	0.21
Japan	Osaka Gas	Ex-ship	2004	2024	0.12	0.17
Japan	Toho Gas	Ex-ship	2004	2024	0.22	0.30
Japan	Toho Gas	Ex-ship	2004	2024	0.07	0.10
Japan	Toho Gas	FOB	2004	2024	0.08	0.11
Japan	JAPEX	Ex-ship	2004	2024	0.50	0.69
Japan	Hiroshima Gas	Ex-ship	2005	2013	0.08	0.11
South Korea	KOGAS	Ex-ship	2005	2008	0.50	0.69
Japan	Tohoku Electric	Ex-ship	2005	2025	0.90	1.24
Japan	Toho Gas	Ex-ship	2007	2027	0.52	0.72
South Korea	KOGAS	Ex-ship	2008	2028	2.00	2.76
Japan	Osaka Gas	Ex-ship	2009	2024	0.92	1.27
China	CNOOC	Ex-ship	2009	2024	3.03	4.18
Japan	Shikoku Electric	Ex-ship	2010	2025	0.42	0.58
Japan	Chubu Electric	Ex-ship	2011	2031	0.54	0.75
Japan	Saibu Gas	Ex-ship	2013	2028	0.39	0.54

The Malaysian LNG projects are split ventures, in which the upstream transfers feedgas to the liquefaction projects (which includes pipelines) at a price equal to approximately 30% of the ex-ship LNG sales price (table 10–46).

Table 10–46. Malaysia: LNG project business structures

Business Structure	MLNG Satu	MLNG Dua	MLNG Tiga
Shareholdings in the LNG plant:	Petronas 90% Mitsubishi 5% Sarawak State 5%	Petronas 60% Mitsubishi 15% Shell 15% Sarawak State 10%	Petronas 60% Shell 15% Sarawak State 10% Nippon Oil 10% Mitsubishi 5%
Entity responsible for marketing LNG	MLNG	MLNG	MLNG

There has been little action to expand the Bintulu LNG complex to include a potential fourth project (MLNG Empat). Petronas stated in 2004 that any such undertaking was on hold and that the timing for development would depend on markets and further reserves allocations to LNG, domestic production, and pipeline exports. Yet various debottlenecking activities are taking place, and more are planned.

The Malaysian government has also been promoting Malaysia as a potential supply hub for the Trans-ASEAN Gas Pipeline—a regional gas infrastructure development project that aims to connect eight major gas-producing/consuming nations by 2020 (Thailand, Malaysia, Singapore, Indonesia, Brunei, the Philippines, Myanmar, and Vietnam). Such a development would increase gas reserves intended for regional pipeline exportation.

The United States

Alaska is home to the world's second-oldest liquefaction facility, located at Nikisi, on the Kenai Peninsula (table 10–47). The Kenai facility started operations in 1969. Kenai LNG was the first project to deliver natural gas to Japan, which has remained the destination for the vast majority of its LNG. As no additional trains were ever added, Kenai is small in comparison to most liquefaction facilities. It is consistently the world's second-smallest

LNG exporter, after Libya. Unlike Libya, the plant's continuous operations have produced at close to design capacity for decades.

Table 10–47. Alaska: LNG export project summary

Project	Start-up	MMt/y	No. Trains	Ownership
Kenai LNG Project	1969	1.4	1	ConocoPhillips 70% Marathon 30%

Kenai LNG is owned by ConocoPhillips (70%) and Marathon (30%). Each partner separately produces and transports natural gas for sale to the liquefaction facility. A ConocoPhillips subsidiary produces gas from an offshore platform in the Cook Inlet, while Marathon produces from the onshore Kenai field and the offshore River field. Kenai LNG owns two Marathon-operated 88,000 m^3 LNG carriers, which transport the gas to Japan (table 10–48).

Table 10–48. Alaska: Signed LNG sales contracts

Buyer	Terms	Start	End	MMt/y
Tokyo Electric	Ex-ship	1969	2009	0.98
Tokyo Gas	Ex-ship	1969	2009	0.33

Existing fields dedicated to the Kenai LNG project are in decline, and there are no plans to expand this facility. However, ConocoPhillips and Marathon applied to the U.S. Department of Energy in January 2007 for permission to extend Kenai's LNG export license from March 31, 2009 through March 31, 2011. The application followed written assurances from Tokyo Electric Power Co. and Tokyo Gas that they were still interested in renewing their sales contracts for Alaskan LNG in line with the license extension. However, fresh feedgas must be found to underpin any LNG contract extensions supplies. Alternatively, new terminals planned for the west coast of the United States and Mexico could take spot volumes as Kenai winds down. Failing to find new gas resources, the facility could be reconfigured as an LNG receiving terminal to bridge the gap between growing south-central Alaskan gas demand and the start-up of North Slope pipeline gas deliveries

NOTES

[1] All graphics used in this chapter are from Poten & Partners.

[2] In August 2006, EGLNG awarded a FEED contract to Bechtel for a second, 4.4 MMt/y liquefaction train. FEED work will be completed in the first quarter of 2007. EGLNG is in discussions with gas resource holders in Equatorial Guinea, Nigeria, and Cameroon to secure the necessary gas supplies.

[3] In December 1997, NLNG and Enel signed a revised SPA that calls for NLNG to deliver 3.5 Bcm/y of LNG to Gaz de France's Montoir de Bretagne receiving facility starting in October 1999 for 22.5 years. ENEL receives the equivalent of gas delivered via pipeline to Italy following appropriate swaps with third parties.

THE ECONOMICS OF AN LNG PROJECT 11

INTRODUCTION

Unlike oil or most other gas monetization schemes, LNG requires specialized and highly expensive equipment along the entire value chain. LNG is not a commodity like petroleum. Crude oil is, by definition, a fungible commodity; it can, with few restrictions, be loaded onto vessels at any oil export point and discharged into virtually any market. The development of an oil export project therefore does not need to be linked to a particular trade or anchored by a particular buyer. The assumption of developers is that a market can be found once the oil is flowing (although the global price of oil or the price in the potential market for the oil will be taken into account when making an investment decision).

Getting LNG to market, by contrast, requires specialized facilities for liquefaction in the exporting country and for regasification in the importing country, linked by a fleet of specialized ships. Committing to an LNG export facility without having secured a buyer (with import capacity) and adequate transport would represent an enormous risk. Historically, LNG projects have been meticulously laid out from the gas field in the exporting country to the gas distribution grid in the importing country before ground was broken on facilities.

The number of participants in an LNG project requires that the entire chain be secured before the project is advanced. Unless a project is financed by a sovereign state (as was the case with Algeria's Bethioua and Skikda LNG plants), participation in LNG projects is usually shared among two or more entities, one of which may be the host government, often in the form of a national oil company. In some instances, such as Indonesia's Bontang project, a single national oil company controls the liquefaction facilities, while a number of oil companies operate the upstream acreage that supplies gas to the project. Participation in the first two trains of the Oman LNG project was spread among seven distinct entities, including the Omani government.

Although the involvement of many participants lightens the burden on any single investor, the sheer enormity of the costs of a grassroots LNG project means that each contributor's commitment is still substantial. This further encourages projects to reduce risks as much as possible by locking in buyers, import capacity, and transport before the final investment decision is made. Often, specific gas reserves are set aside specifically for the LNG project, further reducing any risk or uncertainty.

Capital expenditures for LNG projects are categorized as either upstream or liquefaction costs. Upstream costs are incurred in the production of project feedgas and are similar to the gas production costs associated with any gas project. Liquefaction costs are associated with converting feedgas to LNG for export. Pipeline costs between the production facilities and the liquefaction plant can fall into either category, depending on whether pipelines are governed by a production or a manufacturing tax regime.

UPSTREAM CAPITAL COSTS

Generally, wellhead and field production costs account for most of the upstream costs, including flow lines and transmission networks. The characteristics of the field are obviously important. Gas fields with high sulfur content or fields in remote areas can incur high upstream expenditures. Offshore gas fields often require expensive platforms, although developers are increasingly using cheaper subsea completions for such reserves. These involve wellheads on the seabed that feed gas to a central manifold, which combines the produced gas flows and sends them to a central processing unit located either on a single platform or onshore.

The more remote a gas field is, the more expensive its development will be. The Qatargas project's first trains cost only in the range of $700 million to $750 million each including the upstream development, because the feedgas comes from Qatar's North Field, a shallow gas reservoir of very good quality that is close to the Qatari mainland. This contrasts sharply with the costs for Russia's Sakhalin II project, where total project costs have escalated to at least $20 billion. This project has been developed in a very remote area of the Russian Far East, with enormous infrastructure investment required in order to produce and transport gas from offshore fields off northern Sakhalin Island to the ice-free port and liquefaction plant located in the south.

In addition to production facilities, upstream costs will also include the supporting utilities needed for feedgas production, housing for both construction labor and field operations personnel, and other temporary and permanent infrastructure. Owners' costs and preproduction expenses are also incurred. In some cases, exploration and delineation expenses are considered part of the upstream costs, although initial exploration costs are usually considered sunk by project developers. These can differ widely from project to project, ranging from almost nothing to $200 million or more.

Upstream costs are largely dependent on downstream gas volume requirements. Producing sufficient feedgas for a two-train, 10 MMt/y (14 Bcm/y) facility will obviously require more investment than for a single-train, 3 MMt/y (4 Bcm/y) facility. For this reason, capital costs are usually compared across LNG projects as unit costs—dollars per ton of annual production.

Local labor and materials markets will also have an impact on upstream costs. Upstream projects in developed nations, such as Australia and Norway, may be more expensive than comparable undertakings in emerging markets, such as West Africa or Southeast Asia. While labor productivity in developed nations may be higher, this benefit is usually not sufficient to compensate for the higher wages and benefits in these locations, driving up construction costs.

Not all upstream capital expenditures are incurred prior to start-up. Project participants will usually quantify the reserves available to the project before the final investment decision. Often, new wells will need to be drilled, or new processing facilities will need to be put in place during the life of the gas field as the reservoir is depleted. These forward capital expenditures must also be taken into account in the initial budgeting process.

PIPELINE CAPITAL COSTS

Pipelines are needed to deliver feedgas from the producing fields to the LNG plant. Generally, they are considered separate cost centers from the segments of the production and liquefaction chain.

Pipeline costs are highly site specific. A pipeline built through a flat, empty, seismically inactive desert in a developing country where there is cheap labor will be substantially less expensive than an offshore pipeline or a line built across a mountain range. The number and capacity of compression stations needed along the pipe's length also affect total cost. Generally, pipeline costs are between $1 million and $3 million per mile, although more expensive projects have been built in challenging environments. LNG projects with associated liquids production will often build separate condensate pipelines, further increasing total capital investment.

Liquefaction plant facilities typically represent an LNG chain's most significant capital investment. Until early this decade, technological advances and the application of economies of scale led to substantial lowering in the unit capital investment levels for liquefaction.

LIQUEFACTION CAPITAL COSTS

While most upstream expenditures are similar to those incurred by any gas monetization scheme, liquefaction capital costs are unique to LNG projects. Liquefaction plant facilities typically represent an LNG chain's most significant capital investment. Until early this decade, technological advances and the application of economies of scale led to substantial lowering in the unit capital investment levels for liquefaction. Unit costs for grassroots projects fell from as high as $600 per ton of annual capacity to below $200 per ton, with typical values falling in the range of $200–$350 per ton-year.

However, this downward trend has reversed in recent years. Significant increases in raw materials costs across key commodities such as carbon and stainless steels, nickel, and cement, combined with increasingly constrained availabilities of experienced EPC contractors, skilled labor, and equipment suppliers, have caused unit costs for upcoming LNG projects to balloon to the $500–$700 per ton range. Whether these increased costs will slow the LNG industry's recent high growth rates remains to be seen. These recent cost increases have been accompanied by a sharp rise in global oil prices, which are either directly linked to or strongly related to long-term LNG prices.

Project developers have their choice of a number of different liquefaction technologies, including APCI C3-MR and AP-X, Shell DMR, Phillips Optimized Cascade, Statoil-Linde MFC, and Axens Liquefin (for details, see chapter 5). The choice of technology will usually depend on project participation (e.g., Shell and ConocoPhillips would generally choose their own proprietary processes) or on the EPC company that wins the bid. EPC contractors commonly license a specific technology. Project costs will typically be assessed on a life-cycle cost basis to allow for trade-offs between capital and operating costs between different processes.

LNG storage tanks are another aspect of the downstream capital costs that are specific to LNG projects. Storage facility costs are highly dependent on the liquefaction plant location, the distance to market, the total production, and the choice of containment system. Storage capacity is intimately linked to ship scheduling: If there is less storage space for production, the risks that stem from a delay in shipping become greater. Usually, SPAs will allow for the resale of LNG by a producer in the event that the buyer cannot provide shipping for a cargo (if the cargo is FOB). However, if another ship is not available, or if the sales are ex-ship and storage is not sufficient, a lapse in ship scheduling could lead to full storage tanks (also called tanktops) and a resulting production shutdown. Decisions on capital investment for storage therefore depend in part on how the developer addresses risk.

In addition to the equipment needed for the LNG liquefaction and storage, the downstream portion of the project encompasses the marine facilities needed for LNG exportation. These facilities include the LNG jetty, to load ships, and the materials jetty, to off-load construction and operations material. Other marine costs are heavily dependent on project geography. LNG plants built on exposed coastlines may require expensive breakwaters to provide a protected area for ship operations. LNG ships require water depths of around 12 meters; thus, in areas with high rates of sedimentation (e.g., the Niger Delta, in Nigeria), dredging requirements for both initial construction and channel maintenance can substantially add to costs.

In an effort to defray these infrastructure costs, project developers have been considering the use of floating LNG plants. These plants would be placed on floating barges around the size of supertankers. This would save on marine and pipeline costs but would add somewhat to the costs for the trains themselves.

Although much of the water and acid gases is usually stripped out of the feedgas stream at the producing fields, LNG projects typically require some additional gas processing capability to further reduce impurities or to strip out heavier hydrocarbons. Some projects (e.g., expansions to Nigeria

LNG) incorporate LPG facilities as part of the downstream project. As part of efforts to reduce emissions, Norway's Snøhvit project and Australia's proposed Gorgon project plan to reinject CO_2 into underground reservoirs.

As with the upstream, construction costs should be included in the assessment of liquefaction economics. Again, local wage and productivity factors play a role. Downstream costs will include utilities and support infrastructure. Owners' and preproduction costs should also be taken into account.

If reserves are sufficient and enough buyers can be lined up, LNG developers typically plan for more than one train in a grassroots project. This is because of the economies of scale that come from building a second train of the same capacity. If the infrastructure for the first train is sufficient to handle the additional feedgas, power demand, and marine traffic, a second train can double a project's LNG output while increasing capital investment by only about 50% (depending on local factors). Building two trains initially can therefore greatly improve a project's unit costs.

These economies-of-scale advantages also apply to later expansions of existing facilities. Again, provided that the existing infrastructure is sufficient to handle the increased production, new trains can be built for much less than the original trains. The second and third trains at Trinidad's ALNG project, for example, cost around $1.1 billion. The cost of the third train in Oman is estimated at less than $750 million, compared to the $2 billion required to establish the first two trains.

OPERATING COSTS

Generally, operating expenses for both the upstream and the liquefaction portions of an LNG project are approximately 2%–5% per annum of the total project capital cost. Grassroots projects in harsh or remote environments are at the higher end, and expansions are at the lower end.

Like construction costs, operating expenditures (OPEX) are highly dependent on location. In developed countries, such as Norway or Australia, labor and materials costs are substantially higher than in developing regions. Operations are more difficult in challenging, remote environments, and the costs to bring in materials are also higher. Overall unit OPEX costs are lower for expansion projects, since many facilities or tasks are shared among trains, and economies of scale become more pronounced at higher output.

LIQUIDS PRODUCTION

A project's condensate and/or LPG production can provide a separate revenue stream, alongside LNG production, and can have a very positive effect on a project's economics. Liquids production and exports do add capital costs to a project for extraction, pipelines, storage, and ship-loading infrastructure. Nonetheless, for many projects (including Indonesia's Arun and Bontang plants, Australia's NWS project, and Abu Dhabi's ADGAS project), the relative ease of production and handling of liquids compared with LNG makes them a valuable second income source. Liquids production can benefit a project substantially; income for LPG or condensate exports can, in some cases, lower a project's cost of service by $0.50/MMBtu or more. LPG production can also benefit the project when propane can be used as a refrigerant gas in the LNG production cycle.

In the aforementioned cases, liquids production is an adjunct to the LNG chain. In associated gas or gas liquids-based projects, it is the LNG that is almost an afterthought, a way of monetizing the methane produced by liquids recovery projects. An example is Australia's Darwin LNG project, which is supplied by the Bayu-Undan field, controlled jointly by Australia and Timor-Leste. The field's gas liquids reserves are being developed via an offshore production platform and a floating storage and off-loading (FSO) facility. A gas pipeline to shore will feed the LNG plant.

Since the liquids portion of Bayu-Undan's development is a stand-alone project, the LNG project can be viewed as a separate entity. How does this affect the decision to proceed with the LNG project? Initially, when the developers analyzed the economics of the project over its lifetime, they could not credit the liquids produced upstream to the LNG project. (However, the liquids project does derive economic benefits from LNG production, since piping the gas to shore instead of reinjecting it allows faster extraction of the liquids and eliminates the operating costs associated with reinjection. The incremental liquids production can be considered a credit to the LNG project.) By contrast, the upstream development of the Bayu-Undan field, including construction and well completion, is part of the gas liquids project, so that the LNG project is accountable for very little of the upstream capital costs. In other words, Darwin LNG does not receive any credit for the liquids, but it does not bear any of the upstream costs either.

When developers analyze the effect that liquids production has on a potential LNG project, they need to be very careful as to what they deem to be within the bounds of the project. For example, in West Africa, one of the main drivers of LNG development has been the desire of national governments to eliminate gas flaring. Much of the feedgas for LNG projects is, therefore, associated gas generated as a by-product of oil production. Such cases are similar to Darwin LNG: Crude oil is being produced from the same wells that supply the LNG project with gas, but this crude certainly cannot be considered as a credit to the LNG project. At the same time, the cost of upstream production platforms cannot be attributed to the LNG plant.

A project's development can be hampered by an absence of liquids. Delays in the progress of the Greater Gorgon LNG plant in Western Australia are partially due to the dryness of the project's gas fields. A stream of LPG or condensate would considerably improve the overall project economics. The trains at Indonesia's Bontang LNG plant and Qatar's two LNG projects, by contrast, enjoy substantial liquids credits. Projects such as Darwin LNG and Marathon's Equatorial Guinea proposal were driven by the production of liquids, rather than gas.

FISCAL TERMS

Most countries have established tax structures for hydrocarbons that cover oil exploration and production. The difficulty in finding markets for gas meant that many petroleum producers flared or re-injected gas, so that no specific fiscal terms were necessary in the countries where they operated. Now that global gas production is increasing and countries have a wide range of gas monetization choices, governments are spelling out explicit fiscal terms for upstream gas and, in certain cases, LNG facilities. The investment required in order to commercialize gas is usually substantially higher than for oil, so that typically the total profits are lower for gas projects at least during the initial years, even though the total impact on the local economy is greater.[1]

Like capital costs and liquids output, taxation costs are highly dependent on location. The tax regime under which a project is structured depends on the sophistication of the government, the openness of the local economy, the government's desire to spur further gas production, and the need to develop certain regions, among other considerations. There is no set template for LNG fiscal terms.

Generally, two sets of fiscal terms apply to an LNG project. In the simplest cases, terms similar to those used for oil production apply to the upstream. They can include royalties, domestic market obligations, petroleum resource taxes, and a number of other devices. Upstream taxes within countries are usually higher than taxes on manufacturing or services, since the oil and gas produced are viewed by the host country as part of a national birthright. Downstream LNG fiscal terms are usually simpler. Often the terms applied to the natural gas liquefaction venture are the same as those for a typical manufacturing or refining concern—usually a set corporate income tax rate and depreciation schedule and possibly value-added tax (VAT) or import duties on imported equipment, depending on the host country.

In the upstream, royalties are a common device by which governments can secure a share of a project's revenue. High royalties can be onerous to an LNG project, since they involve a payment to the sovereign made directly out of the sales revenues irrespective of the project's actual earnings. These royalties can be on oil and/or gas; in the case of an LNG project, any liquids produced are often subject to the same royalties as oil production. Royalties are usually expressed as a percentage of initial revenue. For current LNG projects, they generally fall in a range of 5%–20%. Less commonly, they can be calculated as a fixed unit cost ($/MMBtu).

After royalties are exacted, the producer establishes the expenses for the previous year that are subject to cost recovery. Costs that can be recovered usually include operating expenses and capital costs, which are recovered according to some specified depreciation schedule. Some governments permit full expensing of upstream expenditures against revenues before any taxation is levied. Others use depreciation schedules that can be straight-line, in which an equal amount of the total capital spent on the project is deducted over a stipulated number of years (which may or may not attempt to mirror the expected life of the assets), or accelerated, in which a high percentage of the capital costs can be deducted in the first years of the project and lower percentages can be deducted in subsequent years. Brunei, Malaysia, and Trinidad all use accelerated depreciation. For all other current projects, straight-line schedules are used, generally ranging between 25% and 10% per year (i.e., over a four to ten year period). Norway's Snøhvit project was granted a special tax regime in 2002 by the Oslo government that allows 33.3% per year depreciation.

A number of governments provide the upstream segments of LNG projects with additional tax incentives in the form of uplifts, which are additional percentages that can be added to the total recoverable costs. Most LNG fiscal terms around the world allow developers to recover 100% of the previous year's costs; countries that have implemented uplifts (e.g., Nigeria, Norway, and, in its more recent fiscal packages, Indonesia) allow projects to recover between 105% and 120% of costs. Uplifts are only one potential fiscal incentive that governments can offer. Some projects, such as Nigeria LNG, have been given multiyear tax holidays as an inducement for foreign companies to invest.

Other governments, however, actually cap the costs that a project can recover. Recent legislation in Malaysia has capped the total recoverable costs at 60% for gas and 50% for condensate. In Egypt, the caps vary between about 30% and 50%, depending on the nature of the upstream fields. Trinidad's cost-recovery scheme is adjusted according to total production. Importantly, in both the uplift and the cost-recovery scenarios, the total expenses and depreciable capital costs that the project has incurred are eventually recovered; the different schemes primarily affect the timing of expense recognition and hence the payment of income taxes.

Once applicable royalties are levied and cash operating costs are covered, the net project revenue is subject to some sort of taxation. There are several different ways that taxation can apply in the upstream (including the varying depreciation approaches described above), depending on the agreed tax structure between the host government and the project sponsors. Commonly, governments levy a corporate income tax (CIT); the CIT is similar in structure to the one imposed on all concerns in the country, although the CIT for oil and gas projects usually has a higher rate. For LNG projects, those countries that do impose a CIT on profits typically take between about 30% and 50%. The Snøhvit project in Norway is subject to a 78% tax for both the upstream and the liquefaction segments. The average for all current and prospective LNG-exporting countries is about 40%.

A profit-sharing tax can be a straight percentage or linked to production. In a recently applied Malaysian fiscal regime, the government's share of profits increases once a set cumulative volume of gas has been produced by the project. In Trinidad, the upstream fiscal take increases progressively with daily gas production.

Another flexible method for governments to obtain revenue from gas extraction is the use of a resource rent tax. Such taxes allow the sovereign government to share in the upside if a project is very profitable, but does not front-load the project with a high tax burden if profitability is weak. Resource rent taxes link the project's tax burden to the economic rent that it receives, which is defined as any revenue that it receives over and above costs and some specified rate of return (RoR) approved by the government.

There are two main types of resource rent tax: R-factor-based systems and RoR systems. R-factor terms are based on the ratio of the project's total cumulative receipts over its total cumulative costs (the R factor). When this ratio exceeds one, the tax is levied. Algeria is an example of an LNG-exporting country that uses such a system.

RoR taxes apply after some target RoR has been realized by the upstream investment. This target rate is usually the return on a risk-free investment (i.e., U.S. bonds) plus some country-specific risk premium. The cash flow, which is initially negative owing to the up-front capital costs of development, is increased by the target RoR until it turns positive, after which the tax applies. In some countries, the tax is stepped up with higher returns.

In associated gas- or gas liquids-based projects, it is the LNG that is almost an afterthought, a way of monetizing the methane produced by liquids recovery projects.

Australia uses a petroleum resource rent tax (PRRT) that applies a set tax on income over a certain RoR plus the long-term bond rate. The RoR threshold depends on the nature of the income: 5% for development, versus 15% for exploration. For example, a development project would be liable for tax if its RoR rose above 9% in a period when the long-term bond rate was 4%.

One of the drawbacks of a resource rent tax is that, taken on its own, it has a tendency to delay the government's income until later in the development's life. Some countries therefore use both a rent tax, which does not penalize a project with low profitability and therefore discourages investment, and a royalty, which front-loads at least some of the tax revenue. With recent increases in oil and gas prices, governments are now also imposing or considering forms of windfall profits taxes which would apply additional taxes on production if the price of the oil and gas produced rises above stipulated thresholds.

Indonesia, historically the world's largest LNG producer, has an innovative system for receiving up-front income. Upstream projects in Indonesia are subject to a first tranche petroleum (FTP) obligation, under which the government receives a set percentage of the initial oil and gas production. In addition, projects have a domestic market obligation (DMO), which compels them to sell a certain proportion of oil and/or gas into the Indonesian market at a set (less than global market) rate. Both of these mechanisms are, in effect, royalties. Indonesia has applied a number of different vintage fiscal terms packages to upstream developments since the 1970s. Jakarta has proven to be adept at encouraging development in times of lower investment by adjusting fiscal packages.

In addition to formal taxes such as those outlined previously, governments can assure themselves returns from oil and gas developments by becoming participants. Production-sharing contracts (PSCs) are agreements under which a foreign company develops a project jointly with a national oil company. The foreign entity assumes all preproduction risk, and recovers costs out of production. Many upstream Indonesian contracts are PSCs, as is the agreement between Shell, Mitsubishi, Mitsui, and the Russian government for the Sakhalin II project.

Governments can also take direct equity in a project. States can buy project equity outright (either on market or, more likely, on concessionary terms), can be granted a carried interest (in which the government's share is paid out of production proceeds), or can offer some kind of noncash incentive (possibly tax concessions or infrastructure). This kind of arrangement can, however, become an economic burden for developing countries. Equity positions can also lead to conflicts of interest within a government.

The majority of these complex tax structures apply to upstream exploration and production. In most cases, the liquefaction segment of the LNG chain, where it is legally separated from the upstream, is subject to the same tax regime as any other manufacturing concern in the host country. In some cases, the liquefaction and pipeline segments are incorporated within a larger special tax package, along with production facilities (e.g., Australia's NWS and Norway's Snøhvit), but when liquefaction is separate from the upstream, the host's normal fiscal terms for manufacturing enterprises usually apply.

BUSINESS STRUCTURE

As briefly discussed in chapter 9, a variety of commercial structures are available to participants when setting up an LNG venture. The choice of business structure can have a profound effect on the project's total economics, since it affects the project's total tax burden, division of ownership, and distribution of risk. The main difference between business structures is the division between upstream and liquefaction assets and how gas transferred from one to the other is priced. Chapters 9 and 12 discuss this in greater detail.

SHIPPING COSTS

Shipping costs were, until the late 1990s, the most opaque of all costs in the LNG chain. Some observers went as far as to describe them as black boxes, into which revenues disappeared with no clear understanding of how or where they were subsequently distributed. Many LNG tankers were owned by the shareholders in the liquefaction plant (Australia's NWS project and Brunei), chartered from independent owners (Bontang and Arun), or owned by affiliated state companies (Sonatrach). For ex-ship or CIF arrangements, the commercial specifics of the project's shipping arrangements were not normally of great concern to the customers. However, more recently, the shipping segment has become the most transparent element of the chain. This transformation has been driven by many of the same influences experienced in the land-based facilities: open competition between shipyards for the construction of LNG tankers, a growing number of yards technically capable of building the vessels, and the entrance of many new shipowners willing to compete in tender bids to supply shipping to LNG projects. The project sponsors themselves have been more inclined to see shipping as less of a core activity and contract it out to independent shipowners. The competitive tendering process has driven down shipping rates to a level at which it rarely makes sense for the project sponsors to own the ships, since the implied return on capital embedded in the current charter rate appears to be well below the cost of capital for the project sponsors.

Today's standard LNG tanker has a cargo capacity of about 150,000 m^3. The capital cost of a vessel of this size has ranged in the high \$100 millions to the low \$200 millions between 2000 and 2006, with recent cost increases being driven by the weakening U.S. dollar exchange rates and the rising costs of raw materials, primarily steel. Charter rates for vessels of this size have generally been in the range of \$55,000–\$60,000 per day. These charter rates imply financial returns in the high-single-digit range, but these returns are often amplified by highly leveraged borrowing or tax-advantaged lease arrangements for the vessels, secured by long-term charters with the LNG suppliers or buyers. Most owners of LNG ships enjoy favorable tax treatment and pay little or no corporate tax, as many are located in tax-advantaged countries. A further component of value is the residual value of the LNG tanker following the end of the primary term of the charterparty. Even after 25 years, a well-maintained LNG tanker can be traded profitably and at rates that, based on experience to date, are not much below the rates paid for new buildings. Charterers have also become conscious of this value and in some cases have negotiated rights to share in it at the end of the charter term. The charter hire payments include the costs of crewing and maintaining the vessel, which can each run about \$2 million per year, with another \$2 million annually going to insurance and other operating costs on the owner's account. Charter hire will often be adjusted to allow the owners to pass through these costs to the charterer, although in recent years, some owners have been bidding these components on fixed escalation factors.

Other operating costs, such as bunker fuel, port charges, and canal tolls (for ships coming from the Middle East to the Mediterranean and the Atlantic), are passed through to the charterers, and can account for a considerable portion of the transportation expenses, along with boil-off, which is a charterer's cost as well. Representative marine transportation costs for an LNG project can run from around $0.25/MMBtu (from Algeria to France or Spain) to as much as $1.50/MMBtu (from Qatar to the Gulf of Mexico). The introduction of larger LNG tankers (Q-flex and Q-max) could lower this latter rate by as much as 20%.

While these figures reflect the terms negotiated for term charters, there are several vessels that have been built and are being operated on a more speculative basis. Depending on trading conditions (supply availability and pricing in various markets), these vessels (along with other, older ships released from their original charters) have traded under spot charter arrangements for as little as $25,000 per day and as much as $125,000 per day, with a corresponding impact on unit shipping costs.

IMPORT TERMINALS

The last leg of the chain is the import terminal. Traditionally, import terminals were owned by utilities in the importing countries and were operated as integrated components of the utilities' networks. As such, their commercial terms were generally not ascertainable on a stand-alone basis. However, as a part of the utility, the terminal was included within the rate base and its costs and return were included within the rates charged by the utility to its customers. On this basis, the implied cost of terminaling would be on the order of $0.50–$1.00/MMBtu, with the more expensive terminals being in Japan, where high land costs and the need to maintain large storage capacity tend to drive up the required investments to construct a terminal.

More recently, with the advent of open access and the development of terminals on a proprietary but stand-alone basis, it is possible to assess these costs more accurately. For example, the terminals developed by Cheniere Energy in the Gulf of Mexico have a terminaling cost to third parties of around $0.35/MMBtu, plus the cost of vaporizer fuel (about 1.75% of throughput). Pipeline costs to tie into the transmission grid are usually add-ons, on the order of $0.05–$0.10/MMBtu. Older U.S. terminals with their depreciated rate bases, now operated on a third-party access basis, can have terminaling costs less than this. The costs of terminaling services in Europe, where these are available, are comparable to U.S. costs.

NOTES

[1] Baunsgaard, Thomas. 2001. Primer on mineral taxation. IMF working paper.

UPSTREAM GAS SUPPLY AGREEMENTS 12

INTRODUCTION

All LNG projects require a sale and purchase agreement (SPA) and usually a gas supply agreement (GSA) before actual implementation. The LNG chain begins with natural gas reserves that must be produced and delivered to the liquefaction plant as feedgas and fuel for the production of LNG. The terms and conditions for the delivery of gas to the LNG plant are spelled out in the GSA. Its specific terms are heavily influenced by the energy policies of the host government, the agreements that give the upstream venture the right to produce and sell gas to the LNG plant, the ambitions of the national oil company, and the LNG business structure established by the project sponsors in consultation with the host government.

The purpose of the GSA is to formally establish the conditions under which gas will be supplied to the liquefaction plant. Key issues that must be agreed on and formalized include the following:

- The party(s) responsible for supplying gas to the LNG plant (the gas supplier[s]). That party may be the government (or national oil company) of the host country or a producer that has been awarded contractual rights to produce, deliver, and sell natural gas owned by the host country
- The precise quantity of natural gas to be delivered to the plant, which will include the reserves committed to the LNG project and the daily and annual production

rates that the upstream venture will maintain for the feedgas supply and permitted variability of deliveries. Natural gas reserves and production commitments are essential to assure the LNG project sponsors, their buyers, and lenders that the project has sufficient natural gas resources to fulfill all the LNG delivery commitments.

- The period of the natural gas supply agreement. The starting date and the duration of the gas delivery commitment must correspond to the obligations to deliver LNG.
- The price of natural gas supplied to the plant. This is a key element that establishes the allocation of project revenue between the liquefaction and upstream ventures. Project participants should expect this term to be heavily scrutinized, because the LNG revenue allocation will have a major impact on the government's receipts. In most countries, taxation rules for manufacturing and processing industries, such as liquefaction, are quite different from the fiscal regime that applies to upstream natural gas production.
- The natural gas delivery point, which determines whether the upstream or the downstream venture has the responsibility to construct, operate, and maintain a pipeline from the gas field(s) to the liquefaction plant.
- The amount and allocation of damages in the event of an unexcused failure either upstream or downstream of the liquefaction plant.
- The provisions of force majeure, which excuse one of the parties from performance under the GSA owing to events beyond the affected party's control.

LNG BUSINESS STRUCTURES

While all GSAs are expected to address the issues listed in the previous section, the business structures that can be chosen for the LNG chain present different issues that must be addressed in the GSA(s). The business structures currently adopted in LNG projects can be grouped into three categories (as described in chapters 9 and 11):

- Separate upstream and downstream ventures
- Fully integrated ventures
- Liquefaction tolling arrangements

Separate upstream and downstream ventures

Most LNG projects are organized into separate upstream and downstream ventures, a structure that requires the most comprehensive GSA. In this case, there is an upstream/production venture that may have different participants or different participation interests than the downstream/liquefaction venture. A variation is when two or more upstream ventures supply gas independently to a liquefaction plant. In either case, a comprehensive GSA is needed to establish the parameters of the gas supply deliveries. However, even though there are separate upstream and downstream ventures, the parties engaged in the upstream are most likely to be the participants in the downstream liquefaction venture.

When participants in the upstream and downstream segments of the LNG project are different, it is important that the GSA clearly define the commitments and obligations of the upstream gas suppliers and the liquefaction venture as the gas user.

Fully integrated LNG ventures

There are only a few fully integrated LNG ventures, where the participants have the same ownership interest in natural gas production facilities, liquefaction, and LNG production and sales. When there is equal ownership in all phases of the LNG project, the participants' interests are aligned. Therefore, all the parties face similar risks and rewards for the overall performance of the project, and a formal GSA may not be required. Instead, gas supply arrangements and gas utilization issues can be addressed in shareholder participation agreements and/or project operating agreements. Notwithstanding the common interests of the participants, establishing the transfer price of natural gas from the production phase to the liquefaction phase may require a formalized GSA to satisfy the host government's requirements.

With a fully integrated structure, the natural gas transfer price—the price at which gas is transferred from the upstream venture to the liquefaction venture—does not arise from the bargaining between independent interests that characterize an arm's-length transaction. Therefore,

When participants in the upstream and downstream segments of the LNG project are different, it is important that the Gas Supply Agreement clearly defines the commitments and obligations of the upstream gas suppliers and the liquefaction venture as the gas user.

the tax authorities will carefully review this price and the method used to establish it. The government may require that LNG revenues be "netted back" to the production venture, paying the equivalent of tolling fees for pipeline transportation to the plant and for liquefaction. This requires an explicit GSA, to formalize these terms, and the government may well be a party to or an approving authority for the terms of the GSA.

Natural gas tolling ventures

Natural gas tolling agreements are based on the premise that liquefaction plants and ships are tools for monetizing remote natural gas assets and transporting gas to markets. The upstream and downstream participants must agree on the rates of return that are appropriate for liquefaction and shipping investments. The LNG sales revenue is then allocated to the upstream/production venture(s) after the agreed payments are made for the operating expenses and the capital investments in shipping and liquefaction. In this business structure, the gas supplier owns/controls the LNG at the tailgate of the LNG plant and is responsible for marketing the LNG. Thus, the gas supplier receives benefits for its commercial skills in lining up the LNG sales.

The tolling-facility structure limits the scope of the GSA because the party selling LNG is also responsible for supplying gas to the LNG plant. Nevertheless, some form of gas supply and processing agreement is required, and the scope of an individual agreement depends on the specific nature of each arrangement.

The issues covered in the agreement will be somewhat different than in the agreements described previously and may have more of the characteristics of a processing agreement, including the following:

- Obligations of the operator of the liquefaction facilities, including LNG daily and annual production capacity, scheduled start, and duration of operations
- The gas suppliers' rights to utilize LNG production capacity, storage, and loading facilities, including accommodating the rights of other gas suppliers
- Scheduling the delivery of natural gas into the liquefaction plant and the production and loading of LNG
- Payment obligations for the liquefaction capacity, which may include a capacity charge for the allocated capacity and a volume-based processing fee for its use

- Feedgas and LNG quality specifications and liabilities for supplying off-specification gas or LNG
- Rights or obligations of the unaffected suppliers to supply gas in the event of a failure of one of the gas suppliers

Beyond these issues, the tolling agreements can quickly become much more complex, providing terms and conditions for, among other issues, rights under future plant expansions or debottlenecking of the existing plant, adjustments to the tolling fees for changes in operating expenses or additional capital expenditures, obligations of the operator, and mechanisms to replace a nonperforming operator.

TYPICAL TERMS IN A GSA

Quantity

Perhaps the most critical part of the GSA is the dedication of adequate proven natural gas reserves and production capacity. The long-term ability of the project to meet its LNG delivery obligations depends on the reserves committed to the project. One million tons of LNG is equal to about 47–50 Bcf (1.3–1.4 Bcm) of natural gas (depending on gas composition). An additional 8%–10% of the gas is needed as fuel for the liquefaction plant. Thus, a 20-year sale of 1 MMt/y (1.4 Bcm/y) of LNG will require about 1.05–1.15 Tcf (30–33 Bcm) of gas over the life of the contract.

Since liquefaction plants typically operate about 340 days per year, the production of one million tons of LNG per year requires a feedgas rate of 150–160 MMcf/d (1.5–1.7 Bcm/y); this rate has to be sustainable from the first day through the last day of the GSA. The reserve base required in order to support this production rate throughout the term of the contract is about 20% larger than the natural gas consumed, allowing for the natural decline in reservoir performance at the end of its plateau production period.

Producers dedicate specific natural gas reserves that are certified by an internationally recognized third party, such as DeGolyer and MacNaughton, Gaffney Cline, or Netherland-Sewell. Moreover, the producers commit to construct and maintain production facilities and to produce and deliver natural gas at the specified production rates over the life of the project. Hourly, daily, and annual production rates must be agreed on, as well as procedures to coordinate maintenance periods. If there are multiple suppliers, the specific quantities delivered by each supplier must be agreed on, as well as procedures for suppliers to substitute for one another and to balance uneven deliveries.

Natural gas tolling agreements are based on the premise that liquefaction plants and ships are tools for monetizing remote natural gas assets and transporting gas to markets. The upstream and downstream participants must agree on the rates of return that are appropriate for liquefaction and shipping investments.

The volumes are usually dedicated under a take-or-pay arrangement, closely mirroring the take-or-pay arrangements between LNG supplier(s) and LNG buyer(s), and in turn, the GSA may provide for claims arising against the supplier in the event of an unexcused failure to deliver gas as required. The LNG SPAs will contain obligations to deliver LNG in specific quantities within a specified schedule and with tightly defined quality conditions. The SPAs will also establish the commercial terms of an LNG sale, including damages for failure to perform (i.e., to deliver LNG). In addition, if the LNG SPAs provide for volume flexibility on the part of the buyers (e.g., downward quantity adjustments or rights to excess quantities), the GSA must in turn reflect these provisions to match the supply commitment with the LNG sales commitment.

The GSA also spells out the expected schedule for the development and commissioning of the project facilities (production, pipeline, and liquefaction) and provides mechanisms for coordination of these efforts (as well as rights and obligations if one of the parties fails to complete their required facilities on time). Also important are the obligations to supply gas during the plant's commissioning and start-up period (often described as the initial supply period) when the LNG production process will be somewhat uncertain, and the LNG buyers may not be obligated to purchase all the output. Generally, the full obligation for purchase and any corresponding take-or-pay obligations do not commence until the liquefaction plant passes all its performance tests and is declared commercial by the operator.

Quality

The LNG SPA contains specific composition and heating-value ranges with which the delivered LNG must comply; it also imposes upper limits on impurities permitted in the LNG. The liquefaction plant will be designed to process feedgas with a range of compositions, and it is important that the feedgas conform to the composition that the liquefaction plant is geared to accommodate. In addition, impurities in the delivered gas must be within ranges that were anticipated in the design of the front-end gas processing of the LNG plant, where impurities are removed. These quality specifications must be spelled out in the GSA.

Delivery point

It is important to establish which party is responsible for building, operating, and maintaining the pipeline system (which may in fact be developed and operated independently of both the upstream and the liquefaction ventures) that delivers feedgas to the liquefaction plant and where title to and risk for the gas are transferred. In some cases, the upstream gas-producing venture is responsible for the pipeline and must arrange to deliver the feedgas to the liquefaction plant. In other cases, the liquefaction venture is responsible for the pipeline and purchases the gas at the inlet of the pipeline.

Measurement and delivery conditions

To determine the volume, heating value, and composition of natural gas at the delivery point, one party must install and operate measurement devices. In the GSA, the parties agree on the following: who will install, operate, and maintain the measurement equipment (usually the liquefaction plant); the accuracy of the equipment; how and by whom measurement will be conducted and checked; and who will set procedures for periodic verification of the measurement equipment. It is also necessary to agree on procedures that will be followed to adjust past measurements in the event that a measuring device is found to be inaccurate.

Delivery pressure plays an important role in the efficient operation of the liquefaction plant, as all of the gas cooling and refrigeration is applied to the gas at high pressure. At higher gas pressures, gas liquefaction takes place at higher temperatures, reducing the required refrigeration power and improving the process efficiency. The LNG flow is finally flashed to near-atmospheric pressure by passing the flow through a throttling valve or an expander after all the refrigeration has been applied. Specifying the minimum delivery pressure is a key component of the GSA and is a significant consideration in the design and operation of the liquefaction plant.

Natural gas sales price

This provision establishes how LNG revenues are allocated to the segments of the LNG supply—specifically between the upstream/production and the downstream/liquefaction (including shipping, in the case of an ex-ship or CIF sale) ventures. Equally important, this allocation of revenue also has an impact on the taxes and other payments to the government resulting from the LNG sales. The natural gas sales price can be set in a variety of ways and is often the subject of significant debate between the LNG project sponsors and the host government.

Governments tend to view gas production as having great intrinsic value and perhaps as the most valuable portion of the LNG supply chain. The liquefaction venture, which is usually led by a multinational oil and gas company, often takes the view that its technological and commercial know-how, market access, and financial support for the LNG project bring significant value when combined with a previously stranded gas resource, which it may have discovered. Both views have validity. Clearly, there can be no LNG project without a large gas resource that can be dedicated to the liquefaction venture. Likewise, stranded gas could well remain undeveloped without the technical, commercial, and financial support of international sponsors.

The goal of negotiation between a government and commercial parties is to find a commercial basis on which to develop the LNG project. To accomplish this, the project's commercial agreements must reward the international sponsors for the skills and financing that they bring to the venture and the risks that they will take, while recognizing the value of a large gas resource. Many of these terms may be incorporated in the original concession terms under which the gas exploration and discovery was carried out, but these concession agreements are rarely sufficient to include all the terms necessary to define the shares of revenues and costs (although the fully integrated project model based on production-sharing agreements comes close, since all the costs, including liquefaction, are generally treated as development costs).

Delivery pressure plays an important role in the efficient operation of the liquefaction plant, as all of the gas cooling and refrigeration is applied to the gas at high pressure. At higher gas pressures, gas liquefaction takes place at higher temperatures, reducing the required refrigeration power and improving the process efficiency.

Some GSAs price the gas as a percentage of the sales price of the LNG. This method implicitly values each segment of the LNG project, assigns a relative value to each segment, and allocates revenue based on the proportion of each segment to the whole project. This method is used in Nigeria LNG, Malaysia LNG, Brunei LNG, and the first train of Atlantic LNG.

Other agreements set a floor price for the feedgas and establish percentage sharing of the LNG price whenever the resulting gas price exceeds the floor. Examples of this are the Qatargas and RasGas projects. Oman LNG purchases feedgas from the government of the Sultanate of Oman at a fixed price that is adjusted periodically. As a variation on this approach, these price mechanisms may also provide that when the percentage sharing yields a price below the floor price, the difference is banked, and the gas buyer is then allowed to recoup the overpayment when the price rises above the floor. Once the bank balance reaches zero, the regular net back mechanism applies. This approach provides a more stable flow of revenue to the gas producer and, in turn, to the government interests through royalties and taxes.

For tolling facilities and some integrated ventures, the feedgas price is essentially a pure net back from the sales price of LNG. That is, producers deduct operating and capital expense for shipping and liquefaction from LNG revenue, and the remainder is allocated to upstream gas. This method is used in the Indonesia projects, Atlantic LNG Trains 2 and 3, Kenai, Egyptian LNG (Idku), and the new Darwin LNG venture.

Allocation of the value of by-products

Valuable by-products, such as NGL and condensate, are often recovered during the production and treatment of natural gas before liquefaction. They may be recovered by the upstream venture when natural gas is treated in the field, before being delivered into the pipeline, or at the LNG plant, when gas is treated before liquefaction. In the latter case, an explicit allocation of the value derived from those by-products may be included in the GSA or the government's concession or PSC terms. It may not be appropriate to value NGL and condensate on the same basis that is used to value feedgas, and a separate measure tied to the market value of the by-products may be developed.

Liabilities

If the plant does not receive its properly nominated feedgas supply, the liquefaction venture will not be able to meet its contractual delivery obligations and may be subject to a claim for damages from its customers. Similar claims may arise where the liquefaction plant or LNG ships do not perform. On the other side, the liquefaction venture may be entitled to receive take-or-pay compensation from its customers or damages from its EPC contractors or other contractors if they fail to perform. In both cases, the GSA must allocate risks, liabilities, and recoveries between the upstream and the downstream. The allocation and treatment of payments received by the liquefaction venture for take-or-pay obligations is the most complex to address, as issues of alternative sales, makeup, and other provisions of the LNG SPA must be, in turn, reflected in the GSA in a balanced fashion.

Force majeure

Force majeure is an issue closely negotiated in both the GSA and the LNG SPA. Force majeure excuses a party from performing its obligations, wholly or partially, under a contract if events beyond its control prevent it from doing so. The ability of the LNG seller to be excused from its GSA obligations under force majeure for a downstream failure (a problem affecting the liquefaction plant, shipping, or the customers' facilities) is an important concept. A hotly debated topic is whether damage to natural gas reservoirs or loss of reserves that result in the upstream not being able to perform should constitute a force majeure event that must be resolved in the GSA.

CONCLUSION

The GSA is a critical agreement in the LNG supply chain and should be given as much attention and effort as the LNG SPA. The host government will be particularly interested in transfer pricing issues, as this has a major impact on the government's tax realization from the LNG project.

It is difficult to characterize the specific terms that must be covered in each GSA of each LNG supply chain. The nature of preexisting agreements between the gas suppliers and the host government will set the tone for the GSA. The LNG SPAs will set the terms by which LNG is purchased (volume, price, and flexibility in off-take), which in turn will flow back to the upstream producers. The specific business model selected for the LNG supply chain will dictate the types of terms that are needed in the GSA to clarify the rights, obligations, and liabilities and to allocate the risks and rewards of the producing and liquefaction segments of the supply chain.

SALE AND PURCHASE CONTRACTS 13

INTRODUCTION

The sale and purchase agreement (SPA) is the commercial cornerstone of an LNG project. The SPA is the key agreement in apportioning the risks and the rewards along the LNG chain, coming as it does at the intersection of the upstream (where production and liquefaction still remain very closely integrated in most projects) and the downstream, with the meeting point being either the loading port, in the case of an FOB contract, or the unloading port, in the case of either an ex-ship or a CIF contract. The SPA incorporates provisions governing pricing, volume commitments, LNG specifications, shipping arrangements, payment terms, governing law, scheduling (initially of the project and ultimately of the cargo loadings or discharges), and force majeure provisions, which excuse one or more parties from their obligations.

The arrangements for shipping the LNG cargoes are usually spelled out in summary terms in the SPA, but the shipping itself will often be the subject of separate agreements, including LNG tanker charters. LNG tanker charters and similar agreements constitute a subject worthy of separate discussion, and the specifics are covered in chapter 14.

HISTORICAL CONTEXT

The LNG industry has traditionally been characterized by long-term contractual relationships between buyers and sellers. When the LNG industry developed these long-term contracts, two major elements emerged almost immediately. The first element reflected an adaptation from the then-prevailing practices in the pipeline industry, namely, the take-or-pay gas sales contract. In the 1960s and '70s, virtually all pipeline gas contracts involved a take-or-pay commitment on the part of the buyer. (Most of these contracts were found in the U.S. and Canadian markets, where the natural gas industry was more developed and more diversified than in other parts of the world.) Under take-or-pay provisions, the buyer is obligated to lift a specified volume of natural gas or LNG each year or pay for the shortfall.

The second element was the adoption of pricing mechanisms that tied the price of LNG to oil prices. This was not the first LNG pricing model; the first models (early Alaska and Algeria) treated the liquefaction project almost as a utility undertaking, providing the seller with a price mechanism that tied the price of LNG (either ex-ship or FOB) to a fixed price with escalator mechanisms, often including elements of labor and steel pricing as a proxy for the underlying costs of building and operating the projects and recovering an appropriate return on investment. This was not dissimilar to the pricing mechanisms that had evolved on the U.S. interstate market, where gas prices and transportation services were set by reference to the recovery of just and reasonable costs and returns.

This pricing structure broke down rapidly under the combined (and, to some degree, linked) impacts of rapidly increasing inflation and oil prices in the mid-1970s. Following the oil shocks and the energy crises of the 1970s, oil exporters who were also LNG exporters (and many were also members of the Organization of the Petroleum Exporting Countries [OPEC]) could not ignore the temptation to argue for a linkage between oil and gas prices. This move also had the additional benefit of providing several projects that found themselves in financial difficulties a way to enhance their revenues and avoid collapse. The early contracts were adjusted to reflect new terms at the insistence of the sellers, with a few notable exceptions; for example, in the case of El Paso's contract with Algeria, the parties were unable to reach a final agreement, and the contract then collapsed.

By 1980, virtually all LNG sales contracts included take-or-pay provisions and pricing formulas directly linked to crude oil. The establishment of this pricing structure was aided by the position of the buyers, who almost without exception tended to be utilities—and, in the case of non-U.S. companies, utilities that were either owned directly by the host government or strongly influenced in their energy purchase policies by these host governments. In all cases (the U.S. buyers included), the utilities' cost structure and financial drivers did not mitigate against this behavior. Under the rules generally in place at that time, utilities' earnings were a function of their invested capital base, and provided that if the costs for LNG supply acquisition were deemed reasonable, the cost of LNG supplies would be treated as a direct pass-through to the end-use consumers. As might be imagined, this did not reflect competition in the end-use market (since utilities at that time were thought to be natural monopolies and not susceptible to competitive forces of the marketplace), nor did it lead to particularly hard bargaining between buyers and sellers. Buyers were more concerned about the security of supply for what was generally believed to be a finite and diminishing commodity (gas was seen in similar terms to oil) than about the price of that commodity. Reinforcing this tendency was a belief that the acquisition of LNG represented a diversification of national energy supply, away from a dependence on crude oil (dominated then by supplies from the Persian Gulf and OPEC), and the securing of a new source of gas where (in the case of the United States and Europe) conventional domestic supplies were seen as being on the verge of exhaustion. Finally, because many of the importing countries had a high degree of dependency on crude oil and oil products for much of their energy mix, natural gas (whether in the form of LNG or otherwise) could be seen as being in direct competition with oil and therefore could be reasonably priced on the same basis. For a period beginning in 1964 and continuing without hesitation or interruption through 1976, the LNG industry experienced rapid and sustained growth almost independent of the pricing of the LNG supplies.

Beginning with a series of legislative and regulatory changes in the United States, however, this model came under increasing pressure, leading to its eventual modification and even collapse in some markets. In 1978, the United States passed the Natural Gas Policy Act, which allowed dramatically higher prices for newly discovered reserves of natural gas and set the domestic producing industry on a path toward total price decontrol at the wellhead by 1985. While gas consumption in the United States had been rising steadily until the early 1980s, higher prices, coupled with a collapse in industrial demand following the severe recessions that occurred during the same time, began to take their toll. A sharp fall in gas demand resulted, even as supply was increasing under the stimulus of higher wellhead prices, and the infamous gas bubble emerged in the United States (later characterized as more of a gas "sausage").

In 1984, FERC issued Order 380, which permitted the customers of the gas pipeline companies (who in turn were the buyers and resellers of virtually all gas transported in interstate commerce) to refuse to purchase gas for which they had been otherwise contractually obligated. However, Order 380 did not afford the same opportunity to the pipeline companies, which remained bound to their agreements with their suppliers. The result was a severe financial crisis that saw the major pipeline companies doing everything in their power to escape their purchase obligations, leading producers to assert major claims under the take-or-pay provisions of these contracts. Several pipelines entered bankruptcy (some more than once), and all suffered serious financial consequences in settling take-or-pay claims. The sole LNG supplier to the United States, Algerian state-owned petroleum company Sonatrach, also saw each of its contracts collapse under the same pressures, and between 1979 and 1985, the United States went from being the largest to the smallest LNG importer in the world.

Europe was much less affected, since the universe of suppliers and buyers was much smaller and the market was less developed than in the United States. However, the effect that oil pricing had on LNG contracts—and the loss of the U.S. market—led European buyers to exert much stronger downward price pressure on their LNG suppliers (essentially only Sonatrach). When oil prices collapsed in 1986, LNG prices fell sharply; in many cases, price indexation was renegotiated and tied to oil product pricing (distillate and heavy fuel oil), rather than crude oil pricing, since products were seen as both less volatile than crude oil and more reflective of the prices that would be experienced by end users competing against natural gas (eliminating the impact of gasoline, diesel, and jet fuel on the price mix, since natural gas did not compete directly against these products). Asia (for all practical purposes, Japan) initially continued to experience steady economic growth and did not seek the same form of price restructuring as was seen in Europe and the United States; however, the rate of growth slowed as costs in the LNG chain escalated and global economic growth slowed.

Many of the contractual terms seen in the industry today reflect experiences from the previous three decades. Also reflected in these terms are the emerging realities of deregulation in each of the major LNG end-use markets.

LNG contracts are lengthy documents and have tended to become lengthier with the passage of time. To a degree, the technical provisions of these contracts have become standardized over time. The procedures for measuring and testing LNG volumes and quality are one example. In other respects, though, these contracts remain highly specific to the individual trade being covered, and this aspect is unlikely to change while LNG is supplied into disparate markets. The following discussion is an attempt to summarize the key factors that characterize LNG SPAs.

LONG-TERM CONTRACTS

About 90% of the LNG traded is bought and sold under long-term contracts. In the most simplistic view, the value of the trade is established by the quantities, price, and duration of the LNG sales under the SPA. The other fundamental commercial considerations in the SPA are the terms of sale—FOB, CIF, or ex-ship—and the resulting obligation to provide shipping. We now will consider the individual components of LNG SPAs.

Quantities

Most long-term LNG contracts contain very specific provisions regarding the quantities of LNG to be bought and sold. Most are subject to take-or-pay provisions. Typically, the contract will provide for an *annual contract quantity* (ACQ), which is the quantity of LNG, usually expressed in millions of British thermal units (MMBtu), that the buyer must purchase and take or pay for if not taken. However, the ACQ is subject to other significant requirements and adjustments that must also be taken into account in the contract.

Most contracts covering new trade arrangements contain provisions that govern the *buildup* of deliveries during the initial period of the contract. These buildup provisions are designed to accommodate both the buyer and the seller. On the seller's side, very often the start-up of a liquefaction plant will require a certain period of reduced production in order to fully test the plant's technical systems, accommodate any delays in plant completion, and address the delivery of LNG tankers to be used in the trade. On the buyer's side, the *buildup period* is designed to address the need to grow the downstream market to handle the full ACQ. For mature projects or projects delivering to mature and liquid markets (e.g., North America), there is today generally little or no need for a buildup period on the buyer's side, and as the technology of liquefaction plants has improved, the technical window needed for plant testing has also narrowed, reducing the need for buildup on the seller's side. Most contracts, however, do provide for the supply and purchase of LNG during the start-up period, when the volume and timing of LNG that can be produced at the liquefaction plant is uncertain. Generally, LNG sales and purchases during the start-up period are not subject to take-or-pay requirements but are governed by reasonable efforts to deliver and take LNG on both sides.

Once the buildup period has ended, the contract generally enters a plateau period, during which the ACQ remains constant over an extended period of time. As described earlier, the ACQ is normally expressed as a fixed quantity (in MMBtu) to be delivered on an annual basis, However, the

ACQ is subject to a variety of adjustments. Among those adjustments are the following:

- *Volume flexibility, or downward quantity adjustment.* This may permit the buyer to reduce its ACQ obligation by a fixed amount of the ACQ. Generally, this is a small quantity, normally around 5% of the ACQ, and some contracts limit the number of adjustments, or the aggregate adjustment, that the buyer can make over the term of the contract.
- *Round-up/round-down provisions.* These provisions are designed to address the reality that while the ACQ may be expressed as a fixed quantity (in MMBtu), such a fixed quantity cannot be delivered precisely during each contract year. The variations in the actual quantities delivered can arise through scheduling provisions of the contract. For example, a cargo that is loaded or delivered on the day after the contract year ends may actually be attributed to the delivery obligation of the prior contract year, and vice versa. Other factors relate to variations in cargo sizes (because different sized vessels are used or because the MMBtu content of the LNG varies slightly during the period) and to permit reductions in ACQ obligations to allow for scheduled maintenance of the facilities (including the LNG tankers).
- *Excess quantities.* These arise when the plant performs better than expected or when a buyer in a multiple-buyer project exercises a downward quantity adjustment. Most LNG plants are designed with a margin of technical conservatism, which results in the plant's ability to produce more LNG than the aggregate of the seller's ACQs with all its buyers. The treatment of excess quantities in SPAs can vary dramatically and can be the focus of hard bargaining during the SPA negotiations. Normally, these excess quantities are highly profitable for the seller, and they may also be profitable for the buyer, especially for buyers who can earn a profit margin on each LNG delivery. The SPA must address whether the buyer has any preferential rights to these excess quantities and, if so, whether these rights are subject to the same terms and conditions as the ACQ.
- *Incorporation into the* ACQ. Another consideration is whether, once confirmed, these excess quantities become incorporated into the ACQ and covered by take-or-pay obligations. The treatment of excess quantities is also driven by the control of shipping in the SPA. An FOB buyer may be in a much stronger position to argue for preferential rights to the excess, as the buyer could have the shipping to lift these

quantities. For a CIF or an ex-ship contract, the leverage may be with the seller, who is in a better position to control excess shipping. Excess quantities can have different characteristics. Predictable improvements in plant performance result in predictable excess quantities, while other excess quantities may be less predictable (arising from a buyer's force majeure or seasonal variations in plant performance). The former are often treated as if they are part of the ACQ (and some contracts even provide mechanisms for increasing the ACQ to formally incorporate this), whereas the latter require different treatment owing to the inability of either the seller or the buyer to predict them.

- *Makeup quantities.* These constitute a class unto themselves. In the unfortunate circumstance of a take-or-pay contract where the buyer is unable to receive the ACQ and is not otherwise excused from performing (as a result of a force majeure incident, for example), the buyer will nonetheless be obligated to pay for the quantity shortfall at the price specified in the contract (which may or may not be at the full contract price). In return, the buyer is usually afforded the opportunity to take delivery of the equivalent quantities at a later date. The makeup quantities are normally given scheduling priority over all other quantities (e.g., excess quantities) after the firm delivery obligations. The makeup quantities can be taken in subsequent years, including during a period calling for the extension of the primary term of the contract. In some instances, there may be a limit (five years is typical) during which the makeup quantities must be taken or else be forfeited. When the makeup quantities are taken, they may also be subject to a price adjustment (either to make up any price discount given when the makeup quantities were incurred or to take into account any price difference between the time of incurrence of the shortfall and the time of delivery).
- *Force majeure makeup quantities.* These are not always found in LNG contracts. These are quantities that have not been delivered following a force majeure incident but that the parties agree can be delivered at a later date. In this respect, they are treated much as take-or-pay makeup quantities, although they usually have a lower priority in scheduling.

From this description, it should be clear that the quantity provisions can become very complex, especially when there are multiple buyers and/or sellers in the project. This is particularly true in the case of the interaction between the quantity provisions and the scheduling provisions (which establish the cargo delivery programs), which will require addressing the priority rights between different types of quantities and flexibilities, as well as tracking of the quantities attributable to each buyer by category.

Another element of the quantities section of the contract is the treatment of *expansion quantities*. Generally, in contracts that are negotiated for the start of new projects, the parties may reasonably expect that the liquefaction plant will be expanded at a subsequent point in time. For buyers, access to these expansion quantities can be a valuable right, which they will naturally seek to negotiate in the contract. There is no standard treatment of expansion quantities. They may be quantities taken at the buyer's option (subject to demonstration that the buyer has adequate terminal capacity to take them); they may be quantities that are treated as obligations of the buyer and the seller; they may be treated as quantities added to the basic quantities of the contract; or they may be subject to the negotiation of an entirely new contract (which may or may not incorporate many of the provisions of the original contract). Sellers may be less inclined to offer rights over the expansion quantities, as they wish to be free to market these on their own terms. The contract generally spells out the buyers' and sellers' rights with respect to any expansion, along with notice periods, negotiating periods, and any conditions precedent, which must be satisfied before the commencement of negotiations.

Prior to the end of the 1990s, when the LNG market was more of a seller's market, the buyers were generally the parties seeking rights over expansion volumes. The sellers were generally resistant, because they hoped to obtain more favorable sales terms in their expansion sales contracts. This dynamic shifted with the advent of a buyer's market in the late 1990s, and the issue of expansion quantities became less important and less controversial (and disappeared from the SPAs). By 2004, the pendulum began to swing in the opposite direction, once again in favor of sellers. Clearly, the treatment of these provisions becomes a function of the buyers' and sellers' relative bargaining leverage.

Pricing

While quantity provisions in most long-term SPAs generally share common characteristics, the same cannot be said of the pricing provisions. The pricing formulas tend to be tied to specific markets. They also tend to be set by reference to prices of other fuels (including natural gas). These generally reflect perceived market conditions in the three largest regions of the LNG market: Asia and the Pacific, Europe, and the United States. The influence of the industry's history, as described earlier in this chapter, also factors into the evolution of pricing mechanisms in LNG SPAs.

Asia and the Pacific. Generally, LNG prices in the Asia-Pacific region are set with reference to crude oil prices. Because this LNG is being sold into markets where competing supplies of natural gas are otherwise unavailable, this mechanism has been well established for many years. In Japan, LNG is pegged to crude oil prices by a formula consisting of indexation to the Japan Customs Cleared price (JCC; also called Japan Crude Cocktail), although Indonesian LNG is priced against Indonesian crude oil. Meticulously compiled by the government, the JCC consists of more than 200 types of crudes from about 30 oil-producing countries. This combination makes it highly immune to manipulation and very reliable. It also captures the cost and distance required in order to ship fuel supplies to the region. The original concept tied the landed cost of LNG in Japan quite closely to the landed price of crude oil imported into Japan. This price would be further adjusted downward if the LNG was delivered FOB, to take into account the cost of LNG shipping assumed by the buyer.

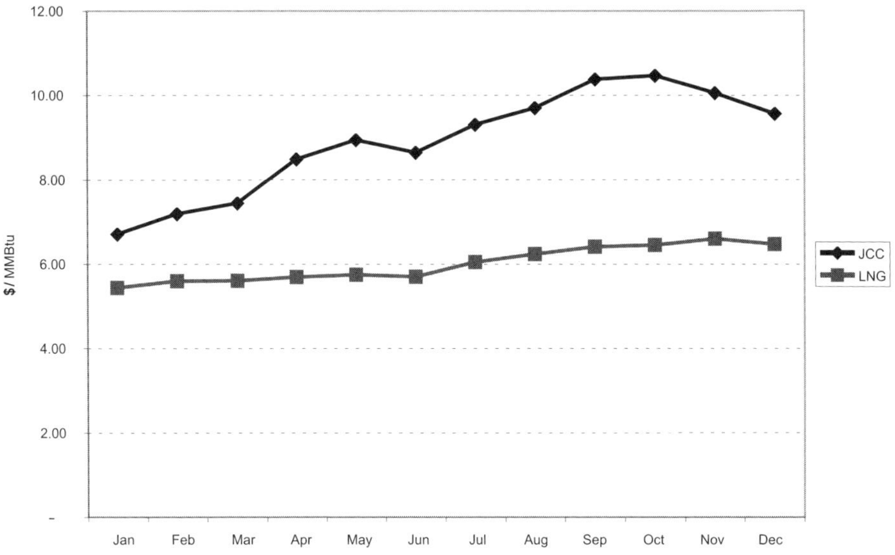

Fig. 13–1. LNG pricing in Japan, 2005: JCC vs.weighted average LNG price

As figure 13–1 shows, Japan's LNG prices closely followed the JCC's movements. The time lag is a result of averaging several preceding months' JCCs to calculate a single month's LNG price. This delays the immediate impact of sudden changes in the oil price on the LNG price and smoothes out the fluctuations.

The volatility of oil prices over the past decades has, however, led to modifications of the original formulas, to reduce the associated volatility in LNG prices, which was beneficial to neither buyer nor seller. Volatility was reduced through the adoption of dampening mechanisms, the best known of which is the S-curve (fig. 13–2). In this formulation, the rate of increase (or decrease) in the LNG price is reduced relative to the rate of increase (or decrease) in the crude oil price above (or below) a certain price level, often with built-in floors and ceilings. This gives the seller downside price protection, and a corresponding benefit is given to the buyer on the upside. From the seller's perspective, this also makes the upstream project more readily financeable, as the lenders (focused on the downside) can count on a more predictable flow of revenues. Korea and Taiwan have followed the Japanese approach to the pricing formula.

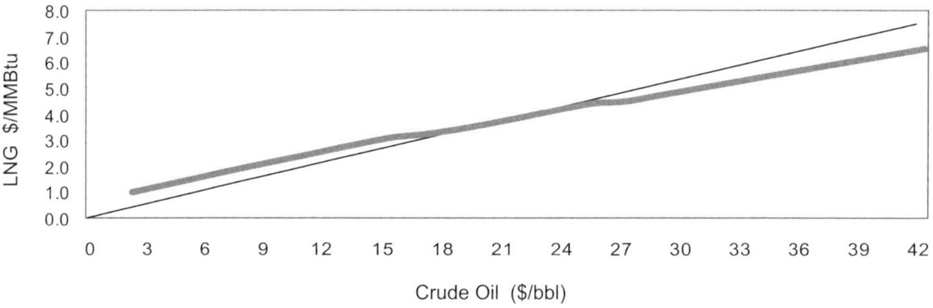

Fig. 13–2. S-curve moderation of price increases and decreases

More recently, these mechanisms came under pressure as the rate of growth in the traditional markets slowed down, just as LNG supply costs were falling. New customers in China and India have been more aggressive in seeking lower LNG prices. China has held competitive bidding, which has resulted in LNG prices for the Chinese market that are reportedly as much as 25% lower than Japanese prices (depending on the crude oil price assumptions). India had been seeking to import more LNG and has been seeking to lower prices as well. Initial Indian contract prices included price mechanisms which are largely fixed over the initial life of the contract or are subject to very minor adjustment—an ironic shift back to the pricing formulas of the earliest days of the industry. India is somewhat different than the other Asian markets, since it has access to domestic gas production and significant gas-based industrial demand.

Europe. European LNG markets outside the United Kingdom do not have significant domestic production. As in the Far East, LNG prices are set by reference to oil, but to both oil products and crude. The pricing structures tend to follow the pattern of a base FOB price indexed to a single crude oil (e.g., Brent), or a basket of crudes, or a basket of products that compete with natural gas in the end-use market, including low-sulfur light and heavy fuel oils.

Most European-oriented contracts do not have S-curves, but many have floor prices. The use of a floor price in any contract raises the issue of whether the contract should also include a ceiling price or, alternatively, a recoupment mechanism that kicks in when the floor price payments exceed the formula price payment that would have otherwise applied. This recoupment provision would allow the buyer to reduce the contract price to recover the overpayment once the contract price moves above the floor price.

The sample formula in table 13–1 is typical in Europe. It contains references to several fuel alternatives with different weightings that reflect a particular market's proportion of alternative fuel uses. Moreover, instead of pegging the LNG price solely to current prices, the formula compares the changes in the various alternative fuels from a base period.

Table. 13–1. Pricing formula for LNG in Europe

$P_n = P_0 \times (W_1 \times F_1/F_{1_0} + W_2 + F_2/F_{2_0})$	
P_0	Original negotiated price (at time 0).
W	Weighting factors/percentages of alternate fuels.
F_1, F_2	Alternate fuels' prices published by third parties. Gas oil, low/high sulfur fuel oil, and coal are common alternatives.
Inflation component	May be added.

Alternative pricing mechanisms

In the Atlantic Basin market, gas is increasingly expected to provide the fuel for gas-fired power plants, which need to compete in increasingly open and short-term electricity markets. As such, the electricity produced from gas must compete on a dispatchable basis with electricity generated from other fuels, such as heavy oil, coal, and even nuclear. To ensure a reasonable level of dispatch, the pricing in power-oriented gas contracts may also include factors indexed to high-sulfur fuel oils, coal, inflation, and even power prices. These indexation factors tend to produce a less volatile gas price and in turn permit the power generator to dispatch the plant(s) on a reasonably high load factor. The advantage of these indexation factors from the seller's perspective is that they provide a more stable cash flow. Note that such indexation does not necessarily translate into lower gas prices, since often the base price can be higher than in a conventionally indexed contract given the high efficiency of modern combined-cycle gas turbine power plants.

North America. Given the more liquid gas markets in North America, LNG pricing mechanisms are generally set with reference to price indices in those markets. For LNG terminals in the Gulf of Mexico, the natural price point is set by reference to Henry Hub or Houston Ship Channel pricing, both of which are viewed as liquid and transparent reference price points. In 2005–2006, it appeared that ex-ship or CIF sales were being made at prices between 85% and 93% of Henry Hub, irrespective of the discharge terminal. On the West and East Coasts, the pricing may be more complex, since the basis differentials between those regions and the Gulf of Mexico may be taken into account in the price formulas. Historically, East Coast prices have been at a premium relative to the Gulf of Mexico, while West Coast prices have been at a discount.

Generic price provisions

There are certain provisions that are often, but not universally, applicable across pricing provisions, regardless of the specific trade. For example, many contracts allocate the responsibilities for payment of taxes, fees, and customs duties on LNG sales between buyers and sellers. Generally, the sellers assume the obligation for these payments in the exporting countries, and buyers assume them in the importing countries. Assessments on LNG tankers depend on whether the terms of trade are FOB, CIF, or ex-ship. Port and harbor dues are treated as transportation costs and generally are not reflected in LNG pricing terms.

Irrespective of the expected LNG sales destination, many LNG contracts provide mechanisms for the renegotiation of the price terms to reflect changes in the end-use markets. These renegotiation mechanisms can be open ended or may contain specific guidelines that limit the range of new prices that can be established. They also provide for the ability to refer price re-openers to third parties (including arbitration provisions) when the parties are unable to reach agreement on their own. Generally, LNG SPAs provide specific intervals during which prices can be re-opened; however, if these occur frequently, it is conceivable that one re-opener provision may still be in negotiation/arbitration by the time the next scheduled re-opener comes along. These provisions are less prevalent where gas markets are liquid and there is little dispute over how to determine the value of competing fuels, which are inevitably other gas supplies (e.g., in the United States and the United Kingdom).

Contract duration

Traditional LNG contracts have durations of 20 years or longer, to provide a balance between the gas reserves required to be proven up front to support the sales commitment and the need for a period long enough to ensure that the appropriate investment return can be achieved and term financing can be secured. The primary terms of the contracts do not include the start-up and buildup periods, which are treated separately (as described earlier). As discussed in the "Quantities" section, the primary term of the contract may be extended to allow the buyer to recoup makeup LNG quantities, whether arising from a take-or-pay obligation or force majeure. Other mechanisms can also result in an extension of the primary term. For example, the contract may provide for an extension mechanism automatically or at either the buyer's or the seller's option for a certain period (e.g., 5 years). This extension may be on the same commercial terms as in the initial term of the contract, may provide for limited reopening of key commercial terms (price or quantity), or may simply offer one or the other party the exclusive right to a limited period of negotiation for the extension quantities. Normally, such extension provisions are conditional on the buyer and the seller's being in compliance with the contract at the time when the extension right is exercised.

OTHER TERMS AND CONDITIONS

Unlike those previously discussed, other terms of LNG SPAs have more in common across different markets. These provisions include gas quality, transportation, scheduling, invoicing and payment, measurement, transfer of risk and title, force majeure, choice of law and dispute resolution, allocation of liabilities, and termination rights. Each will be addressed briefly in the following sections.

Gas quality

Whereas gas quality was once almost a formality, it has become more of an issue as the LNG trade has expanded and diversified. Traditionally, the Pacific customers look for LNG that has a richer or heavier blend of constituents (a higher proportion of ethane, propane, and higher hydrocarbons) than is sought by other buyers. Without domestic gas supplies, the issues of interchangeability and blending are of little concern, and as a practical matter, heavier LNG means that more MMBtu are transported for each cubic meter of LNG, thereby reducing the transportation costs per unit of energy, as well as making life simpler for the LNG producer, who would otherwise have to deal with these constituents as by-products with limited markets. Conversely, the North American market looks for a much leaner product that typically reflects the composition of domestic pipeline gas, which is stripped of the aforementioned components (which are utilized as petrochemical feedstock). Europe falls somewhere between the two extremes. This issue, known as gas interchangeability, continues to evolve, especially in the United States and the United Kingdom. Regulatory authorities on both continents are attempting to find a balance between attracting new LNG supplies and assigning cost responsibility for ensuring gas interchangeability between the suppliers and the customers. At the same time, the introduction of increasingly advanced gas turbines and tighter emissions standards in the power generation sector has placed an increasing emphasis on LNG composition, since these power plants are designed to run with very limited variability in gas quality.

As the trade has grown more globalized, the balancing of these market requirements has become more of an issue for LNG sellers and buyers. SPAs now reflect tighter gas quality specifications, and the risks associated with dealing with off-quality, or off-specification (off-spec), LNG have increased. Typically, the contract remedy for a cargo of off-quality LNG has been to give the buyer the right to reject the cargo, but this remedy is so draconian that it has never been used. Rather, contracts incorporate provisions that require the buyer and the seller to cooperate in dealing with off-quality LNG, usually by mandating that the seller reimburse the buyer for the costs of treating the LNG to bring it into the desired specification range. For rich LNG entering a lean market, this can be achieved by blending nitrogen into the regasified LNG, and for lean LNG entering a rich market, this can be achieved by spiking the LNG with heavier hydrocarbons.

Major LNG sellers are now designing and modifying their liquefaction plants to produce differentiated streams of LNG, often with segregated storage, to enable them to customize LNG blends for different markets. What has not changed is a limited tolerance for impurities entrained within the LNG, which in any event is much less of a concern, since liquefaction plants typically remove these impurities as they would interfere with the liquefaction process.

Transportation

In the context of an SPA, transportation is, in its simplest terms, the obligation to provide sufficient shipping of an agreed specification to deliver the ACQ. On the basis of the earlier discussion, it is clear that the issue of transportation becomes more important in the flexible world that is evolving in the industry. The responsibility for transportation is very different between an FOB contract (buyer provides transportation from the loading port) and an ex-ship or CIF contract (seller provides transportation to the discharge port). Contracts of affreightment occasionally appear in the LNG trade, but for practical purposes, these are similar to CIF contracts. The onus for providing sufficient and suitable shipping lies with the seller or the buyer, depending on whether the contract is ex-ship or CIF (seller responsibility) or FOB (buyer responsibility). Generally, LNG contracts afford the party not providing the transportation the right to inspect or vet the ships.

In consideration of other aspects of the transportation provisions, the following section is written from the perspective of an FOB contract. In the case of a CIF or ex-ship contract, the obligations and undertakings are essentially the same but the roles of seller, buyer, load port, and discharge port are reversed. In an FOB contract, the seller is obligated to provide a safe berth, which the LNG tanker can access and leave from under all normal conditions. The buyer is obligated to ensure that the tankers are compatible with the berth, meet the operating standards (cargo loading times), have up-to-date measurement equipment (since quantities are measured by gauges in the cargo tanks), are of the proper size (or size range), and satisfy the operating standards and quality specified in the SPA. The buyer is responsible for compensating the seller if the LNG tanker remains on the berth for longer than the allowed period as a result of a problem with the LNG tanker (excess berth occupancy time), and the seller is responsible for compensating the buyer in the event the tanker's loading is delayed owing to a problem with the seller's facilities (demurrage), including the failure of an earlier-arriving tanker to have completed loading and departure on schedule. The buyer is also responsible for ensuring that the tanker provides notices to the seller in advance of its anticipated arrival time. When the tanker arrives at the loading port, it will serve a notice of readiness to the seller, confirming that it has cleared all customs and immigration checks and is ready to proceed to the berth and load the cargo.

A unique aspect of FOB transportation relates to the temperature of the tanker's cargo tanks when it arrives at the loading port. If the LNG tanker has failed to retain sufficient heel on board since its last cargo discharge (and almost certainly if it has just left a shipyard where it has been gas freed), then the cargo tanks must be cooled to cryogenic temperatures before the tanker can begin accepting cargo at full loading rates. The cooldown process not only extends the normal loading time but also requires that the liquefaction plant provide LNG, which is returned as excess vapor, requiring further liquefaction, as a result of being warmed in the cooling process. Typically, the buyer must compensate the seller for the extra time and the cost of the LNG used in cooling down the cargo tanks.

Other miscellaneous terms include the provision of liquid nitrogen or bunkers for the tankers, and/or facilities to load ship's stores at the berth.

Scheduling

In the traditional LNG project model, scheduling was a relatively straightforward process, given the inherent spare capacity in almost every element of the LNG chain. In a typical Asia-Pacific contract, schedules were agreed between the buyers and sellers months in advance of each contract year and varied little during the year, if at all—and even then only for unusual circumstances, such as a typhoon disrupting the loading, transportation, or discharge of a limited number of cargoes.

In the trading world, scheduling takes on critical importance. A failure to optimize schedules can result in idle liquefaction, shipping, or terminal capacity and the loss of an associated financial opportunity, but given the potentially different incentives and objectives of buyers and sellers, one party's opportunity may come at another party's cost. No one wants to leave idle capacity anywhere in the chain, and as a result, spare capacity is squeezed out of the system. Most contracts still provide for annual scheduling, but of more importance are the provisions that allow for the annual schedules to be updated on a rolling basis. It is not unusual for schedules to be reset every 30 days to cover the upcoming 90-day period. Although scheduling provisions often call for mutual agreement, the issue of what happens if the parties fail to agree takes on much greater importance, and with take-or-pay provisions hanging over the parties, the consequences of schedules leading to shortfalls in ACQ obligations can carry significant financial penalties. The situation becomes far more complicated when multiple buyers and sellers are using the same facilities (whether liquefaction plants or import terminals). In some cases, plant operators have appointed independent experts or referees to sort out scheduling conflicts between the parties. The SPA scheduling provisions interact heavily with the ACQ obligations and become even more complex when addressing makeup quantities. The SPA scheduling provisions must further take into account scheduling of deliveries to the designated import terminals, and vice versa.

Invoicing and payment

When LNG buyers were typically major, stable, creditworthy utilities, this aspect of the contracts was less of a concern. Typical terms called for payment for a cargo of LNG within 10–30 days of title transfer (obviously differing for FOB and ex-ship contracts). With more diversified and often less creditworthy buyers emerging, the payment obligations of buyers are now increasingly underwritten by requiring buyers to post a letter of credit from a financial institution or provide separate guarantees. These provisions often require separate negotiation, which can be complex: for example, when and how are LNG sellers allowed to draw down letters of credit (especially irrevocable standby letters of credit) or claim against guarantees, and what consequences then arise if the drawdown is subsequently judged to have been unjustified? Increasingly, such guarantees carry limits (driven by accounting rules that require disclosure of such contingent commitments on the issuer's balance sheet), raising further questions as to what will happen if and when the limits of these guarantees are reached.

Measurement

LNG cargo measurement has become increasingly standardized. Generally, measurement has two components. The volume is measured by gauges in the LNG tanker's cargo tanks, by determining the LNG level in the tanks before and after loading at the liquefaction plant and discharge at the import terminal. The composition of the LNG is established by taking samples of the product as it is being loaded or discharged and measuring the density and constituent elements of the LNG. The sampling information can then be used in conjunction with the volume to calculate the quantity of energy loaded or discharged (usually expressed in MMBtu). Sampling also permits the buyer and seller to confirm that the LNG quality meets the specifications in the SPA.

Title transfer

In an FOB agreement, title to the LNG occurs as the product passes onto the tanker at the flange where the tanker's manifold is connected to the loading arms. At the same time, the buyer assumes the risks associated with the cargo, usually covered by cargo insurance. In an ex-ship agreement, the reverse situation occurs, with the title and risk transferring to the buyer as the cargo is unloaded from the tanker.

CIF contracts can be more complicated. In a CIF contract, the seller is usually responsible for securing shipping and cargo insurance, but the costs of both are passed on to the buyer in the LNG sale price. However, there is no absolute rule as to where the title and risk transfer. In several agreements, title and risk transfer on the high seas, outside the territorial waters of both seller and buyer. This is often done to ensure that the buyer is not subject to taxation or liability in the exporting country, with the same being true for the seller in the importing country. While the seller has obtained the insurance for a CIF cargo, once title transfers, the benefit of the insurance in the event of a cargo loss also has to be transferred to the buyer, who will be liable for paying for the cargo once title transfers, regardless whether the cargo is delivered. Often the agreement will call for the buyer to assign the insurance proceeds to the seller in the event of a cargo loss and then be absolved of making payment for that cargo. In a CIF contract, there is no requirement that title and risk be transferred simultaneously.

Force majeure

Force majeure provisions are included in SPAs to address the situation where one of the parties fails to perform for reasons beyond their control. Most force majeure provisions enumerate examples of circumstances beyond the parties' control, such as storms, floods, hurricanes, wars, failure to complete facilities on time because of uncontrollable events, inability to obtain permits or licenses for the construction or operation of the facilities, or damage to any of the facilities involved in the delivery chain (from gas field to receiving terminal). These provisions have become increasingly complicated as the trade has become more complex and as the world has changed. Most force majeure provisions today would cite terrorism as an event. Strikes and industrial disturbances are usually classified as events of force majeure, and the party being subject to the strike is under no obligation to settle the strike and bring the force majeure situation to an end (to avoid giving undue leverage to the strikers in an industrial dispute). In the more complex traded world of LNG, physical events affecting third parties downstream of the import terminal may also be classified as events of force majeure if they prevent the buyer from being able to move the LNG or gas to its customers or if the customers are unable to purchase the LNG.

Somewhat more controversial are provisions that state that acts of governments, agencies, or changes in rules and laws can also be events of force majeure. Very often the effects of these types of actions may be unclear, and the parties may disagree as to whether they prevent one party from performing or simply result in much higher costs or even losses to that party. In the case where a party is a state energy company, there is always a question as to whether the actions of the state can be seen as truly separate from the energy company and thus whether the state company can claim force majeure as a result of an action of its shareholder.

Not classified as force majeure are events that render the agreement uneconomical for one of the parties, no matter how these arise. These events are often described as "price majeure events," giving rise to economic losses by one of the parties as a result of changed circumstances. Force majeure fundamentally means that a party is physically prevented from performing, not economically prevented from performing.

Force majeure provisions also dictate that the affected party notify the other party as to the extent and expected duration of the event and require that the affected party take measures to remedy the problem (the one exception being industrial disputes mentioned earlier). Where an event of force majeure reduces the capacity of the facility (liquefaction plant or terminal), the provisions also cover allocation of any available product or capacity between the various buyers and sellers who may be affected. During a force majeure event, the unaffected party is usually permitted to sell LNG to or buy LNG from third parties, to mitigate any damages the seller or buyer respectively would otherwise incur.

Choice of law

The choice of law is not always as straightforward as it might seem. Earlier LNG contracts tended to be governed either by U.S. or English law. A party rarely accepted governing law from the home country of another party. Today many more legal regimes are being applied to these agreements, increasingly including the adoption of the laws of the exporting country, which may not be as well understood or as well developed as those of importing countries. Understanding the implication of the choice of law is important for understanding the standards of performance under a given provision of an SPA. For example, under English law, the term "best efforts" means to leave no stone unturned in correcting a problem encountered in the commercial relationship, and cost is no object; U.S. law tends to interpret this phrase as meaning commercially reasonable efforts. Parties then often negotiate a standard of commercially reasonable efforts to further define this issue.

Although there are examples and court precedents that can be used to understand how take-or-pay is interpreted in the U.S. legal system, almost no take-or-pay claims have ever been adjudicated in the English courts, most having been addressed in sealed arbitration decisions. The parties to an agreement also have to understand when they choose a legal regime whether they are also incorporating other standards into the agreement; for example, the Uniform Commercial Code in the United States and the English Sale of Goods Act. Suffice it to say that this subject is beyond the scope of this book but requires the careful attention of legal advisers during contract negotiation and drafting.

Dispute resolution

Disputes are rarely left to be resolved in the courts, as most parties prefer more confidential handling of their differences and are not comfortable with going to courts outside their own country. As a result, most legal disputes are handled by international confidential arbitration, with several different standards available to address the mechanics of the arbitration process. Arbitration can be brought using the rules of the United Nations Commission on International Trade Law (UNCITRAL), the International Chamber of Commerce (ICC), the Latin American Arbitration Association, and the American Arbitration Association (AAA), to name but a few authorities. There are also provisions to establish an appointing authority, or a party who will appoint the third arbitrator (the first two being appointed by the parties to the dispute) if the parties cannot agree on the appointment. Again, this can be a body such as the ICC or AAA. Finally, the locus of the arbitration must be designated—New York City, London, Paris, and Geneva being among the common choices.

For disputes of a purely technical nature, the SPA will often provide for the appointment of a single expert who will settle such disputes. Examples of technical disputes include measurement errors, invoicing errors, and LNG quality issues.

In both cases, the costs of the dispute resolution must be determined. Usually, the agreement calls for the parties to split the costs of arbitration or expert determination (apart from their own legal and witness costs), but it is also possible to use the English system of loser pays. The enforceability and collection of an arbitration award must also be given consideration and may require that the agreement reflect the right of the winning party to go into the courts of the losing party's host country to enforce and collect an arbitration award. Arbitration proceedings tend to be lengthy and expensive, and most contract disputes are normally resolved through negotiated settlement.

Allocation of liabilities, liquidated damages, and termination

As is evident from the historical discussion, some companies in the LNG industry have incurred very large financial costs associated with disputes and contract failures. A growing trend in the industry is the use of caps and other limits on liabilities and/or financial guarantees. When one party reaches the cap on liability as a result of a failure to perform, the other party then often has the right to suspend or terminate the SPA. In the case of a suspension, the SPA can be resumed once the nonperforming party makes good on its liabilities. In the case of termination, the contract ends and the nonperforming party loses any further rights under the SPA, with the other party then being freed to do business with other buyers or sellers.

As well as liability limits, SPAs also may introduce provisions for liquidated damages for the failure of one party to perform. These are more usually applicable to the seller for failure to deliver, while the buyer's liability is normally take-or-pay; however, liability arising from the buyer's failure to take may also be resolved by the payment of liquidated damages. These damages are often calculated by following a formula in the contract (e.g., the volume not delivered by the seller times the additional costs incurred by the buyer to replace these volumes), thereby removing the uncertainties associated with leaving damage calculations to the arbitration process.

In the most extreme instances, the resolution of a dispute may be to give the performing party the right to terminate the SPA unless the other party cures the nonperformance in a certain time. However, this gives rise to further issues, such as where the nonperformance arises from another underlying dispute. If one party terminates the contract but the other party is later determined to have acted correctly, the consequences may be unclear, but could be very painful. Even provisions that appear to be straightforward, such as termination, turn out not to be quite so simple in practice!

Spot contracts

As mentioned earlier, spot transactions are increasingly being carried out under so-called master agreements. Master agreements contain many of the same provisions as SPAs, although they tend to be less elaborate, covering only a limited number of cargo deliveries and limited time periods. The typical master agreement will include standards for measurement and testing, invoicing, payment and associated security requirements, marine transportation and shore-based facilities, force majeure, choice of law, and dispute resolution. The key commercial terms—including quantities, price, delivery schedule, LNG quality specifications, and the identification of the loading and discharge ports—are handled in short schedules or memoranda of agreement, which are agreed and executed as each LNG cargo or group of cargoes is committed for sale and purchase.

Given the critical nature of the LNG SPA in determining the commercial underpinnings of a relationship that may last for decades and involve the delivery, sale, and purchase of billions of dollars of LNG, there is no substitute for obtaining good legal advice on both sides of the negotiations.

LNG TANKER CONTRACTS 14

INTRODUCTION

There are two types of contracts for the carriage of goods by sea: the bill of lading and the charterparty. The bill of lading covers the sale and ownership of the commodity being shipped. It is a document of title to the goods and serves as a receipt for the cargo, stating its quantity and condition. It is also evidence of the contract of carriage. The charterparty contract addresses the transportation service. It is a contract between one party, the charterer (or shipper), and the vessel's owner by which they agree to the terms and conditions under which the charterer has the right to use the owner's tanker.

CHARTERPARTY OVERVIEW

In the past, charterparties were drawn up by notaries to cover each voyage or series of voyages of a particular vessel. However, with the expansion of the world's merchant marine, many charterparties are now negotiated around standard forms published by various shipping organizations, especially major oil and gas companies, in the context of chartering oil and oil product tankers and certainly not drawn up by notaries. Each type of charterparty incorporates a standard set of clauses. Any divergence (additional clauses and/or amendments to the standard forms) is dictated by the physical nature of the commodity and the negotiations between the contracting parties.

The charterparty is, in essence, the framework for a long-established set of rules, rights, obligations, and remedies that leaves ample room for the negotiation of terms and conditions between the contracting parties. The emphasis on standardization reflects the unique features of admiralty law that have been developed over centuries of merchant trading on the high seas. Unlike other assets involved in the LNG chain, the LNG tankers are mobile and pass through many legal jurisdictions during their lifetime and even on individual voyages. Many aspects of the marine transportation industry are covered by international legal conventions to which most countries subscribe. In turn, these conventions spell out many of the legal requirements that must be recognized and addressed within the charterparty.

Figure 14–1 shows typical charterparty contracts in the ocean transportation link of an LNG project chain. A number of transportation contracts or charterparties are available to the charterer and shipowner. To determine the most appropriate type of charterparty, the project participants must evaluate their LNG supply and purchase obligations and the operational requirements that these obligations place on the project's shipping requirements. Until recently, the LNG tanker industry has used variations of standard tanker charterparty contracts, which have usually been significantly amended to meet the LNG industry's technical and commercial requirements and standards. However, as the commercial model has changed and the industry has developed more spot and short-term trading, the contractual terms appear to be moving toward the more standard formats that are characteristic of the oil tanker industry.

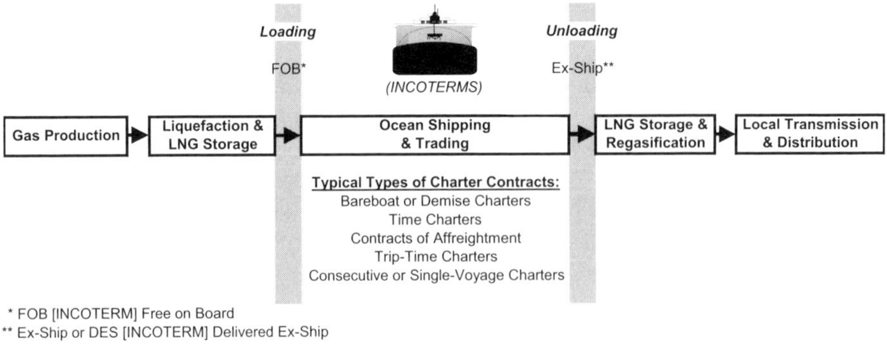

Fig. 14–1. Ocean transportation phase and typical charterparty contracts (*Source:* Poten & Partners)

The main charterparties used in LNG shipping are bareboat charters, time charters, and trip-time charters. Single-voyage charters and contracts of affreightment are a recent development. The obligations, liabilities, and remedies of the contracting parties will vary depending on the charterparty employed. The key commercial terms are described later.

EVOLUTION OF LNG CHARTERPARTIES

Unlike oil and most other bulk shipping segments, traditionally there was virtually no spot charter market (single voyages) for LNG tankers because of the technical and commercial structure of the business. The LNG trade was based on long-term SPAs, which in turn required that the shipping capacity be locked in under long-term time charters, for the duration of the SPA (typically 20 years). Although long-term charterparties remain dominant, there have been some changes owing to the availability of short-term LNG supply and import capacity, and a growing number of LNG tankers have been built and delivered on a speculative basis, unassociated with any long-term trade.

LNG charterparties in the traditional shipping model

Traditionally, LNG tankers were dedicated to specific LNG projects, because the long-term SPAs required the provision of a fleet of tankers of sufficient capacity in order to meet the sales and purchase obligations for the duration of the SPA. The high capital cost and specialized nature of the LNG tankers offered project participants little maneuverability in the SPA terms and very limited flexibility in shipping, which was fully integrated into the project. The tankers were perceived as a moving pipeline. Tankers always called at the same terminals, and their loading and discharge schedules were programmed well in advance with great precision. This is still true for many older ongoing contracts.

The most commonly used charterparty template in the traditional LNG shipping model is Shell Time 3. (There have been subsequent amendments to this template, and today Shell Time 4 and 5 are available.) The industry incorporated a lengthy set of standard clauses found in this oil tanker charterparty and amended them to fit the LNG trade. However, in the early projects, shipping was such an integral part of the project that in many instances, it was owned one way or another by the project itself. Under such an arrangement, there were no true charterparties as such; rather, the shipping conditions were implicit in the LNG SPA, which contained FOB or ex-ship delivery terms. An example of this type of arrangement can be seen in the fleet of Brunei LNG (started in 1972).

Notwithstanding the integrated nature of these projects and the shared ownership of the tankers, the fleets themselves were often organized into affiliated companies, and charterparties were still established between the affiliates just as if they were independent third parties. This reflected the unique taxation and liability regimes covering shipping and served to insulate the other segments of the LNG project from the legal risk of an incident involving an LNG tanker. The existence of affiliated charterparties also helped to establish appropriate transfer pricing mechanisms within a given project, to ensure the agreed sharing of revenues, costs, and risks. When the shipping company is an independent entity, the fleet is chartered in under long-term charterparties (time or bareboat charters) to the project.[1]

The time charterparty. This is a contract under which the charterer hires the LNG tanker from the shipowner for a specified length of time, ranging from months to years. The charterer enjoys full control of the ship for the contracted period. The shipowner is responsible for keeping the vessel in a seaworthy condition, compliant with international regulations and conventions; ensuring that it is manned by a competent and experienced crew; assuming the risk of operations; and bearing all operating costs other than those reserved in the charterparty as being for the charterer's account. The money paid by the charterer to the shipowner, called the hire (daily rate payable on a monthly basis, usually in advance), is divided into two main components: the capital expenses (CAPEX), which represents the reimbursement to the shipowner for the capital cost of the vessel, and the operating expenditures (OPEX), consisting of the daily cost of the crew, stores, management, maintenance, insurance, and all other agreed expenses. The charterer must also pay for the voyage costs (including fuel oil [bunkers and diesel], port charges, canal dues, and nitrogen). Boil-off incurred during the voyage is also a cost borne by the charterer, though the boil-off gas may be made available at no cost to the shipowner for use in the ship's boiler or engine.

CAPEX costs are generally fixed for the term of the charterparty, although they can be revisited in the event that, for example, new regulations or a change in loading or discharge port terminal or berth configurations require that significant modifications be made to the tanker. OPEX costs generally change over the contract term to reflect changes in the underlying costs, although charterers and shipowners have recently begun agreeing to formulaic approaches to OPEX, rather than direct cost pass-through.

One exception tends to be insurance, where the costs are established by the market and may under certain circumstances vary dramatically (e.g., additional premiums are assessed for war risks in areas subject to armed conflict).

The charterparty also spells out the obligations of the parties, with most of the obligations being assumed by the shipowner, who is the service provider. The shipowner will be required to crew and maintain the vessel to high standards and to guarantee the tanker's performance in areas such as the boil-off rate, service speed, fuel consumption, and rate of cargo pumping, all of which can fundamentally affect the costs of the LNG transportation. Failure to maintain these standards can result in the assessment of financial penalties against the shipowner by the charterer and, in extreme cases, can lead to the termination of the charterparty. The charterer may also have the right to terminate the charterparty in the event that the tanker suffers excessive off-hire. Off-hire is any period when the tanker is unable to perform the service required by the charterer, during which time the charterer is under no obligation to pay charter hire (e.g., for a breakdown). The charterparty will spell out the provisions for dry-docking the vessel (intervals, time allowed, etc.). The charterparty also specifies the location where the vessel is to be delivered to the charterer and the location where the vessel is to be redelivered to the owner at the start and end, respectively, of the charterparty term. The charterparty can further specify the right of the charterer to subcharter the tanker to a third party. In this instance, the original charterer now takes on the role of the owner vis-à-vis the new charterer, yet his rights and responsibilities toward the shipowner remain unchanged. Choice of law and arbitration is often England, since the English legal system has extensive experience and precedent in handling maritime disputes, usually through arbitration. Charterparties can also go into more arcane (and often sensitive) areas such as the naming of the tanker, the flag state, the ship registry, and even the paint scheme.

In November 2005, Shell issued their Shell LNG Time 1 charterparty, which is mainly based on the Shell Time 4 oil tanker charterparty. Shell LNG Time 1 is adapted specifically for LNG tankers. The main changes from Shell Time 4 relate to the unique nature of the cryogenic cargo in LNG tankers. Among the important issues are cargo boil-off rates, forced vaporization, spray cooling of tanks, and heel retention (to keep the tanks cooled). For example, the clause titled "Key Vessel Performance Criteria" (Clause 26(g) and (h)) specifies the vessel's guaranteed maximum daily boil-off rate for both the laden and ballast voyage. Shell LNG Time 1 represents a meaningful step toward the development of a standard LNG charterparty across the industry.

The bareboat (or demise) charterparty. Under this type of contract, the shipowner hires out the tanker (i.e., the physical ship itself) and bears no operating or maintenance responsibilities. It is the charterer's duty to fully man, operate, maintain, and insure the tanker; obtain the appropriate certifications and flag registry; and pay the associated administrative costs. For the duration of the charter, the tanker is in the full possession of—and under the absolute control of—the charterer. There is often a tanker purchase option on the expiration of the bareboat charter. In this case, the hire paid to the shipowner is the equivalent of the CAPEX of the time charter, as the charterer assumes all the operating and voyage costs. At the end of the charterparty, the contract spells out the obligation of the charterer to return the tanker to the owner in a specified condition and at a specified location.

LNG transportation contracts in the new era

Short-term LNG trading activity is giving rise to different forms of transportation contracts that are new to the LNG industry, albeit utilized in other merchant marine sectors. The following charterparties are increasingly being considered both for strategic purposes and to adjust the transportation costs and risks.

Trip-time charterparty. This contract runs for a short period of time, generally for one trip. The money paid to the shipowner is based on a daily hire rate that incorporates voyage costs but excludes fuel and port costs, which are for the charterer's account. There are no demurrage claims, since the charterer continues making daily hire payments until the cargo has been discharged.

Voyage charterparty. This is a shorter contract than a time charterparty, although the physical movement of the ships is the same. It usually does not include clauses related to the long-term operations or management of the ship, such as dry-dock provisions or maintenance. The money paid to the shipowner is normally based on a currency amount per ton of cargo loaded, which incorporates all the voyage costs. There are also consecutive-voyage charters.

Contract of affreightment (COA). This is a voyage-charter variation that offers flexibility when a shipper (the charterer) agrees with the shipowner to transport a specified quantity of LNG on a ship-or-pay basis. No vessel is specifically designated, and the time interval between cargo loadings is not necessarily linked with round-trip voyage time, since the shipper usually has multiple destination options. A certain volume of cargo is contracted for loading and delivery, usually at regular intervals, for a specific time period.

The shipowner can nominate any capable and available tanker from its fleet or charter in a vessel for this purpose, provided that the tanker is approved by the charterer. If the shipowner has access to vessels of differing cargo capacities, then their utilization and its impact on shipping schedules must also be accounted for in this agreement. The payment to the owner takes the same form as for voyage charters.

CONTROLLING LNG TANKERS: ADAPTATION TO AN EMERGING MODEL

Historically, suppliers looked to control the LNG tankers, through outright ownership or charterparties, to have consistency in newbuilding designs, operations, and maintenance. LNG supply projects, which had the greatest capital exposure in the chain and were perceived to have more limited options in the event of a shipping failure, generally sought to control their own LNG tankers.

This trend is changing. The reliability of LNG tankers has been well established (subject to proper maintenance practices), and the perception that control equates to reliability appears to be less of a concern. Buyers have become more interested in controlling shipping, and in some instances, sellers have been more willing to cede this control. Reasons for this shift include the following:

- Improved control over tanker expenses and residual values (if the tanker is owned, not on charter) that may lead to a reduction of transportation costs
- Greater flexibility to meet operational requirements, as buyers contract with multiple sellers and their downstream markets become less predictable
- Destination flexibility to deliver at multiple locations
- Capability of sourcing alternative LNG supplies, if required
- Capability of securing extra cargoes
- Concerns on the part of the sellers over legal and fiscal liabilities arising from tankers underway in foreign jurisdictions (e.g., the United States is notoriously litigious and has onerous antipollution laws)

In addition, buyers with higher credit ratings can generally secure lower charter rates (through reduced finance costs for shipowners) than suppliers, who may be project financed and have lower credit ratings.

The traditional LNG business model committed tankers to specific trades and to carrying predictable quantities. Given the very high capital costs of LNG tankers, only a limited number were available on short notice and for limited duration to meet sellers' or buyers' opportunistic or seasonal requirements. Most parties felt that more assured access to these opportunities was best achieved through the control of tankers. This struggle over control of shipping has become a major issue in many LNG sales negotiations.

With a growing fleet of uncommitted tankers, the actual spot charter rates during any given period may be higher or lower than the long-term charter rate, and spot chartering avoids the need to make long-term commitments. For transient business opportunities, *not* controlling shipping and incurring the attendant fixed costs may in fact be an advantage. The commercial allocation of the risks and rewards, including the factors mentioned previously, associated with a long-term SPA between buyers and sellers will probably be more reflective of the relative bargaining power of the parties during the negotiation process than the particulars of who controls the transportation link of the chain. The only compelling reason to seek shipping control is if one party is concerned that the other party will default, in which case the party controlling the shipping may have more ability to mitigate its risks than if the shipping control rested with a defaulting party. Of course, one might ask why any party would enter an LNG SPA where a potential for default by the counterparty was a primary consideration. Regardless of the type of LNG sale, one of the parties to the SPA will be obligated to provide the necessary oceangoing transportation and thus will be faced with the decision of whether to own or charter the tankers.

Owning LNG tankers

Under this option, the future owner (buyer or seller, not independent shipowner) contracts for a new LNG tanker to be built by a pre-selected shipyard; funds the vessel with equity, debt, or both; and contracts with an independent manager to operate and maintain the vessel and provide technical management services (unless the owner has an in-house shipping department). Even though the owner may not necessarily operate the ship, he or she would need to establish a shipping organization to monitor the manager's performance.

The following are some of the main considerations in choosing to own an LNG tanker:

Financial. Ownership exposes the company and its balance sheet to the capital cost of the tanker (including finance and owner's costs during construction). For a non-shipping company, tankers may not be regarded as core assets, and balance sheet exposure to the tanker's capital expenditure may be an issue. However, the financial and balance sheet implications of a tanker can be partially mitigated through project financing, leasing, or tax-advantaged sale/leaseback arrangements. If structured carefully, they may require only a footnote to the balance sheet and have a lower impact on the company's leverage.

Liability. Tanker ownership exposes the party to liabilities associated with shipping. Tanker owners carry substantial protection and indemnity (P&I) insurance for third-party liability claims and insure the value of the ship through what is termed "hull and machinery" insurance. Nevertheless, one of the most serious risks that cannot be insured is the risk of damage to the company's reputation and name in the event of a serious casualty or a significant pollution incident (although LNG tankers are much less risky in this regard than oil tankers). In addition, liabilities are associated with a failure to meet the shipping obligations under an SPA, if the tanker does not perform as expected.

Residual value. This has taken on increasing importance in light of the longer-than-expected trading lives of LNG tankers, which are now approaching 40 years. Ownership provides full rights to the residual value at the end of an LNG SPA or charterparty, unless some sharing arrangement was agreed on in the initial charterparty. The owner benefits if, at the end of the initial employment period, the tanker continues in service at market rates, is chartered to a third party, or is sold.

Control. Ownership ensures control of the operating and maintenance standards of the tanker. A company without in-house ship-operating capability would usually employ a ship manager to be responsible for the operations and maintenance of the LNG tanker to agreed standards (which are usually in excess of the regulatory minimums). The shipowner has the right to replace the manager if these standards are not met. Since most ship managers are responsible for a large number of vessels, they usually have access to a larger crew pool, have more leverage with shipyards and insurance providers, and have in place all the systems and controls that are required in order to run a large fleet. As such, they can usually perform ship management services at a lower cost than an owner's in-house operation, unless the owner controls a large fleet of ships.

Technical and market risks. Owning LNG ships exposes the company to all the technical risks and their associated responsibilities, such as failures or breakdowns. Similarly, technical obsolescence of the ship is the owner's problem and could result in early withdrawal of the ship from service and a reduced residual value, although this has not been an issue for LNG tankers. Mitigation of this risk comes from shipyards' guarantees. At delivery, there are liquidated damages if the tanker does not meet the owner's specifications. The shipyard guarantees the tanker for the first one or two years, and breakdowns and failures are repaired at the yard's expense. However, the shipbuilding contract typically does not allow consequential damages; thus, lost cargoes are the owner's responsibility (although these losses can be insured).

An owner takes little market risk after signing a shipbuilding contract with a shipyard if the owner intends to utilize the vessel in his or her own long-term service. The price of the tanker is locked in, and the only remaining item is the management cost. This introduces an element of market risk, as crewing and shipyard maintenance costs rise and fall with the demand for LNG-related services. However, this is only a small part of the total shipping cost and is seldom avoided if chartering is selected as an alternative. The owner is sheltered from short-term market conditions and charter rate cycles during the primary term of the vessel's utilization and need consider these aspects only if the LNG tanker is released from the SPA commitment before the end of its useful life.

Chartering LNG tankers

An alternative to direct ownership is the chartering of LNG tankers from a third-party owner for the duration of an SPA. In this case, the LNG tanker owner is responsible for contracting for the construction of the tanker, management, technical operations and maintenance, and insurance. Even though there is a third-party owner in the equation, it is still necessary for the charterer to establish a shipping organization (although it will be a smaller one than for ownership) to monitor the owner's performance.

The main considerations in choosing to charter LNG tankers are as follows:

Financial. The charterer is exposed to a long-term financial obligation to pay monthly charter hire to the owner for the duration of the contract. The commitment from the charterer underpins the financing of the tanker(s); the owner is responsible for securing the financing. Because many shipping companies are private, they are often willing to assume more debt than might be the case for a public company and consequently have a lower cost of capital than the charterer might have. As a result, the cost of chartering, when considered solely on financial grounds, may be lower than the cost of ownership.

Liability. Chartering tankers places the liability on the owner of the tanker. While the owner will provide certain performance guarantees for the tankers, with liquidated damages for underperformance, this may not be sufficient to offset liabilities associated with breaching the lifting obligations of an LNG SPA. Furthermore, the charterer's control over the LNG tanker management is weaker than an owner's, and the charterparty usually constrains the charterer's ability to force improvements in the tanker's operation. Therefore, the charterer must carefully consider the choice of the owner, his operating record and practices, and the incentives (and penalties) built into the charterparty and their influence on the owner's behavior.

Residual value. In typical time charter arrangements, the owner benefits from any residual value of a tanker at the end of the charter period. However, the charterer can negotiate to receive a portion of this value at the end of the charter period, and most recent charterparties reflect such potential value-sharing mechanisms.

Control. Chartering the tanker puts management in the hands of the owner. The shipowner generally has control of the operating and maintenance standards employed on the tanker. However, the charterer may be able to negotiate limited rights to require a change in tanker management in the event that the operating and maintenance practices are not satisfactory. Another tool to address potential operating and maintenance concerns is to include a tanker purchase option at a predetermined price at specified points in the charterparty. This gives the charterer the ability to take control of the tanker if necessary.

Technical and market risks. The responsibility for technical problems of the tanker shifts from the charterer to the owner. The owner is responsible for any failure or breakdown and must pay for the repairs. The tanker would be off-hire (the charterer makes no payment of hire) during the repair period, and this would be the only mitigation that the charterer receives. The charterer's claims arising as a result of lost charter hire or lost cargo deliveries would be solely compensated by the off-hire provision. Some of the consequential risks from off-hire, such as the risk of take or pay, may be mitigated by force majeure provisions in the SPA or through the purchase of off-hire insurance or business interruption insurance. Obsolescence of technical onboard machinery is usually the owner's concern, as the charterer will have no risk of economical and technological obsolescence at the end of the charterparty. However, for mandated changes to an LNG tanker (e.g., those arising from regulatory measures or from the need to fit new port conditions), the costs are either shared or passed through to the charterer, in whole or in part, by means of an increase in the CAPEX component of the charter hire. Table 14–1 defines the key commercial terms that have a financial impact on either party to the charter.

Table 14–1. Key commercial terms in an LNG time charterparty (*Source:* Poten & Partners)

Term	Description
Duty to maintain	Requires the owner of the vessel to provide the charterer with a plan to ensure operational reliability of equipment that affects a ship's performance, safety, and availability. This includes an understanding of the owner's plans and budget for maintaining the ship throughout the charter service. The owner must maintain the vessel in a seaworthy condition at all times during the charter period.
Period/trading limits	Details the duration of the charter arrangement, the location of the vessel's redelivery, the nomination process of the vessel's redelivery, and the geographic limitations of where the vessel is able to trade. The clause also details the procedures to be taken should the vessel not be authorized to enter a terminal because of size.
Delivery/canceling	Details the start of the charter, the condition of the vessel at her delivery, and the charterer's right to terminate the contract if the vessel does not meet the conditions. With respect to newbuildings, the shipowner would request that the canceling details of the charterparty mirror that of the newbuilding contract. The vessel's delivery positioning is important, as the charterer would seek to minimize any ballast time paid before the first loading.
Owners to provide	Determines the owner's responsibilities and expenses through the duration of the charter period.
Charters to provide	Determines the charterer's responsibilities and expenses through the duration of the charter period.
Rate of hire	Details the daily rate of hire that the charterer agrees to pay the owner of the vessel for the use of the vessel subject to the terms and conditions of the charter agreement.
Bunkers at delivery/redelivery	States which party is responsible for the cost of bunkers at the time of the vessel's delivery and redelivery and stipulates the minimum bunkers to remain on board.
Subcharter	Spells out the conditions under which the charterer can subcharter the vessel, i.e., charter the ship to a third party.

Term	Description
Off-hire	This clause details the conditions under which the charterer is absolved from paying the hire rate. Conditions that trigger an off-hire are generally related to occasions that result in the vessel's interruption of service in any manner, apart from periodic drydockings. An off-hire will tend to have a negative knock-on effect along the LNG chain, resulting in a delay in loading under a tight schedule and a delay in LNG delivery.
Periodic dry-docking	Details the procedures for the vessel's dry-docking obligations. The clause provides a program nominating the dates of dry-dockings and describes exactly when the vessel becomes off-hire during the actual dry-dock period. Dry-dockings for LNG ships are typically completed over a 25-day spread every 2 1/2 years. There is, however, some flexibility in the timing. An owner will use best endeavors to time the dockings when gas sales are not critical (during the low season). As the number of dockyards capable of handling LNG ships is limited (particularly in the Atlantic Basin), the vessel's deviation and time to reach the yard can be costly. Thus, the timing of the off-hire is an important element generally covered in negotiations.
Vessel's performance	Details the owner's guaranteed operational parameters under which the vessel will operate given specific circumstances and set parameters. The main components include the guarantees of vessel speed, bunker (fuel-oil) consumption, and boil-off quantity.
Laying-up	Covers the circumstances under which the vessel can be laid-up and the various terms and conditions of doing so. Laying-up is extremely rare in LNG and is a very negative sign of a bearish market due to an oversupply of ships.
Financial responsibility for pollution	Details the owner's responsibility to ensure that the vessel is legally covered and compliant with all pollution regulations from the start of the charter and throughout the charter period. For example, a vessel navigating in U.S. waters will need to have a Certificate of Financial Responsibility (COFR), which is a record attesting that the owner has the financial ability to pay for any (oil) pollution damages.

Term	Description
Cool down	Defines the temperature the vessel's storage tanks must be at when the vessel is ready for cargo loading. This clause takes effect at the beginning of a charter, after an offhire period, or a dry-docking. There is a cost associated with cooling down the tanks,(purchase of LNG and time), which is negotiated between the parties. It is common for the expenses to be debted to the owner's account.
Boil-off	Determines the acceptable limit of LNG that turns into its gaseous state and highlights the method of boil-off measurement for each laden and ballast sailing.
Bareboat charter and purchase options	These two clauses are backups for a charterer. If, for any reason, the owner defaults from his duties or obligations (e.g. loss of licenses, change in classification status), the charterer is entitled to terminate the charter or to exercise his or her option to gain full control and management of the vessel. Similarly, should a charterer be unsatisfied with the owner's management of the ship, the charterer has an option to purchase the ship. This option is generally exercisable at the end of an original charter period or any other option period.
Substitution	Details the condition under which the owner or charterer may provide or request an alternative vessel to fulfill the charter obligations.
Insurance	There are two distinct and obligatory types of marine insurances. Hull and machinery (H&M) and protection and indemnity (P&I). H&M insurance covers physical damage to the vessel itself (e.g. to the hull and machinery, such as engine, boilers) under the Institute Time Clauses. The P&I Club coverage (offered by mutual nonprofit association of shipowners) provides third-party coverage of human injuries or fatalities, collisions, groundings, pollution, wreck removal, and towage operations. Insurance is generally a cost pass-through to the charterer in an LNG charterparty. There are other optional insurances, such as loss of hire, which protects the shipowner from potential loss of earnings as a result of a casualty.

NOTES

1 For further reading on charterparties, please see Tusiani, Michael D. 1996. *The Petroleum Shipping Industry*. Vol. 2. Tulsa: PennWell.

SHIPPING CONVENTIONS AND REGULATIONS 15

INTRODUCTION

To participate in the movement of goods and commodities in international trade, LNG tankers, like other vessel types, must comply with a large number of international rules and regulations, as well as those of their home nations. These rules and regulations are embodied for the most part in international laws. International conventions governing shipping are passed through the International Maritime Organization (IMO), an arm of the United Nations.

The IMO itself does not have enforcement powers. Every signatory nation to an IMO convention must pass a domestic law for a regulation or standard to have force within its territorial waters. Through this domestic legislation, each nation is responsible for the enforcement of international conventions within its maritime jurisdiction via its port state control authorities. For example, in the United States, an international convention must first be passed as a law by Congress. The U.S. Coast Guard, now under the Department of Homeland Security, is charged with the enforcement of those domestic laws that reflect international conventions. The United States and other nations are free to pass maritime legislation that may differ from an international convention or is unique in nature. Generally, the domestic legislation mirrors the wording of the international convention.

The International Chamber of Shipping (ICS) is not a regulatory body but, as the international trade association for merchant ship operators, represents the collective views of the international industry from different nations, sectors, and trades. The ICS has consultative status with a number of intergovernmental bodies, including the IMO, which is a major focus of ICS activity. The stated objective of the ICS is the maintenance of a sound, well-constructed global regulatory environment in which well-run ships can operate safely and efficiently. The ICS is committed to the principle that maritime regulation is formulated at an international level. The International Association of Ports and Harbors (IAPH) also holds IMO consultative status and has a major focus on safety and security issues.

To promote consistency, the IMO works through numerous international shipping organizations, to clarify and explain existing international conventions to nations that want to write their own legislation. Most organizations involved in commercial shipping use the IMO's procedural code as a guideline for their own laws and rules and employ IMO publications that explain the codes and conventions. For example, the Oil Companies International Marine Forum (OCIMF) assists the shipping industry in implementing IMO conventions as they apply to tankers in general. The Society of International Gas Tanker and Terminal Operators (SIGTTO) performs a similar function specifically for the owners and operators of liquefied-gas (LNG and LPG) tankers. The IMO, the ICS, OCIMF, and SIGTTO are all headquartered in London, and IAPH is headquartered in Tokyo.

THE RISE OF MODERN SHIPPING REGULATIONS

Establishment and structure of the IMO

The growth of international trade in the 19th century created a need for an organization that would institute a standard set of laws for international commerce. The development of international trade would be impeded if each nation inaugurated its own standards. The first international maritime organization, the Comité Maritime International (CMI), was established in 1897 as a common center for national maritime law associations. For many years, the CMI remained the main coordinator of maritime law.

In 1948, a United Nations conference in Geneva passed an international convention to create a body solely for the purpose of governing the shipping industry. The convention was adopted in 1954. Four years later, the Inter-governmental Maritime Consultative Organization (IMCO) was created, which in 1982 was renamed the International Maritime Organization. Today the IMO is recognized as the official international governing body of maritime law. Other organizations, including the CMI, continue to play an important role in drafting maritime conventions and cooperate with the IMO to achieve their mission.

The purpose of the IMO is as follows:

- To facilitate cooperation among governments in all shipping matters
- To encourage the adoption of the highest practicable standards of maritime safety, security, navigation, and prevention and control of marine pollution

The organization—which summarizes its objectives as "safe, secure, and efficient shipping on clean oceans"—consists of five main committees:

1. **Maritime Safety Committee.** This is the IMO's prime committee dealing with all safety-related matters, including navigational safety, search and rescue, lifesaving, standards of training and watchkeeping, carriage of dangerous goods, fire protection, and radio communications.
2. **Marine Environment Protection Committee.** Established in 1973, this committee is responsible for the prevention and control of all forms of pollution of the marine environment by vessels.
3. **Legal Committee.** Established to deal with the legal issues raised by the world's first major tanker disaster, the 1967 sinking of the *Torrey Canyon*, this committee started the IMO's active involvement in international conventions dealing with liability and compensation.
4. **Technical Cooperation Committee.** This committee assists governments, primarily of developing nations that lack the technical knowledge needed to operate a shipping industry, and to improve their compliance with international standards.
5. **Facilitation Committee.** The purpose of this committee is to address and simplify formalities and bureaucratic documentation, which can delay vessels entering or leaving ports and terminals.

The IMO also produces codes, which are adopted as amendments to conventions and cover a wide range of marine issues. Several codes govern the construction and equipment of specific ship types, including a code for ships carrying liquefied gases. The ship Classification Societies, charged with establishing and applying technical standards, produce designs that either reflect or exceed the IMO's code requirements.

The five main committees are supported by specialized subcommittees that deal with technical and legal matters and prepare resolutions and recommendations. The governing body of the IMO is the Assembly, which meets every two years to establish policies and adopt resolutions;

if required, special meetings may be called at any time. Over the years, a set of comprehensive international maritime laws have been developed, prompted at times by large-scale disasters that focused attention on certain aspects of vessel design or operation. These laws continue to evolve. The IMO has adopted more than 40 international conventions and protocols, and currently the emphasis is on trying to ensure that these conventions and other treaties are properly implemented by the countries that have accepted them. To do so, the IMO works with the flag state and port state control agencies, which have the direct responsibility of regulating shipping and promoting safety. The basic idea is that every vessel must comply with the same set of standards of design and operation regardless of where it is built, the nationality or nationalities of its crew, or its nation of registry.

To pass an international convention, a series of hearings are held with interested parties, after which the IMO prepares draft legislation that meets the demands of maritime nations. The IMO then proposes an international convention that is again reviewed by the world community. A final version is produced and presented to each nation for signature. Most international conventions circulate until a requisite number of signatures are obtained, typically from two-thirds of the signatory nations. However, some conventions are passed when they are signed by a number of contracting governments or signatory nations that represent a certain percentage of the fleet of vessels affected. Once an international convention enters into force, domestic legislation is needed for its enforcement. The process can at times appear to be painfully slow, although improved procedures have ensured that changes can now be enacted more quickly following specific incidents.

Major IMO conventions and codes applicable to LNG tankers

A detailed list of international conventions, codes, and regulations with which LNG tankers must comply is given at the end of this chapter. The following six have the most impact on the LNG shipping industry, although only the International Gas Carrier Code (IGC Code) is specific to LNG tankers:

- The International Convention for the Safety of Life at Sea (SOLAS Convention)
- The International Code for the Construction and Equipment of Ships Carrying Liquefied Gases in Bulk (IGC Code)
- The International Convention on Standards of Training, Certification, and Watchkeeping for Seafarers (STCW Convention)

- The Convention on the International Regulations for Preventing Collisions at Sea (COLREGs)
- The International Safety Management Code (ISM Code)
- The International Ship and Port Facility Security Code (ISPS Code)

The STCW and COLREGs are stand-alone conventions, while the IGC, ISM, and ISPS codes are all amendments to the SOLAS Convention. These are not the only regulations in existence, but they are indicative of the nature of international controls that have been placed on ship design, management, and operation.

SOLAS. The IMO's first achievement was the passage of a new version of the SOLAS convention. The initial SOLAS Convention dates back to 1914 in response to the sinking of the Titanic two years earlier, in 1912. This was an early example of the influence of public opinion in shaping international conventions. The loss of the Titanic resulted in the death of more than 1,500 people by drowning or freezing in the icy waters of the Atlantic. In light of this highly publicized disaster, maritime nations met and established SOLAS, a set of laws responding to safety concerns associated with the Titanic. SOLAS was brought under the auspices of the IMO in 1960 and has subsequently been revised several times.

The original set of SOLAS laws came into force as a direct result of a number of problems highlighted by the Titanic disaster. The shipbuilder had installed lifeboats for less than half the passengers. Once the ship began sinking, confusion reigned among the crewmembers as to how to lower the lifeboats. There was no loudspeaker system to notify all the passengers of the danger they faced, nor were the crew trained to evacuate passengers from the vessel. The Titanic was the first vessel to send out the newly introduced SOS distress signal; however, at that time vessels in the area were not required to monitor their radio receivers to pick up distress calls.

The initial SOLAS Convention addressed each of these concerns. Technological advances over the years took care of others. Ships now carry sufficient lifeboats and life rafts for all passengers and crew, and the crew must be trained and conduct drills covering a wide range of emergency situations. Lookouts must be posted at all times, and ships must continuously monitor radio frequencies dedicated to distress calls.

SOLAS also stipulated that passenger ships must be divided into watertight compartments so that the vessels remain afloat and stable, assuming a certain degree of damage to the ship's hull. This requirement has been extended to all types of ships, including LNG tankers, the design of which must ensure stability in normal and emergency conditions; this is known as intact stability and damage stability. Machinery such as steering gear and electrical installation are required to remain in service under stipulated emergency conditions. Other areas covered by SOLAS include fire protection, detection, and extinction; design of lifesaving appliances; and conditions associated with the carriage of dangerous goods.

Of particular significance to LNG tankers is Chapter V, Regulation 22 ("Navigation bridge visibility"). This sets requirements for achieving good visibility from the bridge of a ship, including specifications for the field of vision from various positions. The elevated level of LNG cargo tanks, especially Moss-type spherical tanks, together with their associated relief valve vent stacks and risers, poses a challenge to naval architects in complying with the visibility regulations. The situation is exacerbated where LNG ships are required to trade into ports having relatively low bridges spanning the access channel. To comply with SOLAS regulations and provide good visibility, the navigating bridge needs to be raised well above the cargo deck, but this can conflict with the air draft restrictions imposed by low bridges. The net result is that larger LNG ships designed to comply with SOLAS navigational safety regulations cannot access certain ports where channels are crossed by low bridges.

The actions required by signatories to the SOLAS Convention are not applicable only to ships that fly their flag or enter their ports. Governments are required to establish and maintain aids to navigation, such as lighthouses, buoys, and radio aids. They are also required to ensure that necessary arrangements are made for the rescue of persons in distress off their coasts. This requirement was supplemented in 1979 by the International Convention on Maritime Search and Rescue.

The IGC Code. Of the six IMO standards discussed here, the most specifically relevant to LNG ships is the IGC Code. It forms Chapter VII of the SOLAS Convention. The latest amendments are contained in the 1993 edition, which applies to ships, regardless of size (including those of less than 500 gross tons), that are engaged in the carriage of liquefied gases and certain other hazardous substances. The 1993 edition is applicable to all ships whose keels were laid on or after October 1, 1994. The earlier (1983) edition, named the Code for the Construction and Equipment of Ships Carrying Liquefied Gases in Bulk (not the IGC Code), applied to ships built on or after December 31, 1976. An even earlier version, called the Code for Existing Ships Carrying Liquefied Gases in Bulk (the 1976 edition), applied to ships constructed prior to December 31, 1976. This first edition of the code was in fact applied retroactively, many LNG ships having already been in regular service for more than 12 years when it was published.

The purpose of the IGC Code is to provide an international standard for the safe carriage of liquefied gases at sea by prescribing design and construction standards for ships and the equipment they carry, all aimed at minimizing the risk to the ship, to its crew, and to the environment. The Code, which takes into account present knowledge and technology, is under a constant state of review, and is supplemented by amendments incorporating latest experience and technological developments. The original 1976 code served to approve the LNG fleet as it existed at that time, rather than to require significant modifications to ships already in service. The fact that many of the ships that predated the 1976 Code remain in safe and reliable service some 30 years later is testament to the competence of those who designed and constructed the first-generation LNG tankers and to the appropriateness of the subsequent versions of the Code by which they have been maintained and updated.

The IGC Code prescribes the safe location of cargo tanks, survival standards under various conditions of damage and flooding, and requirements for ship stability and freeboard. It is especially concerned with the various cargo containment systems, the design of the tanks, their construction materials, welding, and testing. It establishes requirements for cargo tank pressure control and relief, environmental controls, instrumentation, and monitoring systems. Fire protection and extinction, personnel protection and operational procedures, and other special requirements are all comprehensively addressed.

Ships that comply with the requirements of the IGC Code are issued with an International Certificate of Fitness for the Carriage of Liquefied Gases in Bulk, commonly known by its abbreviated name, the Certificate of Fitness. The certificate is issued under the authority of the government of the ship's country of registry and is valid for a maximum period of five years. It is mandatory for a ship in service to undergo annual surveys and an intermediate survey, at which times the Certificate of Fitness must be endorsed to retain its validity. Renewal of the certificate requires a full survey of the ship, and this is usually performed to coincide with the ship's five-yearly special survey cycle. For an LNG tanker, a Certificate of Fitness issued under the IGC Code is the primary document attesting that the ship has been constructed and maintained to accepted international standards. Without a Certificate of Fitness, the ship cannot trade.

STCW Convention. The 1978 STCW Convention established minimum standards with regard to training, certification, and watchkeeping for seafarers on an international level. Prior to its implementation, each individual nation had its own set of standards, usually established without reference to the practices in other countries. As a result, standards and procedures varied widely. The original STCW Convention entered into force in 1984 and recognized that safety lies primarily with the crew, not just with the ship.

An unusual and significant feature of the STCW Convention is that it applies to ships of nations not party to the Convention when visiting ports of nations that are party to it. This ensures that ships of nonparty nations do not escape the control measures applied to ships that fly the flag of a party nation under the Convention. The potential difficulties that could arise for ships of a nonparty nation are among the reasons that the Convention has been so widely adopted. By December 2000, it had been adopted by nations representing more than 97.5% of the world's shipping tonnage.

The STCW Convention has individual chapters addressing the requirements for masters and the deck department, the engine department, the radio department, and special requirements for tankers. Within this latter chapter, there are special requirements for liquefied-gas tankers. These cover training related to the cargo and the cargo-handling equipment, as well as the requirement for officers to have completed an appropriate shore-based firefighting course and to have had a specific period of shipboard service or other approved familiarization commensurate with rank.

The STCW Convention was subjected to a major revision in 1995 (STCW 95). This revision incorporated many lessons learned as a consequence of the 1994 sinking of the Estonia in the Baltic Sea. More than 850 lives were lost when this trans-Baltic ferry sank after its bow doors failed during a storm. The amendments corrected weaknesses in the original Convention, particularly in ensuring proper training of crewmembers. The revised STCW Convention places greater obligations on shipping companies to demonstrate that seafarers are competent and qualified to carry out their assigned duties.

STCW 95 requires the following of every vessel-operating company:

- Each seafarer holds an appropriate certificate
- Ships are manned at safe levels
- Necessary documentation of seafarers is maintained and readily accessible
- Seafarers are properly trained to perform their specific duties
- Seafarers are trained to handle routine and emergency situations
- Communications are in a language that the crewmembers understand (this can be a problem on vessels where the officers and the crew are of different nationalities)
- Minimum rest periods are applied to ensure a safe and alert crew

A significant feature of the revised STCW Convention is the establishment of uniform standards of competence, minimum seagoing time, and experience for specified shipboard functions. This is now required for all types of vessels, not just for tankers. This brings the regulations for all vessel types into line with requirements that have applied to liquefied-gas tankers, including LNG tankers, since the 1978 introduction of the STCW Convention.

STCW 95 also recognizes the contribution of technical innovations such as simulators for training and assessment purposes. Ship-handling, cargo-handling, and engine room control simulators have all become important tools in the training of officers who serve on LNG tankers. Ship-maneuvering simulations are now an essential item in the submissions required by the U.S. Coast Guard in carrying out a waterway suitability assessment (WSA) for any new LNG project.

It has been estimated that some 80% of marine casualties are due in some part to human error. To quantify the application of STCW 95, as distinct from its adoption, in 2000 the IMO published a White List of countries deemed to be giving "full and complete effect" to the revised convention. The White List is a significant step forward in the global effort to rid the world of substandard ships and shipping and marks the first time that the IMO has given a seal of approval to countries that have properly implemented the provisions of an international convention. It also focused attention firmly on those nations not effectively applying the law to which they were a signatory.

In an ever-changing world, amendments to the STCW Convention in 2006 have added mandatory training and certification requirements for designated ship security officers. This is yet another regulatory measure of significance to LNG tankers, which have become a focus of attention as potential targets of terrorism.

COLREGs. This convention, introduced in 1972, was the first to recognize traffic separation schemes. The first such scheme was established in the Dover Strait in 1967 but was operated solely on a voluntary basis. With the introduction of COLREGs, the observance of traffic separation schemes became mandatory.

It is recognized that a high-energy collision, sufficient to affect the integrity of a cargo tank, would be a serious incident for an LNG ship. The risk of such an incident occurring in a port area is virtually eliminated by the strict safety zones applied around the ships and by the escort craft deployed ahead of their transits. However, observance of the COLREGs by all shipping is required to ensure safety of ships proceeding on passage at sea. Of special importance is Part B, Rule 10, which addresses the behavior of vessels in or near traffic separation schemes adopted as mandatory by the IMO. It is in these congested areas, often with local shipping operations involving cross-channel services at right angles to transiting international traffic, that the COLREGS have been effective in substantially reducing collision risk. To date, no LNG tanker has been involved in a collision sufficient to impair the integrity of its cargo containment system.

New LNG Tanker Construction Rules and Regulations

The following extract is adapted from a typical LNG tanker newbuilding technical specification, detailing all the relevant rules and regulations with which the design and construction of the ship must comply. The list covers construction requirements but not operational requirements. However, it illustrates how shipping in general—and LNG shipping in particular—is a highly regulated business.

Classification Society

The Vessel, including hull, machinery, equipment and outfittings, shall be constructed in accordance with the rules and regulations of the nominated Classification Society and under survey of the Society's surveyors.

Rules and regulations

The Vessel shall comply with the following rules, regulations and requirements of the regulatory authorities in force at the date of contract and in accordance with any rules and/or regulations officially ratified but not in effect at the date of contract provided they are scheduled to come into effect as compulsorily applicable for the Vessel prior to the delivery date and IMO amendments coming into effect and becoming compulsorily applicable to this type of Vessel:

- Maritime regulations of the registered country
- International Convention on Load Lines 1966, as modified by the 1988 Protocol, amendments up to and including the 2006 amendments and later amendments
- International Convention for Safety of Life at Sea (SOLAS) Consolidated 2004 and later amendments
- International Code for the Construction and Equipment of Ships Carrying Liquefied Gases in Bulk (IGC Code)
- International Convention for Prevention of Collision at Sea 1972 and later amendments, including IMO Resolution A.464 (XII)
- International Convention for Prevention of Pollution from Ships 1973 (Annex I, IV, V, and VI), as modified by the Protocol of 1978 relating thereto (MARPOL 73/78) and later amendments
- International Telecommunication Union radio regulations 2004 and SOLAS Chapter IV, as amended
- International Convention on Tonnage Measurement of Ships 1969, as amended by IMO Resolutions and later amendments
- IMO Resolution A.468 (XII): Code of noise levels on board ships

- U.S. Coast Guard rules for foreign-flag LNG tankers, for LNG ships operating in U.S. navigable waters and involves compliance with U.S. Coast Guard: Code of Federal Regulations 33 Parts 155, 156, 159, and 164, and Code of Federal Regulations 46 Part 154 excluding Alaskan waters and without Certificate or Inspection
- International Ship and Port Facility Security Code (ISPS Code), 2005
- OCIMF, Guidelines and Recommendations for the Safe Mooring of Large Ships at Piers and Sea Islands," 1994
- ICS, Guide to Helicopter/Ship Operations, 1989
- CAP 437 U.K. Civil Aviation Authority (if helideck fitted)
- SIGTTO, Guidelines for the Alleviation of Excessive Surge Pressures on ESD, 1987
- International Electro-technical Commission (IEC) Publication 60533: Electrical and electronic installations in ships—electromagnetic compatibility"
- ISO 4406:1999: Hydraulic fluid power—fluids—method for coding the level of contamination by solid particles"
- ISO 10816 Parts 1 and 3: Evaluation of machine vibration by measurements on non-rotating parts
- IMO Resolution A.272 (VIII) and A.330 (IX): Safe access to and working in large cargo tanks and ballast spaces"
- IMO: Code on alarms and indicators (1995)
- IMO Resolution A.601 (XV): Provision and display of manoeuvring information onboard ships
- IMO Resolution A.708 (XVII): Navigation bridge visibility and functions
- IMO Resolution A.751 (XVIII): Interim standards for ship manoeuvrability
- ISO 8861: Shipbuilding—engine room ventilation in diesel engine ships—design requirement and basis of calculation (1998(E))
- ISO 484-1: Ship screw propellers—manufacturing tolerances
- OCIMF, Guidelines on the Use of High-Modulus Synthetic Fibre Ropes as Mooring Lines on Large Tankers, 2002 (if fitted)
- Suez Canal navigation regulations and tonnage measurement of ships
- ILO Convention 92: Concerning crews' accommodation (1949)
- ILO Convention 133: Concerning crew accommodation on board ship (1970)
- OCIMF, Mooring Equipment Guidelines, 1997
- OCIMF, Recommendations on Equipment for the Towing of Disabled Tankers, 1981
- OCIMF/SIGTTO, Recommendations for Manifolds for Refrigerated Liquefied Natural Gas Carriers (LNG), 1994
- ICS/OCIMF/SIGTTO, Ship-to-Ship Transfer Guide (Liquefied Gases), 1995

- SIGTTO, Recommendations and Guidelines for Linked Ship/Shore Emergency Shutdown of Liquefied Gas Cargo Transfer, 1987
- SIGTTO, Recommendations for the Installation of Cargo Strainers on LNG Carriers. 1992
- IEC Publication 60092: Electrical installations in ships
- ISO 6954:1984: Guideline for the overall evaluation of vibration in merchant ships
- IMO Resolution MSC.137 (76): Standards for ship manoeuvrability
- OCIMF recommendations for the tagging/labelling, testing and maintenance, documentation/certification for ships' lifting equipment (May, 2005)

IMPORT-RELATED PROJECT SITING AND REGULATORY ISSUES 16

INTRODUCTION

Governments, energy consumers, and policy makers around the world do not question the need to secure access to reasonably priced, clean, and abundant supplies of energy—whether crude oil, natural gas, coal, nuclear, wind, solar power, or electricity produced from one of these sources. However, this does not necessarily mean that they embrace the infrastructure through which energy is delivered. Ideally, energy transportation and infrastructure should be "close, but not too close" to customers—that is, close enough so that transportation and distribution costs remain moderate, but not so close that it is on top of them. However, over the past few decades, what constitutes acceptable closeness has been evolving. Increasingly, local communities embrace the concept of "not in my backyard" (NIMBY).

When it comes to the siting and construction of unsightly and potentially hazardous energy-producing or delivery infrastructure, the policy dilemma is that the negative impacts from the infrastructure are felt most acutely by the host community while the benefits are spread over a much wider spectrum of the population. Opposition to these projects is increasingly the norm as opposed to the exception and is not simply limited to a few environmentally sensitive and wealthy areas such as Southern California. Cynics have observed that the NIMBY movement is evolving into a BANANA (build absolutely nothing anywhere near anyone) or even a

NOPE (nowhere on planet Earth) movement with regard to controversial infrastructure siting.

Even so, the public's attitude toward the construction of LNG import terminals in the vicinity of their communities is only one of the concerns that terminal sponsors must consider when scouting for locations. While it is difficult to build an LNG terminal in a designated location without the support of the local community, it is impossible to do so if the site does not have certain physical and economic characteristics. This narrows dramatically the list of suitable sites. The onus is on terminal developers to identify locations that have the appropriate physical characteristics, that are located in a high-value market (assuring the developer that a profit can be made through the sale of gas in the region), and perhaps most important, that minimize the opposition of local residents and municipal, state, and federal authorities.

LNG IMPORT TERMINAL DESIGN BASIS

Codes and regulations

Different countries have different standards and specifications that govern the design and construction of LNG facilities. Given the potential for a major incident arising from the improper handling and storage of large quantities of energy, government authorities in every LNG-importing country have enacted codes and regulations regarding the design, construction, and operation of LNG facilities and the tankers that serve them. Countries that are considering the introduction of LNG into their national energy mix usually borrow regulations from countries with established codes of practice. Such regulations include the following:

- In the United States, the major design and operating criteria are found in the National Fire Protection Association's (NFPA) "Standard for the Production, Storage, and Handling of LNG" (NFPA 59A) and "LNG Facilities: Federal Standards" (49 *Code of Federal Regulations*, part 193). In addition, the United States has codes governing the waterfront facilities and LNG tanker transits administered by the U.S. Coast Guard (33 *Code of Federal Regulations*, parts 127 and 165).
- In Japan, provisions for LNG facilities are detailed in the High Pressure Gas Control Act (HPGCA), the Gas Utility Industry Act (GUIA), and the Electricity Enterprises Act (EEA). The GUIA applies if the LNG facility is used only for the gas industry; the EEA is applicable if the

LNG facility is used only for the electric industry; and the HPGCA covers all cases that do not fall under the first two categories.[1]

- In Europe, the primary governing standard is EN 1473, "Installation and equipment for liquefied natural gas—design of onshore installations." EN 1473 covers many of the same aspects of LNG siting as NFPA 59A does in the United States. However, the European standards do not generally provide for prescriptive exclusion zones for public protection, but rather require that the developer undertake a site-specific hazard analysis in support of the final design and siting. Under the umbrella of EN 1473, individual countries may have their own additional codes and requirements.

Although host countries have unique siting and permitting regulations, they incorporate many common requirements. Each country mandates that LNG receiving terminals operate according to the highest safety, environmental, and security standards. A prospective site must meet or exceed these regulatory criteria while providing a technically and commercially viable location on which to construct an LNG import terminal. The focus of the regulatory review can also vary among jurisdictions. For example, in the United States, primary siting authority for interstate facilities (which covers all LNG import terminals) is vested in FERC to ensure uniform national siting standards. However, in the United Kingdom, the siting authority usually rests with local county council planning boards, which will consider the national or transnational siting standards and will also turn to other national agencies (e.g., the United Kingdom's Health and Safety Executive) for technical input.

Although host countries have unique siting and permitting regulations, they incorporate many common requirements. Each country mandates that LNG receiving terminals operate according to the highest safety, environmental, and security standards. A prospective site must meet or exceed these regulatory criteria while providing a technically and commercially viable location on which to construct an LNG import terminal.

Location, location, location

Sufficient available land—that can be used for industrial purposes and is close to a deepwater port that can accommodate LNG tankers—is an absolute prerequisite for short-listing a location for an LNG terminal. The site must be able to accommodate the planned LNG storage and sendout equipment (including future expansions) and have reasonably close access to the pipeline grid. Usually, LNG terminal developers identify multiple sites as potential locations and then enter into a process of elimination based on various criteria to determine the most suitable location. These criteria include the following:

Land area. LNG import facilities are composed of tanker berthing facilities, storage tanks, vaporization and sendout equipment, pipelines, and miscellaneous facilities (e.g., power generation and gas-metering equipment). Even though these installations take up a lot of space, it is difficult to pinpoint the minimum amount of land needed, because that will be contingent on several details, including the following:

- The number and size of the LNG storage tanks, the type of containment system, and the size of the resulting tank footprint
- The host country's thermal radiation and vapor dispersion exclusion zone requirements or other hazard assessment protocols
- The adjacent land uses

The terminal developer must also be able to identify and secure a corridor for the pipeline spur that connects the regasification facility to the regional pipeline grid.

Seismic. It is important to determine whether the site under consideration will be affected by seismic activity. In parts of the world—in particular, Japan—some existing terminals are located in earthquake-prone areas. The plant can be designed to counter the effect of seismic shocks or peak ground accelerations, although these adaptations can translate into expensive civil and structural designs requiring elaborate foundations under the critical equipment and tankage.

Safety. LNG is considered a hazardous material because of its cryogenic properties, dispersion qualities, and flammability.[2] According to a staff report by the California Energy Commission,

> The extreme cold of LNG can directly cause injury or damage. Although momentary contact on the skin can be harmless, extended contact will cause severe freeze burns. On contact with certain metals, such as ship decks, LNG can cause immediate cracking. Although not poisonous, exposure to the center of a vapor cloud could cause asphyxiation due to the absence of oxygen. LNG vapor clouds can ignite within the portion of the cloud where the concentration of natural gas is between a 5 and 15% (by volume) mixture with air. To catch fire, however, this portion of the vapor cloud must encounter an ignition source. Otherwise, the LNG vapor cloud will simply dissipate into the atmosphere.[3]

On the ocean, LNG disperses and evaporates at a much faster rate than on land, since water acts as a heat source for the liquefied gas, and a spill at sea cannot be contained. On land, terminals employ a series of impoundments and other designs to contain spills and limit their effects on other equipment—especially to reduce or eliminate the possibility that the spill effects will travel outside site boundaries. Spills on land evaporate much more slowly as heat transfer is inhibited by the freezing of the ground beneath the spill.

The design must ensure adequate distances between the following parts of an LNG terminal: the storage tanks, the berthing and unloading facilities, the vaporization process area, and the other parts of the facility. LNG facilities may be required to have a prescribed exclusion zone—that is, an area surrounding a facility in which an operator legally controls all activities. Exclusion zones ensure that public activities and structures outside the immediate LNG facility boundary are not at risk in the event of an LNG fire or the release of a cloud of flammable vapor.[4]

There are two types of exclusion zones: thermal-radiation protection (from LNG fires) and flammable vapor-dispersion protection (from LNG clouds that have not ignited but could migrate to an ignition source). Thermal-radiation exclusion distances vary by country. In the United States, they are determined by applying the NFPA standard for the production, storage, and handling of LNG and by using a computer model that accounts for facility-specific and site-specific factors, including wind speeds, ambient temperature, and relative humidity. The required distances ensure that heat from an LNG fire inside the storage tanks' bunds, for example, would not be severe enough at the property line to cause serious public injury. Computer models that consider average gas concentration in air, weather conditions, and terrain roughness are used to determine safe distances to ensure that vapors created by an LNG spill will be diluted below flammable levels before leaving the site.[5]

LNG import terminal developers always prepare an LNG spill prevention, containment, and countermeasure plan that describes spill prevention practices, spill-handling and emergency notification procedures, and staff-training requirements. All of a plant's safety and security manuals are submitted to the host country's energy regulatory authorities for review and comment before the relevant regulatory body gives permission for terminal construction to go ahead. Notably, the safety and security parameters of the terminal sponsor are likely to be even more stringent than those prescribed by energy regulatory bodies. No multinational or state-owned petroleum company or gas and power utility would be willing to risk its reputation or endanger life and property by designing a terminal with less than the highest safety and operating standards, in addition to the financial consequence of being held accountable in the event of an accident.

LNG receiving terminals have excellent safety records and consistently meet the stringent safety and environmental requirements that are imposed. However, as M.W. Kellogg noted in its feasibility study for a proposed LNG receiving terminal in Turkey, "One should not overlook the probability of opposition by local and national groups that may not fully understand the nature of the process."[6] Usually, LNG import terminal sponsors will consider possible objections from such groups and attempt to establish lines of communication with the local community and other interest groups very early in the development process, to demonstrate that the impact of the proposal on the local environment and community has been carefully considered. Without question, LNG safety is hard to explain to the public as it involves elaborate technical analysis and design; the opposition to LNG terminals is rarely concerned with factual discussion and can readily scare the local population with nightmarish scenarios of conflagration and destruction. A general distrust of government agencies and energy companies can make siting LNG facilities a challenging experience, notwithstanding the presence and enforcement of highly protective regulatory requirements.

Port access. To be considered for location of an LNG terminal, a prospective site must be near a deep shipping channel with a suitably sized turning basin. Because LNG tankers are very expensive to operate, the proposed location should be relatively unaffected by or protected from extreme weather conditions and severe oceanographic conditions that could delay tanker transit and unloading operations for more than a few days of each year.[7]

Although it is possible to dredge both the ship channel and the unloading berth, dredging can be extremely expensive and may add significantly to the project's construction costs. It can also be very difficult to find a nearby disposal site to dispose of the dredge spoils (particularly if it is contaminated with toxic material). The environmental aspects of dredging can raise issues during the permitting process. Other environmental considerations include air quality (from gas-fired vaporizer and tugboat and LNG tanker emissions), water quality (from ORV discharges and ship and tugboat operations), and the environmental impacts associated with the construction of the pipelines connecting the terminal to the transmission grid.

REGULATORY ISSUES

Terminal-licensing procedures

The first step taken by a company planning an LNG import terminal at a designated location is to sign a basic engineering and design contract and employ an environmental consultant. The contractors will work with the developer to determine whether the designated site is suitable, by conducting technical and environmental assessments of the site and by comparing and contrasting it with other nearby locations. After a site is chosen, a contractor will determine the extent of the civil work required in order to prepare the site and prepare preliminary designs of the terminal's berthing, storage, and regasification facilities. The developer will also design the pipeline that connects the terminal to the gas grid, assessing alternative routes from an environmental and safety perspective, unless arrangements are made with the grid operator to perform this work. At this point, the import terminal sponsor will generally also have opened an informal dialogue with the regulatory agencies.

The developer will usually establish a line of communication with local political officials to address and allay their concerns as early as possible. In addition, the developer will initiate contact with other interested political, community, and/or environmental advocacy groups. Organized interest groups often view an LNG import terminal in their community as inimical to the interests of the local population. If they feel that their concerns are not being adequately addressed by the company and local elected political officials, a project could easily be derailed.

Once the design scope and environmental assessments are in hand, the developer usually submits an application to the national energy regulatory body or appropriate government entity for a license to build the terminal. This application will provide a detailed description of the project, including its safety and security features and its environmental impacts, especially effects on water use and quality, air quality, vegetation and wildlife, cultural resources, geological resources, soils, land use, recreation, aesthetics, and noise. This assessment will also look at the impacts associated with the terminal's construction activities. It may discuss alternatives, including alternative means of supplying gas, alternative sites considered and the reason for choosing the specific site, alternative layout considerations within the chosen site, and alternative pipeline routes. The regulatory authority generally takes an applicant's environmental report as the starting point for preparing the government's own environmental review. The relevant national regulatory body will solicit additional information and/or clarification from the applicant as needed, and will accept public comments on the application.

Provided that all the safety, security, and environmental criteria of the host country are met, the energy regulator will usually issue a final authorization approving the construction of the project. This authorization will generally incorporate conditions with which the developer must comply during both the construction and the operational phase of the project. The authorization for the 1.5 Bcf/d (15.5 Bcm/y) Cameron LNG terminal in Hackberry, Louisiana, required that Cameron LNG meet over 50 conditions, covering design, construction, other permits, and so forth; these conditions have to be satisfied before the terminal was permitted to begin construction and start operations. Particular concerns included the proposed location of the terminal, dredge disposal arrangements, and LNG storage and containment provisions and the attendant thermal-radiation and vapor-dispersion exclusion zone calculations. These authorizations can also be the subject of legal challenges by aggrieved parties; once seen as limited to the United States alone, such legal challenges are spreading rapidly to other host countries, notably the United Kingdom and Italy.

Terminal access

Historically, LNG import terminal sponsors had proprietary access to the receiving facilities that they built. Proprietary access to LNG receiving terminals was—and in many cases still is—considered to be essential by participants in the LNG chain, who are understandably reluctant to sign a 20-year take-or-pay LNG purchase contract with an LNG importer without a guaranteed market outlet. Traditionally, Asian city gas and power utility companies, either publicly owned (e.g., Taipower in Taiwan) or privately owned (all utilities in Japan), built LNG terminals to ensure a steady supply of gas to their own customers.

Proprietary access to LNG receiving terminals also has been one of the underpinnings for financing the entire project. As described in chapter 2, the regulatory bargain granted proprietary or monopolistic rights to a utility in exchange for being subject to government regulation of the prices or tariffs charged to customers, including the profits that the utility could earn from the infrastructure it developed. In this scheme, the need for nonproprietary access was unclear.

The opening of gas and power markets to competition is effecting dramatic changes in LNG import terminal access in Europe and North America—and even in the more conservative Asian markets. Pipeline gas and LNG imports are no longer the sole province of the state gas and power monopolies. Other firms are claiming the right to import gas and/or generate electricity for sale into the market, rather than purchasing gas or power from a state monopoly. In Korea and Spain, private companies are building their own terminals to secure the gas supplies that they need. These companies generally have the blessings of their host governments, which are anxious to promote the private construction of gas delivery infrastructure to meet burgeoning gas demand forecasts.

One of the drivers for the development of offshore terminals was that they avoided many of the more controversial aspects of onshore facilities, especially when it comes to overcoming the concerns about safety and security that factor heavily into onshore terminal siting.

Nevertheless, market liberalization is a double-edged sword for LNG import terminal sponsors. Gas market liberalization is generally characterized by the requirement that transmission—and often distribution—pipeline operators offer open access or third-party access on a nondiscriminatory basis to any qualified participant, often under terms and conditions, including prices, regulated by the government. While host governments appreciate the need for new LNG import infrastructure, they are also becoming aware that few companies will bear the risk of investing in a liberalizing gas market and invest the vast sums of money needed to build an LNG import terminal unless they are guaranteed some access to the facility or they are allowed to charge access fees that reflect the risks they have taken. Some companies will not consider going through the laborious process of siting and licensing a receiving facility and spending hundreds of millions of dollars to build it if they are required by regulations to permit other companies—in many cases, their competitors—to use it. Other terminal developers have positioned themselves as infrastructure operators, willing to build terminals for third parties on the premise that the terms of access can be freely negotiated and allow the developer to profit from his or her efforts.

To that end, governments and regulatory bodies worldwide are looking for ways to create a regulatory climate that is not only conducive to the construction of new LNG terminals but also respectful of the spirit of gas market competition. In Europe, for example, some governments appear amenable to the idea of an import terminal sponsor's using most of its terminal capacity on a proprietary basis. However, the remainder must be made available to third parties on a nondiscriminatory basis.[8] Other European governments have granted exceptions to third-party access on a use-it-or-lose-it basis; the terminal operator can use the terminal for its exclusive importation, but if the terminal capacity is not fully utilized, the regulator reserves the right to revisit the terms and conditions of the authorization and may require the granting of third-party access, as has happened in the United Kingdom. The United States has a stronger history of ensuring third-party access to LNG receiving infrastructure but also needs additional sources of gas to meet soaring demand. In 2002, FERC exempted LNG terminal sponsors from having to provide open-access service. In addition, the U.S. Congress passed legislation in 2002 that granted owners of *offshore* LNG import terminals exclusive access to their facilities. The onshore terminal open-access exemption was codified in the U.S. Energy Policy Act of 2005.

Offshore terminals

One of the drivers for the development of offshore terminals was that they avoided many of the more controversial aspects of onshore facilities, especially when it comes to overcoming the concerns about safety and security that factor heavily into onshore terminal siting. However, while these concerns may be lessened, they are not ignored by the relevant agencies. Most offshore terminal proposals are subject to rigorous safety reviews, although the approach used is more akin to that applied to other offshore energy infrastructure, such as producing platforms, as opposed to onshore terminals. Public concerns are not always assuaged by offshore siting. The U.S. Coast Guard has indicated that it will subject the Broadwater Energy offshore terminal (a permanent floating terminal) in Long Island Sound to safety and security measures similar to those applied to LNG tankers transiting to onshore terminals—in some measure responding to strong local opposition, even though the terminal is nine miles from the nearest land.

Offshore terminals also may incorporate novel technologies, including ship-to-ship or similar cargo transfer methods, that require separate certification and approval before they can be deployed. In contrast, onshore terminals tend to use relatively well-developed technologies that do not require additional certification.

Finally, offshore terminals face unique environmental issues that do not apply to onshore terminals. Offshore pipelines, connecting the terminals to the mainland, raise their own sets of concerns and issues that must be addressed. The selection of vaporization technology has proven controversial, even in the normally industry-friendly Gulf of Mexico state authorities have threatened to veto projects that use ORVs because of potential impacts on local fisheries, thereby forcing a move to gas-fired vaporizers and consequently undermining the projects' economics.

NOTES

[1] There are several cases in which the GUIA applies even though LNG is used both as a residential and as a public utility fuel source for electric power generation. In addition, requirements in the Factory Location Act and the Petroleum Industry Complex Casualty Prevention Act are enforced for all LNG plants and facilities. The Labor Safety and Health Law (for boiler, pressure vessels, etc.) and the Fire Prevention Law (for facilities handling hazardous materials, e.g., petroleum) are also enforced to ensure the safety of all LNG facilities. The Japan Gas Association (Standards for Safety of Facilities and Recommended Practice for LNG Inground Storage), Japanese Industrial Standards, Japanese Petroleum Institute, and Steel Structure Calculation Standards are also specific codes and standards that supplement these laws.

[2] California Energy Commission. 2003. Liquefied natural gas in California: History, risks, and siting. Staff paper, p. 2.

[3] Ibid.

[4] Ibid.

[5] Even if an LNG storage tank is breached, this does not automatically mean that a fire will result. This can happen only when the concentration of LNG in the atmosphere is between 5% and 15% and there is a source of ignition to light the vapor cloud.

[6] M.W. Kellogg. 1993. BOTAS *Petroleum Pipeline Corporation* New LNG *Receiving Terminal Study*. Volume 1, p. 82.

[7] Ibid., p. 84.

[8] See, e.g., BG Group and Enel become partners in Brindisi LNG. 2003. BG press release, June 24. BG Group and Enel will share 80% reserved capacity in their 6 MMt/y receiving terminal at Brindisi, located in southeastern Italy. The remaining 20% will be subject to regulated third-party access by Italian energy authorities. (In June 2005, BG announced that it had bought out Enel's share of the Brindisi LNG project.)

LNG IMPORT TERMINAL USE AGREEMENTS 17

INTRODUCTION

With third-party terminaling services increasingly prevalent in the LNG industry as a result of open-access policies and other regulatory changes, the terms and conditions covering these services are becoming incorporated into agreements between the terminal owner (operator) and each company seeking to contract for throughput capacity in these terminals. Many LNG suppliers such as Shell, Total, and ConocoPhillips have elected to contract for terminal capacity with third-party operators. By joining an LNG terminal project with other suppliers, they hope to gain economies of scale from larger terminals while also building a more diversified market portfolio. Some suppliers, notably Qatar Petroleum and ExxonMobil, have chosen to develop entirely proprietary terminals to maintain schedule and cost control for the downstream aspects of their Qatari mega-trains.

These arrangements fall into two general categories. In the first case, where access is required by regulatory agencies (regulated third-party access), the access terms and conditions are usually spelled out in tariffs approved by the relevant regulatory authority (they may be subject to comment and challenge by interested parties) and are then published by the terminal operator for the use of prospective customers.

In the second case, the terminal is operated on a proprietary basis, and the terms and conditions are covered by either a terminal use agreement (TUA) or a terminaling service agreement (TSA). (There is no discernible difference between a TUA and a TSA.) Such agreements are negotiated between the terminal operator and each customer (capacity user), and their terms are not usually subject to regulatory oversight.

The following discussion summarizes the key considerations in these agreements. Note that while there is operational precedent for regulated access, mainly in the United States, there is very little for proprietary access. The U.S. experience came about as a result of the failed utility model of the legacy LNG terminals, where requiring the operator to offer open access as a condition of reopening these terminals did not threaten any underlying throughput rights and was consistent with the conditions being imposed on the gas pipeline business. Proprietary access came later in the regulatory scheme and was applied initially only to new terminals, then subsequently to expansions of existing terminals. Given this limited history, the ultimate durability of these agreements cannot be judged in the same context as other agreements in the industry, already operational over longer periods of time.

REGULATED ACCESS

In many respects, the tariffs governing third-party access at LNG import terminals are modeled on those employed by gas transmission companies and adapted for the unique attributes of LNG. Usually, the tariffs are designed to apply to throughput rights at the terminals, although in one notable case, the Lake Charles (Louisiana) terminal, the tariff is based on storage rights, creating some complexities in tariff design and operation.

Many of the tariff provisions cover the same aspects of the LNG trade that are covered in SPAs, and often they mirror standard SPA terms and conditions—especially in technical areas, such as LNG measurement practices. The tariff provisions will cover elements such as quantity entitlements (annual and daily); fees (or rates), including the retention of LNG for vaporizer fuel; marine transportation and terminal technical specifications; scheduling, receipt, and measurement of the LNG; quality of LNG and vapor; delivery and measurement of the vapor downstream of the terminal; force majeure; payment terms; liabilities and insurance; governing law; and dispute resolution. The tariffs are usually accessible either through the Web site of the terminal operators or through the regulatory bodies. The tariffs for the Cove Point (Maryland), Elba Island (Georgia), and Lake Charles terminals are available on the FERC Web site, as well as on the operators' Web sites. The same is generally true for the European terminals with open access, including the Fluxys (Zeebrugge, Belgium), National Grid (Grain LNG, England), and Enagás terminals. Rather than summarizing the terms of these agreements here, we encourage the reader to review these documents in their entirety.

More important than the tariff details are the ways in which the tariffs operate and their implications for the LNG business from a commercial perspective. A brief historical review may assist in understanding the evolution of these tariffs. The first issue to consider is the process of firm capacity allocation. In the case of the U.S. terminals (except Everett [Massachusetts]), all of which had been effectively shut down during most of the 1980s and into the '90s, there were no existing customers, suppliers, or users who were adversely affected by the requirement for open access. The following description provides a generic overview of the typical process by which open access was established in U.S. terminals.

Even if the operator would have preferred an alternative business model, open access was a condition to receive regulatory approval to reopen the terminal. The operator filed the proposed tariff terms and conditions with FERC and posted informational notices advising interested parties that the operator was going to conduct an open-season, or a regulated auction through which firm capacity would be awarded. The potential bidders could comment on and seek changes to the tariff on file with the regulators or include such proposed changes as part of their bid submission. Unlike most auctions, however, FERC regulated the maximum rate that the operator could charge for capacity, using classical rate-making procedures, with full cost recovery and a return on investment component. These rates are usually structured as a monthly demand charge per unit of capacity and a small commodity charge per unit of throughput to recover variable costs. Because these terminals had been effectively carried by charges passed through to the downstream customers, even though no LNG had flowed, the rate bases had declined to low levels, and the effective rates were quite low—less than \$0.30/MMBtu plus fuel.

In the bidding process, the regulated tariff set a ceiling on the maximum rate that the bidder could pay (although there was no minimum bid except for the recovery of variable costs). The maximum term was also set out in the bid documents prepared by the operator, but the bidders could propose a shorter term. On the capacity side, the bidders could bid up to the full offered capacity of the terminal. Bids were submitted and then were ranked on a net present value (NPV) basis, with the highest value going to the bidder(s) who bid the maximum rate and the maximum term (i.e., whose bid yielded the highest NPV). If more than one bidder bid the maximum and the aggregate capacity bids exceeded the capacity offered, the bidders were allocated the available capacity on a pro rata basis. The result of this process was that Elba Island and Cove Point, with low maximum rates and access to more attractive markets than the U.S. Gulf Coast, attracted multiple bidders and, through the capacity award process, now have multiple firm customers.

While the tariff terms and conditions would not usually pose a problem if the terminal's entire capacity was awarded to a single bidder (as was the case with BG at Lake Charles), matters become and remain much more complex when there are multiple firm customers. LNG terminals rarely have sufficient storage capacity to offer multiple customers dedicated storage rights (and in any event, the terminal operator is marketing throughput, not storage); therefore, the terminaling activity inevitably involves the commingling of LNG from the individual customers' cargoes and their natural gas sendout. LNG cargoes arrive in discrete lumps, but the sendout is ideally made at a reasonably even rate between cargo deliveries (and this is one reason why the attempt to apply pipeline standards to LNG terminals can be fraught with difficulties). Inevitably, this structure results in LNG inventories being effectively swapped and loaned among the customers (whether through operation of the tariff or as a result of agreements between the customers) as the cargoes delivered by each capacity holder are scheduled according to the terms of the various SPAs. When the LNG delivered by one or more of the customers requires Btu stabilization treatment before it is delivered to the downstream pipelines, the issue of who pays for the stabilization costs of the blended product adds further complexity.

In addition to having tariffs covering firm capacity, the U.S. terminal operators are required to post terms and conditions for interruptible terminal capacity, with maximum rates equal to the firm rates calculated at 100% load factors. Usually, the terms of the tariff provide for revenues received from interruptible terminaling services to be largely credited back to the firm customers. This ensures that the operator does not make an excessive return on investment but provides, at best, only a modest incentive to offer these services. Once interruptible cargo deliveries are factored into the equation, capacity scheduling becomes even more complex. This explains why so few (if any) interruptible LNG terminaling transactions have ever taken place. Rarely do the original tariffs filed by the

In addition to having tariffs covering firm capacity, the U.S. terminal operators are required to post terms and conditions for interruptible terminal capacity, with maximum rates equal to the firm rates calculated at 100% load factors.

operator take these considerations into account, and the operator is under no obligation to modify the tariffs to accommodate such concerns.

These factors generally result in significant efforts being expended after the open season to clarify the rights and obligations of the parties among one another and the operator, especially in the areas of cargo delivery scheduling and downstream pipeline nominations and sendout. When allowance has to be made for force majeure events, such as bad weather that delays vessel arrival and unloading, the scheduling process takes on even more commercial implications through the knock-on effects of scheduling delays on ship demurrage or the risk that take-or-pay claims will be asserted against the customers.

Consequently, customers may have to negotiate operational agreements among themselves to manage these issues. The terms of these agreements are often unknown at the outset, although the customers are under a long-term firm obligation to make the capacity payments even if the effective capacity is degraded by poorly designed tariff provisions.

The tariff rates themselves are subject to change under the guidelines of the regulatory regime, although the operator's right to file for tariff changes may be limited by agreements reached with the customers with regard to rate freezes or caps established as part of the initial service offering. Since the operator is permitted to recover a just and reasonable (in U.S. regulatory parlance) return on his investment, any increases in costs, new capital expenditures, or under-recovered prior costs or investments can be recouped through future rate cases in which the operator seeks approval from the regulators to increase the rates charged for the service. The operator may seek to alter other terms and conditions of service, and even if opposed by the customers, these changes may be accepted by the regulators.

Other features of the open-access regime as practiced in the United States are less than appealing. For example, unused capacity may not be freely released or assigned to third parties by the customers on a short- or long-term basis, but may have to be offered through a public bidding process designed to preserve the principles of nondiscriminatory open access. At the end of the primary term of the agreement, the capacity holder may have the right of first refusal on continuing the agreement but at terms that might not be as favorable as could have been negotiated privately.

In the United States, the open-access regime applied to LNG terminals has resulted in at least three undesirable features: uncertainty over the reliability of capacity rights in multi-customer terminals, rate uncertainty, and obstacles to trading or assigning capacity to third parties. As discussed previously, LNG suppliers are most interested in the security of their downstream arrangements to protect the upstream investments, and open access did not achieve this end. Other regulatory regimes that have adopted open access have followed many of the principles applied in the United States but have moved more carefully given the need to protect the rights of the incumbent capacity holders who had largely enjoyed the unfettered use of the terminals prior to the adoption of open access principles.

Proprietary access

Given the potential problems associated with open access, it is not surprising that prospective LNG suppliers began pressing regulators for different approaches to the regulation of terminaling services. The first break occurred in the United States in 2002 with the passage of an amendment to the Deepwater Port Act, which extended that legislation to cover gas in addition to oil ports located offshore beyond state waters (generally three miles or more). Since the Deepwater Port Act already allowed for proprietary access to oil ports (of which, to date, the Louisiana Offshore Oil Port [LOOP] is the only one), the same rights were automatically extended to offshore LNG terminals.

At the same time, Dynegy was developing a new LNG terminal, the Hackberry Terminal, now Cameron LNG, in Cameron Parish, Louisiana, and had requested that FERC waive its open-access rules and permit Dynegy to negotiate terms and conditions of access with interested parties. While FERC did not accept Dynegy's arguments in favor of the open access waiver, it did issue an authorization in the Hackberry decision allowing Dynegy the right to develop a proprietary-access business model and indicated that it would permit other terminal developers to pursue the same approach, while retaining the right to reassert jurisdiction if proprietary access was later found not to be in the public interest. FERC's justification of this decision was that LNG import terminals serve much the same purpose as large gas-producing fields and could therefore be allowed to compete freely in the market. Cynics might note that agencies, like commercial companies, hate to lose market share, and no doubt FERC noted the rush of announcements of offshore terminals following the amendment of the Deepwater Port Act—terminals that were outside FERC's jurisdiction. The Hackberry decision was further reinforced by provisions in the Energy Policy Act of 2005, permitting onshore terminals to retain proprietary access for a period of at least 15 years. FERC subsequently permitted the Hackberry approach to be applied to expansions of the three existing open-access terminals, provided that these expansions did not adversely affect the rights of the customers who had signed up earlier for open-access capacity. In Europe, as noted previously, the United Kingdom adopted a similar approach as in the United States, although the final decision rests with EU regulators in Brussels, who have so far consented to the terms approved by national regulators. Variations on this theme have also been adopted in Italy and Spain.

With the advent of proprietary access, there is also a need for the development of appropriate agreements under which the operator will offer capacity to third parties. It may not be necessary to have such agreements between the operator and the capacity holder when the terminal is developed as a de facto extension of an integrated project's upstream development, as in the case of South Hook in Wales, where the operator and customer are essentially the same entity. However, other considerations may argue in favor of the development of such a formal agreement between affiliated but legally independent operators and customers—to manage, for example, tax or other legal liability exposures in the host country of the terminal.

In many respects, TUAs will contain terms and conditions that are very similar to those found in tariff structures. Common terms generally include LNG and gas quality specifications, LNG and gas measurement, downstream nominations and dispatch (since these are generally governed by national standards, e.g., the North American Energy Standards Board (NAESB) in the United States and the Network Code in the United Kingdom), technical specifications of the terminal and the LNG tankers, governing laws, and dispute resolution. However, when addressing commercial terms, the agreements can often vary significantly from the practices seen in tariffs. The discussion that follows focuses on U.S. terminals, since some of these agreements are in the public domain, which is not the case in Europe.

The fee for service is a key consideration in the agreement. Generally, this negotiated rate will be high enough to allow the operator a financial return above that which could be earned in the regulated environment. (Sempra Energy has declared that it is seeking rates that would allow it to earn 14% after-tax returns on its investment, well above regulated returns, which tend to be closer to 9%–10%.) The fee is usually fixed for the duration of the agreement's primary term (generally 20 years), but there may be provisions to adjust the fee to recover new investment obligations of the operator as a result of subsequent regulatory requirements, to cover new or increased taxes, or possibly to provide adjustments for increases in construction costs of the facility that are beyond the operator's control. The fee may contain components that track operating expenses and that are adjusted for general inflation or actual expense pass-through. It will also provide for vaporizer fuel retention by the operator. The fees are generally collected in advance and are subject to few, if any reductions, even if the terminal is unavailable

It is in the allocation of spare capacity that matters become more interesting. Free of regulatory prescriptions that can limit the operator's commercial interest in providing the service, the potential value associated with spare unloading capacity in the form of incremental cargo slots can become a major point of negotiation.

for force majeure reasons. In this respect, the fees for service are very similar to the payments made to a shipowner under a charterparty. However, in the case of extended force majeure affecting the terminal, the customer is often given the right to terminate the agreement. In this way, the customer has secured rate (and cost) certainty, which also benefits the operator, who is probably using the payment stream from the customers to secure highly leveraged project financing for the terminal. Lenders are as fond of commercial certainty as customers are.

In the area of scheduling cargo deliveries, the key provisions of TUAs generally mirror those found in tariffs. Cargo-scheduling provisions can be tailored to match (or align closely with) the terms of the LNG SPAs. However, capacity allocation and scheduling among multiple customers becomes more involved, and often the TUA will anticipate the creation of a separate agreement, sometimes called an operation and cooperation agreement (OCA), or another similar coordination mechanism. The OCA is negotiated among the customers, and the operator may or may not be a party to it. Tariffs in open access terminals rarely stipulate such an arrangement, and although they may not expressly prohibit it, the regulators may be skeptical as to whether such arrangements among the incumbent customers will act as a barrier to access by other parties.

It is in the allocation of spare capacity that matters become more interesting. Free of regulatory prescriptions that can limit the operator's commercial interest in providing the service, the potential value associated with spare unloading capacity in the form of incremental cargo slots can become a major point of negotiation. Does the operator retain the unilateral right to sell such slots when they become available? Do the customers have any special or priority rights to these slots—and if so, at what price: the contract rate or a rate negotiated at the time? Do the customers see any financial benefit from the operator's sale of this capacity? How do the rights of a spot or short-term customer affect those of the long-term customers? Can customers freely assign or sell slots to third parties?

With regard to sendout capacity, again the TUA can afford the parties more flexible terms than usual open-access provisions. Most terminals have spare vaporization capacity, which can be made available to customers so that they can use it to vary their throughput rates over short or long periods; alternatively, spare vaporization capacity can be made available to customers or third parties in conjunction with the delivery of extra cargoes, above the aggregate ACQs. Again the issue of rates arises. Does the customer pay an extra charge for the right to utilize vaporization above his daily maximum sendout rate?

Another area fraught with complexity is the balancing of customers' unloading and sendout rates. Clearly, the sendout rate must be balanced in some fashion with the unloading rates, as the terminal will not have unlimited or dedicated storage for each customer. Does the operator impose mandatory borrowing and lending in the TUA with commingled LNG in the tanks, or do the customers negotiate among themselves, through an OCA? What rights accrue to a third party who has acquired spot or short-term unloading slots? How do these spot deliveries affect the sendout rights of the firm long-term customers?

Another advantage of negotiated access is that it avoids the regulatory requirement of mandatory capacity release postings, and the customers can generally sell their slots to third parties on negotiated terms. Extension of the TUA beyond the primary term is also a subject of negotiation, without regard to regulatory policy, which generally imposes conditions on such extensions for open access terminals.

TUAs can provide more flexible approaches to Btu stabilization, through either the stripping of LPG or the injection of nitrogen to meet individual customer requirements, rather than being limited to uniform conditions often required under nondiscrimination provisions of open-access tariffs. Other additional terms that would normally not appear in a tariff can be incorporated into a TUA. An example is the development of a port liability agreement, addressing the respective liabilities of the terminal operator and the LNG tanker operator during shipping operations. These agreements are common in the Far East but are not normally part of a tariff since the LNG tanker operator is not a party to the terminal throughput service covered in the tariff.

Other provisions that are not usually present in tariffs may be found in TUAs. Since TUAs are normally formed in the context of developing new capacity (either by the construction of a new terminal or by the expansion of an existing one), a TUA may provide for a process of coordinating the construction and start-up schedules of the terminal with those of the upstream facilities (again, assuming that there are specific upstream projects dedicated to specific downstream terminals). The customers may gain rights to inspect the terminal plans and construction and may comment on or otherwise influence the terminal's design and operations. TUAs may provide for the removal and replacement of the terminal operator if the operator's performance is repeatedly substandard and for the payment of damages when the operator fails to meet specific performance measures, resulting in losses to the customers. Such provisions are rarely if ever found in tariffs. It is also generally easier to incorporate termination provisions in TUAs than in tariffs, providing more clarity to the parties should serious problems arise.

Since terminals can be expanded readily and generally inexpensively (at least compared to their initial cost), the rights and obligations of the parties to an expansion may be spelled out in a TUA. Do the existing customers have any rights over future expansion capacity, or can this be freely sold to third parties by the operator? How do parties to an expansion interact commercially and legally with the initial customers? In this general context, it is also important to understand whether the operator intends to enter the LNG-importing business and how any conflicts between the operator's and customers' commercial interests will be resolved. While the TUA may be silent on these issues, this should be viewed as a reflection of the parties' intentions and not as a result of ignoring these aspects of the agreement.

A final consideration in the multi-customer negotiated TUA should be whether and to what extent the individual TUAs with each customer need to contain identical terms and conditions. A clear advantage of the TUA approach is that the TUA can be more closely matched with the upstream agreements, but most customers have different upstream agreements with different supply projects that they are trying to optimize in the downstream market. The development of a common TUA for all customers will almost certainly require compromises between the customers; tailored TUAs for each customer may lead to coordination problems down the road while the terminal is in operation. There may be even more critical issues in designing these agreements to address problems which could arise for project start-ups in the present atmosphere of delayed upstream projects and an apparent overbuilding of U.S. LNG terminal capacity.

Terminaling agreements are an emerging and evolving area for the LNG industry. There is certainly experience with the regulated open-access model; however, negotiated proprietary-access agreements, especially those that involve multiple customers, have yet to be operationally tested, let alone stressed. However, proprietary access appears to be the way of the future. LNG buyers and sellers, at least in the Atlantic Basin, have yet one more set of commercial considerations and negotiations to consider as they put together their LNG projects.

CONCLUSION: THE FUTURE OF LNG 18

INTRODUCTION

LNG is moving rapidly from the fuel of the future to the fuel of the present, with a dramatic upsurge now under way in every aspect of the industry. At the same time, the historically cozy LNG club is being shaken by shifting global demand and supply patterns, sharp upswings in energy prices, and an onslaught of new entrants and changing business models. Many of these trends and issues have been covered in some detail in this book. As we look to the future, we feel it is appropriate to summarize our views as to where these trends may lead us.

GLOBAL DEMAND AND SUPPLY

The world's appetite for hydrocarbon fuels continues to grow as the global economy expands. While the relative market shares of the various primary energies may shift, these changes will, in the absence of a major recession, take place over very long time horizons, as a result of earlier market and supply choices. Natural gas demand is steadily increasing, with the rate of growth being a function of the price of natural gas relative to competing fuels. Concerns over global warming will certainly influence the future consumption of hydrocarbon fuels, but natural gas, with its more benign environmental characteristics (compared to coal or even oil) will be favored over its competitors. While an ideal world might be one in which energy consumption begins to decline, it is unclear how this could be achieved given continuing global economic growth, especially in developing countries, which are less likely to favor conservation as an energy policy alternative. Even when alternative energy is considered, natural gas once again plays a prominent role. At present, hydrogen is produced largely from natural gas, given the chemistry of the methane molecule. The increased demand for ethanol for vehicle fuel requires the expansion of corn production, in turn requiring greater use of fertilizer, for which natural gas is the primary feedstock. Given these and many other factors, there seems to be little debate whether natural gas demand will increase for the foreseeable future, with only the locus of demand and the rate of increase remaining arguable.

As the production of natural gas in the major consuming regions falls further short of local demand, the uneven distribution of the world's natural gas resources will ensure that LNG demand will grow even faster than the total gas market. Yet the way ahead for expanded LNG supply is not devoid of problems. New LNG supply projects have, in many recent cases, experienced significant cost increases, schedule delays, or both. Resurgent resource nationalism, spurred by sharp increases in oil and gas prices, has led host countries, including Russia and Algeria, to reassert greater control over their oil and gas reserves and pull back from some of their more ambitious development plans or create uncertainty regarding projects already under way. With higher energy prices, resource conservation takes a higher priority for these countries, which cannot readily absorb the inflow of more foreign currency and lack the management ability to undertake many new energy development projects. For many producing countries, preserving oil and gas for future generations becomes an affordable option.

This tension between growing demand and supply uncertainty will likely characterize the next decade of the LNG industry. Moreover, the recent shift from a buyer's to a seller's market is not likely to be reversed for some time.

TECHNICAL OUTLOOK

One relative constant of the LNG industry is the technology itself. The early decades were characterized by a strong focus on technical excellence and project reliability and safety, recognizing the unique aspects (especially the very high capital investments) of the industry itself. It was an industry largely focused on engineering and construction (or, in the words of the late Malcolm Peebles, "plumbing"), enabling the facilities to achieve extraordinary levels of safety, reliability, and longevity. In this regard, the industry succeeded beyond its wildest dreams.

> **This tension between growing demand and supply uncertainty will likely characterize the next decade of the LNG industry. Moreover, the recent shift from a buyer's to a seller's market is not likely to be reversed for some time.**

Technical innovation has not halted. LNG train sizes continue to grow, and LNG tankers are becoming ever larger, producing economies of scale and lowering LNG supply costs. The LNG shipping industry is adopting slow-speed diesel and dual-fuel diesel/electric engines, but these propulsion systems are already found in many other merchant ships. The result is that LNG is more cost and price competitive and can reach more markets than was possible a decade ago. Still, the underlying facility designs have not changed in any fundamental way, and there is no evidence that the industry will witness anything other than continuing incremental technical improvements.

The major technical challenges are likely to arise around the development of offshore technology for both export and import facilities. The higher costs of offshore development appear to constitute a major obstacle, but niche opportunities, as seen in some of the more flexible designs (e.g., Excelerate), may prompt further development where market size and siting issues make onshore terminals uneconomical or infeasible. Yet even here, it is difficult to classify the offshore efforts as technically innovative, as again they generally represent extensions of existing energy technology to LNG applications.

COMMERCIAL TRENDS

This base of technical stability has afforded the industry the opportunity to evolve and innovate, straining the very conservative links of the LNG chain. Increasing volumes of LNG will move under short-term or spot contracts. LNG sales contracts will increasingly incorporate terms permitting buyers and sellers to divert cargoes from their primary destination so as to take advantage of long- and short-term commercial opportunities, including interregional market arbitrage. The wider adoption of tolling liquefaction plants will permit more flexible and often faster upstream development and will allow companies with conflicting commercial ambitions a means to cooperate and bring their costs down. Import terminals are being developed by third parties who, in turn, lease capacity to LNG importers. Trading companies, often housed within major financial institutions, are seeking

Perhaps the real question is this: Will there ever be a world gas (and therefore an LNG reference) price? Within the next decade, this seems unlikely. Key markets such as Japan will continue to follow the more classic utility model, given their geographical and political constraints to market liberalization.

ways of exploiting these trends and are offering new financial instruments to the market. Finance costs are decreasing because new forms of financing, including Islamic, public and private bond, and tax leasing, are becoming available, alongside traditional project finance and bank debt vehicles.

Much future speculation is focused on LNG pricing. Since 2004, a tightening LNG supply market, combined with a high-oil-price environment, has created a seller's market. Resurgent economic growth in Asia led to increased LNG demand in traditional markets, such as Japan, Korea, and Taiwan; in addition, new importers emerged during these years. High U.K. and U.S. natural gas prices raised LNG prices throughout the Atlantic Basin and influenced the prices of short-term cargoes sold worldwide. In the face of this demand upturn, constrained LNG production translated into higher prices for LNG. This is reflected in the pricing terms for long-term contracts concluded since 2004.

Tenders were being held for LNG sales (long and short term), rather than for LNG purchases, and this was clear evidence that the pendulum had swung in favor of sellers. Scarcity equals value, and supply tendering has shifted from buyers to sellers. For example, the sellers of Nigeria's Brass LNG venture held a tender for supplies in the summer of 2005. Bidding by interested parties was fairly aggressive, with buyers reportedly offering ex-ship prices between 84% and 86% of Henry Hub for sales into the U.S. Gulf Coast. Other tenders for U.S. Gulf Coast deliveries have reportedly resulted in ex-ship prices approaching 90% of Henry Hub.

In the Asia-Pacific region, a sign of tightening market conditions came from Australia's North West Shelf, where Chugoku Electric and Toho Gas tentatively agreed in late 2005 to extend their contracts beyond their 2009 expiration date. These renewals incorporated straight-line formulas without the benefit of ceilings or S curves to dampen the impact of high oil prices, although the two sides agreed to review the situation if crude prices rose above $60 per barrel. Significantly, LNG buyers have been unable to obtain price ceilings since Kogas awarded its tender in early 2004.

Even importers who previously obtained very favorable LNG pricing terms have come to recognize that they will be unable to duplicate their efforts in this new supply-tight, high-oil-price environment. Buyers in mainland China accepted in late 2005 that their insistence on demanding low LNG prices cost them the opportunity to acquire LNG supplies in Australia following non-responsive seller offers during 2005. Chinese buyers have requested a ceiling of $5.00/MMBtu for LNG purchases, a far cry from Guangdong-era deals that capped delivered-LNG prices at just over $3.00/MMBtu. Even the $5.00/MMBtu ceiling may prove difficult to achieve.

Another emerging trend is the use of Atlantic Basin pricing mechanisms in Asia-Pacific markets. For example, in 2005, Japan and Korea accepted cargoes that were pegged to the Henry Hub gas price, rather than the JCC. During 2006, Indian buyers were forced to pay U.S. prices for spot LNG imports. While Asia-Pacific markets will continue to rely on crude oil indexation as the basis for much of their future long term LNG purchases, it is increasingly likely that we will see buyers and sellers worldwide with LNG portfolios that embrace a variety of pricing indices. This is partly because of the management of LNG price risk and partly because a wider range of LNG buyers and sellers will have access to market and supply outlets, both east and west of Suez, and need or want LNG supplies that have corresponding price indexation provisions.

Perhaps the real question is this: Will there ever be a world gas (and therefore an LNG reference) price? Within the next decade, this seems unlikely. Key markets such as Japan will continue to follow the more classic utility model, given their geographical and political constraints to market liberalization. The high cost of LNG shipping will not change. The established LNG supply contracts and their legacy pricing will not disappear quickly from the industry. Furthermore, while the numbers of liquefaction plants, import terminals, and tankers will certainly grow dramatically, they will still be a long way behind the breadth and depth of the world's oil market.

A more realistic proposition is that there will probably be several strongly correlated regional prices that will interact in the same way that benchmark crude oils (Brent in Europe, WTI in the United States, and Dubai in Asia) do on the oil market. Henry Hub should remain the primary reference point for U.S. LNG transactions, and the NBP and Zeebrugge hubs should assume a greater importance for European LNG contracts. It is unclear whether and where such a benchmark price would appear in the Asian market, creating less motivation on the part of sellers or buyers to change the status quo. The portfolio approach to LNG sales and purchases was originally developed to increase physical security of supply. Because natural gas and LNG prices have distinct regional components and do not necessarily show a high short-term correlation, the development of a supply portfolio with diversified prices can reduce the volatility of LNG pricing for both buyers and sellers, increasing price security. However, the long-term pricing trend will almost certainly remain reflective of long-term oil prices, given that oil is and should remain natural gas' closest competitor.

REGULATORY TRENDS

Governments in host nations have largely recognized that LNG import and export projects cannot materialize without fiscal and legal certainty. Mexico is an excellent example of a nation that until very recently lacked a regulatory framework governing the siting, construction, and operation of LNG import terminals. However, the Mexican government was cognizant that prospective LNG developers would not be attracted to invest in Mexico without such a framework and that this could adversely affect Mexico's long-term energy supply outlook. To that end, the federal government was quick to establish regulations required by prospective LNG sponsors. We can expect prospective new members of the LNG club to act in a similar fashion, either adapting their existing petroleum regulations to include LNG or creating a regime specifically dedicated to it, modeled after other countries.

A somewhat surprising trend that has been observed in the Atlantic Basin importing countries is the reemergence of quasi-monopolies for LNG importation. The United States has, since the early 1980s, pursued energy policies based on nondiscriminatory, third-party access to infrastructure under regulated terms and conditions, including the rates charged for such services. Europe's gas liberalization decrees were based on similar provisions. However, regulatory agencies have apparently acknowledged that LNG developers are unlikely to make multimillion-dollar investments in new LNG import capacity without guaranteed access under terms and conditions that accommodate the required security and certainty needed to support the upstream investments.

To that end, regulators have largely exempted new import terminals from third-party access requirements, often based on the theory that these facilities are more akin to production assets than to pipeline and storage infrastructure. In turn, the investors in these facilities and the holders of capacity have forgone the right to assured recovery of their investments through the classical utility business model. There also appears to be an implicit or explicit recognition that different project sponsors will follow different business models and that few barriers to entry exist in the terminaling business. Granted, regulatory authorities have implemented certain provisions (e.g., use-it-or-lose-it strictures in the United Kingdom) to prevent the possibility of market abuse, but the casual untrained observer could be excused for thinking that the gas market liberalization clock has been somewhat reversed! The surge of proposed terminal developments in the U.S. Gulf Coast illustrates that this approach is clearly working.

We expect that governments and energy regulatory agencies in the Asia-Pacific region, where market liberalization has developed at a much slower pace, will take note of the North American and European trends. After all, utility companies that have invested large sums in their respective nations' gas and power infrastructure cannot be expected to freely surrender market share to newcomers and allow them to erode the utilities' profit and customer bases. In any event, these monopoly companies also fulfill their respective nations' energy security objectives, which cannot simply be relinquished in the name of market liberalization. Downstream liberalization is also hard to foresee, given that LNG imports form the basis for nearly all the downstream gas markets in countries such as Japan, Korea, Taiwan, and China.

In any event, regulations tend to follow industry developments, not to lead them. Should less intrusive regulation be perceived to result in sharp increases in natural gas prices, it will be politically difficult for the regulatory authorities to maintain the current posture even if the perception is unsupported by facts. In an energy crisis (however it is defined), regulators must be seen to be acting, even if they cannot actually change the fundamentals leading to the crisis. With natural gas prices driven by factors beyond the regulators' control, political necessity may tempt regulators to regulate what they can—namely, the import terminals. A combination of high LNG prices and underutilized LNG terminals could lay the groundwork for a re-regulation of these assets. Indeed, U.S. and U.K. regulators have made clear references to this possibility in granting recent approvals to import terminals.

CONCLUSIONS

The future of the LNG industry seems assured for the next two decades. Gas demand will grow, supply will expand (even with the uncertainties described in this book), technology will evolve, and continuing commercial innovation will characterize this period. The tension between the traditional utility model and the emerging commercial, trading model will be increasingly resolved in favor of commercialization. These trends will create new challenges and uncertainties, but fundamentally the industry will retain much of what makes it so appealing—that is, a size large enough to be very exciting, but small enough to be quite personal—while also operating in an international and political climate dynamic enough to keep interests alive. For those of us lucky enough to be part of it, we can look forward to challenges, opportunities, risks, and rewards aplenty.

APPENDIX A: UNITS OF MEASUREMENT

Barrel (bbl) of oil: A common unit of measurement for the daily volume of crude oil produced by a well or from a field. The volume of a barrel is equivalent to 42 U.S. gallons.

Billion cubic feet (Bcf): A common unit of measurement for large production rates of natural gas. One billion cubic feet of natural gas is 10^9 cubic feet of gas. A single cubic foot is an imperial/U.S. customary (nonmetric) unit of volume, used in the United States, Canada, and the United Kingdom. It is defined as the volume of a cube with sides of 1 foot (0.3048 m) in length.

Conversions: One Bcfd (billion cubic feet per day), is approximately equal to 10 Bcm/y of gas, which is in turn approximately equal to 7.2 MMt/y of LNG. Bcf and Bcm are commonly used when discussing gas production, import terminals and pipelines. Bcm and MMt are more commonly used when discussing liquefaction plants.

Cubic meter (gaseous): Unit of volume or pipeline capacity. The unit generally favored is the normal cubic meter (Nm^3), measured dry at 0°C and 760 mm Hg. One billion cubic meters (**Bcm**) of natural gas is 10^9 cubic meters of gas.

Cubic meter (liquid): Unit of storage tank volume or LNG tanker capacity. One cubic meter of liquid LNG contains the equivalent of about 610 cubic meters of gas. In this book, when used in reference to LNG tanks' storage volume, cubic meters is always written in longhand; when referring to an LNG tanker's containment capacity, it is expressed as m^3.

Knot: Unit of speed in navigation for ships. One knot is one nautical mile (6,080 feet or 1,852 meters) per hour.

Million Btu (MMBtu): A measurement of the energy content of natural gas, commonly used for pricing LNG and natural gas, equal to 10^6 Btu. A **Btu** is the amount of heat energy needed to raise the temperature of one pound of water by 1°F. One thousand cubic feet (**Mcf**) of natural gas contains approximately one MMBtu of energy.

Million metric tons per year (MMt/y): A measurement commonly used when discussing LNG plant capacity. Sometimes expressed as MMtpa (million metric tons per annum).

Nautical mile: Unit of length used around the world for maritime and aviation purposes, also known as a sea mile. There is no official international standard symbol for the unit nautical mile. One nautical mile is equivalent to 1.150779 miles (statute).

Quad: One quadrillion Btu (i.e., 10^{15} Btu), roughly equivalent to 1 trillion (10^{12}) cubic feet.

Therm: Unit equal to 100,000 Btu.

Tonne: One metric ton, equal to 1,000 kg or 2,204.6 pounds.

Trillion cubic feet (Tcf): 10^{12} cubic feet, commonly used to express gas reserves or a country's gas consumption.

GLOSSARY

Annual contract quantity (ACQ): The quantity delivered in each contract year, as specified in a gas or LNG sales contract.

Annual delivery program (ADP): The annual program for the delivery and receipt of LNG cargoes. The ADP is usually agreed on between sellers and buyers before the beginning of each contract year.

Associated natural gas: Gas found mixed with oil in underground reservoirs. Associated natural gas comes out of solution as a by-product of oil production.

Ballast: Weight added to a ship to improve stability. On an LNG tanker, ballast is provided by seawater carried in the ballast tanks which are found between the cargo tanks and the ship's outer hull. Ballast water is usually taken on board as the cargo is unloaded.

Bareboat charter: A shipping charter (contract) in which the ship is chartered bare (i.e., without crew).

Baseload: The volume of gas designed to be delivered by a system that does not fluctuate significantly.

Boil-off or Boil-off gas: The gas produced when LNG in a storage vessel evaporates as heat leaks into the liquid. This vaporized gas can be recovered and used as energy. The evaporation process keeps the liquid cool and is called auto-refrigeration.

Burner tip: The ultimate point of consumption for natural gas.

Cargo containment system: The method of storing LNG in a ship.

Charterparty: A contractual agreement between a shipowner and a cargo owner, whereby a ship is chartered (hired) for a single voyage or over a period of time.

CIF (cost, insurance, and freight) contract: An LNG sales and purchase agreement in which the buyer of the LNG takes ownership either when the LNG is loaded onto the vessel or during the voyage to the receiving terminal. Payment is made at the time of the transfer of ownership; however, the seller remains responsible for the transportation and the transportation cost.

Civils work: Ancillary construction tasks related to the construction of a plant, including earthworks, foundations, roads, and dredging.

Classification society: A private organization that inspects and advises on the hull and machinery of a ship, supervises vessels during construction and thereafter, and places them in classes according to its rules for each type.

Cogeneration: The simultaneous production of electrical energy and another form of useful thermal energy (such as heat or steam) from the same fuel source, often used for industrial, commercial, heating, or cooling purposes.

Combined-cycle gas turbine (CCGT): The combination of gas turbines with a waste heat recovery steam generator and a steam turbine in an electric power generation plant.

Compressed natural gas (CNG): Natural gas compressed under high pressures, usually between 3,000 and 3,600 psi. CNG may be used as a vehicle fuel.

Condensates: Hydrocarbon liquids, existing as vapor in a natural gas reservoir that condense to liquids as their temperature and pressure decrease during production. Natural gas condensates consist mainly of pentanes (C_5H_{12}) and heavier components. They are usually blended with crude oil for refining.

Daily average sendout: The total volume of natural gas delivered over a defined period of time divided by the total number of days in the period.

Debottlenecking: The process of increasing the capacity of a plant by making relatively minor modifications to individual systems.

Deliverability: The amount of natural gas that a well, field, pipeline, or distribution system can supply in a given period (typically 24 hours).

Downstream: Oil or gas operations that are closer to the end user (see *upstream*).

Draft: The vertical distance from the waterline to the lowest point of the ship, or stated another way, the least depth of water needed for the ship to float.

Engineering, procurement, and construction (EPC) contract: The EPC contract defines the terms under which the detailed design, procurement, construction, and commissioning of an LNG export or import facility will be conducted.

Exclusion zone: An area surrounding an LNG plant in which an operator legally controls all activities. The exclusion zone creates a buffer in the event of an LNG incident. It provides thermal-radiation protection from fires and flammable vapor-dispersion protection from un-ignited vapor clouds.

Ex-ship contract: An LNG sales and purchase agreement in which title to the LNG is transferred to the buyer when the LNG is unloaded at the receiving terminal and payment is made. Also referred to as delivered ex-ship contract.

Feedstock gas (feedgas): Dry natural gas used as raw material for LNG, petrochemical, and gas-to-liquids plants.

Flaring: Burning off unwanted natural gas under controlled conditions.

Force majeure: French for "greater force." Force majeure is a common clause in contracts that essentially releases one or both parties from liability or obligation when an extraordinary event beyond the control of the parties, such as war, strike, riot, crime, act of God (e.g., flood, earthquake, or volcano), prevents one or both parties from wholly or partially performing their obligations under the contract.

Free on board (FOB) contract: An LNG sales and purchase agreement in which the buyer takes title to the LNG on loading at the liquefaction plant and is responsible for transporting it to the receiving terminal.

Front-end engineering design (FEED): The engineering phase that defines the design parameters of a project in sufficient detail to permit an accurate assessment of the project's costs prior to the final investment decision and to provide the basis for the competitive bidding of an EPC contract.

Gas reserves: Gas deposits that geologists and petroleum engineers know or strongly believe can be recovered given today's prices and drilling technology. The term "reserves" is distinct from the term "resources," which includes all the deposits of gas that are still in the ground.

Gas-to-liquids (GTL): A process that converts natural gas into high-value liquid fuels similar to diesel, distillate or heating oil.

Greenfield plant: A brand-new facility built on a parcel of land which has not previously been used for that purpose.

Heads of agreement (HoA): A document outlining the main issues to be included in a subsequent contract or agreement (e.g., the sale and purchase of LNG). It serves as a guideline for both parties negotiating the final documents. HoAs may be binding or non-binding.

Heating value (HV): The amount of heat produced from the complete combustion of a unit quantity of fuel. The gross HV occurs when all the products of combustion are cooled to standard conditions and the latent heat of the water vapor formed is reclaimed. The net HV is the gross value minus the latent heat of the vaporization of the water.

Henry Hub: A point on the U.S. natural gas pipeline system in Erath, Louisiana. Henry Hub is owned by Sabine Pipe Line LLC and interconnects with nine interstate and four intrastate pipelines. It is the standard delivery point for NYMEX natural gas future contracts in the United States and is the point at which the benchmark natural gas price is set for the Gulf Coast.

Hydrocarbon: An organic chemical compound of hydrogen and carbon in gaseous, liquid, or solid phase.

Interchangeability: The ability to substitute one gaseous fuel for another in a combustion application without materially changing operational safety or performance and without materially increasing air pollutant emissions.

Interruptible gas: Gas made available under agreements that allow curtailments of delivery by the supplier or of receipt by the buyer.

Liquefied natural gas (LNG): Natural gas, consisting mainly of methane (CH_4) that has been liquefied by cooling to –258°F (–163°C) at atmospheric pressure. LNG is odorless, colorless, non-corrosive, and nontoxic. LNG occupies 1/600th of the space required for the vapor state at standard conditions.

Liquefied petroleum gases (LPG): Hydrocarbons that are gases at normal temperatures and pressures but readily turn into liquids under moderate pressure at normal temperatures, including propane, propylene, butane, isobutane, butylenes, or mixtures in any ratio.

LNG chain: The components of an LNG project that link the natural gas in the ground to the ultimate consumer. The main links are natural gas production and processing, liquefaction, shipping, regasification, and distribution.

Manufactured gas: Gas produced from oil, coal, or coke.

Natural gas liquids (NGL): Liquid hydrocarbons extracted from natural gas in the field, typically ethane, propane, butane, pentane, and natural gasoline.

Natural gas processing: The treatment of field gas for use as pipeline-quality gas or as a feedstock for a liquefaction plant. Processing includes removing liquids, solids, vapors, and impurities.

Net back price: The price that the producer of natural gas receives at a defined point. The net back price is derived from the market price for the gas minus delivery charges to the market.

Nonassociated gas: Gas located in a reservoir that does not contain oil.

Open access: A pipeline transportation or LNG terminaling service that is available to all shippers on a non-discriminatory basis, subject to capacity availability.

Peakshaving: The supplementing of the normal supply of gas during periods of peak demand with gas taken from LNG storage facilities, or produced from a mixture of propane and air. These facilities are usually located near load centers (market areas).

Peakshaving plant: A plant that liquefies gas from a pipeline during off-peak periods and stores it as LNG for future use, usually for local markets in cold climates.

Project financing: A common method of financing the construction of industrial infrastructure whereby the value of the plant and part or all of its anticipated revenues are pledged as collateral to secure financing from lenders, who have limited or no rights to seek debt repayment (recourse) from the owners. Also know as non-recourse financing.

Receiving terminal: A large facility capable of receiving and storing the cargo from an LNG ship and vaporizing it for delivery to a pipeline system.

Regasification: Converting LNG back to its gaseous state by the application of heat. Also known as vaporization.

Rollover: The rapid release of LNG vapors from a storage tank, caused by the uncontrolled mixing of stratified layers. Layers of LNG of different densities (owing to different LNG compositions) can be created in an LNG tank as a result of insufficient mixing within the tank.

Royalties: A payment to an owner, often a government, for the right to produce oil and gas resources, usually calculated as a percentage of the revenues obtained at the point of production.

Sale and purchase agreement (SPA): A contract between a seller and a buyer for the sale and purchase of a certain quantity of natural gas or LNG for delivery during a specified period at a specified price.

Sendout: The volume of gas delivered by a plant or system in a specified period of time.

Spot sales: The sale of natural gas on a short-term basis.

Stranded gas: Gas that is not close to the market and requires significant infrastructure to deliver it to the market.

Take or pay: A commitment by the buyer of natural gas or LNG to pay for a minimum quantity in a defined period regardless whether delivery is accepted.

Time charter: A contract for a specified period of time or a particular voyage, in which the shipowner provides the vessel and crew while the charterer supplies the cargo.

Upstream: Oil or gas operations that are closer to production.

Vaporization: See regasification.

Weathering: The change in LNG composition over time as a result of the preferential evaporation of nitrogen and methane in the boil-off of stored LNG.

BIBLIOGRAPHY

Andrews, Alex. 1994. Time charterparties. Paper presented at session 9 of a seminar organized by the Cambridge Academy of Transport. Cambridge, November.

Gardner, David. 2001. LNG charter. *Shipping World & Shipbuilder.* http://www.cdg.co.uk/content/files/news/2003%20Intro%20to%20LNG%20Ship%20Agrts%20DAG.pdf. January 1, 2003.

———. 2003. An introduction to LNG shipping agreements. LNG *Journal*. March/April.

Mackin, Stephen. 2003. LNG. Paper presented. London, March 14.

Massey, Eugene A. 2000. LNG time charters—the negotiating issues. Paper presented at the LNG Transportation Contract Seminar, organized by the Institute of Gas Technology. London, January.

Short-Term LNG *Trades: Challenges and Opportunities*. 1998. New York: Poten & Partners.

Spot and Short-Term LNG *Trades and Shipping (through* 2003). 2001. New York: Poten & Partners.

Tanker chartering and documentation. 1994. Papers presented at seminar organized by the Cambridge Academy of Transport. Cambridge, November.

Tusiani, Michael D. 1996. *The Petroleum Shipping Industry*. 2 Vols. Tulsa: PennWell.

Walker, Andrew. The LNG "spot" trade. LNG *Journal*. March/April 2001.

INDEX

A glossary is provided beginning on page 399.

A

aboveground tanks, 122, 170
Abu Dhabi
  to Asian-Pacific markets, 242
  C3-MR cycle in, 115
  early plant development, 14
  financing of, 242
  government gas sales, 238
  imports from, 242
  Japanese imports from, 50, 53, 155, 200
  liquids production, 303
  short-term trades, 222n6
  upstream project financing, 247
Abu Dhabi Gas Liquefaction Company (ADGAS)
  Das Island ADGAS plant, 278–279
  LNG sales contracts, 279
  project ownership, 279
access fees, 381
accident, 256
accounting guidelines, 90
acid gas, 105
acid gas removal, 111
admiralty law, 346
AES, 42
air cooling, 121
air emissions, 8, 180
air quality, 58, 378
Alaska
  to Asian-Pacific markets, 242, 281
  Cascade process in, 113
  early LNG in, 14, 53
  early plant capacity, 71
  financing of, 247
  imports by, 200
  imports from, 242
  investment in, 64n4
  Japanese imports from, 53, 155, 200
  Kenai facility in, 293
  LNG export project summary, 294
  pricing terms renegotiated, 251
  signed LNG sales contracts, 294
  upstream project financing, 247
Alaska Gas Project, 64
Algeria
  C3-MR cycle in, 115
  contracted LNG volumes, 258

early LNG history, 33–34
early plant capacity, 71
early plant development, 14
early pricing models, 324
existing LNG export projects, 257
GTL projects, 23
non-associated gas reserves, 70
pipeline gas supplies to Belgium, 49
pipeline gas supplies to Italy, 48
pipeline gas supplies to Western Europe, 43
pipeline gas to Spain, 46
planned LNG projects, 257
production from, 92, 255
resource nationalism, 396
R-factor-based resource rent tax, 306
Sonatrach in, 256–258
supplier to Europe, 43, 200
supplier to Turkey, 223n13
supplier to United States, 205
transportation costs of, 310
turbine drive technology choices, 131
Algeria-Sardinia Galsi pipeline, 49
alignment of participant interests, 248
allowable rate of return (RoR), 239
ALNG (Atlantic LNG), 240
Altamira, 38
Altamira terminal, 240
ambient air-heated vaporizers, 181
Anadarko Petroleum, 37
APCI AP-X process, 117–118
arbitrage, 245
Argentina, 8, 62
Arun LNG facilities, 286–287
Arzew, 256
Asia
imports by, 200
monopoly utility buyers in, 228
natural gas and liquefied natural gas markets in, 49–62
spot trading in, 220
Asian crisis in 1999, 163, 206, 280
Asia-Pacific market
flexible trading in, 230
project development, 242–244
Asia-Pacific region, 281–284
associated gas, 70, 265
assumption, 246
Atlantic Basin
LNG demand growth prospects, 240
market project development, 240–241
proprietary access import terminals, 394
Sonatrach in, 240
Australia
to Asian-Pacific markets, 242, 281
C3-MR cycle in, 115
Cascade process in, 113
CO_2 reinjection, 302
Darwin business structure, 282
Darwin LNG sales agreement, 282
delivered sales (ex-ship or CIF) from, 78
early LNG history, 15
gas dryness, 304
GTL projects, 23
imports by, 200
integrated projects, 237
Japanese imports from, 50, 53, 200
liquids production, 303
LNG projects in, 281–284
mixed-refrigerant processes, 118
North West Shelf (NWS) LNG project, 282–284
North West Shelf (NWS) LNG project export facilities, 283
ownership structure, 76–77
petroleum resource rent tax (PRRT), 307
pricing to China, 234
reserves in, 90
shipping capacity, 82
signed North West Shelf (NWS) sales contracts, 284
siting considerations, 110
subsea development in, 103
supplier to China, 60

tanker ownership, 308
turbine drive technology choices, 131
uncommitted liquefaction capacity, 222n10, 229, 233
Australian NWS project, 77
Austria, 252n4
auto-refrigeration, 13
Axens Liquefin DMR process, 118–119

B

backward integration, 86
Bacton terminus Interconnector pipeline, 45
Bahia de Bizkaia Gas, 47
Balgzand Bacton Line (BBL), 45
Baltic LNG project, 269
basis, defined, 222
basis of design (BOD), 126
Bear Head Project, 37
Bechtel, 81
Belgium
imports by, 200
imports from Algeria, 200, 257
import terminals in, 14
in-pit tanks in, 175
market liberalization investigations, 252n4
open access input terminals, 387
regasification terminals, 212
short-term trades, 222n6
Zeebrugge liquefied natural gas terminal as pipeline hub, 49
benchmark prices, 208
Bethouia, 256
BG LNG Services, 34, 388
Big Sweep technology, 193
Bintulu LNG complex, 293
Bishop process, 193–194
Bishop Process Exchanger, 194
boil-off, 13, 73, 154, 158–159, 164, 181–182, 348, 349
boil-off rates, 82
Bonny, 205
Bonny River plant, 263
Bontang (Badak) LNG facility, 287
Boyle, Robert, 13
BP, 35
branded liquefied natural gas, 42
Brass LNG (planned), 264, 266
Brazil, 8, 201
break-even costs for a greenfield LNG project, 84
Brent crude, 208
British Gas, 44
British Gas Council, 14
Broadwater Energy offshore terminals, 382
Brunei, 285–286
to Asian-Pacific markets, 242, 281
C3-MR cycle in, 115
delivered sales (ex-ship or CIF) from, 76, 78
depreciation schedules, 305
early LNG history, 14
early plant capacity, 71
financing of, 242
GSA pricing, 320
imports from, 242
Japanese imports from, 50, 53, 155, 200
LNG project structure, 285
LNG sales contracts, 285
vs. Malaysia, 286
pricing terms renegotiated, 251
shipping per SPA, 348
split-revenue ventures, 237
tanker ownership, 308
turbine drive technology choices, 131
upstream project financing, 247
Brunei LNG (BLNG), 285–286
Btu-stabilization equipment, 183
build absolutely nothing anywhere near anyone (BANANA), 373
business interruption insurance, 355
business strategies, 211–216

C

C3-MR system, 115
Cabot, Godfrey, 14
Cabot LNG, 270
California Energy Commission, 376
California energy crisis, 30, 208
calorific values, 182
Calpine, bankruptcy of, 7
Cameron LNG, 390
Cameron, Louisiana, 36
Cameron Parish, Louisiana, 390
Canada, 253
  domestic production declines, 32
  future import terminals, 201
  liquefied natural gas developments in, 37–38
  LNG developments in, 37
  market liberalization, 26
  market liberalization in, 26
  production and consumption, 92
  production from, 92
Canadian Arctic gas, 32
Canaport LNG, 37
capital costs decreases, 208
capital expenses (CAPEX), 348
carbon dioxide, 105
carbon sequestering, 8
cargo-handling systems, 143
cargo loading/discharge, 159–160
Caribbean, 41
Cascade process, 113
casing, 99, 100–101
charter hire, 349, 354
charterparty contracts, 346
charterparty overview, 345–347
Cheniere Energy, 36
Chicago Bridge & Iron (CB&I), 81
Chile, 21, 62, 201
China
  Australian exports to, 283, 284
  coal production costs in, 61
  energy demand, 1, 7, 281
  gas demand in, 60
  Guangdong terminal, 50, 58, 201
  hydroelectric power generation, 9
  imports by, 200
  imports to, 242
  LNG buyers in, 228
  LNG pricing, 74, 231, 399
  LNG projects in, 60–61
  LNG shipbuilding, 143, 150
  LNG ships by, 61
  LNG shipyards in, 148
  LNG trading, 198
  market liberalization, 85, 401
  natural gas pipelines growth in, 8
  pipeline imports access, 57
  pipelines in, 57
China National Offshore Oil Company (CNOOC), 284
Chogku Electric, 398
Christmas tree, 102–103
Cinderella, 139
Classification Societies, 363
Clearwater Port, 191
closed-access, 187
club rules, 204
CMS Energy, 34
CO_2 emissions, 8
coal-fired generation, 5
coal production costs, 61
Code for Existing Ships Carrying Liquefied Gases in Bulk, 366
COLREGs, 369
Columbus Gas, 35
combined-cycle gas turbine (CCGT) power plants, 5
combined-cycle gas turbine (CCGT) technology, 2–3
combined heat and power vaporizers, 181
Comisión de Electricided (CFE), 39
commercial and financial chain, 78
commercial banks, 247
commercial risks, 69
commercial structure, 69
commodity-trading operations, 245

Common Business Practice, 184
community interest groups, 378
competitive lenders, 78
competitive tender, 60, 74
completion and testing procedures, 128
completion risk, assumption by, 246
compressed natural gas (CNG), 23
compressed natural gas (CNG) vs. liquefied natural gas, 23–24
compressor stations, 107
concession or license agreements, 70
condensate credits, 252
condensates, 70, 105, 111
conflicts of interest, 77
ConocoPhillips, 37
consequential damages, 354
Consolidated Natural Gas, 35
construction budgets, 127
construction jobs in exporting countries, 133
construction site teams, 152
construction standards, 153
Continental Oil Company, 14
contract durations, 229
contract failure, 218
contract flexibility, 218
contract of affreightment (COA), 350–351
contract quantity (ACQ), 235
Convention on the International Regulations for Preventing Collisions at Sea (COLREGs), 369–370
conventions and codes applicable to LNG tankers, 364–370
convertibility issues, 248
cooldown, 158
cost and cost reduction along LNG chain, 79
cost-based liquefaction, 238
cost of capital, 236
cost-of-service tariffs, 25
cost overrun subsidies, 269
cost-plus-return system, 239
cost reduction trends, 130–132
Cove Point, Maryland, 35
Cove Point terminal, 183, 201, 241, 386, 388
credit ratings, 351
creditworthy buyers, 214, 228
creditworthy contracting parties, 231
critical paths, 153
Croatia, 49
crude oil as proxy price, 74. *See also* LNG pricing
cryogenic connections, 134
currency, 248
Cyprus, 49

D

Dabhol LNG import/power generation projects, 58, 218, 252
Dabhol plant, 274
Dabhol Power Company, 280
Daewoo Marine Engineering and Shipbuilding, 81
Dahej terminal, 58
damage stability, 366
Damietta, 258–260
Darwin LNG project, 281–282
Das Island ADGAS plant, 278–279
debottlenecking, 128, 271, 283
debt financing sources, 246
dedicated shipping, 203
Deepwater Port Act, 187, 390
default concern, 352
delivered (ex-ship or CIF) sales, 78
demand forecast, 198
demonstrated resources, 232
demurrage, 350
dense-phase gas, 193
deregulation. *See* market liberalization
design and construction standards of ships, 367
destination flexibility, 229, 250
destination restrictions, 229
developing countries, natural gas pipelines in, 8
development drilling, 100, 104

disasters
- East Ohio Gas Company tank rupture, 14
- Estonia, 368
- Titanic, 365
- Torrey Canyon, 363

discharging operations, 160
distribution pipelines, 11, 12
Distrigas Corporation, 33–34
diversification strategy, 21–22
diver technology, 121
divestiture, 26, 29–30
DOE gas demand forecast, 32
Dominican Republic
- blackouts in, 64n6
- LNG development in, 42
- opens terminal, 201
- serves powerplant, 168

Dominion Resources, 35
double containment tanks, 123
Dow, 37
downstream customers, 61, 85, 210, 351
downstream integration, 214
downstream merchant function, 245
downstream pipelines, 388
downstream sales agreements, 58
Dragon LNG, 46
dredging, environmental aspects of, 378
drill bits, 98
drilling mud, 99
drill ships, 100
drill string, 98
dry gas, 70
dual-fuel diesel/electric propulsion, 162
Duke Energy, 34
Dynegy, 390

E

East-West pipeline, 60
economic rent, 239
economics, of power generation, 5
economic trade-offs, 20–21
economies of scale, 79
EGLNG, 295
Egypt
- aggressive growth in, 258
- C3-MR cycle in, 115
- Cascade process in, 113
- contracted Idku volumes, 260
- cost recovery caps, 306

existing LNG export projects, 259
existing LNG project shareholdings, 259
- feedgas purchases, 232, 238
- new projects in, 241, 256
- production from, 255
- SEGAS (Damietta) allocations, 260
- supplier to Europe, 43
- tolling liquefied natural gas, 229, 239
- train ownerships in, 77

El Andalous (Gassi Touli) project, 256–257
Elba Island, Georgia, 34
Elba Island terminal, 201, 240, 386, 388
Electricity Enterprises Act (EEA), 374–375
electric power liberalization
- in Korea, 244
- in Spain, 228
- in United Kingdom, 228
- in United States, 207, 227

electric-price indexing, 234
El Paso, 34, 35, 205
El Paso Merchant Energy (EPME), 35
En 1473 (European LNG siting code), 375
Enagás, 47
Energia Costa Azul, 39
Energy Bridge, Gulf of Mexico, 36
Energy Policy Act of 2005, 187, 390
energy sales growth, 197
energy supply diversity and security, 9
English legal system, 349
Enron, 42
Enron collapse, 208
EPC award, 126
EPC bidding, 126
EPC contractors, 81, 127, 232, 246
EPC costs, 131

Equatorial Guinea
Cascade process in, 113
development in, 260–261
liquids production in, 304
new projects in, 256
planned projects in, 242, 295
Estonia, 369
Europe
gas and power sector liberalization, 252
gas liberalization, 207
gas market liberalization, 207
gas market liberalization in, 227
imports by, 200
LNG buyers in, 226
power market liberalization, 207
privatization of energy markets in, 44
proprietary access import terminals in, 228
spot trading in, 219–221
Everett, Massachusetts, 33
Everett terminal, 33, 168, 183, 201, 387
Excelerate Energy, 36
excess capacity, 227
exclusion zones, 185, 195, 377
expansions, 128
experience curve, 79
exploration and production, 79–80
export credit agencies, 76, 251
export credit agencies (ECAs), 235–236
export-import (ExIm) banks, 251
exporting and importing countries, 199
exporting countries, construction jobs in, 133
export projects, 228
expropriation, 248
ExxonMobil, 385

F

Facilitation Committee, 363
facilities construction, 232
Factory Location Act, 383
fault-bounded gas trap, 94
Federal Energy Regulatory Commission (FERC), 375, 382, 387, 390
feedgas purification and pretreatment, 111–112
FEED proposals, 232
FEED work, 169
FERC Order 380, 29, 33
FERC Order 636, 29
final acceptance, 128
final investment decision (FID), 225
financial advisers, 247
financial chain, 225
financial statement disclosure, 248
financing costs, 209
Finima, 205
Fire Prevention Law, 383
first tranche petroleum (FTP) obligation, 307
Fischer-Tropsch (FT) reaction, 22
fixed-price feedgas, 238
flammable vapor-dispersion protection, 377
flaring, 88–89, 265
flexibility, barriers to, 203
floating LNG (FLNG), 133
floating-pipeline model, 203, 214
floating production, storage, and off-loading vessel (FPSO) designs, 134
floating production units, 190
Floating Storage and Regasification Units (FSRUs), 189
FOB sales, 78
force majeure provisions, 127, 355
forward integration, 86
Fos II terminal, 48
Foster Wheeler, 81
four-dimensional seismic technology, 97
fracing, 100
fractionation system, 112
France
gas demand, 48
imports by, 200
imports from Algeria, 14, 257
imports from Nigeria, 266
LNG shipping development, 139, 148, 149, 162

market liberalization investigations, 252n4
natural gas and liquefied natural gas markets in, 43
new LNG terminal, 241
pipeline imports, 47–48
shipping costs to, 310
Freeport LNG Development, 36
Freeport, Texas, 36
front end engineering design (FEED) request, 126
frontier natural gas resources, 32
Fuel Act of 1978, 6
Fuijan, 60
full-containment tanks, 123–124
futures contracts, 30
future trends, 186–195

G

gas and LNG swaps, 245
Gas Authority of India Limited (GAIL), 59
gas bubble, 33
gas business, development of, 25
gas club, 245
gas-condensate fields, 89
gas consumption
by country, 92
in United Kingdom, 43
gas demand
China, 60
DOE forecast, 32
France, 48
Italy, 43
Japan, 198
Mexico, 38
South Korea, 55–56
Spain, 43, 47
United Kingdom, 43, 45
gas distribution systems, development of, 25
gas-fired power generation, 30
gas-fired vaporizers, 83, 378, 382
gas market liberalization, 49, 381
deregulation of merchant roles, 207
deregulation of natural gas industry, 29–30
in Europe, 44, 227
in United States, 227
Gas Natural, 42, 47
gas pipeline systems, elements of, 11
gas production by country, 92
gas quality and treatment, 182–184
gas reinjection, 89
gas reserves
described, 89
liquefied natural gas projects, elements of, 16
natural gas, 2, 89
non-associated gas reserves, 70
offshore stranded-gas, 133
proven gas reserves, 10, 91
reserves to production ratio (R/P ratio), 10
stranded, 10, 21
worldwide, 26
gas reserves, by country
Algeria, 70
Australia, 90
Iran, 90
Nigeria, 261
Qatar, 3, 70, 90, 92, 210, 222n9
Russia, 10, 90
Saudi Arabia, 91
Trinidad, 70
United States, 91
gas shrinkage, 80
gas supply, adequacy of resources, 232
gas-to-liquids (GTL) process, 22–23
gas-to-liquids (GTL) projects, capital costs for, 22
Gastor, 205
gas trading, 244–245
gas trading hubs. *See* hubs
gas trading policies, 26
gas transmission pipelines. *See* pipelines
gas transportation and supply functions unbundling, 30

gas trap, 94
gas turbine compressor drive, 71
gas turbines, 121
- GE frame gas turbine, 129–130
- peaking, 6
- simple-cycle, 5
- vs. steam turbines, 131

Gas Utility Industry Act (GUIA), 374
gas window, 93
gathering systems, 11, 12, 103
Gaz de France terminal, 48
Gazprom, 44, 45, 242, 268
GE frame gas turbine, 129–130
geophysics, 95
Germany, 49, 252n4
global demand and supply of liquefied natural gas, 395–396
global gas and liquefied natural gas markets, 25–66
global liquefaction projects, 255
global liquefied Natural Gas, 3
global LNG trade growth, 210
global natural gas industry, 5–10
global oil resources, 10
Global Positioning System (GPS) technology, 100
global warming, 395
Golar LNG, 164
Golar Spirit, 146
Golden Pass LNG, Texas, 37
government support, 77
Grain LNG, 46
gravity-based structure (GBS), 133, 192
Greece
- imports by, 200
- imports from Algeria, 257
- in-pit tanks in, 175
- pipeline gas supplies to, 49

greenfield projects, 18
Green Stream pipeline, 48–49, 262
Groningen gas field, 43
Guangdong Dapeng LNG Company, 60
Guangdong LNG Transportation Group, 148, 201
Guangdong pricing, 60
Guangdong terminal, 50, 58, 201
GUIA, 383
Gulf Gateway terminal, 188, 194, 201

H

Hackberry Terminal, 390
Hassi P'Mel gas field, 256
Hazira terminal, 240
heating value range, 196
heating values, 88, 182
heavy hydrocarbons, 112
heel, 73, 82, 158, 173
helium, 88
helium gas, 13
hell or high water provisions, 77
Henry Hub, 26, 75, 234, 398, 399
High Pressure Gas Control Act (HPGCA), 374–375
HiLoad offshore LNG-unloading solution, 190
the hire, 348
Honduras, 201
horizontal drilling, 104
horizontal drilling technology, 80, 100
host country agreements, 231
hubs
- Henry Hub, 26, 75, 234, 398, 399
- Henry Hub pricing, 234
- Henry Hub pricing in Japan, 399
- Main Pass Energy Hub, 191
- Zeebrugge hubs, 399
- Zeebrugge liquefied natural gas terminal as pipeline hub, 49

Hungary, 252n4
Hurricane Katrina, 31
hybrid terminal, 189
hydrocarbon fuels, 395
hydrocarbon traps, 95
hydroelectric power generation, 9
hydrogen gas, 396
hydrogen sulfide, 105, 111
Hyundai Utopia, 147

I

Idku, 258–260
IGC Code, 366, 367, 370
import and regasification plants, 33
import capacity, 212
import-related project siting and regulatory issues, 373–383
import terminal commitment, 225
import terminals, 33–41, 186. *See also* by specific terminal (e.g., Everett terminal)
  codes and regulations for, 374–375
  costs of, 360
  design and construction of, 169–171
  design basis, 374–378
  downstream terminals, 393
  existing and proposed North American, 40
  main components of, 172–184
  in North America, 39
  opposition to, 378
  regulated access of, 386–394. *See also* proprietary access import terminals; third-party access
  use agreements, 385–394
  import terminals, by country
  in Belgium, 14, 212, 387
  existing, in United States, 33
  future import terminals in Canada, 201
  in Japan, 51
  in Korea, 14
  proposed, in Mexico, 241, 266, 294
  in Spain, 14
  in Taiwan, 14
  in United States, 164n15, 241
incremental expansion, 168
India
  Algerian exports to, 234
  ambient air-heated vaporizers, 181
  competitive tendering, 60
  Dabhol project, 50, 58, 79, 210, 218, 252, 274, 280
  energy demand growth, 1, 7, 273, 281
  gas trading with Iran, 21
  imports by, 200
  imports to, 242
  labor costs, 81, 171
  liquefied natural gas imports by, 50
  LNG buyers in, 228
  LNG pricing, 74, 234, 332
  LNG trading, 198
  LNG train costs, 79
  market liberalization, 85
  merchant buyers, 245
  natural gas pipelines growth in, 8
  Nigerian exports to, 241
  pipeline imports access, 57
  risk, 59
  spot trading, 210, 218, 399
  state subsidiaries in, 58
  suppliers to, 243
Indonesia
  Arun LNG export project, 287
  Arun LNG sales contracts, 288
  to Asian-Pacific markets, 242, 281
  Bontag LNG sales contracts, 288
  Bontang (Badak) lng facility, 288
  C3-MR cycle in, 115
  cost-based liquefaction, 238, 243, 247
  cost trends, 80, 110
  early LNG history, 14
  exports to China, 60
  exports to Korea, 55, 56
  exports to Singapore, 63
  feedgas difficulties, 252n1
  feedgas pricing, 321
  first tranche petroleum (FTP) obligation, 307
  imports from, 242
  Japanese imports from, 50, 53, 155, 200
  liquids production, 303
  LNG development in, 286–290
  LNG export expansions, 15
  LNG pricing, 234
  national oil companies (NOCs) participation, 298
  ownership structure, 76
  project financing, 236

ships built for, 145
short-term trades, 206
spot-purchases, 220
Tangguh LNG project sales, 290
Tangguh LNG project structure, 289
turbine drive technology choices, 131
uplifts allowed, 305
wet gas, 304
Indonesian Crude Price (ICP), 234, 331
industry transformation, 215–216
inflexible contract terms, 227
infrastructure costs, 110
insurance, 127
insurance costs, 349
intact stability, 366
integrated joint venture, 202, 283
integrated projects, 237
International Association of Ports and Harbors (IAPH), 362
international banks, 76
International Certificate of Fitness for the Carriage of Liquefied Gases in Bulk, 367
International Chamber of Shipping (ICS), 361, 362
International Code for the Construction and Equipment of Ships Carrying Liquefied Gases in Bulk (IGC Code), 366–367
international commercial banks, 250–251
International Convention on Maritime Search and Rescue, 366
International Convention on Standards of Training, Certification, and Watchkeeping for Seafarers (STCW Convention), 367–369
International Conventions for the Safety of Life at Sea (SOLAS), 365
International Conventions for the Safety of Life at Sea (SOLAS) convention, 364–365
International Gas Carrier Code (IGC Code), 153
international legal conventions, 346
International Maritime Organization (IMO), 19, 361, 362–364
international oil companies (IOCs), 236
international pipelines, development of, 43
International Power/Mitsui, 42
International Safety Management Code (ISM Code), 365
International Ship and Port Facility Security Code (ISPS Code), 365
interstate pipelines, 12
investments banks, 247
Iran
exports to Pakistan, 62
exports to Turkey, 223n13
gas trading with India, 21, 58, 60
GTL projects, 23
imports from, 242
LNG pricing and Dabhol, 59
natural gas reserves, 90
production capacity, 92
Irving Oil, 37
Islamic militants, 287
Italy
early LNG history, 14
floating offshore terminal, 164n17
gas demand in, 43
gas market in demand, 48–49
imports from Algeria, 257
imports from Libya, 200, 261, 262
imports from Nigeria, 266
market liberalization investigations, 252n4
pipeline deliveries, 295
proposed terminal in, 241
rollover accident, 196n7
siting considerations, 380
third-party access, 383n8, 391

J

jack-up rigs, 99
Jamaica, 201
Jamal, 164
Japan
Abu Dhabi exports to, 279
American ships for, 145
Australian exports to, 283
Brunei exports to, 285
calorific values control, 172

competition for gas by, 61
crude oil proxy pricing, 74
daytime harbor transit, 173
domestic competition in, 245
downstream liberalization, 401
early LNG history, 14
gas buildout, 8
gas demand in, 198
gas powered generation, 6
Henry Hub pricing, 399
imports by, 200
imports to, 242
import terminals costs, 360
independent power producers (IPPs) and domestic competition in, 243
Indonesian exports to, 50, 288
in-pit tanks in, 175
Japanese banks, 251
Japanese Customs Clearance price (JCC), 234, 331
Japanese shipbuilding, 57, 143, 144, 146, 149
Japanese Three (J3) consortium, 164n16
vs. Korean shipbuilding, 150
liquefied natural gas import terminals, 51
liquefied natural gas project development, 53–55
LNG buyers in, 226
LNG development decisions, 170
LNG development in, 20, 21
LNG industry, 398
LNG shipyards in, 147
LNG trading, 206
Malaysian exports to, 290, 291
market growth, 281
market liberalization, 49, 85, 207
markets in, 21
Moss licenses, 163n10
nuclear power generation, 54
oil exposure, 52
Omani exports to, 274
power generation fuels, 53
price restructuring, 326
primary energy resources, 52
proprietary access, 380
Qatari exports to, 275
and Russian gas, 111, 270
security of supply, 22
seismic considerations, 376
shipping costs to, 84
shipping distances, 164n13
ship safety, 160
ship size, 82, 155
siting considerations, 374, 383n1
spot trading, 220
storage segregation, 177
terminal costs, 171
terminal size limits, 162
trading house equity, 246
uncommitted liquefaction capacity, 211, 212
United States exports to, 293, 294
wedge volumes, 229

Japan Customs Cleared price (JCC), 234
Japan, gas turbines in, 6
Japan, liquefied natural gas in, 21
joint venture structure, 246
Jules Verne, 139

K

Kansai Electric, 54
KBR.JGC, 81
Kenai, 242. *See also* Alaska
Kenai facility, 293–294
Kenetech, 42
Kogas, 147, 398
Korea. *See also* South Korea
imports to, 242
import terminals in, 14
infrastructure development, 381
LNG buyers in, 226, 228
LNG industry, 398
as major LNG shipbuilder, 156
unbundling and privatization of gas and electric power, 244

Korea Electric Power (Kepco), 56
Korea Gas Corporation (Kogas), 55
Korean shipyards, 235
Kyoto Treaty, 8

L

Labor Safety and Health Law, 383
Lagos, 205
Laieta, 145
Lake Charles, Louisiana, 34
Lake Charles terminal, 201, 240
  tariffs, 386
Legal Committee, 363
lenders, requirements by, 249
liberalization. *See* market liberalization
Libya
  early LNG history, 14
  early plant capacity, 71
  early plant development, 14
  existing LNG export projects, 262
  exports to Italy, 200, 261, 262
  exports to Spain, 200, 261, 262
  gas reserve of, 263
  LNG development in, 261–263
  NOC involvement, 247
  pipeline exports from, 48
  production capacity factor, 294
  production from, 255
  proposed LNG import terminals, 242
  supplier to Europe, 43
  Libyan National Oil Company, 262
licensing, 169
limited-recourse debt financing, 246, 247
liquefaction, 71–72
  process equipment, 71
  unit costs of, 233
liquefaction centers, 256
liquefaction commitments, 203–204
liquefaction complex
  in Damietta, 258–260
  in Idku, 258–260
liquefaction facilities, by country, 255
liquefaction plant
  cost of, 80
  feedgas and flow to, 252
  financing of, 247
  in Marsa el Brega, 261–262
  or tolling facility, 245
  as tolling facility, 76
liquefaction plant costs, 130
liquefaction plant design, 218
liquefaction plants, early, 14
liquefaction process, 109, 112–120
  at LNG export plants, 113
  technology overview, 111–120
liquefaction projects
  in Bethouia, 256
  in Mediterranean region, 255–273
  in the Middle East, 273–281
  liquefaction trains, 71
  mega-trains, 129–130, 385
  size increase of, 54, 128–129
  as tolling facilities, 229
  train size, 211
  unit train capacities, 71
liquefaction units, mega-sized, 211
liquefied natural gas
  business model, 352
  business model, evolution of, 202
  buyers controlling LNG shipping, 75
  future of, 395–402
  importation in 1970s, 33
  imports, 32
  loading jetty, 124–125
  niche markets for, 62
  plant unit costs, 131
  prices for, 27
  quality, 177
  shipbuilding, 143
  spill prevention containment and countermeasure plans, 377
  spot market for, 207
  storage tanks, 121
  supply contract, 69
  tanks, 72

value chain, 68
liquefied natural gas chain
cost and cost reduction along, 79
integration along, 211
liquefied natural gas charterparties
evolution of, 347–351
in traditional shipping model, 347–351
liquefied natural gas "club" expansion, 209
liquefied natural gas demand, 26, 398. *See also* gas demand
demand uncertainty, 55
Taiwan, 62
Thailand, 62, 201
United Kingdom, 43, 45
liquefied natural gas developments
in Canada, 37–38
in Mexico, 38
liquefied natural gas facilities, 374
liquefied natural gas fleet, 155–157. *See also* ships
liquefied natural gas importers, 397
liquefied natural gas industry
commercial trends, 244, 397–400
competitive tenders, 60
development, 13–24
elements of, 3
Japan, 398
Korea, 398
regulatory trends, 400–401
technical and commercial requirements and standards, 346
technical outlook, 396–397
liquefied natural gas merchants, 227, 228
liquefied natural gas off-take, 235
liquefied natural gas peakshaving plant, 14
liquefied natural gas projects
performance of, 251–252
requirements, 230
liquefied natural gas projects, business, 67, 202
liquefied natural gas projects, elements of, 15
capital access, 17
commercial terms, 18
external advisers, 19
final investment decision (FID), 19
gas reserves, 16
government regulations, 19
greenfield projects, 18
jetties, 72
liquefied natural gas project elements, 16
liquefied natural gas tankers, 16
long-term commitments from buyers, 16–17
price risk, 16
relationships among stakeholders, 17
safety and siting, 18
technical details, 16, 17
volume risk, 16
liquefied natural gas projects, recent, 15
liquefied natural gas SPAS, 233–235
liquefied natural gas vs. compressed natural gas (CNG), 23–24
liquefied natural gas vs. pipeline gas, 20, 21
liquidated damages (LDs), 127
liquidity, 204, 205
LNG pricing
vs. pipeline pricing, 75
pipeline pricing vs. LNG pricing, 75
LNG pricing, by country
China, 74, 231, 399
India, 74, 234, 332
Indonesia, 234
Iran, 59
Mexico, 334
Nigeria, 234
United States, 75, 233, 335, 399
loading arms, 72
loading facilities, 72
local distribution company (LDC), 12
local markets, 20
Long Island Sound, 382
long-term contracts, 217
long-term customers, 392, 393
long-term purchase contracts, 25
Louisiana Offshore Oil Port II (LOOP), 390

M

Maghreb-Europe (GME) pipeline, 47
magnetic surveys, 96
Maharashtra State Electricity Board, 58
main cryogenic heat exchanger (MCHE), 116
Main Pass Energy Hub, 191
major oil and gas companies, merchant trading by, 239
Malaysia
- to Asian-Pacific markets, 242, 281
- vs. Brunei, 286
- C3-MR cycle in, 115
- depreciation schedules, 305
- early LNG history, 15
- financing of, 242
- GSA pricing, 320
- imports from, 242
- Japanese imports from, 50, 53, 155, 200
- LNG development in, 290–293
- LNG export projects, 291
- LNG project business structures, 293
- signed LNG sales contracts, 292
- split-revenue ventures, 237
- turbine drive technology choices, 131
- uncommitted liquefaction capacity, 222n10, 229
- upstream project financing, 247

Malaysia LNG (MLNG) Satu, 290–291
Marathon, 35
Marine Consultative Organization (IMCO), 362
Marine Environment Protection Committee, 363
marine facilities construction, 232
Mariotte, Edme, 13
maritime industry trends, 161
Maritime Safety Committee, 363
market flexibility, 55
market liberalization, 85
- in Canada, 26
- of electric power in Korea, 244
- of electric power in Spain, 228
- of electric power in United Kingdom, 228
- of electric power in United States, 207, 227
- of gas, 49, 381
- gas and power sectors in Europe, 252
- of gas in European countries, 44, 207, 227
- of gas in South Korea, 56
- of gas in United States, 227
- regulatory bargain, 25
- regulatory changes, 252
- in United Kingdom, 26
- in United States, 26
- of wholesale electric power, 6–7

Market Oversight and Investigations, 30
markets, 74
market transparency, 204
Marsa El Brega plant, 263
master contracts, standardized, 221
maturation, 92
Medgaz, 47
Mediterranean region, liquefaction projects in, 255–273
mega-trains, 129–130, 385
membrane containment technology, 149
membrane ship construction, 153
membrane tanks, 73, 124, 141
merchant (gas supply) function, 29
merchant energy firms, 30, 208
merchant trading by major oil and gas companies, 239
mercury removal, 111–112
metering and pressure regulation station, 184
methane, 88, 396
Methane Kari Elin, 160
Methane Pioneer, 14
Methane Princess, 139
Methane Progress, 139
Mexico
- Altamira terminal, 241
- gas demand in, 38
- imports from Nigeria, 266
- liquefied natural gas developments in, 38
- LNG pricing, 334

pipeline buildout, 8
proposed LNG import terminals in Mexico, 241, 266, 294
proposed terminals, 201
regulatory trends, 400
Russian exports to, 111, 270
shipping costs, 310
siting considerations, 400
Middle East, liquefaction projects in, 273–281
migration routes, 93
Mirant, bankruptcy of, 7
Mitsubishi, 37
Mitsui, 38
mixed-refrigerant processes, 118–120
MLNG Dua, 291
monetization alternatives, 20, 23, 304
monopoly-franchised utilities, 243, 244
monopoly operation, 25–26
monopoly utilities, project-chain business model and, 226–227
mooring arrangements, 190
Moss containment technology, 149
Moss licenses, 163
Moss Rosenberg Verft, 149
Moss-type FSRU, 189, 366
Moss vessel construction, 153
Multi-Component Refrigerant (MCR), 115
multilateral agencies, 246
multilateral development banks, 251
multiphase pipeline, 107
Multiple Service Contract (MSC), 38
multiyear SPAs, 202
Myanmar, 63, 293

N

naphtha prices, 59
National Balancing Point (NBP), 26, 234
National Fire Protection Association's (NFPA), 374
national oil companies (NOCs)
forward integration by, 85
gas project participation by, 243
as merchants, 229, 241
project financing role of, 248
toll-based liquefaction, 239
natural gas
demand for, 395
exploration, 95–100
field processing, 105
geology of, 92–94
liquefaction flow diagram, 109
physical and chemical properties of, 88–89
pipelines, 105–108
pricing, 208
production, 100
transportation of, 3
world reserves of, 2
natural gas and liquefied natural gas markets
in Caribbean, 41
in France, 43
in Netherlands, 43
in Western Europe, 43
Natural Gas Fundamentals (Peebles), 159
natural gas industry, deregulation of, 29–30. *See also* gas market liberalization
natural gas marketed production, 2
natural gas pipelines, 8
Natural Gas Policy Act (NGPA) of 1978, 29, 33
natural gas prices, 2, 30–31
natural gas reserves, 89
natural gas, resource development, 10–13
natural gas resources, 10
natural gas resources, alternative methods of monetizing, 20–24
natural gas supply, 10–13
navigation bridge visibility, 366
NBP, 399
Nestor, 205
netback, 78
net back from FOB sales, 239
net present value (NPV) basis, 387
New Brunswick, 37
newbuilding technical specifications, 370

New York Mercantile Exchange (NYMEX), 30
New Zealand, 62, 201
NGL extraction, 262
NGLs, 105
Nigeria
- associated gas, 70
- C3-MR cycle in, 115
- contracted Nigeria LNG volumes, 266
- delivered sales (ex-ship or CIF) from, 78
- destination flexibility, 229
- dredging costs, 301
- early LNG history, 15
- existing LNG export projects, 263
- export clients, 267
- on feedgas supply, 252n1
- gas flaring, 89
- gas reserves in, 261
- GSA pricing, 320
- GTL projects, 23
- infrastructure costs, 18
- LNG pricing, 234
- LNG projects under construction or planned, 264
- NOC involvement, 247
- ownership structure, 76
- pipeline gas to Spain, 46
- production from, 255
- project economics, 84
- proposed projects, 242, 295n2
- shallow water drilling, 99
- ship ownership, 145, 147, 205
- split-revenue ventures, 237, 239
- spot trading, 241
- supplier to Europe, 43
- supplier to Turkey, 223n13
- uncommitted liquefaction capacity, 211, 233
- uplifts, 305

9/11
- offshore terminals since, 186
- security since, 185

nitrogen expander-based processes, 120
nitrogen injection, 183
non-associated gas, 70, 89
non-associated gas fields, 265
nondiscriminatory open access, 389
nonrecourse financing, 127
nontraditional trades, 206
NOPE (nowhere on planet earth), 374
Norman Lady, 145
North Africa, 8, 242
North American LNG import terminals, 39, 41
North European Gas Pipeline (NEGP) project, 46
North Seal oil and gas, 45
North Sea pipeline gas supplies to Western Europe, 43
North Slope gas, 32
North Slope pipeline, 294
North West Shelf (NWS), 282–284, 398
Norway
- CO_2 reinjection, 302
- contracted LNG volumes, 267
- Cove Point terminal, 35
- destination flexibility, 229
- exports to United Kingdom, 45
- HiLoad offshore LNG-unloading, 190
- integrated joint venture, 237
- LNG development in, 267
- LNG export project, 267
- mixed-fluid cascade (MFC) process, 130, 132
- Moss technology, 145
- new projects in, 256
- Ormen Lange field development, 103
- pipeline gas supplies to Western Europe, 43
- split-revenue ventures, 237
- taxation, 306, 308
- uplifts, 305
- upstream costs, 299

"not in my backyard" (NIMBY), 373
Nova Scotia, 37

nuclear power, 1
  generation, 52
nuclear power, development of, 9
nuclear power, generation of, 5

O

obligation to serve, 26
ocean transportation phase, 346
odorizing, 184
off-hire, 349
off-hire insurance, 355
off-hire provision, 355
official credit enhancement agencies, 251
offshore drilling rig, 99
offshore facilities, 382
  environmental aspects of, 382
  permitting obstacles, 194
Offshore Floating LNG Terminal Tascana (OLT), 49
offshore gas production platform, 104
offshore gathering systems, 12
offshore liquefaction facilities, 133
offshore pipelines, 105
offshore regasification, 36
offshore stranded-gas reserves, 133
off-site fabricated modules, 132
oil companies, 85
Oil Companies International Marine Forum (OCIMF), 362
oil crisis of 1973, 52
oil indexed pricing, 226–227, 233
oil-linked pricing, 43
oil, market dominance of, 7
oil prices, 1
oil reserves, proven, 90
oil window, 93
Olokola LNG plant (planned), 264
Oman
  to Asian-Pacific markets, 242
  condensates, 70
  Dabhol project, 218
  early LNG history, 15
  exports from, 242
  exports to Asia-Pacific region, 247
  exports to Spain, 241
  exports to to South Korea, 55, 56
  feedgas pricing, 238, 321
  FOB basis sales, 76
  FOB sales from, 78
  Japanese imports from, 50, 53
  LNG chain costs, 79, 80, 302
  LNG development in, 273–275
  LNG export projects, 274
  LNG sales contracts, 275
  onboard reliquefaction facilities, 164n19
  project structure, 250
  state participation, 298
  supplier to Europe, 43
  train ownerships in, 77
  uncommitted liquefaction capacity, 229
Oman LNG project, 273–274
onboard reliquefaction facilities, 73, 164
onshore drilling rig, 98
onshore gas transmission pipelines, 105
open access, 74
open-access, 187
  policies, 385
open-access capacity, 390
open access input terminals, 212
open-rack vaporizers (ORVs), 83, 178–179
operating costs, 80
operating expenditures (OPEX), 348
operational flexibility, 218, 351
operation and cooperation agreement (OCA), 392
Optimized Cascade process, 113
Ormen Lange, 46
overcommitment, 218
ownership chain, 75–78

P

P&O Challenger, 145
Pakistan, 62–63
  gas market liberalization, 55
  labor costs, 81
  as niche demand market, 62–63, 201
pipeline gas difficulties, 21
Panhandle Eastern Pipeline Corporation, 34
Panigaglia liquefied natural gas terminal, 49
Papua New Guinea, 211, 255
pass-through pricing, 26
patents and licenses, 149
Paul Kayser, 164
peaking gas turbines, 6
peakshaving LNG plants, 186
Peebles, Malcolm W. H., 159–160, 396
permeablility, 93
permitting, 169
Pertamina, 206, 243, 247, 286
Petróleos Mexicanos (PEMEX), 38
Petroleum Industry Complex Casualty Prevention Act, 383
Petronas, 290, 293
Phillips Optimized Cascade process, 114
physical chain, 69–75, 225
pipeline environment, 107
pipeline pricing vs. LNG pricing, 75
pipelines
  distribution pipelines, 11, 12
  downstream pipelines, 388
  international pipelines development, 43
  interstate, 12
  natural gas, 11–13
  offshore, 105
  onshore gas transmission, 105
pipelines, specific. *See also* specific country (e.g., Belgium)
  Algeria-Sardinia Galsi pipeline, 49
  Bacton terminus Interconnector pipeline, 45
  East-West pipeline, 60
  Green Stream pipeline, 48–49, 262
  Maghreb-Europe (GME) pipeline, 47
  North European Gas Pipeline (NEGP) project, 46
  North Slope pipeline, 294
  Trans-ASEAN Gas Pipeline, 293
  TransMed pipeline, 49
  Trans Thailand Malaysia pipeline, 63
  Zeebrugge liquefied natural gas terminal as pipeline hub, 49
point-to-point projects, 163
Poland, 49, 200
political risk insurance, 251
political risks, 111, 237
political unrest, 287
polyurethane foam (PUF) insulation system, 146
porosity, 93
port access, 378
portfolio approaches, 214
Port Harcourt, 205
Portugal, 47, 200, 266
Poten & Partners, 81
power generation. *See also* gas turbines
coal-fired, 5
  combined-cycle gas turbine (CCGT) power plants, 5
  combined-cycle gas turbine (CCGT) technology, 2–3
  diesel/electric propulsion, 150, 162–163
  dual-fuel diesel/electric propulsion, 162
  economics of, 5
  steam turbines, 121, 131, 150, 162–163
power plant siting, 7
price controls, 59
price-driven sales, 219–221
price linkage to oil, 50
price pressure, 58
price risk, 69
price risk sharing, 237
prices vs. security of supply, 210
pricing dispute, 218
pricing risk, 238, 250
Prince, William Wood, 14
prismatic cargo tanks, 139
privately owned LNG import terminal, 56

privatization of energy markets in Europe, 44. *See also* market liberalization
production risk, 238
production risk sharing, 237
production-sharing contracts (PSCs), 70, 269, 286–287
production tubing, 101
project-chain model, 226–227, 244
project completion risk, 246
project development, 240–241
project development and execution, 125–128
project finance
    advantages of, 247–248
    funding, 235–236
    history and motivation, 246–247
    impact of transfer from construction to operation status, 127
    for offshore production platforms, 70
    for regasification terminals, 74
    structure and participants, 250–251
project formation, 225, 231
project management issues, 77
project risk, 239
project scheduling, 151
project structure models, 76
project venture structure evolution, 236–244
project ventures, types of, 237–239
propane-precooled mixed-refrigerant (C3-MR) cycle, 115–117
proprietary-access, 195
proprietary access import terminals, 212, 213, 228, 386, 390–394
proven gas reserves, 10, 91
proven oil reserves, 90
proven resources, 89–90
proxy price, crude oil as, 74. *See also* LNG pricing
public perception, 9
Puerto Rico
    gas powered generation, 42, 168, 201
    Guayanilla import terminal, 42
    Trinidad exports to, 271
pure-refrigeration Cascade process, 113–115
purpose-built commercial ships, 139

Q

Qalhat LNG project, 273–274
Qatar
    APCI AP-X process, 117
    to Asian-Pacific markets, 242
    C3-MR cycle in, 115
    contracted LNG volumes, 278
    Dabhol project, 218
    early LNG history, 15
    existing LNG project shareholdings, 276
    exports to China, 60
    exports to Korea, 56
    FOB sales from, 78
    gas reserves in, 3, 90, 92, 210, 222n9
    Golden Pass LNG, Texas, 37
    gravity-based structure (GBS), 192
    GTL projects, 23
    imports from, 242
    infrastructure costs, 110
    integrated projects, 237
    Japanese imports from, 50, 53, 200
    labor costs, 81
    LNG export facilities, 275
    LNG exports, 286
    LNG projects under construction, 276
    mega-sized LNG projects, 71, 129, 277
    mega-trains, 32
    Milford Haven terminal, 46
    non-associated gas reserves, 70
    ownership LNG projects under construction, 277
    proposed terminal, 49
    proprietary access import terminals, 385
Q-flex and Q-max vessels, 82, 165n23
    RasGas LNG plant, 275–276
    shipping costs, 310
    supplier to Europe, 43
    uncommitted liquefaction capacity, 211, 229, 233, 241
    United States market access, 85
Qatargas LNG plant, 275–276
Qatar Petroleum, 385
Q-flex and Q-max vessels, 82

R

rate of cargo pumping, 349
rate of return (RoR) allowable, 239
receiving terminal, cost of, 171–172
recourse financing, 127
redundancy, 170
Regasificación del Noroeste (REGANOSA), 47
Regasificación de Sagunto (SAGGAS), 47
regasification terminals, 18, 19, 74, 83
regulated access of LNG terminals, 386–394. *See also* proprietary access import terminals; third-party access
regulatory bargain, 25
regulatory changes, 252
relationship-driven sales, 220
reliability, 72
reliquefaction facilities, 159
reliquefaction onboard ship, 82
Repsol, 37
reserves. *See* gas reserves
reserves to production ratio (R/P ratio), 10
reservoir rock traps, 93
resources taxes, 282
retail deregulation, 227
revenue commitment, 226
revenue security, 250
rise of modern shipping regulations, 362–370
risk mitigation, 248
risk sharing, 77, 237
rollover, 177, 196
rotary rigs, 98
rules and regulations, 370–373
Russia
- contracted Sakhalin II volumes, 270
- developments in, 242
- exports to Japan, 111, 270
- exports to Mexico, 111, 270
- exports to Turkey, 223n13
- exports to United Kingdom, 45
- gas buildout, 8
- gas reserves in, 10, 90
- GTL projects, 23
- imports from, 242
- integrated projects, 237
- offshore projects, 232
- pipeline gas supplies to Italy, 48
- pipeline gas supplies to Western Europe, 43
- pipeline infrastructure of, 268
- planned LNG projects, 269
- production from, 92
- resource nationalism, 396
- supplier to Turkey, 223n13
- uncommitted liquefaction capacity, 211, 229, 233

Russia (including the Pacific Basin project), 268–270

S

Sabine Pass, Louisiana, 36
safety, 72
safety and security, 184–185
safety systems, 12
Sakhalin, 243
Sakhalin II venture, 268
Sakhalin I project, 55
sales revenue, guarantee of, 230
salt caverns, 193
salt domes, 93, 95
Santo Dominico, 64n8
Saudi Arabia, 91
security advantages, 21
security concerns, 50
security of markets, 22
security of supply, 22, 74, 203
security systems, 12
seismic survey, 96
seismic technology, 104
seismology, 96
self-supporting, independent tanks, 141
semi-submersible platforms, 100
Sempra, 36, 39, 391
sendout capacity, 167–168
shareholders, Japanese trading companies as, 53

Shell, 35, 38, 39, 59, 349, 385
shell and tube vaporizers (STVs), 180
Shell dual mixed-refrigerant (DMR) process, 118
Shell LNG Time 1 charterparty, 349
Shell's DMR process, 132
Shell Time 3, 347
shipboard maintenance and ship life extension (ship longeivity), 160–161
shipboard regasification, 187
shipbuilding
  capacity, 144
  countries involved in, 144
  evolution of, 144
  Korea as leader in, 156
  projects, 150
ship financing, 235
ship operations, 158–160
shipping, 72, 81–82, 214–215
  capacity acquisition, 229
  conventions and regulations, 351–372
  cost of, 84
  LNG buyers controlling, 75
  ownership of, 78
shipping costs, 84, 310
ship propulsion, 73
ships, 19, 72–73
  capacity and capability of, 153–156
  cargo capacity for, 82
  chartering, 354–359
  by China, 61
  competitive lenders for, 78
  containment and handling systems of, 139–144
  containment systems, 142
  containment tank designs, 141
  contracts, 345–359
  control of, 353
  conventions and codes applicable to, 364–370
  costs, 57
  costs of, 150, 352
  crew training requirements, 368
  design and construction standards of, 367
  emerging model of control, 351–359
  liability of, 353
  market risks of, 353
  new construction Rules and Regulations, 370–373
  ownership, 157–158
  ownership of, 352–354
  propulsion mechanisms of, 73
  Q-flex and Q-max vessels, 82
  residual value of, 353
  safety and accident records, 160
  shipyard prices for, 81
  size range, age profile, and trade allocation, 154
  sizes, 162
  specifications, 154
  technical risks of, 353
shipyard selection, 151
shipyards, LNG
  in China, 148
  in Japan, 147
  in South Korea, 148
short-term customers, 392
short-term LNG market, 216–221
short-term sales, 229
short-term trades, 161, 205, 216–217
Shtockmanov field, 242
Shtokman LNG project, 269
Shtokmanov field, 269
simple-cycle gas turbines, 5
Singapore, 63
single-containment tanks, 122–123
Sirte basin, 263
siting authority, 375
siting considerations, 110–111
Skikda liquefaction project, 256
sloshing damage, 188–189
Snøhvit plant, 267
social infrastructure development, 251
solar power, economics of, 9
SOLAS, 370

Sonat, Inc., 34
Sonatrach, 33–34
  in Algeria, 256–258
  in Atlantic Basin, 240
  vs. El Paso, 205
  in Spain, 258
source rocks, 92
sour gas, 105
Southern LNG, 34, 35
Southern Union, 34
South Hook LNG, 46, 391
South Korea
  electric power liberalization, 244
  gas demand, 55–56
  gas market liberalization, 56
  Indonesian exports to, 55, 56
  Japan vs. Korean shipbuilding, 150, 235
  Korea Electric Power (Kepco), 56
  Korea Gas Corporation (Kogas), 55
  LNG industry in, 398
  LNG shipyards, 148
  LNG shipyards in, 148
  as major LNG shipbuilders, 156
shipbuilding industry, 56
Soviet Union, 43. *See also* Russia
SPA
  force majeure provisions in, 355
  liquefied natural gas SPAS, 233–235
  multiyear, 202
  shipping per, 348
Spain
  electric power liberalization in, 228
  exports from Egypt, 259
  exports from Libya, 261, 262
  exports from Nigeria, 267
  exports from Oman, 274
  exports from Qatar, 241, 275
  exports from Trinidad, 271
  gas demand forecast, 47
  gas demand in, 43
  imports from Algeria, 257
  imports from Libya, 200
  imports from Nigeria, 266
  import terminal capacity in, 240
  import terminals in, 14
  infrastructure development, 381
  liquefied natural gas suppliers to, 46–47
  pipeline proposal, 48
  and Portugal, 48
  proprietary access import terminals, 391
  shipping costs to, 310
  shipping for, 139
  Sonatrach in, 258
special purpose vehicle (SPV), 157
speculation, 157
speculative shipping, 215
speculative ships, 82, 157, 205
spherical tanks, 73
spiral-wound heat exchangers, 129
split-revenue ventures, 237
spot cargoes, 56
spot charter rates, 351
spot LNG markets, 85, 216–221
spot LNG prices, globalization of, 75
spot trading, 205, 206
  in Asia, 220
  challenges of, 221
  defined, 216–217
  in Europe, 219–221
  in Japan, 220
  in United States, 219–221
standardization, 132–133
state oil, 1
state owned and financed projects, 237
state subsidiaries, 58
Statoil, 35, 36, 132
Statoil-Linde mixed-fluid cascade (MFC) process, 119, 120
STCW Convention, 367, 368, 369
steam turbines, 121
  vs. diesel/electric propulsion, 150, 162–163
  vs. gas turbines, 131
steel, nickel content in, 14
storage capacity, 167–168

storage capacity requirements, 121–122
storage tanks, 170. *See also* tanks
stranded gas reserves, 10, 21
stratification, 177
stripping condensates, 105
subcharter, 349
submerged combustion vaporizers (SCVs), 179
Submerged Turret Loading, 36
Submerged Turret Loading (STL), 187
subsidized prices, 59
Suez, 34, 240
Suez Matthew, 145
Sulfinol process, 105, 111
superdeals, 206
supermajors, 85
supply and demand outlook, 32
supply chain, 25
supply forecast, 198
supply interruptions, 21
supply project, 226
supply, security of, 203
surplus capacity, sources of, 217
survival standards, 367
sweet gas, 105

T

Taiwan
  competitive tendering, 60
  downstream liberalization, 401
  gas market liberalization, 49, 50, 85
  imports by, 200
  imports from Indonesia, 288
  imports from Malaysia, 291
  imports to, 242
  import terminals in, 14
  LNG buyers in, 226
  LNG demand, 62
  LNG imports of, 57
  LNG industry, 398
  nuclear power generation in, 57
  pricing formula, 332
  utility buyers in, 245, 380
Taiwan Power Company (Taipower), 57
take-or-pay contracts, 25, 29, 69, 202
Tambeyneftegas, 269–270
Tangguh LNG project, 289–290
tanker cooldown, 125
tanker fleet for crude oil, 222
tanker purchase option, 355
tankers. *See* ships
tanker unloading, 170
tanks
  experimental designs, 140
  fire safety requirements, 377
  insulation, 159
  sizes of, 131
tariffs, 385, 386, 389, 393, 394
taxation, 239, 248
Technical Cooperation Committee, 363
technical risk management, 67
Technigaz, 149
Technip, 81
technology developments, 162–163
terminal capacity, third-party sales of, 215
terminal operations, 161
terminal use agreement (TUA), 385
terrorism, 111
terrorist activities, 18
terrorist targets, 184, 186, 369
Thailand
  LNG demand, 62, 201
  natural gas pipelines growth in, 8
  pipelines to, 63
  potential projects, 201
  the bareboat demise charterparty, 350
  the Netherlands
  Groningen gas field, 11
  natural gas and liquefied natural gas markets in, 43
  pipeline construction, 45
  pipeline gas supplies from, 43
  pipeline gas supplies to Italy, 48
  pipeline gas supplies to Western Europe, 43
  terminal proposals, 49, 200

thermal exclusion, 195
thermal-radiation protection, 377
third-part due diligence, 248
third-part terminal owners, 161
third-party access, 44, 47, 50, 212, 381, 382, 385
three-dimensional seismic technology, 80, 97
time charterparty, 348–351, 356
Tobago, 113, 270–273
Toho Gas, 398
Tokyo Electric (TEPCO), 54
toll-based liquefaction, 239
tolling liquefied natural gas, 59, 76
Total, 38
town gas, 69
Tractebel, Inc., 34
trade matrix, 199
trades, 228
traffic separation schemes, 369
training and assessment, 369
training and certification requirements, 369
trains. *See* liquefaction trains
Trans-ASEAN Gas Pipeline, 293
transfer pricing, 77
transfer pricing mechanisms, 348
TransMed pipeline, 49
transmission lines, 11, 25. *See also* pipelines
transparency, 204
transportation contracts, 350–351
transportation costs, 69, 84, 310, 349
Trans Thailand Malaysia pipeline, 63
Trinidad
  capacity of, 35
  Cascade process in, 113
  contracted LNG volumes, 272
  cost recovery schemes, 306
  depreciation schedules, 305
  development choices, 20
  downstream tolling, 239
  early LNG history, 15
  expansion costs, 302
  exports to Dominican Republic, 42
  exports to Europe, 43
  exports to United States, 145
  FOB sales from, 78
  gas quality from, 182
  gas transmission in, 238, 240
  LNG development in, 270–271
  LNG project shareholdings (existing and under construction), 272
  non-associated gas reserves, 70
  ownerships of, 34, 35, 42
  production flexibility, 218
  production from, 255
  project financing, 247
  tolling liquefied natural gas, 229
  train ownerships in, 77
  transmission lines to be developed, 107
  Venezuela and, 273
Trinidad and Tobago, 270–273
Trinidad's Atlantic Liquefied Natural Gas (ALNG) project, 34, 42
trip-time charterparty, 350
turbine-driven LNG plants, 129
Turkey
  imports by, 200
  imports from Algeria, 223n13, 257
  imports from Iran, 223n13
  imports from Nigeria, 223n13, 266
  local siting opposition, 378
  pipeline gas supplies, 49
turnkey EPC contracts, 246
turret system, 189

U

unbundling, 207, 227
uncommitted liquefaction capacity
  in Australia, 222n10, 229, 233
  in Japan, 211, 212
  in Malaysia, 222n10, 229
  in Nigeria, 211, 233
  in Oman, 229
  in Qatar, 211, 229, 233, 241
  in Russia, 211, 229, 233

Uniform Commercial Code, 342
United Arab Emirates (UAE), 91, 278–280. *See also* Abu Dhabi
United Kingdom
domestic production, 333
early LNG history, 14
electric power liberalization in, 228
gas and power market liberalization in, 44
gas demand forecast, 45
gas demand in, 43
gas interchangeability, 336
gas merchant functions in, 244
gas-on-gas competition, 227
gas prices in, 233
imports by, 200
imports from Algeria, 256
imports from Egypt, 259
Japanese buyers seeking outlets in, 55
labor costs, 171
liquid gas market in, 335
LNG development in, 45–46
LNG ships slated for, 165
market liberalization in, 26
National Balancing Point (NBP), 234
open access input terminals, 387
production decline, 27
production from, 92
regulatory trends in, 400–401
ship purchase by, 144
siting considerations, 337, 380
Sonatrach in upstream sector, 258
terminal construction in, 241
third party access, 382
United States
electric power liberalization in, 227
El Paso experience, 205–206
energy mix, 7
existing liquefied natural gas import terminals in, 33
exports from Egypt, 259
exports from Mexico, 39
exports from Nigeria, 266
exports from Norway, 267
exports from Qatar, 32, 277
exports from Russia, 44, 269
exports from Trinidad, 271
exports from Yemen, 280
exports to Asia-Pacific region, 281
exports to Mexico, 38
gas buildout, 11–12
gas interchangeability, 336
gas market liberalization, 55, 207, 208, 227
gas market, sectors of, 27
gas powered generation, 6
gas properties in, 88
gas reserves in, 91
gas trading, 208
government policy, 8
Henry Hub pricing, 234
imports by, 201
imports from Algeria, 257
import terminal design, 374, 375, 377
Japanese imports from, 50
Kenai facility, 293–294
labor costs, 171
litigation in, 351, 380
LNG buyers in, 226
LNG development in, 13–14, 27
LNG import terminals, 164n15, 241
LNG in gas market, 170
LNG pricing, 75, 233, 335, 399
market liberalization in, 26
markets in, 165n13
natural gas and liquefied natural gas markets, 27–36
Natural Gas Policy Act (NGPA) of 1978, 325
natural gas pricing in, 156
new liquefied natural gas terminals in, 36–37
open-access, 389
peakshaving LNG plants, 186
power market liberalization, 207
production from, 92
project-chain model, 228
proposed LNG import terminals, 36, 39

proprietary access, 386, 390, 391
proprietary access import terminals, 195
regasification terminals, 212
regulatory standards, 183
regulatory trends in, 400
Russian export potential, 242
shipbuilding, 146
shipbuilding industry, 145
ship mothballed, 85
shipping costs, 84
shipping inventory, 146
ship regulations, 361
short-term trades, 283
siting considerations, 18, 186, 375
Sonatrach contract, 326
Sonatrach in downstream, 258
spot trades in, 219–221
spot trading, 79, 218
terminal access, 213
third-party access, 382
Uniform Commercial Code, 342
United States Coast Guard, 369
United States Energy Policy Act of 2005, 382
United States Maritime Administration (MARAD), 206
unit train capacities, 71
upstream exploration and production, 69–70
upstream gas production economics, 79
upstream integration, 214
upstream projects, 394
upstream strategies, 209–210
upstream taxation, 239
use-it-or-lose-it basis, 381
utilities, 121

V

value chain, 68, 83–86
vapor, 376
vaporization, 83, 170, 178–181
vaporization technologies, 83
variable operating costs, 85
Venezuela
natural gas pipelines growth in, 8
potential projects, 255
Trinidad and, 273
volume risk, 69, 250
voyage charterparty, 350
voyage costs, 348

W–X

water quality, 378
waterway suitability assessment (WSA), 369
weathering, 177
wedge volumes, 217
Wellhead Decontrol Act of 1989, 29
Wellhead deregulation, 29
well logs, 97
West Africa, 232, 299, 303
Western Europe, 43
Western Siberia fields, 268
West Texas Intermediate (WTI), 208
wet gas, 70
White Paper on Interchangeability, 183
wholesale electric markets liberalization. *See* electric power liberalization
wildcat wells, 97
Williams Corporation, 35
windows, 93
wind power, economics of, 9
wing, 103
Wobbe index, 183–184, 196
World Bank, 19
world gas consumption projections, 5
worldwide gas reserves, 26
worldwide natural gas consumption, 1980-2004, 28

Y

Yamal LNG project, 269
Yemen, 280–281
Yemen LNG project, 280–281
Yung An LNG terminal, 57

Z

Zeebrugge hubs, 399

Zeebrugge liquefied natural gas terminal, 26, 240

ABOUT THE AUTHORS

Michael D. Tusiani

Michael D. Tusiani joined Poten & Partners in 1973 and has served as Chairman and Chief Executive Officer since 1983. During his career, he has been active in all aspects of oil and gas trading and transportation. He has written numerous articles on energy and shipping matters and two books, the *Petroleum Shipping Industry: A Nontechnical Overview* (PennWell, 1966) and *The Petroleum Shipping Industry: Operations and Practices* (PennWell, 1996). He received a B.A. in economics from Long Island University and an M.A. in from Fordham University.

Gordon Shearer

Gordon Shearer is President and Chief Executive Officer of HESS LNG LLC, a joint venture of Hess Corporation and Poten & Partners, which was established in June 2004. He joined Poten & Partners in January 2001 in the Project Development & Finance group. Prior to joining Poten he was employed by Cabot Corporation from

1978 until 2001, with numerous assignments in the Corporation's energy businesses, culminating with his position as Vice President from 1991 until 2001. His experience includes the appointment as Chief Executive Officer of Cabot LNG Corporation, which owned and operated the LNG import terminal in Boston Harbor and the LNG carrier *Matthew*. During his time with Cabot LNG he was heavily involved in the creation of the Atlantic LNG project in Trinidad and Tobago. He received a B.Sc. in Geophysics from Edinburgh University, and an MBA from Harvard Business School. He was appointed to the National Petroleum Council in May 2005.